# CITIZENS OF SCANDAL

# CITIZENS
# OF SCANDAL

Journalism, Secrecy, and the Politics of Reckoning in Mexico

VANESSA FREIJE

Duke University Press | Durham and London | 2020

© 2020 Duke University Press
All rights reserved
Cover designed by Courtney Leigh Richardson
Text designed by Drew Sisk
Typeset in Minion Pro by Westchester Publishing Services

Library of Congress Cataloging-in-Publication Data
Names: Freije, Vanessa, [date] author.
Title: Citizens of scandal : journalism, secrecy, and the politics of reckoning in Mexico / Vanessa Freije.
Description: Durham : Duke University Press, 2020. | Includes bibliographical references and index.
Identifiers: LCCN 2020008237 (print)
LCCN 2020008238 (ebook)
ISBN 9781478009825 (hardcover)
ISBN 9781478010883 (paperback)
ISBN 9781478012399 (ebook)
Subjects: LCSH: Journalism—Political aspects—Mexico—

History—20th century. | Political corruption—Mexico—History—20th century. | Civil society—Mexico—History—20th century. | Mexico—Social conditions—History—20th century.
Classification: LCC PN4974.P6 F745 2020 (print)
LCC PN4974.P6 (ebook)
DDC 079/.7209046—dc23
LC record available at https://lccn.loc.gov/2020008237
LC ebook record available at https://lccn.loc.gov/2020008238

Cover art: *Reader*: Unidentified man reading the news about an earthquake in Central Mexico, September 20, 1985. Courtesy the Associated Press. *Newsprint*: Courtesy istockphoto.com/Liliboas. *Background*: *La Jornada*, 1985.

*To my parents, Susan Caldwell and Matthew Freije*

# CONTENTS

| List of Illustrations<br>ix | List of Abbreviations<br>xi | Acknowledgments<br>xiii |

INTRODUCTION

1

**CHAPTER 1**
## RECKONING WITH THE REVOLUTION
23

**CHAPTER 2**
## "VEHICLES OF SCANDAL"
51

**CHAPTER 3**
## MUCKRAKING AND THE OIL BOOM AND BUST
79

**CHAPTER 4**
## THE SPECTACLE OF IMPUNITY
107

**CHAPTER 5**
## A MEDIATED DISASTER
138

**CHAPTER 6**
## THE WEAPONIZATION OF SCANDAL
167

EPILOGUE

193

CONCLUSION

199

| Notes<br>207 | Bibliography<br>255 | Index<br>275 |

**LIST OF ILLUSTRATIONS**

Figure 1.1: Héctor García, *Niña con su puerco*, 1965.

Figure 1.2: Gregorio Méndez, untitled photograph, *Sucesos*, January 14, 1967.

Figure 2.1: "El director de la escuela estatal Emiliano Zapata hace declaraciones al reportero," *Excélsior*, December 7, 1974.

Figure 2.2: Iracheta, "Falso rumor," *El Universal*, December 11, 1974.

Figure 2.3: Iracheta, "Los infundios," *El Universal*, December 16, 1974.

Figure 3.1: Reproduction of a leaked CIA report published in *Proceso*, October 31, 1977.

Figure 3.2: *Huele a gas!*, illustration by Naranjo.

Figure 4.1: Rius, "Listos con las listas!," *Proceso*, September 27, 1982.

Figure 4.2: Rius, "Medio siglo de siglas," *Proceso*, November 29, 1982.

Figure 4.3: Cover of *Picardías del Negro Durazo* comic book.

Figure 4.4: "En el Ateneo de Angangueo, 1981," *Nexos*, July 1984.

Figure 5.1: "Ayuda," *Proceso*, September 23, 1985.

Figure 5.2: Pedro Valtierra, "Identificación de cadáveres en el Seguro Social," *La Jornada*, September 23, 1985.

## LIST OF ABBREVIATIONS

| | |
|---|---|
| AMI | Agencia Mexicana de Información / Mexican Information Agency |
| BAY | Banco Agrario de Yucatán / Yucatán Agrarian Bank |
| CCH | Colegio de Ciencias y Humanidades / School of Sciences and Humanities |
| CCI | Central Campesina Independiente / Independent Campesino Organization |
| CDE | Comité de Defensa Ejidal / Ejidal Defense Committee |
| CENCOS | Centro Nacional de Comunicación Social / National Center for Social Communication |
| CIA | Central Intelligence Agency |
| CIASES | Centro de Información y Análisis de los Efectos del Sismo / Center for Information and Analysis of the Effects of the Earthquake |
| CISA | Comunicación e Información, S.A. / Communication and Information, S.A. |
| CNC | Confederación Nacional Campesina / National Campesino Confederation |
| CNOP | Confederación Nacional de Organizaciones Populares / National Confederation of Popular Organizations |
| CROC | Confederación Revolucionaria de Obreros y Campesinos / Revolutionary Confederation of Workers and Campesinos |
| CTM | Confederación de Trabajadores de México / Confederation of Mexican Workers |
| DFS | Dirección Federal de Seguridad / Federal Security Office |
| DGIPS | Dirección General de Investigaciones Políticas y Sociales / General Office for Political and Social Intelligence |
| FBI | Federal Bureau of Investigation |
| FCE | Fondo de Cultura Económica / Endowment for Economic Culture |
| FPI | Frente Popular Independiente / Independent Popular Front |
| IMF | International Monetary Fund |

| | |
|---|---|
| IMP | Instituto Mexicano de Petróleo / Mexican Petroleum Institute |
| JLCA | Junta Local de Conciliación y Arbitraje / Local Committee on Conciliation and Arbitration |
| MLN | Movimiento de Liberación Nacional / Movement for National Liberation |
| NAFINSA | Nacional Financiera / National Finance Agency |
| NIIO | New International Information Order |
| OPEC | Organization of the Petroleum Exporting Countries |
| PAN | Partido Acción Nacional / National Action Party |
| PBS | Public Broadcasting Service |
| PCM | Partido Comunista Mexicano / Mexican Communist Party |
| PEMEX | Petróleos Mexicanos / Mexican Petroleum |
| PERMARGO | Perforadora Marítima del Golfo / Maritime Drilling of the Gulf |
| PFDT | Procuraduría Federal de la Defensa del Trabajo / Office of the Federal Attorney General for Labor Protection |
| PGR | Procuraduría General de la República / Office of the Attorney General of the Republic |
| PIPSA | Productora e Importadora de Papel, S. A. / Paper Importer and Producer, S. A. |
| PJF | Policía Judicial Federal / Federal Judicial Police |
| PMT | Partido Mexicano de los Trabajadores / Mexican Workers' Party |
| PRI | Partido Revolucionario Institucional / Institutional Revolutionary Party |
| PSUM | Partido Socialista Unificado de México / United Socialist Party of Mexico |
| SEDUE | Secretaría de Desarrollo Urbano y Ecología / Ministry of Urban Development and Ecology |
| SEP | Secretaría de Educación Pública / Ministry of Public Education |
| SMGE | Sociedad Mexicana de Geografía y Estadística / Mexican Society of Geography and Statistics |
| SSA | Secretaría de Salubridad y Asistencia / Ministry of Health and Assistance |
| UN | United Nations |
| UNAM | Universidad Nacional Autónoma de México / National Autonomous University of Mexico |
| UPD | Unión de Periodistas Democráticas / Union of Democratic Journalists |
| USIA | United States Information Agency |

## ACKNOWLEDGMENTS

Long before I began graduate school, my interest in Mexican politics and culture was shaped by my own geography. I grew up in a small town known only for its avocado groves and proximity to a military base. It was an hour's drive from Tijuana, thirty minutes from the Pauma Indian Reservation, and fifteen minutes from an imposing immigration checkpoint. So began my education in border politics. I am grateful to friends and teachers, including Tony Acevedo, Everard Meade, and Eric Van Young, who encouraged me to formally study the dynamics that I frequently encountered as a young adult.

Duke University provided the most nurturing environment I could have asked for as a graduate student. Elizabeth Fenn, John French, Nancy MacLean, Peter Sigal, and Philip Stern were wonderful teachers. I was surrounded by supportive peers, and I'm thankful to Angélica Castillo, Libby Cole, Julia Gaffield, Diana Gómez, Sean Parrish, Erin Perish, Bryan Pitts, Yuridia Ramírez, Michael Stauch, Corinna Zeltsman, and many others for their comradery. Sallie Hughes also generously mentored me from afar and offered critical readings. I am forever grateful for the advising and support of Jocelyn Olcott, who continues to share her time and insight.

The Colegio de México offered me an institutional home in Mexico City when I embarked on my research, and the Fulbright–García Robles Scholarship gave critical financial support. New friendships provided not only companionship but also engaging conversation that generated new questions and interpretations. Derek Bentley, Jennifer Boles, Francisco Campos, Luis Francisco, Janice Gallagher, Adam Goodman, Andrea Maldonado, Tore Olsen, Emanuel Rodríguez, Diana Schwartz, Laura Sullivan, and Larisa Veloz were sounding boards on archival discoveries and misadventures and composed an invaluable community.

This book would not have been possible without the support and openness of journalists, scholars, and public officials in Mexico who shared their time, insights, and many meals. Gregorio Ortega Molina, Sergio Rodríguez González, and Jacinto Rodríguez Munguía offered insight and leads. I owe a debt of gratitude to Luis Hernández Navarro, who listened endlessly about this project and enriched it in many ways. I am still astounded that so many people were willing to open their archives to me. I am especially grateful to Luis Fernando Granados for allowing me to be the first to view his father's materials. He not only trusted me to sift through the unorganized boxes that he himself had not yet seen, but Luis also entrusted me with his home, lending me a key so that I could come and go as I pleased. Sara Lovera and Luis Javier Solana also generously shared their collections with me.

The expertise and assistance of many archivists made this research possible. Under the knowledgeable direction of Mariano Mercado Estrada and Marina Villagómez Moreno, the Fundación Heberto Castillo was a wonderful place to work. Omar Raúl Martínez welcomed me into the Fundación Manuel Buendía and offered reflections on Buendía's life. The archivists at the Archivo General de la Nación, the Fondo de Cultura Ecónomica, and the Secretaría de Salud y Asistencia were also exceedingly helpful. After I moved back to the United States, Nidia Olvera Hernández gathered materials when I could not make it back to Mexico City, and I have greatly appreciated her help. Kyle Johnson came to the rescue with images in the last week before this book went into production.

The U.S.-Mexican Studies Center at the University of California–San Diego provided a peaceful space to begin writing what constituted the basis for this book. Melissa Floca was a tireless leader and Greg Mallinger a fearless guide on our outings to Tijuana. I benefited from many informal discussions with Michael Lettieri and Casey Lurtz. Froylán Enciso offered insightful thoughts on translation and encouraged me to allow humor into my writing. Kayla Donato and Sharon Jeong provided respite from the academic world during that year, and they, along with Mary Tharin and Stacie Walsh, have been steadfast companions throughout.

A postdoctoral fellowship with the Dartmouth College Society of Fellows allowed me to begin the research for chapters 1 and 2. Randall Balmer, Robert Bonner, and Laura McDaniel eased my transition to New England and were excellent hosts. Mary Coffey, Pamela Voekel, and Michelle Warren were wonderful mentors. I could not have asked for a better cohort of fellows: Kate Hall, Bess Koffman, Yvonne Kwan, and Caitano da Silva, were tireless cheerleaders and taught me about drones, icebergs, intergenerational trauma, and lightning, respectively. Udi Greenberg and Jennie Miller were great interlocutors and guides. They, along with Izzy Dabiri, Kate Hall, Garnet Kindervater, and Simon Toner, offered humor, meals, and friendship that made the writing process less lonely and reminded me that scholarly work is best when undertaken in conversation with others.

This book continued to develop at the University of Washington, where I started teaching in the Henry M. Jackson School of International Studies. It would be easy in an interdisciplinary school for faculty to remain siloed in their disciplinary camps, but my colleagues have been a rich source of intellectual engagement, have prompted me to ask new questions, and have allowed me to learn more about my own discipline. A special thanks to Mika Ahuvia, Arbella Bet-Shlimon, Daniel Chirot, María Elena García, Liora Halperin, Sunila Kale, Reşat Kasaba, James Lin, José Antonio Lucero, Devin Naar, Christian Novetzke, Deborah Porter, Ileana Rodríguez-Silva, Joel Walker, Adam Warren, Jonathan Warren, and Glennys Young for their support and feedback. A fellowship with the Simpson Center for the Humanities provided space for me to finish the manuscript, and I am grateful to Rachel Arteaga and Kathy Woodward for leading fascinating lunchtime seminars, as well as to the fellows for their intellectual engagement. I have also learned a great deal from my students, particularly Zinaida Carroll who provided feedback on this manuscript.

I was lucky to find friends who were at the same writing stage as me, and Shane Dillingham, Nova Robinson, and Natasha Varner read multiple chapters of this book. Nova and Natasha shared in my setbacks and celebrations, and for that I am especially grateful. Gabriela Alejandra Buitron and Diana Schwartz also offered comments and made this book stronger. Rebecca Herman, Stuart Schrader, and Christy Thornton have been wonderful allies and role models. Corinna Zeltsman has been subjected to reading far too much of my work; in addition to slogging through the entire manuscript, she (and her partner Mattia Begali) consulted on title ideas and image selections, and she has been an endlessly positive sounding board over the last few years.

I have been welcomed into a community of scholars whose feedback has pushed my work to be better. Ana María Serna invited me to join the Seminario de la Esfera Pública at the Instituto Mora, and the group has been an excellent source for ideas. Gabriela Aceves, Benjamin Bryce, Celso Castilho, Mary Roldán, Benjamin T. Smith, Geoffrey Spurling, and Edward Wright-Ríos have offered excellent comments. Mary Kay Vaughan has been an inspiration and a source of honest advice, and Andrew Paxman and Anne Rubenstein read the entire manuscript and gave incisive feedback at just the right moment. I am grateful to scholars like them who give so generously of their time. Thanks also to Martha Espinosa, Robert Franco, Natalie Gasparowicz, Michael Matthews, Jocelyn Olcott, Peter Sigal, Farren Yero, and Corinna

Zeltsman for attending a manuscript review and offering constructive feedback. I am thankful to the anonymous reviewers of this book who greatly strengthened the work. I am also grateful to Gisela Fosado and Alejandra Mejía for their support as they shepherded this project to publication. An earlier version of chapter 2 was originally published in the *Hispanic American Historical Review* under the title "Speaking of Sterilization: Rumors, the Urban Poor, and the Public Sphere in Greater Mexico City" (2019): 303–36, and is reprinted here with permission from Duke University Press.

The community I have found in Seattle has quickly made it feel like home. Thanks to Kathy and Erie for welcoming me into the neighborhood; Sueños de Salsa for keeping me sane and making me part of Seattle's community of *bachateros* and *salseros*; and to Jayadev Arthreya, Julian Gantt, Radhika Govindrajan, Devin Naar, Nova Robinson, Andrea Soroko, Natasha Varner, and Hamza Zafer for sharing so much food and friendship. Daniel Bessner read this research at its various stages and never wavered in his encouragement. I am grateful that I had him as a partner for many years, and remain thankful for his friendship.

Finally, my family has been impossibly supportive through this process. They did not always understand why it took so long to finish and publish this book, but they always believed I was doing something meaningful. My maternal grandmother, Rita (Noel) McGlincy, encouraged me from a young age to read, and my maternal grandfather, Lloyd McGlincy, urged me to see the world. My paternal grandparents, William and Patricia (Kafoure) Freije, provided my first introduction to cultural syncretism. Pen Caldwell joined the family in 2009 but has quickly integrated himself into our large clan. My siblings, Hope, Nicholas, Sophie, and Ethan, are my favorite people; they make everything better and always give me something to aspire to. My parents, Susan Caldwell and Matthew Freije, not only believe in me but also in the power of ideas. They are the reason any of this was possible, which is why this book is for them.

# INTRODUCTION

In Mexico, we inhabit a realm of two truths: one is the people's, they know it because they have seen it, it is what everyone on the street recognizes as reality; the other truth is the official one, the one that is imposed by decree.
—JOSÉ LUIS GONZÁLEZ MEZA AND WALTER LÓPEZ KOEHL, *UN ASESINO EN LA PRESIDENCIA?*

The press, a big gossip, will go off and tell everyone.
—ROBERTO BLANCO MOHENO, *MEMORIAS DE UN REPORTERO*

In July 1979 star journalist Manuel Buendía reported on Acapulco's "decadence" and decline, painting a picture of deteriorated opulence.[1] His nationally syndicated column described blue waters cluttered with bottles and cans and untreated sewage runoff that posed a serious health hazard to swimmers. In addition to producing new environmental threats, the modernization of the resort city in the 1940s had delivered uneven benefits. To construct high-rise waterfront hotels, federal developers expropriated small-scale farmers' land and (with the aid of police) burned their crops.[2] The result was popular protests, housing shortages, and expanding squatter settlements on the surrounding hillside. Social discontent was still evident decades later. Buendía observed protests in the city square, where taxi drivers mounted a hunger strike to demand the *placas* (medallions) that they needed to legally work. The columnist blamed this conflict on the unpopular state governor, Rubén Figueroa, whom he depicted as a thug with a paunch that "shook like a 'sack full of skulls'"—a turn of phrase that humiliated the politician and delighted disgruntled residents.[3] Overall the article suggested that Acapulco's once glimmering exterior, like Mexico's modernization, could no longer mask the ugly reality of violence, impunity, and inequality.

The attention from a prominent Mexico City journalist sparked impassioned exchanges that crossed class divides as local workers, reporters, and public officials responded to the article. In Acapulco's central plaza, the taxi drivers took to megaphones to broadcast the columnist's accusations. Meanwhile, white-collar hotel workers congratulated Buendía on his influential article.[4] Letters and megaphones were just two of the technologies, along with photocopy machines, talk radio shows, telephones, flyers, and graffiti, that readers used to comment on what they read. This engagement exemplifies the emergence of new publics that, while not fully national in scope, connected Mexico City and regional news consumers.

Buendía's was just one of many articles that broke with the long-standing conformism in national broadsheets, the country's oldest and most prominent newspapers. In the 1960s, influential Mexico City reporters of diverse educational and ideological backgrounds increasingly exposed public officials' misdeeds, including embezzlement, torture, police violence, and electoral fraud.[5] Journalists also introduced new perspectives into their reporting, citing the testimonies of marginalized groups and including the views of disaffected officials. Exposés at times erupted into political scandals that circulated between print and broadcast media, electrified debate, and connected different publics, altering the nature of urban political culture.

This book explores contests over knowledge production, political voice, and information access in late twentieth-century Mexico. From the 1960s through the 1980s, the public sphere became more robust and the political arena became more competitive. These decades are popularly and historiographically associated with Mexico's democratization, a gradual process by which the ruling Institutional Revolutionary Party (Partido Revolucionario Institucional, PRI) allowed new spaces for urban political engagement. While independent unions, student movements, and civic organizations flourished, the PRI held on to the presidency until 2000, capping over seventy years in power. To explain this slow decline in political dominance, scholars have emphasized the importance that watershed moments played in reversing the PRI's legitimacy.[6] The 1968 massacre of protesting students, the painful 1982 debt crisis, and the 1985 Mexico City earthquake all figure prominently in scholarly explanations for Mexico's democratic change. A study of political scandals, however, demonstrates that such "watersheds" were themselves a creation of the national press.

*Citizens of Scandal* examines how Mexico City print media critically shaped narratives of political change. It explores what happened when wrongdoing, while common knowledge, became a topic of public debate. I argue that the circulation of critical news and spectacle had two transformative effects on political culture and urban citizenship. First, the national publicity of wrongdoing undermined state attempts to manage public discourse.

Governing officials traditionally made decisions behind closed doors and announced them after the fact. Yet news exposés disrupted this practice by forcing federal officials to respond to public opinion and to reckon with internal party schisms. A study of scandal thus reveals the conflicting interests that divided the PRI, challenging monolithic representations of the party.

Second, scandalous news items provided collective opportunities to revise political expectations and sharpen expressions of dissent. Readers would not have been surprised to learn of the impunity of street cops, the corruption of city bureaucrats, or the absence of effective representation. Yet knowing had not meant reckoning. As Heather Levi instructively writes about secrecy, the boundaries between knowing and not knowing are rarely absolute.[7] Public exposure, especially in print, functioned as "a powerful mechanism both for the enforcement of values and norms and for the rearticulation of those norms."[8] Publicity thus became an important, though unpredictable and inequitable, tool of political representation.

Urban Mexicans were, in this sense, "citizens of scandal." While the law promised equal rights, the reality was a "differentiated citizenship" that was often based on skin color, gender, property, religion, class, or access to the legal system.[9] Scandals could only offer an uneven and similarly inequitable mechanism to deliver justice. Despite these shortcomings, spectacles constituted an important aspect of the meaning-making practice of urban citizenship. The Mexico City press served as a launching pad for scandals that reached a national audience. This study considers both how news coverage outside of Mexico City found its way into the national press as well as how Mexico City journalists reported on political developments outside of the capital. While this focus cannot capture the heterogeneity of regional news and audiences, it is not merely a Mexico City story. As suggested by the opening vignette, scandals circulated through multiple media with national reach, knitting together different publics in moments of shared outrage. By engaging with and reinterpreting scandals, ordinary Mexicans asserted their right to participate in the definition of the country's social and political problems.[10]

Finally, this book challenges long-standing assumptions that a free press and democracy are mutually constitutive. In late twentieth-century Mexico, the work of journalism became more dangerous as the political system democratized, and reporters increasingly faced retaliation from organized crime and public officials.[11] Meanwhile, print media did not equitably deliver accountability and representation. Scandals not only amplified the voices of the powerful but also relied at times on gendered and racialized language to garner broad-based outrage. Even as critical reporters denounced corruption, moreover, they withheld many more secrets from public discussion. These tensions—between free speech and (self-)censorship, representation and exclusion, and transparency and secrecy—defined the Mexican public sphere in the late twentieth century.

## MEDIATED CITIZENSHIP

The 1960s were ripe for deliberation over Mexico's political system. The 1959 Cuban Revolution had catalyzed profound regional change, fundamentally altering expectations about the possibilities of revolutionary uprising. In Mexican cities, Cuba's example inspired massive labor strikes and radicalized university campuses, while motivating the federal government to unleash greater repression against dissidents. Four decades had passed since the 1910 Mexican Revolution forged a new social pact that guaranteed land reform, workers' rights, and sovereignty over natural resources. In 1929, revolutionary generals formed a single party to ensure the peaceful transfer of power, and in 1946 the PRI inherited this one-party state, claiming the revolutionary mantle while pursuing more conservative economic policies. The party governed through three class-based organizations, which mediated the grievances of industrial workers, peasants, and white-collar urbanites. As a testament to the PRI's ideological flexibility, diverse groups from political bosses (*caciques*) to leftist syndicalist leaders could register their demands so long as they did so within party structures.[12] Power sharing among elites allowed Mexico to avoid the military coups and dictatorships that beset much of Latin America in the twentieth century, but political stability also came at the cost of persistent repression in the countryside. By the 1960s the PRI received international accolades for ushering in a uniquely stable, if idiosyncratic, democracy and for overseeing high economic growth.[13]

Popular political engagement was shaped by the spread of new information technologies at midcentury. Urban Mexicans developed a "mediated citizenship" in which their political commitments and practices were forged through everyday interactions with mass media.[14] This was evident, for example, in a 1973 letter from an Acapulco resident to Miguel Ángel Granados Chapa, the opinion editor at the national broadsheet *Excélsior*. The letter writer, named Leonor, thanked the columnist and other journalists for affirming what she already believed: that political leaders did not understand her lived reality and that "corruption is an enormous pit into which nearly everyone falls to some degree."[15] Mexico City media furnished Leonor with a repertoire of images, texts, and vocabularies that she shared with other urban residents and that helped her narrate her political worldview.

The spread of mass media was a Global South phenomenon in the 1950s and 1960s. International development organizations, influenced by modernization theory, saw mass media adoption as a pivotal step in economic development and civic engagement.[16] To this end, the Ford Foundation; the United Nations Educational, Scientific and Cultural Organization; and other nongovernmental organizations sponsored communications studies, funded technology transfers, and provided technical aid to the Global South—especially Africa and Latin America.[17] The Cold War battle for hearts and minds provided another rationale for mass media investment in the so-called Third World, and Soviet and U.S. leaders tried to reach new audiences with radio broadcasts, television programs, and films. Shaped by this context, Mexican leaders saw mass media as essential not only to modernization but also to the creation of a national identity and to their preservation of power.[18] Over the course of the twentieth century, the state invested in radio transmitters, newsprint production, a microwave broadcasting system, and two satellites, making the country a regional front runner in communications development.[19]

Government support for education and culture fundamentally altered reading practices. State-subsidized newsprint and advertising gave consumers access to affordable and diverse reading material. Since the late 1930s, the state-run monopoly Paper Importer and Producer, S. A. (Productora e Importadora de Papel, S. A., or PIPSA) stabilized the domestic newsprint market by purchasing, warehousing, manufacturing, and selling paper. The result was well-stocked corner newsstands that sold popular comic books, sensationalist crime tabloids, and sports dailies alongside mainstream periodicals and political magazines. Urban dwellers lingered at newsstands to skim headlines while they waited for their buses, and political elites pored over the news while they had their shoes shined. By the end of the day, a single copy of a newspaper would be well worn after passing through multiple hands at barbershops, shoeshine stands, or tenement patios.[20]

Official census data charted a considerable growth in primary school attendance between 1940 and 1970, and over these decades literacy climbed from 42 percent to over 76 percent, with even higher rates in Mexico City.[21] Census data likely overestimated literacy by including individuals who could only write their names, but ethnographic research provides additional context for these figures. Researchers in the 1960s and 1970s found that tabloid readership was prevalent in tenements and squatter settlements in greater Mexico City.[22]

Surveys conducted by the U.S. Information Agency (USIA) also indicate that newspaper readership thrived outside the capital. By 1966, 64 percent of residents in midsize cities in central Mexico, such as Irapuato, Pachuca, Puebla, and Toluca, read the newspaper daily or several times per week.[23]

The experience of urban life was one of mass media saturation, even for the very poor. New theaters and government-enforced price controls on tickets popularized moviegoing.[24] A 1952 USIA survey found that 53 percent of urban Mexicans went to the movies at least once per month, and *Variety* reported in 1966 that Mexico had the joint highest per capita rate of film attendance in the world.[25] By the 1960s, storefronts, bus stations, bars, and restaurants boasted television sets to attract patrons. Television viewership began as a public activity, and residents would gather (for a small fee) at neighbors' homes to watch popular telenovelas. It was not until the 1970s that the domestic manufacturing of television sets made ownership possible even for the urban poor.[26] By 1965, 43 percent of residents in Mexico's three largest cities (Mexico City, Guadalajara, and Monterrey) owned a television set and 86 percent owned a radio.[27]

Three decades of urbanization and industrialization between 1940 and 1970 produced dramatic demographic and cultural shifts, and the PRI struggled to adapt with this changing population. Improved public health lowered rates of infant and maternal mortality while contributing to rapid population growth and rising unemployment. The postwar mechanization of agriculture increased landlessness and rural unemployment, driving many subsistence farmers to migrate in search of work, particularly in the 1960s. During that decade, 1.8 million people immigrated to the greater Mexico City area. The city and its environs swelled from 1.5 million people in 1940 to 8.4 million three decades later; by 1970, one-sixth of Mexico's population lived in the capital.[28] Facing strained public services, growing unemployment, and housing scarcity, public officials joined international demographers in blaming economic recession on population growth.

Political magazines and newspapers with small metropolitan readerships, such as *El Día*, *Política*, and *Siempre!*, were among the first Mexico City publications to discuss the problems of landlessness, poverty, and corruption in the early 1960s. These news outlets attacked leading power brokers, rather than midlevel figures, and drove broader debates over policy. While critical articles often began in more rarefied publications, they ignited collective discussion by circulating through a wide network of media. Practices of "borrowing" news items without attribution were common, and established mainstream newspapers frequently reported on exposés first broken by left-leaning outlets. By the late 1970s, syndication services placed critical columns, including Buendía's and Granados Chapa's, in newspapers across the country, enabling distinct readerships to encounter the same news items. News and cultural production were heavily concentrated in Mexico City; television broadcasts centered on events there, and many local publications relied on national news feeds for their stories.[29] Mexico City media were not uniquely confrontational, but they were exceptionally influential in shaping national debates.

Scandalous exposés circulated beyond elite readers, worrying public officials who saw the lower classes as unpredictable and potentially violent. Cheap tell-all memoirs and comic books magnified and reinterpreted salacious stories, and neighborhood organizations diffused articles by reprinting or summarizing them in bulletins or flyers. Radio and television programs commented on scandalous cases and generated greater interest through interviews with aggrieved parties. As politicians found themselves forced to respond to accusations, they also spread the topic to a wider audience. The availability of multiple critical news outlets made this intertextual exchange possible. At the same time, readers encountered the news in different ways depending on their education levels, reading speeds, and insider knowledge.

Mexico City's independent-minded press democratized public debate by widening the topics discussed and the voices represented. In this way, journalism contributed to the expansion of the public sphere, or the arena that "compel[led] public authority to legitimate itself before public opinion."[30] Philosopher Jürgen Habermas theorized the public sphere as a horizontal space for debate that first emerged in eighteenth-century Europe alongside the rise of the bourgeoisie. He lamented, however, that the public sphere was later corrupted by mass culture and the welfare state, which collapsed the boundary between state and society and turned news into a commodity.[31] In his rendering, the rise of the market economy made the public sphere possible but later undermined it altogether.

Habermas's normative prescription has elicited considerable criticism. Feminist scholars have argued that he glossed the gendered and class (not to mention racial) exclusions that underpinned his idealized public sphere.[32] How, they wondered, could these spaces be considered democratic when access to them was premised on being white, male, and middle class? Meanwhile, scholars of the non-European world have adapted Habermas's model to their regions of study by resisting the ideal of "rational" debate. Latin American historians, for example, have shown that seemingly illiberal or irrational forums, such as gossip columns, crime pages, and Catholic radio programs, could constitute spaces for critical deliberation.[33] They have also illustrated that the public sphere could be extended under undemocratic or even authoritarian governments.[34] In effect, these scholars identify how critical deliberation operated under conditions distinct from Habermas's formulation. Indeed, Pablo Piccato usefully frames the public sphere as the "processes" and "interactions" that brought together "private interests, state policies, and social practices such as reading and conversation."[35]

This book shows that even politically and financially compromised journalists could expand the public sphere. For much of the twentieth century, Mexico City publications, reporters, and directors could not survive financially without state subsidies. Newspaper owners were economically dependent on government advertising and state-subsidized newsprint, and reporters relied on the notorious *embute*, bribes in the form of cash-stuffed envelopes from public officials, to supplement their meager salaries. These conditions undoubtedly placed considerable constraints on reporters. State and press entanglements also extended beyond economic dependence. Like North Atlantic journalists, Mexican reporters relied on insider leaks (and thus political goodwill) for confidential information. Meanwhile, as readerships expanded, public officials needed reporters to manage public opinion and to silence damaging stories. Examining how interpersonal relationships undergirded scandals, this book reveals that the opening of the public sphere simultaneously rested on processes of negotiation, alliance, and concealment.

As Mexico City writers pressed to open a closed political system, they did not see all voices as equally deserving of amplification. Politicians and journalists often described knowledge production in gendered terms that cast elite male knowledge as rational news and subversive speech as feminine gossip. Journalists and intellectuals similarly naturalized gender and class inequalities by delineating who could lay claim to knowledge. By raising these contradictions, I push back against Habermas's normative understanding of the public sphere as an inherently democratic realm. Moreover, instances of violence toward Mexican journalists, as in some other parts of Latin America, have only increased under electoral democracy.[36] The outsize role that criminal organizations and private corporations have played in shaping contemporary news also underscores the need to revise Habermas's understanding of the relationship between the market, the state, and press freedom.

## OPEN SECRETS AND THE ONE-PARTY STATE

This book departs from prevailing scholarship on Mexico City print media. Scholars and journalists alike have described the national press as co-opted or complicit in the maintenance of the PRI's decades-long rule.[37] Sociologists and political scientists argue that it was not until the 1990s that economic liberalization, the privatization of PIPSA, and shifting newsroom cultures fostered the development of "civic journalism."[38] Recent scholarship, however, highlights that national media could cultivate critical subjectivities despite state attempts to forge quiescence. Popular songs and films emphasized individual development, cultivating anti-authoritarian mindsets, while flysheets and crime news generated critical discussions of state impunity.[39] Building on this work, my book shows that, beginning in the 1960s, reporters did not have to be fully independent to effect substantial change. In fact, as political insiders they could stoke elite rivalries and launch penetrating investigations into corruption. These exposés were not neutral and often served as weapons for one political faction against another. Indeed, journalists both reflected and generated serious competition inside the party. By moving away from dichotomies of co-optation versus independence, we can better understand how journalists shaped Mexican political culture and engagement.

A study of the national press from the early 1960s through the late 1980s also reveals the PRI's infrapolitics and draws our attention to moments of rupture within the ruling party, underscoring its continued heterogeneity. In so doing, this book revises our ideas about the one-party regime in the late twentieth century. Historians of the postrevolutionary period have shown the decentralized, organic, and local processes of negotiation that produced the modern Mexican state.[40] In recent years, historians of midcentury Mexico have similarly revealed the significant popular opposition and state repression that persisted after the PRI consolidated power. As Paul Gillingham and Benjamin T. Smith argue, the PRI combined an ambiguous mix of "hard and soft power, of coercion and co-option," leading them to characterize the regime as a "*dictablanda*."[41] Demonstrating that the party's control was never complete or even, these studies collectively challenged revisionist historiography that depicted an all-powerful ruling party.[42]

And yet, work on post-1968 Mexico still tends to reproduce the sensibility, if not the language, of contemporary writers who characterized the PRI as an authoritarian "monolith."[43] With few exceptions, studies of this period often depict the ruling party as a unanimous and cohesively acting body. In rural Guerrero, it was a brutal authoritarian regime;[44] in Mexico City and other urban centers, however, the PRI was more flexible and responsive to disgruntled middle classes, independently organized street vendors, and Indigenous leaders who worked within state institutions.[45] This produces the sensation of walking through a hall of mirrors; the party is reflected differently depending upon the location from which one views it. From the vantage point of the Mexico City press, the party appeared beset by challenges. It also struggled to mask its internal divisions, which had become so polarized that disagreement was often resolved by publicizing dissent. Leaking to the press played an important role in stoking internal party divisions and ultimately contributed to the PRI's splintering in 1987, auguring the end of one-party rule.

Airing the party's dirty laundry broke with the open secrets that guaranteed mutual protection among political elites and were constitutive of twentieth-century Mexican political culture.[46] Open secrets, or "that which is generally known, but cannot be articulated," had disciplined governing officials, journalists, and ordinary people by requiring the silencing or dissimulation of knowledge.[47] In practice, of course, this silence was contingent on one's audience and location; behind closed doors, public officials openly gossiped about evident wrongdoing, but they avoided publicly airing the information. Journalists were often privy to these conversations but publicly dissimulated their knowledge to avoid appearing complicit.[48] Writing on the Argentine context, Ieva Jusionyte notes that crime reporters relied on a dense web of relationships, which required them to "develop the social knowledge and skills necessary to recognize where *not* to look and what not to see."[49] Ordinary people, meanwhile, might possess only partial knowledge of official wrongdoing, but lack the protection or access to denounce it. Indeed, secrets perpetuated "separate spheres of knowledge" that served to "create and maintain social difference and relations."[50] This book examines how the interplay between exposure and secrecy shaped the Mexican public sphere while enforcing complicity at multiple levels.

## DENUNCIA JOURNALISM

Many of the journalists in this book clashed personally and ideologically, but they were united by their willingness to expose official wrongdoing, even while their individual motivations and strategies differed considerably. I describe these figures as *denuncia* journalists. In so doing, I reclaim a derogatory characterization that Latin American public officials used to describe those who smeared politicians without real evidence against them.[51] Throughout Latin America, *denuncia* refers both to a general, public accusation and a formal, legal complaint. For example, victims of a crime can file a formal report (denuncia) to initiate a criminal investigation. In the absence of legal safeguards, however, victims historically sought out journalists who transformed individual grievances into issues of common concern. The reference to denuncia thus signals the ways in which journalists connected ordinary people with political elites, capturing reporters' liminal roles as both the tribunals of civil society and the advocates of state bureaucrats.

Midcentury denuncia journalism was predated by a long history of politically committed commentary in the press. Pointed denunciations became particularly visible during the late nineteenth-century dictatorship of Porfirio Díaz when newspapers like *El Hijo del Ahuizote* and journals like *Regeneración* excoriated public officials by name. The repercussions for denunciations were severe, and the Díaz government imprisoned confrontational editors, confiscated newspaper copies, and destroyed printing presses.[52] With the outbreak of the Mexican Revolution in 1910, denuncia journalists and photographers kept readers informed of the violent conflict that would unseat the dictator and claim at least a half million lives. After the fighting subsided, radical leftists and conservative Catholics alike exposed government wrongdoing in periodicals like *El Diario de Yucatán* (Mérida), *El Informador* (Guadalajara), and *El Machete* (Mexico City). Crime news also furnished a space to denounce police incompetence and official injustice. With the consolidation of the one-party regime in the 1930s, officials closely monitored the national press, but denuncia journalism continued to thrive outside the capital.[53]

In the 1960s, many young Mexico City journalists were politicized by experiencing state violence firsthand. Left-leaning culture writer Carlos Monsiváis witnessed the military's violent repression and imprisonment of railroad strikers in 1959. Héctor Gama, Froylán López Narváez, and José Reveles were similarly radicalized after they marched in the 1968 Mexico City student protests and saw plainclothes security forces open fire on an unsuspecting crowd of students, teachers, and professors. Many budding writers considered the Tlatelolco Massacre, as the attack became known, to be the defining event of their political lives. After sustaining a gunshot wound to his leg, reporter Francisco Ortiz Pinchetti embraced conservative criticisms of the PRI. Elena Poniatowska, though she did not participate in the protests, became famous for her interviews with the participants, which she compiled in her best-selling 1971 chronicle *La noche de Tlatelolco*. Heberto Castillo, an engineering professor at the National Autonomous University of Mexico (Universidad Nacional Autónoma de México), was arrested, imprisoned, and tortured for his involvement in the protests. Upon his release two years later, he used journalism to build support for his leftist opposition party. In short, the massacre was a profoundly formative event for many journalists.[54]

Reporters who named and shamed public officials did not represent the average Mexico City journalist. They were exceptional in terms of their influence, moral authority, and, at times, financial security. Exposing wrongdoing implied social, economic, and professional risks. Many of these writers had sufficient means to survive economically if their exposés resulted in their firing. For example, chronicler and novelist Poniatowska was the descendant of Polish nobility and independently wealthy, making it possible for her to take greater risks. Castillo, a professional engineer and leftist activist, was a regular news commentator in the 1970s, but journalism was not his primary source of income. Julio Scherer García earned a reputation for always refusing bribes, but one editor noted that the famous newspaper reporter and director could afford to do so because he came from a wealthy family.[55] Others, like Buendía and Monsiváis, grew up in lower-middle-class families but became influential and respected public figures by the 1970s, which granted them greater latitude for dissent. Financial security or cultural prominence thus allowed these writers to challenge powerful officials in print.

Still, reporters encountered an unpredictable government, which alternatively supported, co-opted, or repressed them. While President Luis Echeverría promised that his "democratic opening" would include press freedom, the boundaries of acceptable dissent were often shifting. Muckraking publications like *Por Qué?* suffered repeated attacks, and in 1976 Echeverría intervened in the nation's prominent broadsheet, *Excélsior*, to remove its editorial team. This experience compelled the ousted editors to found more critical news outlets, including *Proceso* and *Unomásuno*, in the late 1970s. These publications covered numerous high-profile scandals that emerged during the subsequent administration of José López Portillo. In addition to denouncing political corruption, such news outlets also provided spaces for *crónicas*, narrative journalism that foregrounded the voices and experiences of those often marginalized by the press and political power.

These dynamics functioned differently outside the nation's capital, where financial ties were weaker between local and regional newspapers and state governments. As a result, small publications could collaborate closely with civic movements and deliver damning criticism of local authorities and corruption. Yet there also were significant limitations to doing so. Impunity reigned to a greater degree outside Mexico City, and crossing the wrong official could lead to serious, even deadly, consequences. This led to an odd paradox: capital city journalists enjoyed the greatest level of safety but higher levels of scrutiny.[56]

By the 1970s Mexico City denuncia journalists generally had some higher education, which further distinguished them from most working reporters.[57] They established their careers in the capital, though many were born elsewhere in the country, and their worldviews were informed by Mexico City's connection to the wider world. Many had the opportunity to travel abroad; some went for study while others went as agricultural workers as part of the joint Mexican-U.S. Bracero Program that began during World War II. In universities, newsrooms, and publishing houses, Mexico City writers and academics rubbed elbows with Spanish and South American exiles who shaped the political and cultural outlook of these institutions. Mexico City journalists also closely followed regional developments, and some took to the streets to protest the 1961 Bay of Pigs Invasion in Cuba and the 1973 coup that overthrew socialist Chilean president Salvador Allende. Reporters and intellectuals were also influenced by regional religious trends. A 1968 meeting among Latin American Catholic bishops in Medellín, Colombia, resulted in a regional ecclesiastical turn toward liberation theology. Though far from universally accepted within the church, a commitment to social justice filtered into educational institutions, civic organizations, and sermons. Journalists' political expectations thus were shaped by the ideological and political developments in the region.

Mexico City reporters and opinion writers also were influenced by shifting international journalistic norms and genres. The New Journalism movement in the United States informed Mexican literary reporting, inspiring long-form pieces that cultivated readers' identification with marginalized individuals.[58] Chronicles brought new voices and issues into the elite press, introducing the experiences of rape victims, Indigenous activists, and soccer fans, to name just a few.[59] Mainstream periodicals in Mexico City also closely followed the Watergate scandal and lauded the heroic reporters who confronted President Richard Nixon. The prolific output of media and communications studies further articulated ethical expectations, including objectivity and balance, which were diffused internationally in conferences and textbooks.[60] By the late 1970s journalism students in Mexico were well versed in the arguments of U.S. and Western European communications theorists.

In other ways, denuncia reporters were no different from their less confrontational counterparts. Even the most influential reporters understood that their content was subject to negotiation. *Siempre!* magazine director José Pagés Llergo famously articulated the internalized journalistic norms in his pronouncement that Mexican reporters could write about anything save the president, the military, and the Virgin of Guadalupe (that is, the

Catholic Church). The quotable phrase captured the possibilities of journalistic speech while also obscuring how the boundaries of acceptable criticism were always shifting. The minister of the interior frequently called newsrooms to communicate requests for stories or alterations, which editors and directors typically heeded.[61] Officials, from congressional representatives to cabinet members, cultivated relationships with their preferred reporters to generate positive coverage. Journalists and editors thus learned to navigate competing interests and to adjust their coverage accordingly.

In a profession dominated by men, reporters rubbed elbows with police and politicians in spaces of masculine sociability, such as cantinas, shooting ranges, or late-night poker games.[62] Conservative reporter Roberto Blanco Moheno pithily described journalism as "the comradery of drink and the distribution of coin."[63] Relationships were also lubricated with gifts of imported scotch and invitations to family events, such as christenings. Female reporters, meanwhile, were typically excluded from these reciprocal relationships. This made information gathering more challenging while allowing women to avoid the expectations that accompanied personal relationships with informants. Until the late 1970s, most female journalists, including Poniatowska, were relegated to writing for the social pages. Those who gained access to political beats improvised methods for accessing information. Among them was Sara Lovera, who covered labor issues for *El Día* in the 1970s and *La Jornada* in the 1980s. To gain incriminating information, she once wore a disguise to sneak into a closed-door meeting. Poniatowska, meanwhile, avoided official sources and instead interviewed ordinary people for her chronicles. Other women may have used their sexuality to cultivate informants, as Colombian journalists Laura Restrepo and Virginia Vallejo famously did with a member of the guerrilla group M-19 and Pablo Escobar, respectively.[64]

## SCANDAL AND NARRATIVE

One outgrowth of denuncia journalism was the prevalence of political scandals, which galvanized readers' attention and helped sell newspapers. Headlines warned darkly of "The Complicity of Silence" and revealed "A Fashionable Sport: Hunting Journalists."[65] Exposés also took direct aim at powerful figures, lobbing accusations that Mexico City's police chief ran an extortion ring and that the president's family was involved in drug trafficking.[66] High-profile cases could even prompt the resignation and imprisonment of public figures. Scandals were unique in late twentieth-century Mexico because they mobilized national, rather than local, attention.[67]

In the broadest terms, scholars understand scandals as disruptive accusations of transgression. Notably, such accusations demand a response.[68] As Don Kulick and Charles Klein write on the Brazilian context, scandals produce "small-scale and temporary crinkles in the overall social fabric" and can be seen as "political actions that result in both recognition *and* redistribution."[69] This dynamic was evident in the aftermath of Buendía's column, as discussed at the opening of this chapter. His confrontational coverage prompted the Guerrero state director of police and transit to issue a response in national newspapers the following day, discrediting the hunger strikers as disingenuous "whiners" and accusing them of sneaking home to eat dinner.[70] Paid articles delivered similar messages in local and national newspapers and issued veiled threats against Buendía, making him fear for his safety.[71] Despite these ad hominem attacks and this personal intimidation, Guerrero's governor, Figueroa, eventually acceded to the taxi drivers' demands and issued them the medallions they requested.[72] With this Janus-faced response, state officials delivered an episodic and unpredictable form of accountability.

I consider scandals not as abbreviated interactions but as social processes involving a series of amplifying moments that included recirculation, gossip, new revelations, public responses, denials, punishment, remembering, and silencing. This definition foregrounds the echoes evident long after an initial disruption has passed. The social processes of scandals allowed multiple actors to shape the political resonance that these cases would have. These resonances changed over time and were contingent on the social and political conditions of scandals' production and revelation. Scandals were not only interpreted and diffused by media but also through word of mouth, public performances, and handmade signs. Analyzing the circulation of scandals leads me to depart from James C. Scott's influential framing of everyday popular expression, including gossip, stories, and slander, as "weapons of the weak." Scott has argued that these "backstage" expressions revealed disgruntlement but did little to change structures.[73] Scandals, however, collapsed the boundaries between "onstage" and "offstage" expressions, and unattributed accusations could fuel collective action and prompt official responses.

As scholars now recognize, scandals are socially constructed, and most bad behavior does not garner national outrage and attention.[74] Late twentieth-century Mexico was no exception. Reporters often withheld potentially salacious stories because they lacked sufficient evidence or support within the government, which they would need as protection against retaliation. And even when journalists reported wrongdoing, many exposés failed to capture the popular imagination. Those that did ignite outrage could be synthesized into easily digestible sound bites. As "bounded stories," scandals often functioned as cautionary tales or lessons that media, from documentaries to radio, invoked long after the scandals subsided.[75] Through iterative processes, references to a case could evoke a wider set of meanings. For example, a mention of 1968 referenced state violence and illegitimacy; and an allusion to Mexico City police chief Arturo Durazo elicited images of morally depraved and abusive functionaries during the economic crisis. And comments regarding clandestine sweatshops, which collapsed in the 1985 earthquake, recalled employer greed and state complicity in poor labor conditions and shoddy building construction. The meanings behind these political events and figures were undoubtedly contested at the time. But reporters consistently reiterated the stakes, inscribing these transgressions into popular memory as watershed moments.

The corruption of high-ranking officials became an overriding theme of exposés. In the fall of 1982 Mexico defaulted on its foreign debt repayments, catalyzing an economic crisis that reverberated throughout Latin America. Structural adjustment agreements with the International Monetary Fund in 1976 and 1982 inaugurated an era of neoliberal governance characterized by technocracy, deregulation, and market liberalization. Though they differed considerably in their conceptualizations of Mexican democracy, both leftist and conservative journalists and activists concurred that the PRI's corporatist system had allowed political leaders to act with impunity. Reporters collaborated with burgeoning social movements to diversify the voices and demands in their exposés.

The most salient scandals identified a single perpetrator, personalizing political power by reducing a complex web of relations to a solitary individual.[76] Conscientious reporters would flag the structural conditions that perpetuated these issues, and they described corruption as a generalized problem with the PRI rather than the individuals within it. As accusations circulated through media, the narrative structure of scandals made it easy to lose this nuance. Stories often made a spectacle of shaming select individuals and repeating key sensational details. Public apologies, forced resignations, and even indictments became expected outcomes of public accusations. Such performances of justice legitimized the status quo by underscoring that the political system was working. Moreover, these punishments were individualized; the press served as an ad hoc lever of justice that could not possibly guarantee rights for all. With scandals, contestatory publics and a pluralistic public sphere emerged, but government accountability rested precariously upon the publicity of wrongdoing.

## WRITING A HISTORY OF THE RECENT PAST

By centering the press in the study of late twentieth-century knowledge production, I aim to make a familiar source unfamiliar. If archival documents feel rarefied, news publications are the opposite. Internationally, periodicals share a visual style and layout (headlines, columns, sections, and bylines) that make them easily legible and navigable. Scholars and other writers have turned to journalists' accounts to make sense of the post-1968 period because many government archives remain inaccessible. In so doing, historians have tended to deracinate influential press articles from their moments of production, erasing the processes that allowed particular narratives to assume a prominent place in public memory.

Like archives, print media have their own histories of production, curation, and silences. A historian can read periodicals against the grain, searching for telling cracks that reveal divisions among the newsroom staff or coded messages that were only intelligible to a select few. A well-informed observer can discern the various interests at play on any given page. Paid advertising space projected the denunciations of local organizations and unions. Wrapped around news articles were public service announcements informing readers of everything from the availability of housing credit to the accomplishments of the Ministry of Water Resources (Secretaría de Recursos Hidráulicos). Less visible but equally prevalent were *gacetillas*, paid articles that editors masked as real news. Opinion pages frequently featured weekly contributions from politicians, who saw editorials as an alternative means to disseminate their ideas. As president, Echeverría even pseudonymously wrote a regular column, "Granero Político," to project his views.[77] His authorship was an open secret among the political elite, but perhaps unknown to the working-class reader of *La Prensa*, the tabloid where the column appeared. News publications, then, are rich texts that reveal contests over information, political power, and economic resources.

This book brings together a new archive of materials, some of which have never been examined before. I analyze print media sources, including advertisements, photographs, letters to the editor, and cartoons, alongside unpublished documents culled from over seventeen archives, primarily located in Mexico City. While I focus on the print origins of scandals, I trace the circulatory relationships among different media. This illustrates how television and radio reported on print stories, authorities responded, street performances and memoirs offered commentary, and these interventions circulated back to inform print media interpretations. I juxtapose these media sources against materials from journalists' and politicians' private collections, state intelligence archives, presidential papers, and congressional debates. Reading these documents together allows me to consider the relationship between knowledge, secrecy, and scandal, teasing out the bits of information omitted from the public record and dissimulations that accompanied scandalous exposés.

Examining print media alongside unpublished documents also deepens our understanding of how knowledge production and state surveillance functioned. Given the limited archival materials available for the period after 1964, most historians rely on the archives of two intelligence services, the Federal Security Office (Dirección Federal de Seguridad, or DFS) and the General Office for Political and Social Investigations (Dirección General de Investigaciones Políticas y Sociales). These agencies, which operated from 1947 to 1985, were charged by the Ministry of the Interior with identifying political challenges, and both organizations became notorious for their repression and violence. In 2002 President Vicente Fox declassified these intelligence archives shortly after his National Action Party (Partido Acción Nacional) defeated the PRI in a historic election. Both Fox and contemporary observers framed the declassification as a promising sign of transparency that would allow the country to reckon with its authoritarian past. Scholars have since combed through intelligence sources to reveal a greater prevalence of both state repression and popular resistance than was previously associated with the height of the PRI's power. Other historians have used the materials to demonstrate the sources of regime vulnerability and anxiety after 1968.[78]

Historians are aware of the limitations of intelligence reports.[79] State spies typically had little education and were unfamiliar with their subjects of analysis. At times they exaggerated threats to boost their agencies' importance or they simply lied, perhaps to avoid a troublesome investigation. Spies were also notorious for their abuses of power, particularly as funding increased over the 1970s and into the early 1980s.[80] Even while acknowledging these realities, historians have tended to privilege intelligence sources as granting unfettered access to the state's logic and true intentions. Yet as Ann Laura Stoler notes, the arbitrary designation, production, and traffic in secrets is itself a key marker of state power.[81] Paul Christopher Johnson further observes that secrecy raises thorny epistemological issues because one can never know with certainty that they have accessed the entire truth.[82] Indeed, in the late twentieth century ordinary people frequently presumed that official pronouncements and scandalous exposés always hid a larger conspiracy.

A history of the press blurs the boundaries between what historians have considered to be "secret" and "public" sources. Paging through investigative news publications reveals the reproduction of secret documents that were leaked to journalists. Many of the originals can be found across multiple private archives, suggesting that these sources passed through many hands relatively freely. Leaked reports also bear material traces, including signatures and stamps of receipt, that betray widespread knowledge of mismanagement across different organizations. By publicizing these documents, journalists made state secrets public. Intelligence agents also produced reports that relied on thousands of published press articles. By studying the transformative nature of publicity, this book highlights that open secrets were key to the PRI's maintenance of power.

Interviews with twenty-five journalists and politicians helped to shape and identify the archive for this book. These were not necessarily well-known figures, but they had all been active in the press or in politics during the 1960s and 1970s. Some of them, like Gustavo Robles, had been part of the state bureaucracy for decades, moving among different institutions for much of his career. He, like others, pointed me in the direction of more people to talk to and facilitated access to personal archives. While these interviews helped shape my archive and broader understanding of Mexican journalism and politics, they do not make up the empirical basis for my analysis and thus will rarely appear in the references of this book.

The journalists' and politicians' private collections I consulted are generally informal archives stored in family kitchens, home offices, or attics and awaiting organization and curation. Reporters saved leaked documents, correspondence with readers and politicians, drafts and clippings of their articles, and research that informed their writing. Journalists like Sara Lovera amassed smaller collections that centered on the stories and issues that she viewed to be defining of her career. These private archives not only offer a window onto the self-fashioning of the reporters but also their decision-making processes. Juxtaposing leaked documents against published articles reveals that journalists did not merely report leaks as officials wished. At times the reporters saved the leaked materials without ever exposing them, and in other cases they used the documents to reveal a wider network of complicity. While officials always leaked stories with particular aims in mind, the outcomes were not always what they hoped for. Private archives thus offer another window into the press as a site of knowledge production.

## CHAPTER OUTLINE

The book follows widely circulated stories that achieved broad audiences and thus stitched together national publics. Many of the episodes I examine will be familiar to those with knowledge of Mexican history, and I return to these moments in part because of their continued resonance in popular memory. I also chose to examine particular scandals based on the availability of archival documents that could elucidate the production and dissemination of these stories. The chapters take on a variety of temporal and geographic scales. Whereas one chapter covers nearly six years, another focuses on events that unfolded over the course of three weeks. These different time frames capture the multiple ways in which media exposés took shape and the social and political echoes they inspired. The chapters center primarily on Mexico City media. Mexico City was both the seat of the federal government and, by the mid-1970s, home to one-sixth of the country's total population. "Local" corruption investigations could thus have national consequences through federal reforms, and Mexico City media played a disproportionate role in shaping national news.

Chapters 1 and 2 explore the development of a mediated citizenship in greater Mexico City. While denuncia journalism thrived in regional newspapers, it was not until midcentury that critical exposés regularly appeared in capital city publications. Chapter 1 examines how Mexico City journalists and the broader public reckoned with the limits of state-led development, and, by extension, the Mexican Revolution. The chapter analyzes two scandals that shaped these discussions: a 1963 investigative series on the ailing Yucatecan henequen industry, and the 1965 censorship of Oscar Lewis's *Los hijos de Sánchez*, an anthropological exploration of Mexican poverty. Both exposés ignited heated debates about who could disprove narratives of revolutionary progress. The chapter traces the echoes of scandals in letters to the editor, boisterous university roundtables, and peasant protests.

While chapter 1 shows how elite-generated scandals could fuel collective action, chapter 2 demonstrates how popular accusations catalyzed a scandal in elite print media. In 1974, unsubstantiated accounts surfaced claiming that the government was sterilizing poor schoolchildren, leading to widespread panic and school closures in the greater Mexico City area. Denuncia journalists were wary of knowledge that came from the city's impoverished periphery, and they allied with governing officials to discount the accusations as ignorant rumors. Policing the boundaries of rational debate, journalists tried to exorcise popular knowledge from printed forums. Yet residents of greater Mexico City drew on the language and vocabularies of international sterilization scandals to formulate denunciations against state-sponsored violence. Chapter 2 examines how conflicts over knowledge production emerged amid the opening of Mexico City's major broadsheets.

Chapters 3 and 4 focus on the denunciation of corruption, which became a central theme of muckraking journalism in the late 1970s and early 1980s. Chapter 3 examines an embezzlement scheme at Mexican Petroleum (Petróleos Mexicanos, or Pemex) that led to the imprisonment of its director, Jorge Díaz Serrano. At the time, denuncia journalists covered the case to argue for a more equitable distribution of wealth and an end to PRI corruption. But the 1982 economic crisis led public officials and conservative groups to mobilize the Pemex scandal to their own ends: to justify the slashing of the social safety net and the liberalization of Mexico's economy. Chapter 4 takes up the iconic scandal of Mexico City chief of police Arturo Durazo, who was embroiled in drug trafficking, embezzlement, and, most dramatically, murder. The scandal escaped the control of investigative journalists, circulating widely and inspiring new interpretations in comic books, films, and tell-all accounts. These popular media often gave racialized and gendered explanations of corruption. The chapter thus highlights a tension within scandals: they could expose state impunity and wrongdoing even while relying on discriminatory language to mobilize outrage. Together, chapters 3 and 4 consider how the meanings of scandals ultimately escaped the control of their originators.

Chapters 5 and 6 explore how scandals intersected with growing demands from civil society. Chapter 5 analyzes news coverage after the 1985 Mexico City earthquake, which revealed that abusive and unregulated labor conditions had heightened the death toll. The chapter examines the conflicts over how to represent the disaster. State-sponsored radio programs and public service announcements mobilized experts to deflect blame, and government-aligned media produced sensational coverage to depoliticize the scandal. Chronicles traced the affective and individual responses among marginalized groups. Meanwhile, the increasingly visible victims of state corruption, like the survivors of collapsed clandestine sweatshops, struggled to shape coverage in a way that reflected their interests. When they failed to project their own views through bulletins or filming, they could also register their dissent by refusing to speak to reporters. The chapter thus highlights how scandals brought contests over public space and representation into sharp relief.

Chapter 6 analyzes local, national, and international coverage of the 1986 gubernatorial elections in the northern state of Chihuahua. Electoral fraud sparked hunger strikes and civil disobedience from the conservative opposition. While leftist denuncia journalists acknowledged the evidence of fraud, the Chihuahuan elections raised thorny questions about the politics of scandal. Academics, activists, and journalists commented on the case, questioning whose interests were served by the accusations and voicing fears that ill-intentioned groups could weaponize scandals against political opponents. Obvious silences and presumed prejudices elicited angry calls from readers to newsrooms, bitter accusations of co-optation by journalist peers, and on-the-ground confrontations between correspondents. These conflicts highlight the competing standards to which reporters were held by each other and their readers. Confrontations reveal that many readers and reporters understood the press as an advocate that could not (and should not) be objective.

An epilogue concludes with the dizzying scandals of the late 1980s and early 1990s, which linked President Carlos Salinas and his family to narco-trafficking and even murder. Shortly after Salinas's term in office ended, his brother was imprisoned and Carlos went into a self-imposed exile. These seemingly unprecedented events had their roots in the development of Mexico City's denuncia journalism in the 1960s. Collectively chapters 5 and 6 trace the formation of a national public sphere in which the denunciation of powerful figures provided an episodic and unpredictable mechanism of accountability. These scandals consistently revealed and aggravated disunity among regime officials and challenged conventional methods of managing public opinion. They also brought together new publics who reinterpreted the scandals and incorporated them into their narratives of political change. The public sphere permitted new voices and perspectives while revealing the persistent tensions between transparency and secrecy, representation and exclusion, and free speech and censorship.

CHAPTER 1

# RECKONING WITH THE REVOLUTION

On the fifty-sixth anniversary of the Mexican Revolution, *Siempre!* magazine published an anonymous editorial that took stock of the country's political and economic progress.[1] The author (likely *Siempre!* director José Pagés Llergo) acknowledged that problems of landlessness and union corruption persisted and noted that the PRI was "more democratic in substance than in form."[2] He nonetheless deplored the recent "fashion" of "dwelling on the [revolution's] deficiencies and detours." The editorial was a masterful exercise in dissimulation: the author listed the unfulfilled promises of the revolutionary project, even as he disavowed questioning the Mexican Revolution. By carefully addressing the distinct publics who read *Siempre!*—governing officials, university students, and leftist intellectuals—the author maintained the open secret of revolutionary shortcomings.

This chapter examines the challenges and consequences of publicly criticizing the Mexican Revolution in the 1960s. It does so through the exploration of two scandals. The first began in the regional press when, in 1963, Yucatecan reporter Mario Menéndez Rodríguez uncovered a massive embezzlement scheme in agrarian lending institutions. The second scandal erupted in 1965 after federal government officials censored a controversial book about urban poverty, *Los hijos de Sánchez*, which was written by a U.S. anthropologist. In both cases, heated debates ensued about who, and what evidence, could undermine narratives of revolutionary progress. State spies, Mexican government officials, and U.S. consuls all worried that the resulting scandals would generate popular discontent and even lead to violence.

Mexican federal officials had developed sophisticated means to shape and monitor national news coverage. In the early 1950s, President Adolfo Ruiz Cortines created communications offices for each cabinet minister to disseminate press bulletins related to his activities. Under President Gustavo Díaz Ordaz in the mid-1960s, press monitoring was delegated to the Ministry of the Interior, and spies for the Federal Security Office (Dirección Federal de Seguridad, or DFS) and the General Office for Political and Social Intelligence (Dirección General de Investigaciones Políticas y Sociales) reported on the comings and goings of reporters.[3] Wary of the mounting labor and student activism taking over campuses and city streets across the country, DFS agents and federal officials feared that regime opponents would weaponize scandals to discredit the government and mobilize armed opposition. Meanwhile, U.S. consuls feared communist infiltration from Cuba and speculated that scandals would aggravate unrest among peasants. DFS spies and U.S. consuls alike suggested that, absent Mexican government oversight, the press would act as a tool of subversion. In seeking to conceal what was already common knowledge—that the revolution had not solved problems of poverty and landlessness—ruling officials signaled the power of the open secret.

Meanwhile, the elite journalists and academics who pursued exposés on urban poverty and rural neglect believed that their direct intermediation would improve the lives of the poor. Ordinary people also found ways to turn scandals to their favor. Yucatecan peasant leaders used exposés on agrarian corruption to fuel their mobilizations. Urban middle-class readers engaged with press coverage at university roundtables and in letters to the editor, challenging or expanding on published information. These interactions highlight the unequal relationship between journalists, their subjects, and readers but nonetheless show that engagement with scandals extended beyond political elites and created new publics with competing aims in mind.

## "JUDASES OF THE REVOLUTION"

The most confrontational *denuncia* journalism began outside Mexico City, where journalistic exposés directly accused individuals of wrongdoing. Local and regional newspapers received fewer federal government loans, payments, and newsprint, making them more financially precarious. At the same time, less federal oversight and funding translated into greater space for dissenting news coverage. Small periodicals like *Acción* in Chihuahua City or *El Chapulín* in Oaxaca City essentially operated as nonprofit ventures and catered to the concerns of civil movements. Even commercial ventures like the conservative *Sol* newspaper chain periodically covered taboo topics such as electoral fraud, though they did so to extort governing officials rather than from a sense of civic duty. Meanwhile, Mexico City broadsheets generally remained loyal to the federal government, which also kept their operations afloat with subsidized newsprint and loans. Government ministries supplemented low salaries with bimonthly payments (known as the *iguala*) to reporters who covered their organizations. By the mid-1960s, the most prominent political columnists could collect up to twice their monthly salary (four thousand pesos) in such payments, and by the 1970s ordinary reporters could expect a minimum monthly payment of 750 pesos.[4] Beat reporters also made ends meet by correcting proofs for printers and writing articles commissioned by politicians, tasks that could earn them as much as one thousand pesos.[5] These material ties created a symbiotic relationship between private news media and governing officials and encouraged reporters and directors to self-censor.

State spies were most preoccupied with monitoring Mexico City media, but in 1963 an article series published in the southeastern city of Mérida came to their attention. Menéndez Rodríguez, who directed *El Diario de Yucatán*, published an exposé that accused agrarian officials of growing rich at the expense of Mayan peasants who labored in the agave fields.[6] The newspaper figured among the best-selling regional periodicals in the country and was generally oppositional in tone, often siding with conservative business and landowning interests.[7] By exploring enduring abuses in the countryside, the twenty-six-year-old Menéndez Rodríguez suggested that the postrevolutionary agrarian reform had failed to uplift Indigenous peasants.

Such evaluations were not, in and of themselves, threatening to the political order. Governing elites and state spies privately acknowledged the problems of official corruption and rural impoverishment, but they concealed such candor from the public. Instead they limited their criticisms to private conversations, internal memorandums, and political digests. For example, since its creation in 1948 the elite *Buro de Investigación Política* newsletter openly discussed the unfulfilled goals of the Mexican Revolution but labeled the digest "confidential."[8] The supposedly secret newsletter circulated to thousands of subscribers. The *Buro de Investigacion Política*, like the editorial discussed earlier, highlights how the lines between secret and public information were not always easily delineated.

By 1964, the PRI's presidential candidate, Díaz Ordaz, openly declared during his campaign that "the peasant" represented one of the most urgent challenges facing Mexico.⁹ He referred to subsistence farmers, who in the 1960s accounted for most of the migrants that abandoned the economically depressed countryside for job opportunities in cities.¹⁰ The joint Mexican-U.S. Bracero Program, a farm labor agreement signed during World War II, had ended that same year, amplifying concerns that more agricultural workers would return to Mexico in search of employment. Once he assumed office, Díaz Ordaz vowed to "put the brakes on the exodus of farm labor to urban areas" by addressing rural unemployment.¹¹ He suggested that Mexico's development depended on making the agrarian reform effective so that peasants remained in the countryside and continued producing food for the cities. His statements were intended to preempt criticism, but governing officials recognized that publicizing the abuses committed by landed elites and agrarian institutions could produce politically unpredictable results.

In his 1963 investigative series, Menéndez Rodríguez did not limit his criticism to low-level functionaries. Instead he accused the director of the state-run Yucatán Agrarian Bank (Banco Agrario de Yucatán, or BAY), which distributed credit and technical expertise to the *ejidos* (collectively owned and farmed lands), of underreporting the international sale price of henequen and pocketing excess profits totaling some 3 million pesos.¹² Henequen, a tough fiber extracted from agave to make twine, had represented Yucatán's primary export crop since the late nineteenth century. Local authorities had seized Indigenous communal lands for large henequen fields and drafted the state's majority Maya population into debt peonage.¹³ Menéndez Rodríguez suggested that abuses against Indigenous workers continued within the very institutions designed to protect them.

Menéndez Rodríguez crafted his articles with a particular audience in mind: the public officials whom he accused and the authorities with the power to investigate them. He fetishized quantitative data as the most objective, "incontrovertible" evidence of "the fraud committed against the Yucatecan people." With belabored explications of numbers, Menéndez Rodríguez's articles were dry, sober reading. To illustrate the discrepancy between the BAY's advertised and actual sale prices in 1962, he narrated henequen price charts in painstaking detail. This style likely lost all but the most avid readers' attention but served as proof of his documented claims against specific individuals. Menéndez intimated that he had more information he could still reveal, provided by landowners who wanted to see the BAY director fired, and he urged officials to respond "before new 'leaks' become a rushing Niagara."¹⁴ Even as Menéndez Rodríguez claimed to uncover a scandal, he acknowledged that he had concealed information in the process, hoping to pressure political elites with threats of new revelations.

Menéndez Rodríguez hailed from a well-established family and went abroad for his studies, attending an elite Catholic high school in New Orleans and then completing his university degree at Tulane University. Soon after his return to Mérida, Menéndez Rodríguez married the daughter of a wealthy landowning family, solidifying his place among the Mérida elite. He went to work at the family-run newspaper, *El Diario de Yucatán*, which his grandfather had owned since the turn of the century. After Menéndez Rodríguez assumed the directorship in 1961 he steered coverage toward more pointed criticism of local clergy and landowners, taking aim at members of his own elite social circle.[15]

In his exposés Menéndez Rodríguez repeatedly called on the outgoing president to respond to accusations of embezzlement and invoked the executive's stated fight for "the redemption of the campesino," a broad term used to describe politically engaged rural workers.[16] He noted that ejidos had bred exploitation, but he initially avoided an indictment of the entire PRI system, instead framing the agrarian reform as a laudable but unrealized project, and he allowed that corruption could be uprooted by isolating specific individuals, preserving the president's honor and respectability. Menéndez Rodríguez advocated federal intervention to aid Mayan workers, echoing the rhetoric of many state reformers who portrayed Indigenous peoples as backward and childlike and thus in need of state assistance.[17] Employing religious imagery borrowed from his Catholic education, Menéndez Rodríguez emphasized that the "regime asks only that the *Judases of the Revolution*, who have impeded any advancement of the Agrarian Reform, be identified so they might punish them."[18] In this biblical metaphor, President Adolfo López Mateos plays the part of the savior and the errant officials his disloyal disciples. Rather than asking for generalized institutional change, Menéndez Rodríguez called for the punishment of a handful of offenders, undergirding the government's emphasis that individuals, not the regime itself, were responsible for the revolution's corruption.

Menéndez Rodríguez's audience extended beyond the narrow circle that he had perhaps envisioned. Agrarian leader Arsenio Lara Puerto brought Menéndez Rodríguez's most recent findings to the attention of some fifty thousand *ejidatarios* (shareholders of communal land) represented by the Ejidal Defense Committee (Comité de Defensa Ejidal, or CDE), which advocated peasant participation in *ejidal* governance. He promised CDE members, "I will not rest until the swindling thieves and bad bureaucrats of the

Banco Agrario de Yucatán have been imprisoned."[19] The agrarian leader exposed henequen workers to Menéndez Rodríguez's articles, which they likely would not have encountered on their own.[20] Lara Puerto cited new embezzlement figures, "prove[n] with documents," that reached 18 million pesos.[21] This emphasis on documentary proof reflected the widespread understanding that numbers and writing were inherently modern and truthful and thus carried greater political weight than eyewitness claims. Another ejidatario wrote directly to President López Mateos and enclosed clippings of Menéndez Rodríguez's articles as proof of his claims that workers were being swindled by agrarian officials.[22] By demanding accountability, ejidatarios could use the same logic that postrevolutionary reformers (and colonial administrators before them) had employed to insist that peasants better account for their time and thereby maximize their productivity.[23] Lara Puerto now urged them to demand that the government do the same.

Regional newspaper coverage did not always garner national interest, but in March 1963 Mexico City's conservative broadsheet, *Excélsior*, dedicated front-page space to the brewing unrest in Yucatán, which the reporter credited to Menéndez Rodríguez's recent articles.[24] Commenting on rural discontent, an *Excélsior* editorial also acknowledged the "alarming frequency" of fraud accusations, though it suggested that the Mayan peoples were subjected to supernatural, and thus uncontrollable, forces. The opinion editors lamented that ejidatarios "have suffered the curse of swindlers who get rich through the management of agrarian exports, while the wretched Indigenous live in misery on starvation wages."[25] The editors understood the plight of Yucatecan Mayan workers but implied that state intervention would be powerless to reverse rural exploitation.

The symbolism of the henequen industry made it a particularly important measuring stick for agrarian reform, and thus piqued national media interest. Writers and revolutionaries had long identified the henequen industry as representative of the ills that had given rise to the Mexican Revolution. In 1909, one year before the revolution erupted, U.S. reporter John Kenneth Turner published a series of articles detailing how Yucatecan henequen plantations exemplified the enslavement of Mexican Indigenous peoples. Though henequen workers were not at the forefront of revolutionary fighting, they continued to be associated with the conditions, such as concentrated landownership, that necessitated profound structural change.[26]

After the fighting subsided, a coalition of revolutionary generals made the redemption of peasants a key pillar of the 1917 Constitution, which legalized the state expropriation and redistribution of land.[27] Agrarian reform peaked in the late 1930s under President Lázaro Cárdenas, whose government expropriated over one hundred thousand hectares of land and partitioned it into hundreds of communally farmed plots. To appease landowners, however, Cárdenas created the "Great Ejido" (Gran Ejido), a concentration of over two hundred plots to be managed by Henequeneros de Yucatán, a newly created, joint venture between ejidatarios and ex-*hacendados* (owners of large landed estates).[28] Landowners maintained their wealth through their ownership of the henequen rasping machinery, which they rented out for worker use. Complaints of exploitation and mismanagement led the federal government to intervene in 1955, dissolve Henequeneros de Yucatán, and create the BAY in its place.[29] But Menéndez Rodríguez revealed that exploitation and corruption persisted just two years after this reshuffling was complete.

This cycle of corruption, mismanagement, and reorganization would not surprise readers or ejidatarios, but a charged political context led *Excélsior* editors to urge authorities to investigate Menéndez Rodríguez's accusations and punish the responsible parties. The editors noted that "failing to do so would contribute to discontent in the Yucatecan countryside and allow demagogues to capitalize on this general unrest and redirect it in support of ideological extremists of national 'liberation,'" a reference to the pressure group, the Movement for National Liberation (Movimiento de Liberación Nacional, or MLN).[30] This diverse coalition of intellectuals and political leaders, which formed in 1961, lobbied for greater union autonomy and for the revival of economic nationalism. The presence of prominent political figures—most notably, former president Cárdenas—in the MLN signaled that a schism had emerged within the ruling party's umbrella organization. With this larger political context in mind, *Excélsior* editors urged governing officials to defuse pressure by responding to Yucatecan complaints. Federal authorities in the Ministry of Agriculture and Ranching (Secretaría de Agricultura y Ganadería) heeded this warning and fired BAY director Gilberto Mendoza, offering an episodic lever of justice. Mendoza thus became the second official to be dismissed because of Menéndez Rodríguez's revelations.[31]

Ruling party leaders expected that punishing offenders would stem additional press coverage and deflate popular organizing. Mobilizations continued in Yucatán, however, eliciting concern from the DFS. In mid-April 1963, spies produced an eight-page report, *El problema henequenero en el estado de Yucatán*. The "problem" that they referenced was not merely economic but fundamentally political in nature. Spies denounced that Menéndez Rodríguez's articles had "provoked a general unease among diverse sectors of the state," and they observed that long-standing conflicts within the industry had worsened. DFS agents worried that such denunciations "give the regime's enemies ammunition to attack it, claiming that the agrarian reform in the Yucatán has been a failure."[32] To admit failure, they suggested, was to undermine the credibility of the ruling party itself. While acknowledging that the press accusations were true, the agents also revealed ulterior motives behind the exposé. They reported that the story was originally leaked to Menéndez Rodríguez by disgruntled ex-landowners who believed that the BAY director was working against their interests. The spies suggested that Menéndez Rodríguez was a pawn of the landed elite, who wanted the BAY director ousted, but the reporter would soon surprise them by taking aim at ex-hacendados as well.

DFS agents offered surprisingly candid views regarding the exploitation and corruption that plagued henequen production. Their intelligence report admitted that despite the various agrarian programs intended to improve the lives of Mayan workers, the population remained in abject poverty. Agents observed that "campesinos have never enjoyed any real benefit that frees them from the state of misery to which they have been subjected for twenty-five years."[33] By remarking on persistent poverty since 1938, arguably the high-water mark of the agrarian reform, agents implied that revolutionary initiatives did not mitigate rural landlessness and poverty. At the same time, they recognized that to admit the failures of agrarian reform publicly would be politically compromising. They suggested that documented, publicized evidence would empower opponents in a way that an open secret could not.

Indeed, the DFS agents were most concerned that Menéndez Rodríguez's exposés could fall into the wrong hands. The government was wary of another revolution at home and worried that peasants could serve as cannon fodder for an uprising. Leaders viewed Yucatecan Mayans as particularly vulnerable given their desperate poverty and the peninsula's physical proximity to Cuba. The ruling party had another reason to fear losing its peasant support base. In January 1963 a leftist and reformist coalition formed the Independent Campesino Organization (Central Campesina Independiente, or CCI), a lobby for land redistribution, social welfare, and public services. The CCI directly challenged the PRI's umbrella organization for peasants, the National Campesino Confederation (Confederación Nacional Campesina, or CNC), by offering independent representation. For the government, organizing outside the CNC signaled a loss of control that could lead to electoral losses or worse.[34]

In May 1963 U.S. consular officials similarly feared that Menéndez Rodríguez's articles would inflame peasants and galvanize support for growing leftist movements. They reported the Mexican government's "ardent desire to draw attention away from the eighteen-million-peso fraud that has come to light." Though they did not explain how, exactly, henequen workers had learned of *The Diario de Yucatán* exposés, consular officials reported that peasants were "furious" about the fraud. Like DFS spies, U.S. consuls worried that "they, the campesinos, can be mislead [sic] and it would be advantageous to the left to mislead them."³⁵ For consular officials and DFS agents, scandals were a matter of manipulation, not unfiltered facts, as journalists like Menéndez Rodríguez claimed.

Federal government officials saw television, first broadcast in Mexico in 1950, as a promising tool for combating communist infiltration. While a commercial venture, the Telesistema Mexicano monopoly forged strong ties with the government, and news programming (though limited to short, daily broadcasts in the 1960s) supported state efforts to delegitimize labor and social movements. For example, Telesistema Mexicano smeared the massive strike of railroad workers in 1958–1959, while remaining silent regarding the military's arrest of more than ten thousand strikers. The broadcast company also produced a documentary on the Cuban Revolution, narrated by television presenter Jacobo Zabludovsky, which depicted the communist regime as failing and unpopular.³⁶ Television programming thus complemented state efforts to vilify leftist movements.

Challenging official narratives, Menéndez Rodríguez recounted his fight against corruption in his 1964 book *Yucatán o el genocidio*. Freed from the editorial constraints of the newspaper, Menéndez Rodríguez unleashed vitriolic attacks that branded agrarian officials as "pilfering assassins."³⁷ The text consisted primarily of reprinted articles, alongside his personal narration of the events that had surrounded each piece. The reporter figured as the central protagonist, whose writing culminated in an audience with President López Mateos and appearances before the public prosecutor's office. Menéndez suggested that accountability not only necessitated publicity but also physical travel, crime reports, private meetings with the president, and masculine daring.

Menéndez Rodríguez no longer implied that corruption was limited to a few individuals but instead took aim at the entire political system. He introduced his book with the first-person formula of many testimonials, which opened with a witness statement that protested wrongdoing. He affirmed that this was his "protest against a corrupt bureaucracy that is only concerned with its own illicit enrichment at the expense of those who suffer hunger and thirst."³⁸ Menéndez Rodríguez argued that his role was to expose the truth, and promised that the revelations would reveal the sins of public officials. He thus envisioned his journalism as a liberating and judging gospel that would make errant officials pay for their divergence from revolutionary principles. He demanded that the state reclaim its commitment to redeem Mayan henequen workers by lifting them out of their poverty and breaking their reliance on landowners.

Menéndez Rodríguez encountered retaliation for his exposés. The Mérida elite published open letters in the government-owned *Diario del Sureste*, branding Menéndez Rodríguez as a communist, and they visited newsrooms to complain. Menéndez Rodríguez felt that he had become a persona non grata, and that this affected not only himself but also his wife and child. Even his family elders, who were also managers and editors at *El Diario de Yucatán*, distanced themselves and at times refused to publish his articles, indicating that he had moved beyond the acceptable limits of criticism by attracting national attention and attacking the local members of the clergy and economic elite. Ostracized by the Mérida community, Menéndez Rodríguez moved to Mexico City in February 1965.[39]

## REPRESENTING THE COUNTRYSIDE FROM MEXICO CITY

While denuncia journalism thrived in regional newspapers, it was not until the mid-1960s that criticisms of the revolution consistently appeared in Mexico City news publications. A combination of factors facilitated this gradual opening. First, divisions among the ruling elite came to a head in the early 1960s, and prominent leaders mobilized the press to air their grievances. Second, the expansion of university and cultural life, fostered by state investment, provided alternative spaces for public engagement and debate. Finally, political repression and the inspiration of the Cuban Revolution prompted young journalists to distance themselves from the ruling party.

By the mid-1960s select Mexico City publications connected dire rural conditions with failed revolutionary promises. This was the case in the political magazine *Siempre!*, which had published articles on landlessness since its founding in 1953. Director and longtime magazine publisher Pagés Llergo created *Siempre!* with the blessing of President Adolfo Ruiz Cortines. The magazine's glossy covers featured colorful caricatures, and its news content offered pluralistic political analysis, which attracted a wide readership among intellectuals, students, and politicians. *Siempre!* claimed a circulation of seventy thousand, but U.S. consular officials in Mexico City estimated that it was closer to thirty-five or forty thousand.[40] Consular officials also suspected that *Siempre!* received funding from Cuba, the Soviet Union, and the right-leaning Mexican government, suggesting a contradictory cocktail of interests motivating the magazine's coverage. Indeed, director Pagés Llergo was a complicated character; in the late 1930s he had openly expressed admiration for Adolf Hitler and Nazism, but he later offered *Siempre!* as a space to air anti-fascist and leftist ideas.[41] Some magazine contributors, like Portuguese communist Antonio Rodríguez, articulated reformist criticisms that sought to improve, rather than overturn, the PRI's centrality to political life.[42] But *Siempre!* also provided a platform for radical leftists like Víctor Rico Galán, who stridently denounced state violence. The newspaper's ability to host critical perspectives while simultaneously disavowing them (as demonstrated in this chapter's opening vignette), mirrored the ruling party's own strategy of accommodating and disciplining dissent.

*Siempre!* cartoons often delivered the hardest-hitting criticism of state corruption. They were not unique in this regard; cartoons often offered escape valves for dissent, even in otherwise uncritical publications. Leftist cartoonist Eduardo del Río, better known by his pen name, Rius, frequently used simple sketches to parody official discourses of revolutionary progress. In an October 1965 cartoon he built on Menéndez's exposés of corrupt agrarian institutions. Entitled "In This Town There Are No Thieves," Rius's full-page cartoon contrasted government rhetoric with common knowledge of Mayan impoverishment. His title played on a 1965 Alberto Isaac film, *There Are No Thieves in This Village*, based on a short story by Gabriel García Márquez.[43] In Rius's rendering of the "official version," the agrarian reform had given Mayan campesinos land, and agrarian authorities acted as "faithful public servants" of the ejidos. In the "unofficial version," which Rius described as the "reality," elites enriched themselves through their control of state agrarian institutions as Mayan peasants sunk deeper into poverty.[44] By juxtaposing competing representations of agrarian reform, Rius criticized governing officials for refusing to acknowledge the reality that the public knew all too well.

*La Cultura en México*, the cultural supplement of *Siempre!*, also used affecting photos and peasant testimonies to question the gains of the Mexican Revolution. Since the supplement's 1962 creation, it delivered cultural criticism of avant-garde art while providing journalistic exposés on more conventional political issues. The September 1, 1965, issue addressed the fate of Mexico's agrarian reform with a cover that announced "The Agrarian Problem Continues Fifty Years after the Revolution." In the seven-page feature story, Elena Garro, an accomplished playwright and the ex-wife of famous poet Octavio Paz, reported peasants' denunciations of violence and dispossession. Her 1963 debut novel *Los recuerdos del porvenir*, which explored military abuses of rural people, likely lent authority to her report. In Ocosingo, Chiapas, peasants testified that thugs, employed by large landowners and protected by local authorities, seized communal lands, "burned our granaries," and "robbed everything we had in our houses."[45] In some cases, those who resisted were killed. Garro's article underscored how governing officials not only failed to protect peasants but also were complicit in the violence against them.

Sympathetic writers like Garro positioned themselves as intermediaries whose interventions could deliver a degree of justice for marginalized people. Yet such efforts reveal a fraught relationship between reporters and their subjects. Garro had dedicated considerable energies to advocating for land reform and campesino rights since the 1950s. In so doing she was one of the few women to access the world of political reporting. She was also a complicated vehicle for the representation of peasant demands. Her blond hair, glamorous clothing, penchant for drama, and concern for the poor led some of her peers to disparagingly refer to her as Evita Perón, a gendered assessment that trivialized her advocacy. Her unconventional strategies did not endear her to her peers, who complained that Garro used blackmail to get what she wanted professionally. One notorious incident occurred in 1965 when Garro arrived at a literary event in Morelos with one hundred (or, by another account, three hundred) campesinos who were recently dispossessed of their lands. Garro demanded that the attendees sign a pledge that they would represent the peasants' concerns. Garro used the campesinos, who may not have been aware of the scheme, as props to shame writers into signing a symbolic (and obviously nonbinding) agreement. When Mexico's preeminent writers refused to grant her and her guests entrance, Garro slashed their tires. As Rebecca Biron discusses in her biography of Garro, male literary figures recounted this story to suggest "that Garro typically offends, or just irritates, rather than educates those whom she critiques."[46] These gendered assessments elided the most problematic aspect of this episode, which was that Garro manipulated peasants in the interests of proving a point to her peers.

Accompanying Garro's *La Cultura en México* article were black-and-white photographs by Héctor García that depicted an abandoned and depressed countryside. García had a personal commitment to exposing the ravages of poverty, as he himself grew up extremely poor in Mexico City. As a boy, García was sent to a reformatory after he was caught stealing. Upon his release, he traveled to the United States as a farm worker with the Bracero

Program. García's eventual rise to prominence as an award-winning photographer demonstrates that, with some luck and talent, journalism could provide an opportunity for upward mobility. García was instrumental in bringing images of daily life into mainstream journalism; in 1958 he created a new section for *Excélsior*, "F 2.8: La vida en el instante," which for two years featured his photographs of Mexico City.[47] Despite overt representations of poverty, his images appeared in one of the city's conservative broadsheets.

The editors of *La Cultura en México* used image captions to underscore Garro's central argument: that despite official protestations to the contrary, the Mexican Revolution had neither abolished concentrated landownership nor ended indebted servitude. While photographing inner-city slums and rural poverty was not new, by the 1960s it became increasingly common for the editors to frame photographs (with captions and headings) as delegitimizing of the revolution, lest viewers assign their own competing interpretations.[48] Government reprisals had cut short previous efforts to publish photographs that highlighted inequality. For example, in 1947 the famous photographers, the Hermanos Mayo, created *Más*, a magazine that published photo-essays on slums, poverty, and corruption in the Mexico City area, but the venture barely lasted six months before it was forcibly shut down.[49] The combative magazine *Presente* did not fare much better and succumbed to financial pressures five months after its initial publication in May 1948.

Many of García's photographs presented Indigenous peasants as divorced from time and place, undermining government claims of modernization and progress. In one image, a young girl emerges grinning from a small hut with a thatched roof, her shoulders wrapped in a traditional *rebozo* (shawl). The caption, "The new landowners' new indentured servants," allowed the anonymous girl to stand in for the enduring labor abuses and landlessness in the countryside. A closely cropped portrait of a young boy followed a similar script with a caption that explained, "There is no difference between him and his grandfather."[50] In the photograph, the child wears a tattered straw hat and gazes directly into the camera. His face is smeared with dirt and his mouth is slightly agape, as if he is about to say something to the photographer. With the visual markers of rurality (the thatched roof, bare feet, traditional dress, and dirt), these photographs seemingly could have been taken anywhere in Mexico over the previous one hundred years. The anonymized subjects further suggested the universality of their situation. With the help of pointed captions, García's photographs argued that the Mexican Revolution had not brought changes to the countryside, and peasants continued to suffer from abusive labor conditions and landlessness.

Figure 1.1  Héctor García, *Niña con su puerco*, 1965. Courtesy of Fundación Héctor García.

One of the essay's captioned photographs (see figure 1.1) offered a unique glimpse into the way that peasant subjects saw the photographer. The image pictures a two-and-a-half-year-old girl sitting in a field with a pig "as thin as she is." The girl's face is twisted in the middle of a sob. The reader learns that it was photographer García who made her cry because the girl thought that he was going to take her pig away from her. Unlike the other captions, this one is written in the first person. García explains that he snapped two photographs before "I ran away, ashamed of my suit, my tie, my white shirt. I look like the 'master' and the 'master' makes them tremble [with fear]."[51] García names the subject, Estela, whose individual identity becomes legible because of her own recognition of the photographer. While heavily mediated, viewers can briefly glimpse the reactions that peasants had to the intrusion of photographers, who interacted with their subjects to compose the scenes. The caption reminds readers that some peasants did not distinguish between the well-meaning photographer and the abusive landlord, seeing both as similarly bent on violence because of their shared class background.

The Mexican Revolution provided a powerful source of political legitimacy and critique. Photographs of rural poverty and exposés on landlessness represented peasants as litmus tests of revolutionary progress. Menéndez's exposés showed that, for governing officials, henequen symbolized the possibility of irrational uprising, while the photo spread in *La Cultura en México* represented peasants as the victims of predatory landowners. These conflicting imaginaries reflected postrevolutionary narratives, which had framed peasants as both the protagonists and beneficiaries of the Mexican Revolution. In the 1960s the "peasant question" was further complicated by the challenges associated with rapid urbanization. Elite writers and governing officials saw depressed rural economies as threatening modernizing cities. Indeed, peasants generated antipathy when they moved to cities, and elites often blamed the urban poor for overcrowding, traffic, pollution, and crime. Urban poverty became the subject of intense debate in the 1960s when economic growth slowed and the limits of state-led development became apparent.

### *SANCHISMO* AND DEBATES ABOUT POVERTY

Migration from the countryside had increased over the previous decade as farmers searched for employment in the industrializing capital. City housing could not accommodate growth, leading to notoriously overcrowded downtown tenements. Middle-class and elite Mexico City dwellers disparaged recent arrivals as dirty, presumably Indigenous, and criminal—a characterization captured by the derogatory slang term *pelado* for the urban poor.[52] For the ruling party, rural migrants represented a political challenge as corporative institutions struggled to accommodate new residents' diverse and shifting demands. The largest two umbrella organizations represented peasants in the agricultural sector and unionized industrial workers. The third, the National Confederation of Popular Organizations (Confederación Nacional de Organizaciones Populares, or CNOP), was the least developed of the PRI's corporative institutions and captured the heterogeneous array of urban workers, from white-collar bureaucrats to street vendors. In the mid-1960s, PRI officials feared the CNOP was impotent and even considered creating a replacement organization.[53] Like debates about landlessness, discussions of urban poverty challenged narratives of revolutionary progress, which framed PRI legitimacy as rooted in socioeconomic uplift.

Perhaps no work politicized urban poverty and inequality more than one that was written by a U.S. author. In 1964, the Mexican state-sponsored publishing house, the Endowment for Economic Culture (Fondo de Cultura Económica, or FCE), released a Spanish translation of anthropologist Oscar Lewis's book *Los hijos de Sánchez*.[54] Originally published in 1961 with an

English title, *The Children of Sánchez*, the book consisted of lengthy interviews with the Sánchez family, who lived in Mexico City's downtown tenements. The work's publication in Mexico catalyzed fraught debates regarding whose knowledge counted most in the public sphere and what kinds of denunciations carried the greatest authority.

In *The Children of Sánchez*, Lewis framed the Sánchez family history as exemplary of the "culture of poverty," a concept he coined to describe the value systems that perpetuated intergenerational poverty.[55] Reflective of trends in cultural anthropology and psychoanalysis, Lewis underscored the idea that this culture was rooted both in individual choices and structured by the legacies of colonialism and present-day capitalism.[56] His framework became influential in U.S. domestic policy-making circles, which sought to address inner-city poverty. A different set of circumstances shaped the critical reception in Mexico, however. While Lewis did not frame his work as a critique of the revolution, public officials interpreted it that way, fearing the book would provide fodder for mounting criticisms of the ruling party.

Officials also worried that a prominent, U.S.-based critique would undermine Mexico's reputation as an exemplar of Global South modernity and development. The country's international image took on greater importance after 1963, when Mexico won the bid to host the 1968 Summer Olympics.[57] Mexico City mayor Ernesto Uruchurtu undertook a massive infrastructure project to showcase the city's development; construction began on a metro system, and the first station opened in 1967. The city also widened the nineteenth-century thoroughfare, the Paseo de la Reforma, and constructed a freeway, the Anillo Periférico, to better connect the city. These projects removed poor residents and ambulant vendors from centrally located neighborhoods to make space for businesses and middle-class housing.[58] A prominent critique from a U.S. anthropologist, then, threatened to undermine Mexico's international image and raised long-standing resentments of foreign intervention.

Three months after the publication of *Los hijos de Sánchez*, the secretary general of the Mexican Society of Geography and Statistics (Sociedad Mexicana de Geografía y Estadística, or SMGE), Luis Cataño Morlet, brought a lawsuit against Lewis and FCE director Arnaldo Orfila Reynal for slander and libel. In his denunciation, Cataño Morlet voiced nationalist concerns that Lewis's book attacked Mexico's "way of life." The book, based on oral histories, revealed the unsanitary living conditions, inadequate health services, interpersonal violence, and police abuse that the Sánchez family experienced. Lewis limited his own analysis to the prologue, dedicating the main text to curated, first-person testimonials. The anthropologist suggested that these accounts provided unmediated access to the views of the urban poor.

It was this intimate register that most concerned Cataño Morlet. The book was narrated in the expletive-rich language of its protagonists, and the SMGE official worried that such irreverent talk undermined government efforts to showcase Mexico City's modernity. In his denunciation against Lewis and the FCE, Cataño Morlet addressed poverty as if it were a set of social scientific claims that could be disproven by undermining Lewis's research methodology and personal biases. Among the SMGE official's principal accusations was that Lewis had invented his informants; Cataño Morlet argued that ordinary Mexicans would not independently voice such criticisms. He denounced Lewis, claiming that "through the mouth of Alberto Sánchez, he paints a false and depressing picture of the political, economic, and social life in Mexico, saying that we are governed by a 'gang' of thieves; that the people are dying of hunger."[59] For Cataño Morlet, the scandalous content of the oral histories was evidence of their fabrication.

Cataño Morlet also worried that the salacious reading material could become a vehicle for subversive thought, and he accused Lewis of working as an agent for the U.S. Federal Bureau of Investigation (FBI). The SMGE official urged the Mexican government to intervene and protect vulnerable minds. The Sánchez family history included vivid recollections of early sexual experiences, leading Cataño Morlet to compare the book to pornography that circulated illegally throughout the city and to assert that "*Los hijos de Sánchez* is not a scientific book, but rather a clumsy crime novel."[60] He indicated that the book's salacious style would make it an easy source of entertainment, thus undermining its scholarly value. In his presentation to the SMGE, Cataño Morlet described "words so obscene they could make a sailor blush" and warned that readers would "forget about science and continue reading out of morbid curiosity."[61] He urged authorities to intervene before the book became a best seller. He also predicted that "even the illiterate will buy it for their friends to read to them." Fearing that *Los hijos de Sánchez* would politicize marginalized urban dwellers, Cataño Morlet believed that preventing the book's circulation was the only solution.

Ironically, attempts to censor *Los hijos de Sánchez* sparked even greater public interest. The first edition sold out quickly and used copies appeared on the black market for up to six times their original retail price of forty-four pesos. During a visit to Mexico City after the book's release, Lewis encountered at least one dozen taxi drivers familiar with the work. Even those unlikely to pick up an academic book encountered the scandal in their daily media consumption. Intense debate ensued on the Mexican airwaves, and hundreds of print articles discussed the controversy in the first month after Cataño Morlet's denunciation. Public intellectuals, journalists, and governing officials weighed in and alternatively raised cries against U.S. imperialism or accused the Mexican government of censoring criticism. Such discussions centered on whether it was unpatriotic to acknowledge the existence of widespread urban misery.[62]

*Los hijos de Sánchez* was not the first work to discuss Mexican poverty, though it was certainly the most widely circulated. Poverty was a frequent topic in comic strips and films, including Luis Buñuel's 1950 film *Los olvidados*, which dramatized a dystopian Mexico City. The film incited a national outcry but was received to international acclaim, forcing the Mexican government to reverse its initial attempts to censor the movie. Novelist Carlos Fuentes also gave a cynical depiction of Mexico's urban development in his 1958 novel *La region más transparente*. Even if perturbed, officials publicly discounted these creative pieces as interpretative works of art. For consumers, meanwhile, fictional works stirred debate and aroused discontent but were nonetheless difficult to uphold as evidence that the PRI had betrayed its revolutionary values. *Los hijos de Sánchez*, on the other hand, was written by an esteemed U.S. anthropologist. For this reason, the SMGE director attacked the bias of the book and the authenticity of Lewis's informants, suggesting that undermining the pretense to objectivity would disqualify the revelations of the work itself. Myriad public officials joined him and took to the airwaves and print media to defend the country against the perceived insults of the U.S. researcher.

Endemic to debates about *Los hijos de Sánchez* was the question of whether social science offered objective political critique. The rise of the social sciences as a cohesive field of inquiry was relatively new to Mexican universities. In 1951, the National Autonomous University of Mexico (Universidad Nacional Autónoma de México, or UNAM) opened its National School of Social and Political Sciences (Escuela Nacional de Ciencias Políticas y Sociales), reflecting a region-wide trend toward institutionalizing social-scientific inquiry. The school offered undergraduate majors in diplomatic studies, political science, social studies, and journalism, and it grew from 142 students in its inaugural year to 620 by 1961.[63] Though still small, the school soon became competitive with other degrees in the arts and sciences. Reflecting international intellectual trends, economic and social development were central themes of the curriculum, and all majoring students were required to take courses on these topics.[64] The influence of the social sciences was also reflected in select periodicals, which published academic findings. For example, the labor-friendly broadsheet *El Día* reserved a full page (entitled "Testimonios y documentos") for excerpted social science research from academic journals. Both the university and print media thus introduced readers and students to key inter-American social science debates.

*El Día* also dedicated prominent space in its front page and opinion section to the Lewis case. The periodical was founded in 1962 with the support of the progressive PRI senator Enrique Ramírez y Ramírez, and it provided a forum for journalists and intellectuals to counter the government's anticommunism. With around forty thousand copies sold per day, *El Día* became a key site for debates about the course of Mexico's economic development and political democracy.[65] For example, while other periodicals toed the government line and framed strikers as subversives, *El Día* gave ample and generally fair coverage to social protests. The opinion pages regularly featured prominent progressive writers, including Francisco Martínez de la Vega and Fernando Benítez, who contributed editorials on urban poverty and peasant struggles. In the mid-1960s reporter Manuel Buendía also began writing his column, "Para Control de Usted," in which he gradually wrote in more accessible prose directed at the reader. *El Día* exemplified how progressive PRI officials utilized print media to advance their reformist agendas.

In their many commentaries on the book, left-leaning and liberal journalists and academics rejected Cataño Morlet's attempts to undermine Lewis's academic credentials. Instead they grounded their claims in intersubjective knowledge, contending that *Los hijos de Sánchez* did not reveal anything new. They emphasized that quotidian eyewitness accounts confirmed that the Sánchez family could be any poor urban Mexican family. The primacy of commonsense observations was reflected in public intellectuals' interviews with print media. Álvar Carrillo Gil, a Yucatecan pediatrician and art collector, asserted that *Los hijos de Sánchez* simply detailed "what we see every day," and UNAM lecturer Daniel Moreno concurred that officials "denied the reality of the Mexican people" when they accused the book of peddling lies.[66] Essayist Víctor Flores Olea maintained that the SMGE director was scandalized by the public exposure of poverty rather than by the reality of poverty itself.[67] One columnist for *Siempre!* commented on the surrealism of the debate by noting that "either we are in a paradise and complain purely out of idleness and the desire to lament or we are inventing a reality that does not correspond with the actual situation of the country."[68] These commentators challenged officials' epistemological claims with repeated references to a singular "reality," the ontology of poverty, which they established through intersecting eyewitness accounts and personal experiences. In effect, leftist writers emphasized that Mexico City residents did not need Lewis's book to recognize that the state's revolutionary agenda had fallen short.

Many readers concurred with this view, and in February–March 1965, they corresponded with *El Día* to challenge official attacks on Lewis. One woman expressed that the SMGE "would have to disprove that 'one and a half million people' live in Mexico City 'in similar or worse conditions' as those described by the Sánchez children."[69] While most of the published letters came from middle-class Mexico City residents, some letters arrived from labor and peasant groups outside the capital. For example, members of Sindicalist Student Youths (La Juventud Estudiantil Sindicalista) sent a letter asserting that no word or text could be as offensive as the "poverty, hunger, poor health, anguish, insecurity, and unemployment that the absolute majority of our people suffer."[70] Other readers defended Lewis by claiming that he was not the first to highlight urban poverty. For example, Francisco Emilio de los Ríos of the Colonia Santa María la Ribera neighborhood of Mexico City argued that "Lewis has not uncovered anything new."[71] He suggested that social science consensus had already emerged on the issue of Mexican poverty and thus, Lewis's contribution was unoriginal. Readers already understood that miserable living conditions existed in downtown slums and that many Mexico City residents struggled to provide for their families, but it was the official attempts to deny or conceal this reality that most preoccupied them.

University roundtables provided interactive opportunities for the public to intervene in ongoing debates around the Lewis case. Rather than stuffy academic affairs, they reflected the vibrancy of university life and student organizing in the 1960s. Preparatory school and university students mobilized to democratize their institutions and protest the violent repression by the riot police. With these reformist and antiauthoritarian demands, students sought a greater voice in public life. Roundtables also reflected growing opportunities to discuss ideas outside the classroom. New cultural centers at UNAM, including the Department of Cultural Diffusion (Dirección de Difusión Cultural), the Casa del Lago, the revamped Radio Universidad, and the university magazine, the *Revista de la Universidad*, offered novel spaces for political and cultural engagement.

Well-informed readers attended university-hosted roundtables to address intellectuals and public officials through questions, disruptions (booing), or affirmations (cheers). This active engagement reflected the robust development of the Mexico City public sphere and the importance of spectacle within it. This dynamic was evident when a leftist student organization convened a roundtable on the *Los hijos de Sánchez* scandal on March 4, 1965. That day, fifteen hundred people packed into the auditorium at the National School of Economics (Escuela Nacional de Economía), which soon grew hot due to the size of the crowd. The roundtable featured Cataño Morlet and a panel of three intellectuals. *El Día* described a lively environment in the auditorium with a boisterous mixed-age crowd of "serious pipe-and-hat intellectuals" and university students who brought snacks to enjoy during the event.[72] Creating a spectacle, the scandal both incited outrage and provided entertainment.

The crowd's behavior suggested that participants had already reached their own conclusions about *Los hijos de Sánchez* but nonetheless wanted to add their voices to the debate. This was evident when the SMGE secretary general took the podium and engaged in a volley of insults with attendees. In his speech, Cataño Morlet summarized the charges against Lewis and Orfila and reiterated accusations that Lewis was an FBI agent. When Cataño Morlet complained that Lewis's informants had called the government "a gang of thieves," the crowd broke out in cheers. By interrupting and mocking Cataño Morlet, participants rejected norms of extreme deference and expressed their shared criticism. Cataño Morlet lost his composure and shot back that the students were "pro-Yankee" and wanted Mexico to become like South Vietnam, where the United States controlled a foreign government. The public official denounced criticism as evidence of treachery and subversion. The jeers of the crowd, meanwhile, highlighted the audience's refusal to be cowed.

The intellectuals on the roundtable still felt it was important to undermine Cataño Morlet's accusation that Lewis had fabricated the testimonies. When Professor Francisco López Cámara took the podium, he introduced new physical evidence by playing a tape recording of Manuel, the eldest son in the Sánchez family. In his study Lewis had used pseudonyms to protect his subjects, which made it difficult to confirm the identities of the Sánchez family members. Officials pointed to this secrecy as evidence that Lewis had invented his informants and their testimonies. By presenting the tape, López Cámara suggested that mechanically reproduced recordings would prove the authenticity of the Sánchez family and thereby support popular denunciations of poverty.

While the scandal around the book had made Manuel Sánchez and his family into household names, their voices were silenced in the public debate about the book. In an auditorium filled with reporters, photographers, middle-class students, and political elites, the recording was the only representation of the urban poor. Manuel made a plea for political and social recognition: "I want to make clear that I exist." He directly addressed the audience and urged that "the people who can, the best off, should modify the system of life that those of us in the lower classes lead." Such overt political statements rarely appeared in the oral histories of *Los hijos de Sánchez*, and Manuel's formulation suggested that his sessions with Lewis and the subsequent scandal had informed his political sensibility.[73] At the same time, the presentation of a recorded statement prevented Manuel from further engagement in the debate. He was unable to respond, for example, when Cataño Morlet questioned the tape's authenticity. Audience members, by contrast, erupted in protest after the SMGE official attempted to discount Manuel Sánchez's statement. While the recording was curated and mediated just like the accounts included in *Los hijos de Sánchez*, common knowledge and personal experience made the audience believe that the book's claims, and thus the tape, were authentic.[74]

Manuel's recorded appearance highlights the class-based limitations to engaging scandals. The Sánchez family occupied a precarious position, fearing government retaliation yet seeking to gain upward mobility through their newfound fame. Manuel's willingness to intervene in the public debate might have been encouraged by the support he received from López Cámara, who had assisted him in finding housing and securing a medical exam. Family members also periodically dropped by or called the FCE offices to ask for financial assistance. Orfila Reynal made payments (from the book's royalties) on Lewis's behalf, but the FCE director did not necessarily approve of the practice. Indeed, Orfila Reynal noted that the last payment to Manuel's younger brother, Roberto Sánchez, did not last long due to "the excessive carelessness of these kids."[75] The Sánchez family was thus dependent on Lewis (and by extension the FCE) and subject to the publisher's attempts to manage the family's affairs.

For some public officials the roundtable also signaled that the scandal had gotten out of control. Even select SMGE members were embarrassed by Cataño Morlet's behavior, which they believed undermined the academic integrity of the institution. After the roundtable, some of his colleagues denied their involvement in the legal case against the publisher. In a letter to the FCE, they noted that Cataño Morlet had not even consulted the society before making his complaint and that most SMGE officials were against the denunciation and its attacks on free expression.[76] The belated nature of this denial, however, suggests that SMGE officials regretted the unanticipated political fallout of the lawsuit and wanted Cataño Morlet to take the blame.

Notably, however, governing officials defended Cataño Morlet in print, preserving the appearance of unity at all costs.

The *Los hijos de Sánchez* case prompted a months-long debate, which brought together a Mexico City public well versed in the details of the case. The echoes of this scandal were apparent in the creative reinterpretations that continued to surface around the book. The *Diario de México*, for example, published a serialized novel of the drama, complete with illustrations by cartoonist Rius.[77] The scandal also inspired radio commentary, parodic plays and novellas, and a neologism, *Sanchismo*, that referred to defamation or the act of defaming.[78] These cultural afterlives solidified the narrative around *Los hijos de Sánchez*, allowing it to serve as a common political reference point for official censorship and imperiousness. Twelve years later, the scandal inspired the 1978 blockbuster film *The Children of Sánchez*, starring Anthony Quinn and beloved Mexican movie star Dolores del Río.

But the case did not serve as a catalyst for the opening of the Mexico City press or public debate writ large. While the federal attorney general dismissed the charges against Lewis and Orfila Reynal, the FCE board refused to publish a third edition of the book, fearing that a reprint would revive the controversy. This frustrated Lewis, who had promised the Sánchez family a substantial cut of the royalties. He recognized that the scandal could yield significant financial dividends and had estimated that a new edition could have sold forty thousand copies.[79] Six months later, Orfila Reynal was fired from the FCE in an action that many writers interpreted as punishment for publishing *Los hijos de Sánchez*.[80] Editors were reticent to publish news on the firing, presumably having been instructed by communications liaisons that the case would no longer be subject to open discussion.[81] The debate around the book demonstrates the fickle nature of the government, which had permitted open discussion, only to later close it down. As was often the case, though, censorship did not prevent the opening of other avenues for dissent. In protest against the FCE's decision, prominent literary figures like Fernando Benítez, Elena Poniatowska, Enrique Ramírez y Ramírez, and Vicente Rojo started the Siglo XXI editorial house, through which they intended to defend revolutionary ideas, including peasants' and workers' rights.[82]

The scandal surrounding *Los hijos de Sánchez* highlights how a dense mass media landscape created new publics. The discussion of poverty pushed the boundaries of acceptable political discourse while failing to hold public officials accountable. As a generalized accusation against the one-party regime, no single individual could bear the responsibility for the previous four decades of policies that had produced the conditions suffered by the Sánchez family and others. Moreover, the debate raised important questions about accountability and truth. Even as the social sciences achieved greater influence and visibility in Mexican universities and newspapers, readers and students contested official attempts to undermine the veracity of Lewis's account. Instead these individuals argued that firsthand knowledge, particularly when shared by many people, was the most convincing form of evidence.

## THE PRESS AS A TOOL OF SUBVERSION

Many political elites understood the denuncia press to be a tool of subversion rather than one of civic education. Cataño Morlet feared that *Los hijos de Sánchez* would capture and politicize a wider audience, while undermining Mexico's sovereignty. Meanwhile, Yucatecan and federal authorities and DFS spies worried that Menéndez's muckraking pieces were fueling unrest among henequen workers.[83] As the newly appointed director of the Mexico City weekly magazine *Sucesos para Todos*, Menéndez assumed a more radical tone than he had in *El Diario de Yucatán*. *Sucesos* was similar in appearance and format to *Siempre!*, but sold twice as well and was more combative.[84] Printed across the border in El Paso, Texas, *Sucesos* saved money on newsprint, while guarding the print shop against government attacks.[85] As *Sucesos* director, Menéndez frequently covered controversial domestic topics, including peasant and student protests, as well as international issues such as Latin American guerrilla movements and the Vietnam War. He also continued to report on the fate of henequen workers, but he no longer called upon the state to intervene in uplifting Yucatán's peasants.

Agents for the DFS and U.S. consular officials closely monitored the mounting ejidatario unrest in Yucatán. In 1964 and 1965, henequen workers took to Mérida's streets to demand that their stolen funds be returned, wages increased, and unpopular union leaders expelled.[86] By early 1966, ongoing strikes led the governor to announce "an incalculably grave crisis" and U.S. consular officials warned that the state represented "a potential political danger to Mexican and United States interests through leftist exploitation of campesino discontent."[87] Spanish-born journalist and communist Víctor Rico Galán was also convinced that Menéndez's exposé had given peasants "the resources to understand . . . who was truly responsible" for their oppression. Like Menéndez, Rico Galán trusted in the political efficacy of documented evidence, which he believed would empower Mayan peasants with knowledge. He asserted that "long years of lies and excuses . . . ended in the face of irrefutable evidence and the full explanation of the facts."[88] For Rico Galán, publicizing the truth held undeniable political power, though he did not explain how peasants had encountered Menéndez's *Sucesos* articles.

In January 1967, *Sucesos* published a multipart series on Mérida's "state of siege," detailing how the military had occupied city streets since September to quell ongoing strikes. Clashes had ensued between workers and thugs for hire, and police had responded with violence, arrests, and the imprisonment of some protesters.[89] Menéndez inaugurated the series by placing blame squarely on the governor and Miguel Olea Enríquez, the director of Cordemex (the public-private company that exported cordage made from henequen), whom he accused of instigating the violence.[90] Menéndez had radicalized by this point, much to the surprise and confusion of his friends and family.[91] The reporter issued a no-holds-barred, sweeping indictment of the Mérida elite and federal and state officials. He savaged Olea Enríquez by comparing him to the despicable feudal commander who raped and abused his vassals in Lope de Vega's seventeenth-century play *Fuenteovejuna*. Menéndez further seethed that officials had illustrated that the wealth of the Yucatecan people "rests in the hands of incompetent politicians with the character of public women."[92] His moralistic, aggressive, and hypermasculine language recalled the style of denuncia journalists during the dictatorship of Porfirio Díaz. Menéndez warned that the Mayan people suffered malnutrition, illness, and repression, and that they might rise to kill their oppressors, just as the peasants did in the final act of the play. His vision for political change was no longer reform but rather revolution.

*Sucesos* complemented its investigative reportage with photo spreads. In contrast with *La Cultura en México*'s photo-essay from two years earlier, the *Sucesos* images did not represent campesinos in atomized portraits but rather as powerful masses marching through Mérida's city center. One full-page photograph (see figure 1.2), taken by Gregorio Méndez during the protest marches in September 1966 (and published in January 1967), pictures thousands of henequen workers who fill the streets to capacity, suggesting their mobility and organization.

As viewed from a balcony overlooking the march, most of the protesters are similarly dressed in straw hats and traditional white cotton clothing, giving the sense of a uniform mass. The photograph captures a peaceful crowd as workers mill about and chat; some are even looking curiously up at the photographer. Yet the accompanying caption describes the protesters as threatening, noting that, "Today, more than ever, the Yucatecan people feel the violence. Who can control these campesinos who demand what rightfully

Figure 1.2 Gregorio Méndez, untitled photograph, *Sucesos*, January 14, 1967, 16.

belongs to them?"⁹³ In praising the workers' agency, Menéndez departs from his earlier characterizations of Mayans as defenseless and childlike while simultaneously deploying a common trope of Mayan henequen workers as vengeful and violent. The article series connected the unrest in the Yucatán with the "revisionism of the revolution," the cover title for the magazine's January 28, 1967, issue. With images of mobilized workers, the *Sucesos* articles suggested that it was the Mayan peoples themselves who were rewriting the narrative of the Mexican Revolution and its progress.

Publicizing the persistent problems of urban poverty and rural landlessness did not expose readers to new information, but it did change the tenor of debate by forcing a collective reckoning. Press coverage of such issues preoccupied PRI leaders, and one Yucatecan public official wryly quipped that "the greatest mistake of the government was to teach the Indians how to read. Now they're all reading *The Diario de Yucatán!*"⁹⁴ This statement likely exaggerated the influence of the newspaper, but it reveals fears that the PRI would be vulnerable to competition if it lost control over political discourse. While censorship continued, rare moments of publicity still had transformative effects by contributing to the formation of new publics, forcing a degree of governmental accountability, and facilitating collective action.

## CONCLUSION

In the 1960s independent student, labor, and peasant movements challenged the Mexican government's revolutionary rhetoric. Rather than delivering socioeconomic uplift and political enfranchisement, these movements argued, the state had abandoned the poor and used violence to silence dissent. They thus challenged the PRI's discursive legitimacy, which rested on its claims to represent the revolution. While more moderate in tone, denuncia journalists and photographers also discussed rural landlessness and urban inequality to emphasize that the revolution was not merely "unfinished," as some governing officials claimed, but abandoned.

Technological changes facilitated efforts to document poverty while raising additional questions of authorship and intent. Recording technology seemingly offered proof of Lewis's informants while sparking controversy over possible manipulation of the tapes themselves. Photographs similarly provided mechanically reproduced "evidence" of the impoverishment of the countryside while leaving out identifying clues that could situate the subjects for viewers. Captions thus critically laid out the significance of the images for readers. In other instances, recording technology amplified the voices of marginalized groups, while making them targets of government reprisals. For example, even as Manuel Sánchez articulated his position on a voice recording, fear of retaliation kept him from attending the panel and thus from actively engaging in the debate.

Denuncia journalism still challenged top-down attempts to delineate the appropriate spaces for criticism. Broadsheets like *El Día* offered a forum for intellectual debates that furnished evidence and epistemologies to explain the persistence of poverty. In letters to the editor, readers intervened to assert the persuasiveness of their own experiences and personal knowledge. University roundtables also expanded the conversation to include students and intellectuals who wished to talk back against a government official. These rarefied venues restricted access to a sliver of mostly elite and educated individuals, but the scandal around Lewis's censorship also endured through theatrical renditions and satirical novels, which expanded the public that was familiar with the case. Denuncia journalism also offered a tool to Yucatecan peasants engaged in long-standing struggles for fair wages and democratic representation. Ejidatario organizations mobilized documentary proof, published by Menéndez, to undergird and strengthen their claims.

Denuncia journalists' willingness to break with public secrets did not signal the linear opening of the press, but instead highlights the uneven democratization of public debate in Mexico City. After months of freewheeling discussion about *Los hijos de Sánchez*, officials prevented the new edition's publication and shut down press coverage of the topic. Similarly, Menéndez transformed *Sucesos* into a hard-hitting investigative magazine, but he was fired after two years as its director. His rapid radicalization had generated tensions with *Sucesos* owner Gustavo Alatriste, who found a more conservative replacement.[95] Menéndez's resignation came just three months after the leftist magazine *Política* published its final issue, folding after seven years of intense economic pressure. *Política* had distinguished itself from other media by directly criticizing the president, who had been traditionally off limits for the press, and by covering state repression, such as the political assassination of peasant labor leader Rubén Jaramillo and his family in May 1962. To temper criticism, PIPSA frequently withheld newsprint, and *Política*'s leadership was often subjected to intimidation or even violence by government officials.[96] When *Política* finally closed, the U.S. embassy in Mexico City observed that the radical Left was temporarily orphaned without a printed vehicle for dissent.[97] This ebb and flow of vocal dissent, official scrutiny, and economic crisis would continue to define denuncia journalism, even after the incoming president announced an opening of the press in 1970.

CHAPTER 2

# "VEHICLES OF SCANDAL"

In the early 1970s, the federal government dramatically changed its public stance toward political criticism. Eschewing the overt anticommunism of his predecessor, incoming president Luis Echeverría embraced a populist platform, and he even altered his sartorial choices, donning folkloric guayaberas, to signal his commitment to social causes.[1] Ironically, this shift followed the state's repression of the 1968 student movement; that summer Mexico City witnessed the largest street protests in its history, marking the culmination of over a decade of student activism. The Tlatelolco Massacre brought the protests to a violent end just ten days before the opening ceremonies of the Mexico City Summer Olympics. Plainclothes security forces fired from the apartment buildings that surrounded the Plaza de las Tres Culturas, killing dozens, if not hundreds, of students and teachers who had gathered for a rally below. Riot police arrested and imprisoned many more, adding to the lengthy list of political prisoners.

Decades would pass before the state admitted responsibility for the massacre, but Echeverría recognized the need to belatedly address the students' demands. As secretary of the interior under the previous administration he had been complicit in the massacre, but he now presented himself as the progenitor of the PRI's reformation. Upon taking office in 1970 Echeverría declared a "democratic opening" that promised press freedom, a new tolerance for union independence, and the release of political prisoners. Encouraged by the president's overtures, new groups organized for union democracy, squatters' rights to land and water, access to abortion, and protection from domestic violence. Artistic collectives also flourished, producing experimental films and performance art that depicted the struggles of women and workers, among others.² Finally, liberation theology was revolutionizing some segments of the Catholic Church. Mexican Jesuits actively embraced the mission of social justice and formed new organizations to educate and empower poor communities. While new avenues for dissent arose, state violence continued. This was evident when state-hired thugs attacked student protesters, killing twenty-five and leaving dozens wounded in the Jueves de Corpus Massacre on June 10, 1971.

Echeverría tried to co-opt intellectuals and the leftist opposition by increasing the education budget, reinvesting in the film industry, and creating new public offices and academic centers to employ former student movement leaders. He also allowed *Excélsior*, the nation's historically conservative broadsheet, to become a visible symbol of intellectual freedom. As one of the two oldest news publications in Mexico, *Excélsior* had historically undergirded political power. It provided a forum for intraelite quarreling and a platform for state propaganda; front pages printed presidential speeches and lengthy interviews with politicians, and opinion pages featured laudatory editorials on government accomplishments. With Echeverría's permission, however, broadsheets gradually provided spaces for diverse and contrarian opinions. Anticipating that *Excélsior* would offer an "escape valve" for dissent, the president cultivated ties with the new democratically minded director, Julio Scherer García.³

The diversification of publications and perspectives, however, did not discourage the proliferation of informal news, which transcended class and ideological registers.⁴ In the early 1970s rumors, conspiracies, and scandals became a considerable source of concern for spies and government officials. Business leaders and members of the conservative National Action Party (Partido Acción Nacional, or PAN) spread conspiracies of political destabilization, gas shortages, and a peso devaluation to mobilize opposition. Louise E. Walker observes that intelligence agents and opinion leaders alike believed that political and financial uncertainty fueled middle-class rumors.⁵ Growing economic inflation strained pocketbooks, and state repression drove some student movement leaders underground to form guerrilla cells. Headlines and news broadcasts announced that terrorists were carrying out bank robberies and kidnappings, heightening fears of political instability.⁶

In December 1974, a new scandal aggravated these tensions. As residents of Nezahualcóyotl, an impoverished municipality that hugs Mexico's City's eastern border, prepared for Christmas festivities, word spread that public health officials, sometimes with the assistance of foreign doctors, were sterilizing poor schoolchildren under the guise of routine vaccinations. Parents quickly gathered outside local schools to block the path of medical workers, and many of them joined marches to demand that the federal government respond to the accusation. Public health authorities and the Mexico City press intervened by asserting that poor parents lacked the education to understand modern medicine. A typical headline reduced the episode to "ignorance, a barrier to vaccination in Ciudad Netzahualcóyotl."[7] After the allegations spread to Mexico City, opinion leaders lamented that rumors had "invaded" and "devastated" the city by assaulting reason.[8] This chapter considers the distinct reactions to and consequences of a scandal that emerged from popular, rather than elite, sources.

The allegations of forced sterilization proved to be unfounded, and scholars and cultural commentators have since underscored the irrationality of the rumors.[9] As Luise White and Lauren Derby note, however, the "inaccuracies" of ephemeral speech reveal the worldviews and "political imagination" of those who believe and spread them.[10] Building on such scholarship, this chapter shows that the allegations of sterilization were not opposed to informed political engagement but rather an integral component of it. As literacy, readership, television access, and political engagement increased, so too did the efforts to understand and influence the news by talking about it. Ordinary residents drew on media coverage and personal experience to comment on what was politically plausible: racially motivated state violence. The unsubstantiated allegations also had real effects, challenging James C. Scott's formulation of rumors and gossip as weapons of the weak.[11] The sterilization scandal provided a pretext for collective action and community consolidation in Nezahualcóyotl and surrounding Greater Mexico City neighborhoods. It also mobilized a concerted government and media effort to halt the allegations. These elite actors responded to a different scandal: that sinister groups had presumably sown fear and dissension among the credulous lower classes.

Most Mexico City reporters, government officials, and state spies quickly dismissed the allegations as "rumor." While this designation accurately described unconfirmed and unattributed information that often spread by word of mouth, it also evoked gendered, racialized, and classed associations to delegitimize the scandal. To untangle the epistemological from the discursive functions of the term *rumor*, I only employ it when it appears in the documentary record. Instead I refer to the popular commentaries on, reactions to, and imaginative reinterpretations of the allegations as *scandal*, emphasizing the social processes over the veracity of the claims. Unsubstantiated or unattributed claims advanced very different ends depending on who spread them. For example, governing officials and spies surreptitiously seeded disinformation and gossip with devastating effects for independent organizations. Right-wing groups knowingly diffused false information in a conspiracy to undermine the government. I employ this broader vocabulary of disinformation, conspiracy, rumor, and scandal to distinguish between the language used by historical actors and my own conceptual framework.

The sterilization scandal heightened state fears that the urban poor were politically unpredictable and, therefore, dangerous. To make popular worldviews legible, and thus controllable, spies busily reported on each new appearance of the allegations, while both intentionally and unintentionally spreading unsubstantiated information themselves. Mexico City journalists undergirded these efforts by invalidating the allegations and trying to eradicate popular scandal from the public sphere. Contrary to what liberal reporters wished to believe, however, unsubstantiated stories could become scandals with enduring political consequences. Decades later, many of those who once lived in Netzahualcóyotl remain convinced that sterilizations took place, and the scandal endures in popular memory as a delegitimating moment for both the state and federal governments.

### "WARNING CIUDAD NEZAHUALCÓYOTL PARENT"

The sterilization vaccine scandal began sometime during the first week of December 1974 (no one could confirm the actual day), when an unidentified woman appeared at a local primary school in Mexico state, which surrounds the capital city to the north, west, and east. She came bearing ominous news, conveying the findings of her daughter's autopsy report, signed by the Hospital Civil. The mother warned that her eleven-year-old girl had suffered strange and ultimately fatal symptoms after receiving a routine vaccination, which foreigners had administered at her local public school.[12] The autopsy revealed that the vaccine had not only killed the young girl but had also damaged her uterus. The woman disappeared as quickly as she had appeared, leaving the Ministry of Health and Assistance (Secretaría de Salubridad y Asistencia, or SSA) to write a speculative internal report that blamed the anonymous individual for spreading a dangerous rumor. Word quickly spread through the surrounding markets and housing subdivisions that children who had recently received a typhoid vaccine had begun to bleed from the mouth and genitals, turn purple, faint, or even die. According to these accounts, the vaccine was designed to sterilize poor children.[13]

The timing of the allegation was no coincidence. In 1972 the SSA and the Mexican Social Security Institute (Instituto Mexicano de Seguridad Social) had launched family planning programs in health clinics across the country. In March 1974 Echeverría institutionalized these initiatives by authoring the General Population Law, which empowered the secretary of the interior to adjust social and economic policies in accordance with demographic needs.[14] The justification for family planning was simple: the country's demographic growth (3.5 percent per year) was among the highest in the world; without a reduction in population, Mexico would not produce enough food to meet basic needs. This perspective marked a departure not only from longstanding pronatalist policies but also from Echeverría's own 1969 campaign slogan, "To govern is to populate."

Though Echeverría acknowledged that social welfare programs were also necessary to reduce poverty, the president echoed neo-Malthusian claims that high levels of unemployment, illiteracy, and hunger all stemmed from population pressures. Demographers and health workers largely blamed poor women for overpopulation, even though family size varied little by class (and the president himself was the father of eight children).[15] To reform stereotypical moral failings, such as machismo and laziness, advertising campaigns encouraged "responsible parenthood," emphasizing that smaller families could better provide for children's physical and psychological needs. Ultimately, however, family planning followed the international development community in targeting women's bodies as either sites of economic transformation or as barriers to development.

Residents of Ciudad Nezahualcóyotl might have encountered family planning advertisements while listening to the radio, waiting for the bus, or visiting the doctor. They might also have learned of state efforts while watching television, which was becoming a more prominent medium for news consumption. The development of videotape technology had improved the production speed of broadcasts, and preparations for the 1968 Summer Olympics expanded the country's microwave system, which, combined with new satellite technology, made it possible to air the games live and in color.[16] The national manufacture of television sets also lowered the retail price for consumers. The Ministry of Public Education (Secretaría de Educación Pública, or SEP) saw broadcast media as a powerful tool to reach the urban poor and installed more than eight hundred television sets in sixty Mexico City schools.[17] Officials also collaborated with the newly formed Televisa monopoly, which united the country's two broadcasting powerhouses in 1973 to produce educational *telenovelas*. By the late 1960s, this genre of soap operas had reached a mass, cross-class audience, and the government-sponsored series that promoted family planning and literacy, among other initiatives in the 1970s.[18] Nonetheless, Nezahualcóyotl residents soon expressed their wariness toward state efforts to transform their bodies and behaviors.

While SSA officials traced the scandal to the mysterious woman, intelligence agents argued that the panic began with an incendiary leaflet that appeared in Nezahualcóyotl on December 4.[19] Bearing the boldface title, "Warning Cuidad Nezahualcóyotl Parent," the leaflet reported that children in public schools had received a vaccine that caused "inflammation, partial paralysis, and in girls the eruption of the uterus," echoing the claims first expressed by the anonymous woman outside a primary school. The flyer also noted that the vaccine had led to seven deaths. Including these concrete details—the location, the vehicle, and the consequences—undergirded the document's truth value. The authors also identified specific agencies that were reputedly responsible, accusing the Mexico state government, the SEP, and the SSA of conspiring to sterilize poor children. The leaflet urged parents, "Do not allow them to vaccinate your children."[20] Copies of the flyer likely passed through hundreds of hands, appeared on front stoops, and ended, as most flyers do, crumpled on the ground under the many feet that passed by. Intelligence agents from the General Office for Political and Social Intelligence (Dirección General de Investigaciones Políticas y Sociales, or DGIPS) collected copies of the leaflet, tucking them away for further analysis.

The original site where the allegations emerged shaped their broader reception among capital city elites. For many living in Mexico City, Nezahualcóyotl exemplified the rapid urbanization that had brought impoverished residents to the Valley of Mexico over the previous decade. In the 1950s and 1960s, migrants moved from crowded downtown tenements and the depressed countryside to squatter settlements, shantytowns, and low-income subdivisions on the fringes of the capital.[21] While Nezahualcóyotl only had sixty-five thousand residents in 1960, its population soared to 650 thousand in 1970. That number doubled just five years later, making Nezahualcóyotl Mexico's fourth largest urban area. By 1970 the population of Mexico City and its surrounding urban areas also nearly doubled, reaching 8.4 million people and accounting for one-sixth of the nation's total population.[22]

For many middle-class and elite residents of Mexico City, Nezahualcóyotl was a symbol of backwardness and danger. Public services had not kept pace with growth. Nezahualcóyotl had no garbage collection, leading to informal dumps situated precariously close to housing developments. The municipality's residents also suffered from a contaminated and irregular water supply, no functioning sewage system, unpaved roads, and limited public transportation. Built on the nearly dry Texcoco lakebed—formerly the site of a major Aztec city—the neighborhood periodically flooded during the rainy season. Meanwhile, residents were assailed by dust storms during the dry season. They were also embroiled in battles with land developers, who colluded with municipal authorities to defraud and dispossess them of their land. Unlike in squatter settlements or shantytowns, Nezahualcóyotl residents did have their own primary schools, and most could read, but they remained economically, socially, and politically marginalized.[23]

The uncertain origins of the flyer, combined with its potential to catalyze popular mobilization, preoccupied DGIPS agents. In the early 1970s, student movement participants had organized residents in peripheral communities like Nezahualcóyotl for water and land rights. Similarly, Jesuit organizations, including the newly formed Cultural and Education Promotion (Fomento Cultural y Educativo), sent initiates to live on ejidos or in settlements to minister to the poor.[24] Shaped by liberation theology, these organizations advocated social justice, and in some cases revolutionary change, but they may have opposed family planning efforts. Spies quickly linked leftist groups to the accusations, asserting that a squatters' rights group, the Movement for Settler Reinstatement (Movimiento Restaurador de Colonos), had circulated the flyer.[25] The SSA similarly conjectured that neighborhood movements had "taken advantage of this situation to blame the government for a problem created by foreigners," though health officials did not elaborate regarding what, exactly, foreigners had done.[26]

Reactions to the flyer exemplify how new technologies, such as photocopying, made it possible to generate more theories and confusion. The leaflet was signed by the Independent Popular Front (Frente Popular Independiente, or FPI), one of the many leftist grassroots organizations created by ex–student movement leaders after 1968. It was not, however, uncommon for public officials and political parties to falsely sign and circulate broadsides to undermine opponents. Thus the signature does not guarantee the FPI's authorship, and those accusing the government of forced sterilization might have opted for anonymity to avoid retaliation. In any case, middle-class authors probably produced the flyer, given that they were more likely to have access to a typewriter and mimeograph technology.

Nezahualcóyotl residents would not be surprised to learn that various groups sought to manipulate their communities to distinct ends. Community leaders had their own theories about how alleged sterilizations advanced hidden agendas. But the allegations were credible because they drew from stories that greater Mexico City communities had already encountered in their media consumption and daily lives while also reflecting personal experiences of state discrimination or mendacity. Some working-class parents even justified their concerns about forced sterilizations by explaining that they had read about them in the newspaper or heard about them on the popular nightly news program *24 Horas*.[27] The program, which began airing in September 1970, was hosted by PRI ally Jacobo Zabludovksy. Such references to establishment media highlight a skilled ability to cite distinct sources of authority depending on one's audience. Regardless of the source of the information, Mexico state residents reacted as if the information was credible.

## MOBILIZING AS THE POOR

Governing authorities grew alarmed when rumors led to collective action and threats of violence. Soon after the flyer surfaced, confrontations broke out in Nezahualcóyotl neighborhoods as frightened residents tried to ascertain whether strangers were interlopers or innocent passersby. The specter of ambulant medical teams transformed public spaces into sites of potential danger, as it was commonplace for health workers to administer inoculations in markets and busy plazas.[28] Anyone carrying a briefcase or wearing a white lab coat became suspect. Some parents stationed themselves outside their children's primary schools, armed with sticks or knives, prepared to attack vaccinators.[29] Schools were emptied of pupils, and principals reported attendance as low as 10 percent during the week after the flyer first appeared.[30] While some parents feared for their children's safety, others likely understood that a scandal provided a fortuitous pretext for mobilization and an opportunity to briefly consolidate neighborhood opposition.

Spies from the DGIPS filed multiple reports on December 9 and a dozen more on December 10. As if seeking to contain an epidemic, they identified each new school and neighborhood that had been infected by the allegations. Intelligence agents also dutifully recorded the subversive speech they overheard outside primary schools and reported, for example, that some parents "cursed the president" and held Echeverría personally responsible for the sterilizations.[31]

The spies sought not only to identify the instigators but also to capture the political attitudes of the worried parents, many of whom worked in the informal economy and resisted official overtures to join the CNOP. To capture this population, Echeverría had formed neighborhood councils and passed reforms to regularize land usage, though these measures often disadvantaged residents by opening land to private investment.[32] The president had also created new institutions, including the National Workers' Housing Fund (Instituto del Fondo Nacional de la Vivienda para los Trabajadores) and the Department of the Federal District's General Office of Popular Housing (Dirección General de la Habitación Popular, DDF), to construct affordable housing and support low-income home buyers.[33] The poorest individuals who lacked formal employment, however, did not qualify for such loans. In Nezahualcóyotl, moreover, the municipal and state governments countered federal efforts by colluding with developers and refusing to recognize residents' land titles. The federal government also complemented political accommodation with violent dispossession when residents insisted on mobilizing independently. Spy reports thus reflected efforts to understand and control a population that the state deemed politically dangerous.

Meanwhile, community leaders saw the allegations as an opportunity to mobilize outrage and exert political pressure on local and federal officials. On December 9, students of an UNAM preparatory school, the School of Sciences and Humanities (Colegio de Ciencias y Humanidades, or CCH) Oriente, and their parents gathered to address the threat of sterilization. Situated in the working-class Mexico City neighborhood of Iztapalapa, which borders Nezahualcóyotl to the west, the CCH Oriente served as a key base of operations for the FPI, the presumed author of the original flyer. Since the early 1970s, the FPI had organized Nezahualcóyotl residents to demand new schools, water, public transportation, and paved roads.[34] At the meeting hundreds of attendees agreed on several resolutions. First, from that day forward they would not send their children to school until the government clarified the issue. Parents and students also organized two protest marches on December 10, one in Nezahualcóyotl and the other in Iztapalapa, which would culminate in a rally at the SEP's Valley of Mexico headquarters.[35]

While DGIPS intelligence agents produced two reports on the meeting, it is unclear whether the office actually sent a spy to the event, or if agents merely interviewed attendees after the fact. The two reports differed considerably on the most rudimentary details, with one reporting seven hundred attendees and the other two thousand.[36] At a time when basic information was at a premium, agents seemingly relied on imprecise recollections to produce intelligence on the scandal.

A new flyer circulated at the meeting and offered a class-based critique of family planning: "Many functionaries and the rich say that 'overpopulation' is the cause of hunger. They lie! The true cause of hunger is the exploitation that the people suffer." The authors argued that the state should focus on wealth redistribution rather than blaming the poor for underdevelopment. Moreover, they called on Nezahualcóyotl residents to resist, pronouncing, "We the poor won't be sacrificed as guinea pigs for the rich!" The reason for population control, the authors emphasized, was to uproot opposition. The flyer emphasized that "as long as there are exploited residents there will be greater discontent and more revolutionary organizing. This is what many politicians and exploiters fear! That is why they want to avoid more births, more people that are against them!"[37] The flyer effectively framed family planning as a covert project to eliminate leftist political opposition.

Similar rhetoric inflected comparable episodes elsewhere in Latin America, including Chile and Peru. The most notorious episode occurred in Bolivia, after the 1969 film *Yawar mallku* depicted Peace Corps volunteers secretly sterilizing natives. Though fictional, the film sparked outrage among Indigenous and student organizations, which urged political leaders to defend Bolivia's national sovereignty. Protests reached such a pitch that the government finally decided to expel the Peace Corps in 1971.[38] While Bolivian protesters accused foreign aid workers of sponsoring eugenics campaigns, Mexican leftist groups identified federal and state agencies as the perpetrators of class-based sterilizations, perhaps because the Mexican government embraced family planning, while other Latin American leaders had retreated from such policies.[39]

Since the 1960s the British and U.S. governments, international nongovernmental organizations, and the United Nations (UN) viewed the reduction in Third World birth rates as crucial to economic development and the protection of liberal democracy. They feared that increasingly young populations would lead to political rebellion, citing Cuba and Vietnam as cautionary tales, and they often made foreign aid contingent upon meeting population control goals.[40] Multiple cases of sterilization indicated that international aid organizations were motivated by desires to eliminate dark-skinned, poor populations. In Brazil, for example, the military regime gave the International Planned Parenthood Foundation and U.S. aid organizations permission to spearhead population control initiatives that targeted Brown and Black Brazilians, and a scandalous exposé in 1967 linked evangelical missionaries to the sterilization of Amazonian women.[41] In the early 1970s the *New York Times* revealed that doctors in the U.S. South had targeted recipients of welfare, primarily Black women, for sterilization.[42] Reading about this horrific violence from afar, educated Mexican media consumers may have borrowed these images and details in their interpretations of the allegations.

In the 1970s new leftist governments in Argentina, Chile, and Peru denounced population control initiatives as racist and imperialist, and they rejected funding from British and U.S. organizations.[43] Mexico, by contrast, embraced family planning and foreign funding. The decision stemmed from the president's political ambitions. Echeverría was keenly aware that the UN had identified population control as a crucial priority, and he hoped to gain prominence on the world stage by promoting family planning. With a single six-year term permitted for Mexican presidents, Echeverría aimed to continue his political career by becoming the UN secretary-general when his term ended.[44] His efforts were rewarded with international recognition, as Mexican statesman Antonio Carrillo Flores served as the secretary-general for the UN's International Conference on Population.[45]

Speakers at the Iztapalapa meeting thus addressed local and state authorities, not international organizations. Some speakers hypothesized that land developers had paid for the vaccines, while others conjectured that sterilizations were intended to sway the 1975 Mexico state gubernatorial elections. In these explanations, gendered violence was symptomatic of a larger political conspiracy to stem community activism. Coordinators of the Iztapalapa meeting portrayed violated children, particularly girls, as the objects of capitalist exploitation. It was no coincidence that the allegations centered on girls, whose innocence and morality was rooted in their lack of knowledge of what was allegedly being done to them. As Miriam Ticktin writes, "Innocence comes into being in relation to its various binary others, such as guilt, knowledge, and sexuality."[46] If the allegations had focused on the sterilization of adults, discussions would have confronted questions of women's sexuality and, possibly, their hidden desires for such procedures.

The language of class conflict made gender violence a metaphor for ideological and political warfare. For example, one speaker reported that "an autopsy has been performed and found that, in the case of girls, their uteruses and ovaries were destroyed."[47] By citing a medical exam, he mobilized the language of modern science to assert that empirical evidence of sterilization existed, while implicitly critiquing the new technologies that had made it possible for doctors to fuse, remove, insert devices into, or operate upon women's and girls' reproductive organs. Nevertheless, the speaker did not consider how such procedures intersected with women's desires or needs, sidestepping contemporaneous feminist assertions that safe abortions and the Pill would grant women greater autonomy.[48] Instead, he suggested that the state's true intentions could only be revealed through further violence (an invasive autopsy) on girls' bodies.

While their perspectives were silenced by meeting leaders, women were highly visible at the protests the following day. On December 10, more than two thousand mothers stationed themselves at the Los Reyes la Paz municipal palace at 8:00 AM to demand protection for their children.[49] They also marched alongside men in the two protests that had been planned at the CCH Oriente meeting. This political participation was not exceptional. In the early 1970s, women increasingly joined popular neighborhood movements to demand land and water rights.[50] While their political activism broke with established gender norms, they framed their participation as a defense of their families.[51] Without access to their testimonies, it is impossible to know what women felt as they marched that day. Yet juxtaposed against positive attitudes toward birth control, it is reasonable to presume that participants might have spoken with two voices as they responded to the scandal.[52] They were expected to desire children, and to admit otherwise would require admitting many other equally unspeakable desires. Yet by joining protests, women demanded respect for their communities and registered their own claims to power.

Intelligence agents' efforts to track developments in Mexico state were only complicated over the following days as the rumors spread beyond Nezahualcóyotl and Iztapalapa. New flyers appeared farther east in Mexico state and farther west in downtown Mexico City. Signed by another left-leaning grassroots neighborhood association, the United Settlers' Front (Frente Unido de Colonos), the document reiterated assertions that "we the poor will not be used as guinea pigs for the rich!"[53] Trucks also contributed to consciousness-raising efforts, patrolling Iztapalapa and Nezahualcóyotl streets with loudspeakers warning parents not to send their children to school. The vehicles were unmarked, frustrating DGIPS spies' attempts to ascertain who had hired them. Recognizing the need to counter ephemeral speech, municipal authorities deployed their own loudspeakers to assert that the vaccines were harmless. The cacophony of aural warnings suggested an urgency of news that the technologies of print and broadcast media could not accommodate.[54]

Informal news structured political engagement in the Valley of Mexico during the early 1970s. Poor urban residents presented flyers to municipal authorities as documentary proof that sterilizations were occurring. Circumventing editorial gatekeepers, these flyers seemingly offered residents access to privileged information. Yet readers did not interpret this news in a homogenized manner; instead they offered their own competing explanations of motive and authorship. Meanwhile, state spies pieced together oral and printed accounts to render the urban poor intelligible to Ministry of the Interior officials, who oversaw the intelligence services. As the scandal spread to Mexico City, reporters joined efforts to discipline ephemeral speech.

## DISTINGUISHING THE FACTS

Mexico City newspaper headlines soon described "panic" and "psychosis" and warned readers not to believe the "false rumors." Articles suggested that hearsay had led to anarchy and detailed how riot police were deployed after parents attacked teachers in various parts of the capital.[55] Journalists from major broadsheets and sensational tabloids invoked a well-worn discourse of fanatical and irrational parents obstructing the state's modernizing efforts. This language echoed earlier depictions of Catholic protests against the anticlerical education policies of the 1920s and 1930s.[56] Reporters also rehearsed earlier criticisms voiced by public health reformers who had confronted local resistance to smallpox vaccinations.[57] These public health campaigns were often complicated by local contests over power with ordinary people stuck in the middle. In 1949, for example, middle-class actors spread conspiracies that vaccines caused infertility in women, impotence in men, and even death.[58] Information asymmetries required ordinary people to trust that vaccinators were well-intentioned actors injecting them with a benign substance. Print media joined government efforts to disprove the allegations and underscored the shared assumption that the urban poor could not be knowledge producers.

The press offensive asserted that baseless accounts could only be contained through the publication of disqualifying evidence. Noting that objective science proved that the hearsay was false, news articles continually highlighted the presumably flawed theories of parents: How did they know that the vaccinations were really sterilizing their children? Who had seen the doctors enter the schools? Where were the police reports of dead children? Who had experienced the sensationalized symptoms allegedly caused by the vaccine? Reporters not only raised questions of proof but also posed them directly to the concerned parents, acting as vehicles for the government's slowly developing efforts to disprove the rumors. Yet news articles and spy reports suggested that the boundary between fact and fiction was far from clear. Indeed, there are many instances in which politicians, spies, and reporters themselves knowingly or unknowingly spread unsubstantiated accounts.

EL DIRECTOR de la escuela estatal "Emiliano Zapata" hace declaraciones al reportero

## La Ignorancia, Barrera en Contra de la Vacunación en Ciudad Netzahualcóyotl

Figure 2.1 "El director de la escuela estatal Emiliano Zapata hace declaraciones al reportero," *Excélsior*, December 7, 1974, 16.

Newspaper coverage nevertheless modeled the proper way in which readers should respond to dangerous allegations. In an *Excélsior* article, one journalist included the list of questions that he posed to mothers outside a primary school in Mexico state.[59] Each question implied that the lack of empirical evidence, and particularly eyewitness accounts, undermined the mothers' statements. This reporter, like others, deployed a gendered definition of gossip as information shared by women, and he suggested that mothers responded emotionally because they did not investigate the rumors before acting on them.

Images also demarcated the gendered boundaries of who could legitimately claim knowledge by visually conveying the authority of middle-class male voices. The accompanying photograph (see figure 2.1) pictured the journalist taking notes as a local school director spoke. Surrounding the two men are a handful of schoolchildren, presumably waiting to receive more information. By instructing readers to discount parents' voices, the article echoed long-standing public health discourses in Latin America, which cast poor and uneducated women as unfit mothers who required scientific guidance to properly care for their children.[60] Nezahualcóyotl parents likely understood the value of inoculation but distrusted the state health ministry to provide safe vaccinations. Indeed, some parents opted to purchase expensive vaccines from private clinics, and many dispensaries reported scarcity due to the high demand.[61] The photograph also allows for an alternative reading. While most eyes are trained on the two men, two girls in the foreground are turned away and chatting together. One wears a big smile, breaking with the presumed gravity of the situation. While mainstream media described scenes of terror and panic, the image suggests that some students might have experienced it as a source of entertainment and excitement that allowed them to skip class.

On December 10 the SSA issued paid advertisements in all capital city newspapers to disprove the allegations. Under the boldfaced title, "False Rumors about the Vaccination," health officials laid out their argument in a quasi-legal fashion, dividing the text into seven numbered points.[62] The SSA defended the necessity of vaccines by underscoring how immunizations against diseases like typhoid were critical to early child development. The fact that children were the alleged victims of sterilization made the accusations particularly threatening to the state, which since the early twentieth century had asserted itself as the guarantor of childhood development and protection.[63]

Public health officials distinguished between those who believed the rumors and those who intentionally spread falsehoods. The announcement emphasized that a sterilization vaccination did not even exist and thus that the allegations had no basis in fact. The SSA implied that only ignorant, poor, and unmodern Mexicans believed the sterilization allegations, but it characterized middle-class actors who participated in the scandal as subversive masterminds. Presuming that the sterilization allegation reflected an attempt "to create social unrest," the announcement urged Mexico City residents to "report to the authorities any person who, by any means, spreads [these ideas] or incites parents to keep their children out of school."[64] In the context of swirling conspiracies about an impending economic crisis, the SSA implied that the political Right was spreading hearsay to destabilize the government. In some cases, threats against those who spread the accusations were even more pointed. Outside one primary school, a public health official tried to prevent a reporter from recording children's testimonies, warning him that "if he continued writing down 'gossip' it would end badly."[65] The threatening statement feminized popular knowledge and implied that it was incompatible with rational information.

The views of the individuals who believed and shared the allegations were generally mediated through skeptical journalists or spies, who depicted a homogeneous rumor mill. But piecing together disparate accounts allows us to speculate that the scandal contained credible claims that were grounded in personal experience. Allegations of forced sterilization spoke to the plausibility that the government discriminated against the poor and used violence to further its own interests, that modernization had not benefited the economically and socially marginalized, and (perhaps most importantly) that political elites serially lied to the public. At the same time, we should not underestimate the ambivalence that structured popular reactions. For example, communities did not have to believe the allegations were true to react to them. The scandal provided a set of broader critiques that ordinary people could mobilize against local officials.

The SSA also undermined its own claims by combining factual statements with questionable ones. Notably, the announcement denied that a vaccination campaign was taking place in any part of the country, contradicting other newspaper reports of nationwide immunizations against polio, diphtheria, tetanus, measles, typhoid, and whooping cough.[66] Poor communication between government agencies likely produced this contradictory information. Indeed, just two days after the announcement, an internal SSA memorandum reported that a vaccination campaign in the Mexico Valley that was scheduled to end in November had been extended.[67] The SSA did not publicize this updated information, however, suggesting that health officials recognized that doing so would only generate more suspicion. For many greater Mexico City residents, blanket denials merely confirmed that the agency had something sinister to conceal.

Parents recognized that tampering with evidence was a common government strategy to maintain plausible deniability of wrongdoing. This was apparent in one confrontation between a police officer and a concerned mother from the Colonia Ampliación Ramos Millán. When the police officer requested that she provide material proof of the allegations, the woman responded with indignation and asserted that authorities were automatically disinclined to listen to the poor. She suggested that only a spectacular and morbid display could convince authorities that a supposed vaccine was harming schoolchildren, wondering: "Do you need to be presented with a child's cadaver to believe us?"[68] The brief exchange was reported by *La Prensa*, Mexico's best-selling tabloid, which delivered sensationalist crime news. Reading the news article against the grain offers a snippet of women's voices and reveals that the unnamed "housewife" talked back to officials who presumed that they employed more objective epistemologies. A bitter irony also remained unspoken in their exchange: while police asked to see physical proof, state security forces disappeared dissidents to discredit claims of repression. For example, security forces were rumored to have minimized the casualty figures of the Tlatelolco Massacre by burning protesters' bodies.[69] Moreover, in the early 1970s security agents systematically disappeared radical peasants by dumping their bodies into the Pacific Ocean.[70] Under such circumstances, the absence of physical evidence of sterilization might not appear to be disqualifying.

While the police officer suggested that the distinction between rumor and eyewitness accounts was obvious, intelligence agents often struggled to distinguish between substantiated and unverified accounts. This was evident, for example, in a DGIPS report on a labor stoppage at the Ayotla Textil factory in Mexico state. On December 10, intelligence agents reported that workers had collaborated "to 'trap'" a medical team said to be vaccinating children at a nearby school. According to spies, laborers heard that doctors had arrived with bodyguards "armed with high-powered submachine guns," a detail that suggested a highly coordinated and militarized vaccination team. According to DGIPS agents, factory employees declared a work stoppage and rushed home "to find their own guns and defend their children."[71] Given stringent gun laws, it is doubtful that many factory workers would have gained the special permission to carry firearms.[72] The agents likely recorded hearsay in addition to exaggerating for dramatic effect.

The report's embellishments reflect the overriding anxiety about opening the political system to popular mobilization. By raising the specter of armed vigilantism, spies amplified the perceived political and social threat posed by the allegations. Intelligence agents were perhaps more inclined to do so in the case of Ayotla Textil, which was a well-known site of political resistance. After a protracted battle against corrupt union bosses, factory workers had gained their independence from PRI control a few years earlier.[73] Intelligence agents saw the historical rejection of clientelism alongside uncontrollable rumors as a volatile combination. The growing number of independent neighborhood associations deepened concerns that the managed democratic opening was spinning out of control.

Journalists also (unknowingly) blurred the boundary between eyewitness account and hearsay. For instance, *La Prensa* reported an episode in which university students rescued a doctor who "was on the verge of being lynched" by local youths in Iztapalapa. The episode's inconsistencies and implausible details indicate, however, that the boundaries between fact and fiction and eyewitness account and rumor became confused when reporters tried to sort out ephemeral speech in writing. By the journalist's account, the students coolly defused a potentially violent situation by sending the vaccine to a laboratory "so that its contents can be analyzed and objective information can be given to the anguished parents."[74] Invoking the "objectivity" of modern science, the students purported to allay fears with one simple test.

Yet contradictory details in the article suggest that class prejudices inflected the reporter's attempts to determine the authenticity of a story. If, as authorities claimed, a vaccination campaign was not underway, why was the doctor in this story carrying vaccines on his person? If the doctor was an interloper in disguise, as many parents asserted, why would *La Prensa* leave out that detail? Moreover, how did the students have immediate access to a laboratory where they could test the vaccine in question? How did these random passersby happen to know how to identify the chemical composition of the syringe's contents? The reporter may have related this episode because he granted greater credibility to the university students. Alternatively, *La Prensa*, a government ally, could have consciously invented the story to reference scientific proof that the allegations were unfounded. In either case, publishing the story gave it greater authority.

The sterilization scandal generated a dense paper trail of news articles, flyers, spy reports, and official bulletins that mobilized competing claims of scientific evidence. Journalists, police, and public officials asserted that the middle classes could easily distinguish between fact and fiction, but their methods for identifying rational speech relied on classed and gendered assumptions about who was a legitimate knowledge producer. Moreover, they frequently reported unverified information when it confirmed their political views. Meanwhile, residents applied their own well-honed epistemologies to decipher the language of state authorities and journalists. Their reactions to sterilization allegations did not stem from ignorance but from their understanding that politicians serially lied to them and hid evidence to avoid scrutiny.

## A RIGHT-WING CONSPIRACY

PRI representatives and left-leaning opinion leaders assessed the underlying forces behind the scandal, and they quickly and categorically blamed right-wing Mexican business groups and the PAN. The PAN and Catholic civic organizations adamantly opposed family planning measures, and in 1973 they launched a virulent campaign against federally mandated and standardized textbooks, which included discussion of sex education. Protests and pamphlets accused the federal government of promoting radical leftism and impropriety.[75] Allegations of sterilization had first appeared two months earlier in the conservative northern states of Monterrey and Tamaulipas, suggesting that the PAN might have started the rumors.[76] Cognizant that psychological warfare (including misinformation and conspiracy) was a prevalent tool of subversion, PRI public officials and left-leaning writers accused fascists of laying the groundwork for a coup that would reverse Echeverría's progressive reforms. Strangely, they did not speculate about the leftist authors of the flyer, nor did they dwell on the language of class warfare that pervaded the allegations themselves. Instead they presented Echeverría as the last line of defense against fascism.[77]

Political tensions had escalated shortly before the sterilization scandal erupted outside Mexico City. In August 1974 José Guadalupe Zuno, Jalisco governor and the father-in-law of president Echeverría, was kidnapped by leftist guerrillas. In light of this high-profile capture, PRI officials delivered strident speeches denouncing the threat of terrorism, fascism, and foreign conspiracies. The minister of the interior, Mario Moya Palencia, also threatened to take thirty-seven Televisa programs off the air because they allegedly encouraged guerrilla activity.[78] By November intelligence agents reported that Mexico City had descended into "a general state of 'psychosis'" as conspiracies swirled that a political coup or economic collapse was imminent.[79] The PAN aggravated tensions by distributing flyers that urged residents to protest the rising costs of basic foodstuffs. Thus, the sterilization allegations were just one of many scandals that unsettled greater Mexico City residents in the fall of 1974.

Prominent opinion leaders read political polarization through the lens of hemispheric events. At the forefront of their minds was the September 11, 1973, coup that had unseated Chilean president Salvador Allende.[80] Public intellectuals warned that Mexicans must choose between "Echeverría or fascism," aiming their message at leftists who were wary of allying with the state after the Tlatelolco Massacre.[81] Many leftist and liberal journalists took to the streets to protest Allende's overthrow, and they interacted with Chilean exiles who arrived in Mexico City in the days after the coup. Scherer García, for example, welcomed Allende's widow, Hortensia Bussi, into his home. He also traveled to Chile after the coup and recalled witnessing "a country cloaked in blood."[82] Reporters worried that Mexico would succumb to similar violence.

Political observers saw troubling parallels with Chile, where inflation and rising food prices drew middle-class women into the streets, banging pots and pans, to call for Allende's overthrow during the *cacerola* (cooking pot) protests. Echeverría had established a public friendship with Allende, framing their countries as dual vanguards of social democracy. His term, like Allende's, was marked by a tense relationship with the country's business elite, which was based in the northern industrial center of Monterrey. Echeverría's promises of land and tax reforms and his charged leftist rhetoric had alienated powerful interest groups. Mexico City officials worried that the United States would use political instability and the president's populist policies as a pretext to incite a coup.[83] Meanwhile, Echeverría privately reassured U.S. president Richard Nixon of his commitment to defend the hemisphere against communism.[84]

For many left-leaning and liberal journalists, these developments suggested that the Mexican Right had spread the sterilization vaccine conspiracy to incite discontent. One reporter for *El Día* referred to the panic as a "rehearsal" for more troubling things to come.[85] Prominent political columnist Manuel Buendía similarly noted that the rumors originated in the conservative north and ominously warned that "now the fascist escalation has arrived in the [Mexico City] metropolitan area."[86] The PAN, which enjoyed support among middle-class Catholics in the north of the country, fueled speculation by reporting the allegations of sterilization as if they could be true.[87] By reading domestic discontent through the lens of hemispheric instability, journalists silenced the implicit criticisms voiced by organizing residents. Governing officials did the same, reflecting a deeply rooted understanding that the poor were pliable pawns who could be easily manipulated.

### ENFORCING REASONED DEBATE

Amid the scandal, *Excélsior* journalists jealously policed the boundaries of what they considered to be reasoned debate. The young editorial team, comprising Christian democrats and leftists of various stripes, proudly asserted their newfound independence from the government. With Echeverría's permission *Excélsior* became the most prominent national forum for dissent, though it remained much more moderate in tone and content than new oppositional publications like Mario Menéndez Rodríguez's *Por Qué?* But editors regularly adjusted their coverage when necessary and self-censored to avoid political backlash.[88] This was common practice within national print media, which strove to maintain peaceful relations with public officials; doing so guaranteed the state-subsidized newsprint and advertising (some 30 percent of total advertising revenue) that kept newspapers afloat.[89]

But economic considerations were not the only motivation for editors. *Excélsior*'s editorial team also shared governing officials' classist prejudices. In a highly unequal country, upwardly mobile editors and political elites belonged to a privileged stratum that viewed itself as morally distinct from the lower classes. Editors frequented the same bars and restaurants as public officials and had attended the same schools and universities. This class background shaped opinion leaders' visions of democratic opening, which they suggested would be spearheaded by the middle classes. The sterilization vaccination scandal thus revealed the limits, rooted in class and gender privilege, of press opening. When allegations of sterilization surfaced, journalists had only two sources to verify the story: official denials and popular eyewitness claims. While the latter would later be disproven, journalists were quick to discount these testimonies.

*Excélsior* opinion writers depicted those who engaged the sterilization scandal as poor, ignorant, and female. Leftist intellectuals saw the poor as spreading a dangerous irrationality that could lead to fascism. Froylán López Narváez, an opinion editor for *Excélsior* and close confidant of Scherer García, opined that the rumors made public opinion's "childlike susceptibility" and "defenselessness in the face of malicious attacks or unintentional provocation" clear. López Narváez interestingly suggested that it was not the press that constituted public opinion but rather uninformed hearsay. He participated in Mexican protests against the Chilean coup, and he worried that fascists could easily mobilize conspiracies to incite violent opposition against the government. He argued that the lower classes would be easily manipulated because they lacked the education to discern good information from bad.[90]

In *El Universal*, a large broadsheet with a primarily elite and middle-class readership, communist reporter Antonio Rodríguez similarly worried that rumors "fertilized" vulnerable minds for fascism, a reproductive metaphor that feminized the public. A PRI senator echoed this sentiment by arguing that rumors attempted "to sow doubt among Mexicans toward their institutions and to prejudice the people against government policy."[91] Appeals to scientific objectivity overlooked the prevalence of unsubstantiated information that originated from both the government and the press. Tellingly, the authors underscored the "rationality," rather than the truthfulness, of news, suggesting that veracity was determined not by content but by source: educated, elite (and typically light-skinned) men.

Reporters for *La Prensa* also characterized rumors as an uncontrollable and feminine mode of information. The tabloid targeted working-class readers and was one of Mexico City's most popular newspapers; by the 1970s it was known for sensationalist crime pages and government-aligned news coverage. *La Prensa* reporters deployed gendered depictions of the rumor mill, which they compared to the Chilean cacerola protests. They also frequently mentioned mothers, godmothers, and female neighbors when they discussed the spread of rumors, and an editorial even asserted that "slum-dwelling *comadres*" were an "effective vehicle for scandal." The editors contrasted irrational gossip (associated with women) against the rationality of print, which only "the convincing action of a man of reason" (*hombre de razón*) could resolve.[92] Beyond the literal translation, the term *hombre de razón* historically referred to white men, further drawing the racial boundaries of knowledge. The opinion writer disqualified the scandal as mere "rumor," suggesting that the allegations' association with women disqualified them as a rational source of information. In such assertions *La Prensa* contributors demarcated the boundaries of whose knowledge belonged in the gradually expanding public sphere.

*El Universal* cartoons similarly suggested that rumors gained currency among the most economically and socially disenfranchised. Cartoonists undergirded such associations by deploying tropes of indigeneity (barefoot women in traditional dress, often carrying babies on their backs) and workers in the informal economy (especially *pepenadores*, or trash collectors) to signify indigence and ignorance.[93] At the same time, some cartoons captured the ambivalence that undergirded the scandal. One, sketched by *El Universal* cartoonist Sergio Iracheta (see figure 2.2), pictured an impoverished mother complaining that it was "too bad that the sterilization vaccine [rumor] is false. I was going to send my husband to them."

Iracheta feminized the rumors while depicting a woman expressing her desire: by sterilizing her husband, she would gain more control over her own reproduction. The cartoonist suggested that there was a gap between what a woman needed to say publicly and what she might actually want. Indeed, the prevalence of abortions in the early 1970s—an "open secret" according to one social scientist—suggests that women wanted more control over their fertility, and small-scale surveys further indicated that women often sought abortions without their husbands' knowledge.[94] Iracheta suggested that women's protests were simply performances of indignation. When interpreted in this light, the cartoonist's chosen title, "Falso Rumor," refers ironically to the "rumor" that poor women opposed sterilization.

Print media and government officials argued that only the poor participated in the scandal, yet oral accounts suggest that many middle-class resi-

Figure 2.2 Iracheta, "Falso rumor," *El Universal*, December 11, 1974, 4. © Agencia El Universal.

dents of Mexico state also believed the allegations of forced sterilization to be true. For example, when I mentioned this case to archivists and researchers in Mexico City, many had vivid childhood memories of the accusations, which they suspected were true. These anecdotal accounts are bolstered by SEP reports, which noted that 70 percent of Mexico City's primary schools were affected by the scandal, indicating that the panic spread well beyond the most marginalized neighborhoods.[95] By insisting that only the poor believed the allegations, government officials tried to splinter public opinion and avoid a potentially dangerous cross-class rebellion.

Broadsheets were complicit in this effort. Reporters articulated a tautological argument to explain who believed the rumors. In *El Universal*, columnist María Mendoza implied that to believe the rumors was to be ignorant, and therefore to be poor, and that to be poor was to be ignorant. She lamented that the sterilization scare was a symptom of the "miserable ignorance of my people," and maintained that rumors were just one manifestation of superstition, much like Catholic devotees' practice of crawling on their knees to honor the Virgin of Guadalupe at the La Villa Basilica. In a common style for female columnists, Mendoza wrote in conversational

Figure 2.3 Iracheta, "Los infundios," *El Universal*, December 16, 1974, 4. © Agencia El Universal.

prose and recalled that, upon seeing the devotees, "I would yell from my window in Tlatelolco: work!"⁹⁶ This anecdote demonstrated her distance (both physical and intellectual) from superstitious Catholic worshipers. Mendoza identified herself as one of the middle-class beneficiaries of the relatively new Nonoalco-Tlatelolco public housing project for Mexico City's white-collar workers. In the image she conveyed, she literally looked down on pilgrims, whom she presumed not only to be unemployed but also willfully so. Mendoza suggested that the middle classes were the legitimate beneficiaries of mid-century modernization and that their rationality demonstrated their right to wield social and political power.

Iracheta drew another cartoon (see figure 2.3) that subtly questioned this prevalent discourse by acknowledging that the allegations could be true. The cartoon depicts a confrontation between an upper-middle-class couple as the husband arrives home late. He is forced to answer to his wife's accusation, "They told me that they saw you with a blond woman." Cowering with sweat beading dramatically on his brow, he replies, "Good thing no one believes rumors anymore, darling." The emasculated husband can be read as symbolizing the vulnerable and defensive government. While he delivers a de facto denial, his nervousness indicates that the gossip might be true. Under the title "Los infundios" (False news), the cartoon offers an ambiguous depiction of the rumor mill, subtly questioning the defensiveness of blanket denials.

Nearly two weeks after the panic first surfaced, leftist chronicler Carlos Monsiváis offered a characteristically sardonic and ambivalent reading of the scandal. A vocal critic of state power, he paradoxically found himself advocating the government line even as he identified with parents' distrust. At age thirty-six, Monsiváis was a prominent cultural critic and director of *La Cultura en México*. A fixture of prestigious literary circles, Monsiváis was admired by his peers for his massive personal library, which boasted works of literature and social science. In addition to being a voracious reader, Monsiváis was an avid consumer of film and music. He began his writing career in the late 1950s as a television critic for *Excélsior*, and by the 1960s he hosted a popular film criticism program, *La Cine y la Crítica*, at Radio Universidad.[97]

Monsiváis's article brilliantly captured the ambiguity of the sterilization scandal. He opened his *Excélsior* opinion piece with a criticism of the heteronormative and Catholic emphasis on procreation. Referring to parents' fears, he exclaimed that "their children could be robbed forever of the joy of procreation... their children will learn that poverty is not just lack of goods: among the poor, fundamentally, poverty is defined by the absence of children." Monsiváis contradicted himself at every turn, simultaneously mocking heteronormative family values while highlighting the legitimate concerns of poor urban dwellers. He further complained that ephemeral speech was rooted in ignorance and thus inhibited the development of an enlightened public sphere. He noted that "the more fantastical and grotesque the rumor, the more likely that it will be believed, spread, and incorporated in that dense layer of prejudices that make up the solid base of knowledge of a people marginalized from all of the major decisions that affect them." In the piece, he simultaneously argued that rumors emerged from perverse intrigue and from a long-standing political alienation.[98]

Monsiváis's opinion article asserted that official disinformation and systematic oppression led ordinary Mexicans to believe rumors. He argued that not only "massive ignorance" but also "decades of self-satisfied and mendacious language have resulted in a collective deafness toward official words."[99] Moreover, he suggested that rumor was a weapon of the weak, which both the poor and middle classes used because they lacked viable avenues for political change. He lamented the vicious cycle in which the politically and economically disenfranchised believed false information, which in turn contributed to their continued oppression. While identifying with the urban poor, he also revealed a conflicted classism.

Monsiváis offered a unique perspective by treating popular culture as worthy of serious analysis. His writing moved seamlessly between the highbrow discussion of art and literature and the lowbrow analysis of soccer matches and taco stands. This distinctive narrative style likely stemmed from his own outsider perspective. Monsiváis grew up in the working-class Mexico City neighborhood of Portales, where he was raised in a fundamentalist Quaker family that prohibited the consumption of alcohol and tobacco.[100] As a child, he attended Sunday school every week and considered himself a "minority" both within his church and in the predominantly Catholic country. His lifestyle, like his upbringing and narrative style, was also queer. Some of his hypermasculine peers, like Manuel Becerra Acosta, dismissed Monsiváis's cultural supplement as a "ladies's salon magazine."[101] This comment likely referred to Monsiváis's gender performance in addition to his identifying narrative style, which departed from dry, supposedly objective language. While Monsiváis did not publicly discuss his sexual orientation, he never married and avoided the exaggerated bravado of his male literary counterparts. Monsiváis's outsider perspective allowed him to capture the ambiguity of the scandal. He highlighted the tensions between ignorance and knowledge; the desire for scandal and legitimate fear; the vulnerability to outside manipulation and the savvy distrust of official information.

These contradictions highlight a key shortcoming of the gradual opening of the press that was underway in the early 1970s. Even as writers voiced greater criticism of the ruling party by reporting on state repression and corruption, some leftists actively silenced the voices of the poor from public debates. For those who believed and spread rumors, however, the question of evidence only required the belief that the government was capable of using violence against the poor and lying about it.

## CONCLUSION

In 1974, more than one hundred thousand Mexican children did not receive vaccines due to their parents' fear of them being sterilized.[102] After schools closed for Christmas vacation, panic around sterilization abated, allowing public officials and international observers to take stock of the events. The U.S. embassy in Mexico City observed that the government had passed through a "mini-crisis of confidence."[103] Some public officials sought to understand how the Mexican government might avoid similar episodes in the future, and presidential hopeful Porfirio Muñoz Ledo even commissioned a study on the sterilization rumors.[104] In late January 1975, state spies and health authorities reported that similar allegations had spread south to Puebla and Chiapas, signaling that state efforts had failed to quell concerns.[105] Notably, these reports revealed concerns about the political, rather than health, ramifications, of the scandal. Officials saw sterilization rumors as evidence that the democratic opening was escaping top-down control; party institutions could not incorporate the urban poor and manage their dissent. Meanwhile, informal news spread rapidly in Mexico City's densely populated periphery, foiling government efforts to demobilize community organizations.

No conclusive evidence confirms the origin of the accusations that the government was sterilizing poor schoolchildren. However, the scandal can be appreciated apart from the intellectual authorship. As a site of knowledge production, the allegations of sterilization reflected scenarios that were plausible for greater Mexico City residents. The urban poor, by participating in the scandal, argued that the state's intentions for development were not benevolent but rather secretive attempts to eliminate dissent. Rather than signaling ignorance, speaking was an essential way in which residents of greater Mexico City made sense of the stories and events they encountered in film, radio, and other media. Far from depoliticizing Nezahualcóyotl residents, the allegations sparked collective action in a community that had been divided by land developers. By demanding accountability and shaping public debate, scandal formed part of the expanding public sphere.

Reactions to the allegations also reveal a great deal about those who tried to silence the accusations. The early 1970s witnessed an unprecedented, though still moderate, opening in Mexico City broadsheets. Behemoths like *El Universal* and *Excélsior* transformed their opinion pages into rich sites for debate. Yet their reporters joined journalists across the ideological spectrum in attempting to silence the sterilization scandal. Slips in their writing suggest that the ontological distinction between eyewitness account and hearsay often hinged on ideas of whose knowledge counted rather than whether the information was verified. These reporters decided which forms of dissent were permitted in the press and suggested that rational criticism was safest in the pens of upper-middle-class men. Knowledge production was explicitly outside the purview of the urban poor, especially women. Thus, this chapter underscores how denuncia journalism perpetuated gendered ideas of authority and knowledge production in the 1970s.

Journalists' concerns about rumor only grew over the following years, and Monsiváis would later declare 1976 "the Year of the Rumor."[106] By this point, however, he did not blame hearsay on conspiring middle classes or the ignorant poor. Instead he connected rumors to a broader distrust stemming from the betrayal of the 1968 student massacre. After such an event, Monsiváis asked, "Who believes the PRI and who believes the government?" During the presidency of José López Portillo, Monsiváis and other journalists would increasingly pose this question in new muckraking outlets that delivered scandalous corruption exposés.

CHAPTER 3

# MUCKRAKING AND THE OIL BOOM AND BUST

Heberto Castillo, an engineer by training and a longtime leftist activist, pulled no punches in his denunciations of Mexico's oil industry. After a devastating oil spill in the Bay of Campeche, he pronounced, "Pemex is not only physically poisoning the country. Pemex, under the current director, is contaminating the national conscience."[1] The article was just one in a series of combative investigations into embezzlement, mismanagement, and deception in the state-owned and -operated oil monopoly, Petróleos Mexicanos (Pemex). Castillo's reportage was emblematic of the politically committed *denuncia* journalism that became more prominent in the late 1970s.

Castillo's investigative pieces appeared in multiple publications, but most regularly in *Proceso*. The political magazine first hit newsstands in November 1976 and quickly became known for its muckraking. Every Sunday, for ten pesos, readers could discover new political misdeeds announced on the weekly edition's glossy cover. "Corruption" became the magazine's watchword, which the editors wielded to explain the country's ills, including the nation's economic dependence.[2] *Proceso* spearheaded coverage of Mexico's projected rise to become an oil powerhouse and the petroleum sector's subsequent economic collapse. Even with small circulation (relative to the most popular tabloids), the newsmagazine shaped the terms of wider debate and set the national media agenda for discussions of oil policy.[3] This chapter explores scandals around corruption and embezzlement in Pemex.

A steady stream of leaked documents, anonymously filtered by state officials, fueled print media exposés. This practice signaled a trend toward resolving intraparty conflict by exposing disagreements to the reading public. Disgruntled officials often leaked documents to steer the course of internal debates or to undermine a political rival. However, sharing state documents with reporters did not always produce intended results; the public sphere was a constant site of struggle in which transparency was only one of a series of possible outcomes. Evidence of elite divisions heightened tensions within the administration and dispelled the image of a unified party and government, sparking broader demands that decision-making processes be made more transparent.

Muckraking journalism placed regime officials on the defensive and thus disrupted government strategies for managing press coverage. Pemex and public officials responded to printed accusations by orchestrating call-in television programs, broadcasting congressional hearings, and circulating pamphlets. While muckraking appeared principally in elite-oriented magazines and newspapers, journalists also tried to engage a broader public. Castillo wrote for a wide range of publications, including some, like *Ovaciones*, that were directed at popular audiences. He also collaborated with a cartoonist to publish illustrated summaries of his *Proceso* investigations. Castillo's political activism and journalism were closely connected, and leftist party activists further diffused his reported findings.

Muckraking signaled changing professional norms and sparked public debates about journalistic ethics. Some *denuncia* reporters faced accusations that they had stolen or fabricated documents or that they were paid to reveal damaging information. Reporters openly responded to such accusations in print, and editors reproduced leaked documents to prove their authenticity. These discussions intersected with international debates about the social role of the press and established new expectations of how reporters should behave. In the late 1970s, then, national print media served as a platform for open dissent, a forum for intraelite sparring, and a state vehicle for managing public opinion.

## MANAGING ABUNDANCE

Within weeks of taking office on December 1, 1976, President José López Portillo and Pemex director Jorge Díaz Serrano proclaimed newly discovered oil reserves large enough to make Mexico "the new Iran."[4] López Portillo announced that Mexico would become a net exporter of crude oil, and he promised that hydrocarbon sales would spur economic growth and fund social programs. The incoming president had seemingly found the key to resolving population pressures and consequent concerns about food and energy scarcity. Crude prices remained high in the wake of the 1973 Organization of the Petroleum Exporting Countries (OPEC) oil crisis, and López Portillo predicted that petroleum profits would fuel industrial growth, accelerate agricultural production, and allow Mexico to quickly recover from its August 1976 peso devaluation. President Luis Echeverría's term had ended with a financial crisis; the national debt crested at $27.5 billion in 1976, and foreign currency reserves had fallen 85 percent since the beginning of the year. Facing a debt default, Echeverría negotiated a $600 million bridge loan with the U.S. government and also signed a loan agreement of nearly $1.2 billion with the International Monetary Fund (IMF). The IMF agreement required that Mexico reduce the national debt by cutting public spending, an unpopular policy in a country already subjected to rising inflation.[5]

López Portillo viewed oil revenues as a solution to both political and economic woes. He was the first PRI presidential candidate to run unopposed in an election, and high levels of voter abstention made ruling officials worry that the party had lost its popular support base.[6] By August 1977, however, López Portillo was confident that the oil boom would restore popular allegiance, suggesting that the PRI needed to maintain a robust patronage system to remain viable. As the president declared to a room of cabinet members and Pemex technicians, "Mexico, a country of contrasts, has had to manage shortages and crises. Now in Petróleos [Mexicanos] we must accustom ourselves to managing abundance."[7] He asserted that Mexico had once again become a rich country and that oil would act as a social leveler.

López Portillo's plans for oil and gas exportation signaled a dramatic reversal of the decades-long decline in petroleum production. In 1938 President Lázaro Cárdenas nationalized the petroleum industry and expelled British and U.S. firms, making Mexico the first major oil exporter in the world to do so. Pemex was founded the same year and became a powerful symbol of nationalism and independence. Oil represented an important source of government revenue and helped fund postwar development by providing thousands of new jobs and subsidizing gasoline and electricity for new industries and consumers. However, Pemex lacked the equipment, technical know-how, and funds to pursue further exploration, and Mexico was soon importing refined oil to meet the demands of a growing population. It was not until the 1970s that new technological advances and funding enabled Pemex to discover significant oil fields for the first time in decades.[8]

Mexico City newspapers cited skyrocketing reserve figures to underscore the correlation between petroleum, prosperity, and self-determination. By the mid-1970s OPEC member countries demonstrated that oil represented a primary way for the Global South to gain economic and political leverage. Mexico City newspapers drooled with excitement over petroleum's immense profitability, echoing Pemex press bulletins and official statements. *Novedades*, a popular broadsheet, affirmed that "when leveraged rationally, hydrocarbons can prove a solid foundation for reducing the enormous advantages enjoyed by advanced industrialized powers."[9] *El Día* headlines announced the rapidly rising reserve figures, which had increased from 11.1 billion barrels of oil in December 1976 to 14 billion in 1977, with 2.8 billion more expected in the future. Emphasizing the scientific certainty of Mexico's oil wealth, Pemex projected that oil production would increase nearly tenfold from the paltry 150,000 barrels per day in 1977 to 1,105,000 by 1982.[10] *Excélsior* reported that "enormous" oil fields in Campeche and Coahuila would enable the country to pay off all of its foreign debt by 1982.[11] With similar confidence, *El Día* declared that Pemex would create new jobs in many states.[12] By the close of 1977, phrases like *administrar la abundancia* (managing abundance) and *salir del bache económico* (rising from economic depression) became synonymous with the new oil policy.

*Proceso* coverage fell like a wet blanket on the dizzying projections of barrels and dollars. Each issue delivered around forty-five pages of reportage and analysis. Readers would open the magazine to find a six-page lead article written by one of the magazine's prominent reporters, often Carlos Borbolla, Carlos Ramírez, or José Reveles. Black-and-white photographs and cartoons from well-known artists like Naranjo and Rius accompanied the exposés. Meanwhile, *artículos de fondo* (analysis articles) invited academic, intellectual, and political luminaries to lead debates within the press. Longer than opinion columns, these pieces both introduced and analyzed new information. Soon after López Portillo's announcement, *Proceso* questioned the technical soundness of reserve figures and underscored the geopolitical risks of becoming a primary oil exporter.

## THE MAKING OF A POLITICIAN-JOURNALIST

*Proceso*'s confrontational stance was born out of its editors' experience of censorship. In the summer of 1976 lame-duck president Echeverría orchestrated a coup within the *Excélsior* cooperative, catalyzing the removal of director Julio Scherer García and his editorial team on July 8. The president denied any involvement and the new editor-in-chief Regino Díaz Redondo maintained that the editors' removal was the result of a democratic election in the newspaper cooperative.¹³ Divisions had indeed been brewing within the newspaper: press operators, newspaper balers, and other manual workers felt marginalized by Scherer García's intellectualism and favoritism.¹⁴ After Scherer García's defeat was announced at the cooperative meeting, Díaz Redondo's faction reportedly declared that "the riffraff [la *indiada*] has voted!," reclaiming a pejorative, racialized term to distinguish themselves from the elite editorial team.¹⁵ Echeverría had been aware of these internal conflicts and mobilized them to his advantage; he stationed thugs at the cooperative meeting to intimidate anyone who thought to vote differently. This was not his only attempt to secure influence over powerful newspapers before he left office. Credible rumors swirled that he was behind the 1976 acquisition of the popular *Sol* regional chain by the Mexican Editorial Organization (Organización Editorial Mexicana) and that he had used proxies to purchase controlling shares of *El Universal*.¹⁶

In response to the *Excélsior* intervention, some two hundred journalists and printers resigned in solidarity. While the government instructed domestic news outlets to remain silent on the episode, the action was met with opprobrium abroad.¹⁷ The ousted *Excélsior* editors soon organized fund raisers to found a new publication, *Proceso*, though the outgoing administration tried to obstruct their efforts by withholding newsprint.¹⁸ When López Portillo took office in December, he expressed his solidarity with the new venture, hoping this gesture would win him favor with middle-class audiences in Mexico City and distance him from his shamed predecessor.¹⁹

*Proceso*'s new staff of writers included Castillo, who became the most vocal opponent of López Portillo's oil policy. In his weekly contributions, Castillo published evidence of mismanagement, deception, and unscrupulous decision making in Pemex. His analysis articles could be dense and full of technical jargon that would be difficult for the nonspecialist to understand. However, Castillo complemented these specialized pieces with more digestible, but equally combative, opinion articles for mainstream outlets, including the conservative newspaper, *El Heraldo de México*. With stellar engineering credentials, Castillo expected readers to take the information on his authority. He had graduated from UNAM in 1951 with a degree in civil engineering and became well known in his field for his 1962 invention of the Tridilosa; this lightweight, geometric support structure came to be used worldwide in civil engineering because it cut construction costs and provided greater stability in case of earthquakes. As the only Mexican to gain international recognition for an engineering invention, Castillo was a source of national pride.

For Castillo, hard-nosed journalism and political activism were complementary projects. Actively involved in the anti-imperialist movements of the 1960s, he was a founding member of the Movimiento de Liberación Nacional (Movement for National Liberation, or MLN) and led the Mexican delegation to the 1966 Tricontinental Conference in Havana, Cuba. While defending traditional leftist platforms, such as agrarian reform, Castillo also embraced New Left concerns such as decolonization and the release of political prisoners.[20] The 1968 student movement was pivotal to Castillo's development as a political figure. In May 1969 he was arrested, tortured, and imprisoned in Mexico City's Lecumberri penitentiary for allegedly inciting violence as an UNAM professor during the protests. On May 14, 1971, political pressure led President Echeverría to pardon Castillo, along with twenty-three other political prisoners.[21] Soon after his release, Castillo founded the Mexican Workers' Party (Partido Mexicano de los Trabajadores, or PMT) alongside labor leader Demetrio Vallejo. They traveled throughout the country promoting their platform of union independence, national sovereignty, and fair wages.[22] During this time, Castillo began writing regular columns for *El Universal* and contributed occasional articles to *Siempre!* and *Por Qué?* The ideological diversity of these publications—from the government-aligned *El Universal* to the radical leftist *Por Qué?*—illustrates how Mexico City publications offered more pluralistic spaces for debate in the early 1970s.

While Castillo had risen to an upper-middle-class position in Mexico City, he was familiar with the realities of rural life. He was born in 1928 in Ixhuatlán de Madero, a small mountainous town in the southeastern state of Veracruz. The fifth of seven children, Castillo described his parents as "well-to-do peasants"; they owned some land, but "had come on hard times." Neither of his parents studied past primary school, and his father was a mule driver. Yet Castillo acknowledged that being light skinned granted his family privileged status in their majority Indigenous community. He was six years old when the family moved to Mexico City, and Castillo later studied at the same junior high school attended by such luminaries as poet Octavio Paz. Reflecting on this period, Castillo viewed his ability to remain in school as another marker of his privilege. Many of his schoolmates had to end their studies to enter the workforce and support their families.[23]

Castillo's first articles for *Proceso* took issue with plans to build what became popularly referred to as the *gasoducto* (gas line). On June 2, 1977, Pemex director Díaz Serrano announced the construction of a two-thousand-kilometer gas pipeline from the southeastern city of Cactus to the northeastern city of Reynosa, just across the border from McAllen, Texas.[24] The pipeline would enable Pemex to export the abundant natural gas associated with oil drilling. Eager to capitalize on the rapidly growing petroleum reserves, Díaz Serrano planned to import the pipeline's parts rather than constructing it domestically, bringing the total cost to around $1 billion.[25] Castillo warned that the gas line would preempt alternative clients for natural gas and would commit Mexico to selling at prices set by the United States.[26]

Castillo presciently maintained that abundance was a double-edged sword; if political leaders mismanaged wealth, it could lead to serious problems. Distrustful of Díaz Serrano, he accused the Pemex director of "raising oil reserves from his desk," essentially cooking the rising figures by changing the calculation criteria.[27] Claiming high reserve figures would allow the country to borrow against future petroleum sales and bolster trade agreements. Castillo emphasized that misleading foreign investors could sink Mexico further into economic crisis or even lead to geopolitical conflicts. This intervention reflected global concerns about peak oil, the point at which petroleum production peaks and then declines. Committing the country to an unsustainable level of exportation, Castillo feared, would dry out its reserves, leaving Mexico worse off than before.

Castillo's engineering background allowed him to propose alternative policies that, in his opinion, would grant Mexico greater control over its petroleum production. With increased oil drilling, associated natural gas was abundant, but Mexico still lacked the infrastructure to store or export it. Castillo proposed an alternative gas line that would run only ninety kilometers from the southern state of Chiapas to the Gulf of Mexico.[28] He argued that this would save money on construction while enabling Mexico to ship gas in liquid form to multiple countries.[29] Rather than a wholesale rejection of exportation, Castillo urged that decision making be transparent and cautious. With OPEC as a powerful model, he argued that Mexico should use oil to preserve and strengthen its national sovereignty rather than to pursue short-term profits.

Castillo's industry ties positioned him to expose information with real consequences for the making of oil policy.[30] Historically, all oil production decisions were made by Pemex administrators, but López Portillo attempted to bring policy making under the purview of his cabinet. Pemex officials balked at this power grab and often refused to provide basic data to the administration, frustrating government ministers who were scrambling to master the field.[31] Within this context, Castillo's professional background granted him privileged access to informants within Pemex, which employed many of his former university peers and career colleagues. One prominent Pemex engineer publicly complained that Castillo disoriented not only the public but also government officials. Deploying ad hominem attacks, he described Castillo as stubborn, uninformed, and "blinded by ancestral passions against our unavoidable neighbors."[32] He suggested that Castillo sowed doubt and dissension among public officials. At a time when there was a high political premium on oil expertise, Castillo had the technical knowledge crucial to analyzing petroleum data.

Like many Mexico City–based denuncia journalists, Castillo enjoyed financial independence, and his criticisms of the PRI regime were sharpened by years of repression. In other ways, however, he was distinct from many of his journalist peers. First, Castillo had uniquely strained relations with public officials. He violated norms of decorum by naming governing elites in his denunciations, and he humiliated politicians by publicly divulging the content of private conversations. Second, as an opposition party leader, Castillo used his journalism to amplify his political platform. While regime officials understood that they needed to permit some criticism to maintain party legitimacy, Castillo's journalism threatened to siphon voters away from the PRI. The combative and partisan nature of Castillo's denunciations shaped how regime officials would respond to his articles.

## PERFORMANCES OF ACCOUNTABILITY

Pemex engineers and governing officials mobilized media to manage and monitor public opinion. They used a range of public relations tactics to simulate dialogue, suggesting that it was important to maintain the appearance of openness. For example, on September 24, 1977, researchers from the Mexican Petroleum Institute (Instituto Mexicano de Petróleo, or IMP) appeared on the popular Saturday night television program *Jurado Popular* to explain the complexities of oil production. Hosted by well-known television personality Jorge Saldaña, the show invited audiences to phone in questions about contemporary issues. In this particular episode, petroleum experts fielded viewers' inquiries about new oil policies and, specifically, the plans to build a gas pipeline to the Mexican-U.S. border. The IMP experts defended Pemex's export policies without giving callers the opportunity to respond. Television producers also carefully curated the questions, and Castillo complained that the program was "staged" and that Pemex engineers censored most of his phoned-in questions.[33]

By contrast, new talk radio programs sought a more direct and critical engagement with listeners. In 1976 Francisco Huerta began his program,

*Opinión Pública*, on Radio ABC with a goal to raise listeners' political consciousness and critical thinking. Like *Jurado Popular*, *Opinión Pública* used broadcast media to respond to print articles, but Huerta prompted readers to "analyze the gap—the chasm, really—between what was published and our actual needs." This resonated with listeners who suddenly heard their perspectives and criticisms echoed and affirmed on the airwaves. OEM, which owned Radio ABC, and public officials tolerated the program but would not allow callers' voices to be aired, insisting that they remain mediated through the host.[34] Both critical talk radio and government-aligned television series used print media as a foil for their programs, circulating debates beyond a narrow elite sphere.

In contrast to talk radio, print media often offered a platform for governing officials and dissident journalists to verbally spar. This was evident in *Proceso*'s ninth commemorative issue of the Tlatelolco Massacre, in which Castillo self-dramatized his role in the oil debates. The magazine's cover featured his photograph, symbolically linking his oil advocacy to the student protests. Castillo opened the lead article by explaining that his activism had led to "a long national controversy in which I have had to confront media and many government officials, on the one hand, and necessarily painstaking information about oil and gas."[35] He thus constructed his expertise and activism as a compelling basis for making claims. He devoted the article to describing four separate meetings with the president and other high-ranking public officials. In each anecdote, Castillo painted a picture of frustrated political elites seeking him out, and he presented himself as a lone defender against irresponsible oil exportation policies.

Castillo at times failed to spell out the main points for readers. By publicizing official attempts to silence him, he underscored how his work was important precisely because governing officials viewed it as threatening. In one anecdote, he related that Jesús Puente Leyva, chairman of the Commission for Petroleum Studies in the House of Representatives (Comisión de Estudios del Petróleo en la Cámara de Diputados), invited Castillo to his home to discuss the oil controversy. Castillo described the representative's home as luxuriously outfitted with hardwood floors and ceilings from the Chiapanecan Lacondan jungle, suggesting that the official was already accustomed to pillaging Mexico's natural resources. According to Castillo, Puente Leyva told him in English, "You are right, but for the wrong reasons." In response to the deputy's language choice, Castillo quipped: "I am still not ready for the post–gas line era," noting that he himself only spoke Spanish.[36] His retort implied that the use of English, and the loss of Spanish, would become more prevalent with export policies that compromised Mexican independence.

Compared with most Mexico City media, Castillo's articles were remarkably confrontational. While his language could be impenetrable when he wrote on the details of the oil industry, his prose sharpened when he homed in on particular public officials, whom he called out by name. This marked a departure from prevailing political discourse, as public officials typically resisted naming their rivals in speeches. Moreover, Castillo did not subscribe to the common journalistic practice of "writing between the lines."[37] Criticisms in broadsheets were often buried beneath seemingly irrelevant references and mind-numbing detail. This strategy served to distract both readers and public officials, taking the bite out of the more direct accusations. The practice allowed journalists to provide candid opinions while appeasing public officials, who either did not notice the criticism or believed no one else would. By explicitly identifying each official involved in the oil case, Castillo broke with this tradition. Provoked, those he identified jumped to the defensive.

Only two weeks later, Díaz Serrano appeared before the Mexican Congress to explain how Pemex had arrived at its reserves figures and to dispel "cowardly alarmism." Two hundred fifty people attended the congressional session, and a DGIPS spy recorded Castillo's "noticeable" presence in the press section. When his turn came to speak, the Pemex director asserted that "the Mexican people have the right to understand the quantity of their wealth and what its possibilities are." He divulged "confidential" figures, which revealed likely reserves of 29.2 billion barrels of oil. By presenting this as privileged information, Díaz Serrano intimated that he was confiding in the audience by letting them in on the secret. Yet this presumed power also implied associated obligations. Indeed, Díaz Serrano urged unquestioning support and warned that there was "a race against the clock" to cash in on oil's rising global price tag.[38] He weaponized transparency by suggesting that congressional representatives would be responsible for economic losses if they did not support his policy. The Congress was historically supine before the president and dominated by a PRI majority, but the speech signaled that there may not have been universal support for the president's new development program. Indeed, in the elite newsletter *Buro de Investigación Política* Horacio Quiñones responded to Díaz Serrano's speech with the wry observation, "If all we want is dollars, perhaps we should just secede to Texas."[39]

This remark captured the essence of the oil debate. Though congressional representatives discussed the technical merits of the new oil policy, the controversy ultimately centered around whether Mexico should draw closer to the U.S. economy. Following Díaz Serrano's speech, representative Puente Leyva echoed the idea that oil exportation was the key to economic prosperity, articulating a vision of Mexican development that required engagement in the global economy.[40] Unlike the *dependentistas*, whose ideas about dependency theory had gained currency in the Global South, Puente Leyva implied that open trade would naturally benefit the country rather than increasing its dependence. In this way, he signaled the influence of Chile, which in the wake of the 1973 coup adopted a development model rooted in deregulation, austerity, and free trade. Puente Leyva asserted that in the context of the global OPEC oil crisis, Mexico had the opportunity to reverse its fortunes.

Naming names in the press put public officials on the defensive and prompted them to respond to both the substance and the tenor of the attacks. Taking on Castillo's proposal for a shorter gas pipeline, Puente Leyva used his time on the floor of Congress to assert that "the controversy has hinged on an argument that I do not hesitate to label absurd." He also responded explicitly to claims that Castillo made in his October 3 *Proceso* article. To undermine Castillo's self-representation as an ideologue rather than a politician, Puente Leyva accused him of trying to blackmail the government into giving the PMT legal registration. The congressman also sought to defend his own reputation, pronouncing, "This is a frank accusation against the critics of the gas pipeline whom at one time I wished to be my friends." Obliquely referring to his welcoming of Castillo into his home, Puente Leyva suggested that their interactions would no longer be friendly. Chafing at Castillo's rendition of their conversation in *Proceso*, Puente Leyva further stated, "I am going to cite two authors of a work in English, which is not the language of the post–gas line but rather of educated people.'"[41] He indicated that Castillo had violated confidences by making their conversation public.

Pemex also responded to Castillo's criticisms of the gas pipeline by distributing a free informational supplement in October. The insert was distinct from most government publicity, which invoked the ideals of the Mexican Revolution without offering concrete proposals. This supplement, by contrast, systematically addressed each of Castillo's arguments with section headings such as "Its Cost," "By Land or by Sea," and "What Is Its Significance for the Country's Economy?"[42] Castillo and chronicler Elena Poniatowska both published articles on the pamphlet, impressed by the scale and ambition of Pemex's response. Castillo noted that the eight-page, full-color supplement—a fairly costly publicity endeavor—was inserted into all newspapers with national circulation, and Poniatowska remarked how the pamphlet had "arrived to all of our homes."[43] Like letters to the editor and congressional speeches, this leaflet showcased the continued relevance of print in setting the terms of debate, as well as the defensive posture of the Pemex administration and legislators.

Beneath the surface of these speeches and pamphlets was the question of how issues of common concern should be decided. The muckraking press disrupted traditional strategies for addressing popular demands. Castillo's careful reading of Pemex data forced oil officials like Díaz Serrano and Puente Leyva to respond to Castillo's claims that they were concealing information or even lying. Yet Puente Leyva's comments indicated that this was not just a rational debate about oil policy but also an opportunity to defend his reputation. As officials and journalists tried to bolster their respective positions, they made competing attempts to assert their own authority (moral, political, or professional) to speak on matters of oil policy. As a well-regarded engineer, Castillo positioned himself as an expert on petroleum matters in a moment when internal conflicts raged over who could claim industry expertise.

## SECRET DOCUMENTS AND PUBLIC EXPOSÉS

A steady stream of insider leaks foiled official attempts to manage information. Leaking documents revealed cleavages not only among politicians but also between the government and the ruling party, sharpening the lines of disagreement. High-ranking officials increasingly sent confidential meeting minutes, oil reserve reports, and internal Pemex memoranda to trusted reporters. Handwritten notes at times accompanied the documents with exhortations that the journalists use good judgment and avoid revealing identifying information. By 1978 the prevalence of this practice would spark debates about *columnismo*, a neologism that described the proliferation of political columns that attacked political figures.

Leaking was encouraged by the availability of more newspapers and magazines that were willing to report on political wrongdoing. Prominent columns, such as Manuel Buendía's "Red Privada" in *Excélsior* and José Luis Mejías's "Los Intocables" in *El Universal*, became outlets for disaffected officials to force issues by exposing them in print. The Mexican Information Agency (Agencia Mexicana de Información) syndicated these columns in dozens of regional papers, allowing the authors to reach distinct readerships outside Mexico City. The density of critical outlets also facilitated the circumvention of censorship, as one publication was often willing to print articles that others withheld.[44]

Select officials also supported the creation of investigative news publications. For example, when a contingent of former *Excélsior* editors and reporters needed to procure a loan for their new periodical, they sought assistance from the secretary of the interior, Jesús Reyes Heroles. He helped them secure eight million pesos from the state lending institution, National Financial Agency (Nacional Financiera, or Nafinsa), which enabled them to found the tabloid-size daily *Unomásuno* on November 1, 1977.[45] It was not uncommon for newspaper directors to seek government help to access the loans, advertising, printing equipment, or commercial real estate necessary to begin a new publication.[46] But *Unomásuno*'s founders emphasized that this assistance would not compromise the newspaper's independence. The first issue, which reported on popular discontent in Chiapas, highlighted the newspaper's commitment to investigating topics of social justice and inequality.[47] Over the following years, the periodical also sent correspondents to El Salvador and Guatemala and produced some of the best reporting on the Central American civil wars.

The Nafinsa loan did, however, establish a complicated relationship with the secretary of the interior. In February 1978, as part of UNAM's lecture series "Communication and Dependency in Latin America," *Unomásuno* director Manuel Becerra Acosta fielded questions from students who wondered how the newspaper would maintain its independence. He assured the audience of some 450 attendees that "the eight-million-peso loan that I received does not involve any obligation on our part; the newspaper is independent, and that will not change going forward."[48] The open discussion of how financial ties might compromise critical coverage highlights that publications like *Proceso* and *Unomásuno* built their reputations on their accountability to readers. Becerra Acosta also tried to avoid the political corruption of his staff by paying them well. While most Mexico City reporters supplemented their paltry wages with bribes, *Unomásuno* journalists earned twenty-four thousand pesos per month; the best paid among their peers, they made a decent living and could even afford to buy cars.[49]

Becerra Acosta described his relationship with Reyes Heroles quite differently when confronted on a separate occasion by DFS agents. In December 1977, intruders had entered the *Unomásuno* offices, cut the telephone lines, and destroyed ink from the printers. DFS spies initiated an investigation into the attack and visited the newsroom to question Becerra Acosta. In their summary report, agents described the *Unomásuno* director as haughty and confrontational. Becerra Acosta had defensively mentioned his relationship with Reyes Heroles while in the same breath insulting the spies. Becerra Acosta asserted that the newspaper was aligned with the secretary of the interior, which oversaw the DFS, and therefore was "very powerful."[50] While Becerra Acosta had highlighted the newspaper's civic mission during his conference at UNAM, his interaction with spies underscored how newspapers needed powerful figures to protect denuncia journalists from retaliation. The director selectively emphasized different aspects of *Unomásuno*'s founding depending on his audience.

*Proceso* and *Unomásuno* soon became resources for disaffected officials who sent compromising documents to reporters. In October 1977, for example, *Proceso* reporter José Reveles received leaked meeting minutes from the Pemex Administration Advisory Board (Consejo de Administración de Petróleos Mexicanos), comprising cabinet members and Pemex engineers, directors, and union leaders. Like many of his peers at *Proceso*, Reveles belonged to a younger generation of journalists who asserted their independence from the government. The minutes, as edited by Reveles, revealed board members' fears that negative press coverage would diminish popular support for oil policies. In the meeting, Oteyza urged Pemex to publicize information regarding how it calculated oil reserves to "stop the rumors" that challenged these figures. Cabinet members and Pemex officials also cited Castillo's latest articles and worried specifically about his accusations that "Díaz Serrano serves the United States' interests above Mexico's." Leaders rightly recognized that regime legitimacy could suffer with the changed policy direction. Some members urged a broad publicity campaign, including accessible television programming, to avoid the appearance that "we are responding only to the *Proceso* article."[51] Such a direct response, they implied, would grant greater weight to Castillo's claims and make the administration appear defensive. By publicizing these private conversations, Reveles amplified the importance of *Proceso* while presenting officials who simulated transparency rather than actually delivering it.

The publication of confidential documents raised suspicions regarding how, exactly, reporters came by their sources. To head off government denials, news editors frequently presented their documentary evidence by transcribing the incriminating documents or reproducing images of leaked reports. Images of seals, signatures, and receipt stamps made middle-class readers feel that they could access insider information. At the same time, the practice of exposing internal memoranda should not be confused for absolute transparency. Journalists revealed insider information while concealing or simply remaining ignorant of other relevant details.

Skepticism reflected long-standing assumptions that the press was compromised by political power while also signaling a growing interest in journalistic ethics. In the 1970s new journalism programs opened at universities across Mexico, including the Monterrey Institute of Technology and Higher Education (Instituto Tecnológico y de Estudios Superiores de Monterrey), the Autonomous University of Guadalajara (Universidad Autónoma de Guadalajara), and the Autonomous University of Sinaloa (Universidad Autónoma de Sinaloa), among others.[52] Professional journalism associations also grew and newspapers, universities, and the UN, as well as its United Nations Educational, Scientific and Cultural Organization, hosted myriad conferences that centered on the relationship between information and economic development.[53] In Mexico, as elsewhere, the political role of media was a topic of frequent discussion.

At times journalists publicly addressed accusations that they had stolen documents or revealed state secrets. This was the case when Castillo discussed a leaked U.S. Central Intelligence Agency (CIA) report on Mexico's "energy outlook." In his *Proceso* article on October 31, 1977, Castillo took pains to prove the document's existence and to defend himself against charges of improper behavior. Editors reproduced the report's front cover, which included the CIA's seal, and the first page (see figure 3.1).

Castillo underlined sentences to draw readers' attention to the report's key findings, and these reproductions were placed prominently alongside the article so that readers could appreciate the document's authenticity. A copy of the CIA report exists in Castillo's personal archive, confirming that he did indeed have the document in his possession.[54] His article summarized the CIA report's main takeaway: that global petroleum demand would surpass production by 1985 and Mexico would become a major oil provider.[55] For Castillo, this prediction confirmed fears that exporting large amounts of oil would make Mexico more vulnerable to energy scarcity and, possibly, to U.S. intervention. With such compelling documented evidence, he believed that Mexican oil officials would have no choice but to respond to his claims.

In a country where suspicions of the CIA ran high, Castillo's access to the report raised questions. Though he had claimed that the report simply "fell into [his] lap," public scrutiny led him to dedicate his next article to demystifying the process by which journalists accessed documents.[56] The CIA report, he explained, was sent to him at the PMT office, free of cost.[57] Identifying journalistic standards of cross-checking information and protecting sources'

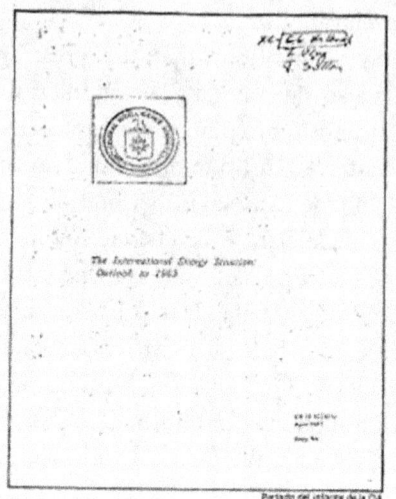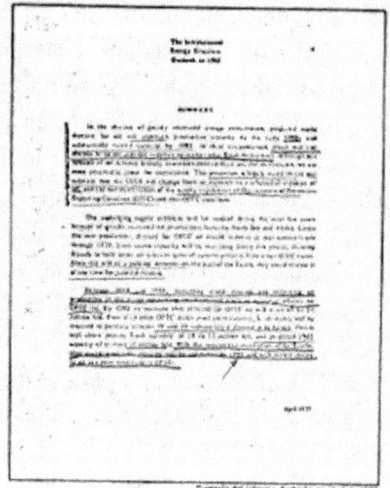

Figure 3.1  Reproduction of a leaked CIA report published in *Proceso*, October 31, 1977, 13.

identities, Castillo wrote, "I confirm my sources. But it is often the case that many Mexicans ask me not to reveal their names." In his unpublished draft, Castillo added, "But I am willing to publish the source [of the document] and give unquestionable credit to whoever provides me with information."[58] Perhaps believing the threat to be too strong, Castillo crossed out that sentence for the final draft.

Castillo believed that he could be more candid precisely because he was not a professional journalist whose income depended on reporting. In 1967 he sold the Tridilosa patents to private companies, and the royalties gave him the financial freedom to devote himself fully to politics while still supporting his wife María Teresa Juárez and their four children.[59] Castillo asserted that "for me, journalism is a weapon, not a source of income, nor a means to distinguish myself."[60] He emphasized that his ideological motivations differentiated him from market-driven journalists who tried to "ganar la noticia" (get the scoop), a play on words that also referred to efforts to make money off what they published. Castillo emphasized that his purpose was "to mobilize the Mexican people to defend their natural, and nonrenewable, resources." While he needed the press as an outlet for his ideas, Castillo argued that he enjoyed greater freedom because he did not have to compromise with public officials. Regardless of the motivations behind their exposure, the publicity of leaked documents changed the nature of journalistic denunciations. By reproducing the documents, editors preempted official denials and forced political elites to issue a response. This strategy naturally led to internal conflicts among regime insiders, who resented that their colleagues exposed them to public scrutiny.

## CREATING POPULAR PUBLICS

Leftist opposition soon surfaced against the gas line, reflecting Castillo's influence. In the fall of 1977, youth members of the Mexican Communist Party (Partido Comunista Mexicano, or PCM) painted graffiti across the urban landscapes of Mexico City and Nezahualcóyotl, asserting, "The Looting of Oil Impoverishes the People" and "No to the Gas Pipeline."[61] Oil represented one of a handful of issues that the PCM took up in public protests. Graffiti also urged "Full Support for the Tendencia Democrática," an independent electrical union; "Attend the PCM's Demonstration October 29"; and "We Demand 25 Percent Salary Increases." As Camilo D. Trumper argues was the case in Santiago de Chile, writing on the urban landscape was a way to "claim city spaces and transform them into arenas of public political debate."[62] Graffiti similarly allowed PCM activists to reach a public beyond rarefied readers and project their message to any city dweller who happened to pass by. In so doing they signaled that oil sovereignty was an issue of public concern.

Regional PMT committees also distributed pamphlets that echoed Castillo's main points against oil policy. Leaflets that circulated in Mexico state argued that oil wealth "is at risk of being 'sold' (almost given away) in order to fix the U.S.'s energy problems rather than contribute to our country's development." The pamphlet also accused Díaz Serrano of "cunningly raising our country's oil reserves to make the people believe that we are swimming in oil." Challenging the skyrocketing reserve figures, pamphlets echoed Castillo's assertions that Díaz Serrano had lied about the oil reserves. The PMT committees noted that public officials could invent numbers, just as they did other pieces of information.[63]

Castillo also circulated his ideas by giving talks on energy policy, and he visited Chihuahua's Regional Technology Institute (Instituto Tecnológico Regional) and the local Tendencia Democrática offices in November 1978. There he accused Pemex of lying about its reserves and deployed juvenile puns as he referred to the gas pipeline as the "ass line."[64] For Castillo, the issue of oil was just another example of how "in Mexico there are [only] two classes: exploiters and exploited." A select few profited enormously from oil exploitation while the majority suffered as a result. Castillo's audience was not universally impressed, and the day before his talk, critics left graffiti on the institute halls accusing Castillo of being an "agent of Soviet imperialism."[65]

Castillo made other efforts to diffuse his arguments beyond *Proceso*'s readership. In December 1977 he collaborated with cartoonist Rius to produce a graphic booklet, *Huele a gas!* (It smells like gas!), which provided an introduction to the gas pipeline debate. The cover attracted readers with its bright yellow color and lowbrow double entendre. Published by *Proceso*'s publishing house, Editorial Posada, *Huele a gas!* engaged broader audiences by repackaging exposés in popular and accessible formats. The booklet could be found in bookstores and on newsstands, sold alongside serialized comic books. Illustrations accompanied abridged versions of Castillo's *Proceso* articles, highlighting the stakes for nonspecialists. For example, Castillo's exposé on the CIA report appeared alongside a Naranjo cartoon that pictured a capitalist wheeling an infantilized Uncle Sam to suckle from a giant bottle labeled "PEMEX" (see figure 3.2).

An accompanying blurb explained that the United States was the world's largest energy consumer but that its supply was "about to run out." The corresponding image underscored the ease with which the United States was being granted cheap access to Mexico's natural resources. *Huele a gas!* effectively simplified Castillo's complicated articles and made them digestible for a wider audience.

While *Huele a gas!* was highly critical of the PRI, the pamphlet also revealed the authors' nostalgia for Cárdenas era social reform. Castillo did not view the Mexican Revolution as an elite project but instead argued that the PRI had betrayed revolutionary principles. One illustrated article identified oil exploitation as emblematic of the PRI's "forty years of sacking, frauds, and thefts to the detriment of our national economy."[66] Castillo and Rius thus connected the oil issue to the endemic regime corruption that reigned after the presidency of Cárdenas, who had acted as a personal mentor to Castillo. Yet Castillo did not believe the PRI could be reformed from within; instead he suggested that it was only by unseating the ruling party that the systemic rot could be uprooted.

Echeverría, had tried to extirpate the PMT, and police had kidnapped and beaten Castillo and Vallejo at various points in their organizing.[67] The steady pressure of guerrilla groups and urban popular movements alongside high voter abstention, however, led López Portillo to take concrete steps to co-opt the leftist electoral opposition. He made Reyes Heroles, a liberal, reform-minded politician, his right-hand man as secretary of the interior. Together they crafted a series of laws collectively referred to as the Political

Figure 3.2 *Huele a gas!*, illustration by Naranjo.

Reform, which Congress passed in December 1977. This legislative bundle granted amnesty to guerrillas and legalized leftist opposition parties, while retaining barriers to party registration. The PCM capitalized on the reform, gaining legal registration in 1978 and winning eighteen congressional seats in the 1979 midterm elections.[68] Even so, the government continued to deny the PMT legal registration until 1984. Castillo nonetheless persisted in disseminating his ideas through his journalism, speaking engagements, illustrated books, and PMT literature. His politicized journalism made it impossible to buy him off: Castillo had a uniquely prominent platform but avoided the financial pressures that journalists typically faced. Moreover, his arguments soon resonated with political insiders, who joined him in denouncing Pemex corruption in 1979.

## A SCANDALOUS OIL SPILL

On June 3, 1979, a massive oil spill breathed new life into the debate. A blowout in the Ixtoc 1 exploratory well caused the drilling rig to catch fire and collapse into the sea, resulting in the deaths of fifty-four workers. Photographs of the Bay of Campeche showed a brown mass of petroleum contaminating normally blue waters. The spill took nearly ten months to contain, making it one of the worst in history.[69] Díaz Serrano waited eight days to hold his first press conference, and when he finally spoke to reporters he reassured them that Pemex was employing the most advanced technologies to control the spill, which flooded the bay with thirty thousand barrels of crude oil, plus associated gas, each day.[70] Over the following days, Díaz Serrano downplayed the environmental destruction and reassured investors that the accident would not slow petroleum production.[71] Two weeks after the blowout, however, 250 square kilometers of water were covered in a slick layer of petroleum.[72]

The spill gave Díaz Serrano's political enemies ammunition to use against him. By the end of 1978 clear divisions had surfaced between cabinet members who wished to continue the brisk pace of oil production and those who feared the effects of petrodollars saturating the economy. Oteyza spearheaded arguments for a production cap, signaling a change of heart since he had defended Díaz Serrano's plans the previous year. On November 21 he submitted to the president the Plan for National Development, which proposed a 2.2-million-barrel-per-day cap on oil production. Of that amount, only around half would be exported to the U.S. market. But the Pemex director had soon pushed to nearly double that proposed limit, amplifying many cabinet members' concerns that he had grown too reckless and powerful.[73]

The Ixtoc 1 oil spill brought to light Díaz Serrano's careless decision making and conflicts of interest. In an *El Universal* opinion column, PAN leader José Ángel Conchello echoed Castillo's insinuations, made two years earlier, that Díaz Serrano had never sold off his interests in a drilling company, Gulf Maritime Drilling (Perforadora Marítima del Golfo, or Permargo), of which the Pemex director was a founding member. Given that Permargo had drilled the Ixtoc 1 well, Díaz Serrano's stake in the company came under heightened scrutiny.[74] Conchello noted that the "dirty practice" of awarding contracts to one's own company was so common among public officials that "it require[d] no explanation."[75] While he explained that such conflicts of interest were already common knowledge, he suggested that the oil spill provided the impetus for action.

In the wake of the Ixtoc 1 spill, many journalists also demanded that the government prove its commitment to information access and transparency. In addition to legalizing leftist opposition parties, the 1977 Political Reform had amended Article 6 of the Mexican Constitution to guarantee the "right to know." Without a corresponding regulatory law, however, there was no mechanism to ensure transparency. The amendment nonetheless sparked animated discussions in the press, and Secretary of Social Communication Luis Javier Solana spearheaded advocacy for a regulatory law. In 1979 the Congress began holding public hearings on a right-to-know law and invited journalists and public intellectuals to share their views.[76]

The day after Díaz Serrano's press conference, mainstream reporters and opinion writers impugned the levity with which he spoke of the spill's environmental and economic impact. The combative tone marked a shifting journalistic culture that demanded greater responsiveness from public officials. Reporters contrasted the government's rhetoric of transparency against the reality of "the systematic misinformation and the minimization of problems."[77] An *El Día* headline announced, "They Are Hiding Information about the Spill's Damage in Campeche."[78] Meanwhile, an opinion writer for *El Universal* noted that "after so much talk about the right to know, will we return to the old practice of leaving things without clarification, hoping [the people] will just forget with time?"[79] The PCM pointed to the spill as evidence that the Mexican people deserved a greater say in the making of oil policy.[80] After affirming its commitment to implementing the right-to-know law, the government was forced to account for why information was not forthcoming regarding the oil spill.

The spill had grave effects on the local economy of Campeche, where 80 percent of families lived off fishing. Plankton were hardest hit, affecting the food supply for other marine animals. At the height of shrimp season, fishermen also saw their catches reduced by 50 percent. Others reported reeling in fish and sharks that had already been partially cooked by the water and oil heated by the blowout. Seeing their livelihoods threatened, residents of Ciudad del Carmen questioned how oil production had benefited them.[81] In the following issue of *Proceso*, Enrique Maza reported that in other oil-rich regions, like the state of Tabasco, Pemex had similarly colonized land and destroyed the lifeways of subsistence farmers.[82] According to Maza, environmental destruction was not limited to occasional oil spills; Pemex flooded dams with chemical waste, contaminated and salinated potable water, destroyed agricultural fields, and burned contaminants that polluted the air.

The Ixtoc 1 spill also provided an opportunity for latent political grievances to be aired in the press. As criticism mounted regarding environmental destruction and Díaz Serrano's conflicts of interest, disaffected cabinet members leaked documents that implicated Pemex in mismanagement or corruption.[83] In July 1979, for example, Buendía received a copy of a document drafted by the Ministry of Commerce (Secretaría de Comercio) that accused Pemex of illegally awarding construction contracts for the gas line without the constitutionally mandated competition.[84] The three-page document was stapled to an unsigned note that alerted the columnist to "another abnormality in the Pemex administration," suggesting that this was not the first time that the informant had given Buendía sensitive information. Receipt stamps indicate that someone within the Pemex administration or the Ministry of Commerce could have leaked the document.

In his *Excélsior* column on July 30, Buendía portrayed the oil spill as a watershed moment for Díaz Serrano's critics, but he relied more on political gossip than the leaked source to make his claim. He opened the piece by cryptically observing that "it appears that in Pemex, something is burning other than the 'Ixtoc' well."[85] Buendía's "Red Privada" column frequently bridged the oral spheres where officials could freely express criticism and the printed forums where the reading public could access them. Here he divulged that the credibility of the Pemex administration was seriously being called into question, even by "public officials close to the president." Perceptions that Díaz Serrano wielded unbridled power aggravated frustrations, and cabinet members referred to the Pemex director behind his back as "the sheik." Buendía observed that Díaz Serrano was no longer invulnerable and noted that "these statements foreshadow the downfall of important figures."[86] Yet the columnist did not accept that corruption was limited to the Pemex director and instead argued that even when Ixtoc 1 was controlled, it would be difficult to "contain the avalanche of criticisms, doubts, revelations, and suspicions that have devastated the current administration of the company." Buendía's column demonstrated a delicate balance of dissimulation, concealment, and revelation. He divulged political gossip while remaining silent regarding the leaked document. At the same time, his reference to an "avalanche of criticisms" implied that he had more information that he could still disclose.

One might wonder whether Buendía and Castillo viewed each other as allies in their exposure of Pemex corruption. Although their efforts seemingly coincided, their personal styles and aims conflicted. Only a few months after Buendía published this column, he received a gun and ammunition as a gift from the Pemex public relations director and an invitation from Díaz Serrano to join him for target practice.[87] Like many journalists, Buendía often accepted such social invitations, recognizing that these connections would enrich his reporting. However, personal ties and fears of losing important sources could lead reporters to withhold criticism. Díaz Serrano meanwhile viewed Castillo as an intransigent adversary whose denunciations could not be softened through outings to the shooting range. Castillo used columnists like Buendía as foils to accentuate his own independence. Even the leftist party leader's choice of dress distinguished him from Buendía, who dressed like a power broker in tailored suits and expensive cuff links. By contrast, Castillo's sartorial choices of guayaberas or other informal tieless shirts signaled his self-presentation as a different type of politician who was aligned with the popular classes.[88] While their dispositions and ideologies were distinct, both disrupted the government's control over political discourse.

In his annual address on September 1, 1979, López Portillo devoted considerable time to attacking print media. Despite his efforts to encourage press opening, he now argued that freedom of expression had only cultivated sensationalism. He denounced that "fear is sold as news; blackmail is used to extort; fame is built by defaming; credit built by discrediting; [the press] . . . lies to make arguments, and it lives to slander."[89] Until that point, the president had allowed the minister of the interior to manage journalists, while the executive maintained an appearance of tolerance. But he now suggested that he had erred in granting too much freedom to reporters. While López Portillo identified a recent devolution of press ethics, he drew on a long-standing discourse that framed press freedom as a privilege too often abused by journalists. Indeed, his predecessors President Miguel Alemán and Adolfo López Mateos had employed similar language in speeches that denounced that "journalists took advantage of freedom of expression" and exhorted that "freedom requires responsibility."[90]

It was no accident that López Portillo's speech followed the Ixtoc 1 spill, and he clearly considered Castillo to be among those journalists who "built [fame] by defaming." In a private meeting one month earlier, López Portillo had accused Castillo of calumny, slander, libel, and giving sensitive information to foreign countries and thus endangering Mexican national security.[91] This openly confrontational stance foreshadowed the president's refusal to grant the PMT legal registration in 1981 and his withdrawal of government advertising from *Proceso* in 1982. His memoirs also indicate his growing frustration with members of his cabinet, whom he believed betrayed him by sending privileged documents to reporters. Reflecting on the frequency of leaking, López Portillo later lamented that his inability to control the government's relationship with the press was one of his "greatest failures."[92]

In the end, Congress subpoenaed Díaz Serrano to appear before the lower house on September 20, 1979, for questioning regarding his illegal awarding of contracts, his shares in drilling companies, and his handling of the Ixtoc 1 oil spill. The interrogation lasted eight hours and represented the first hearing that was televised for a national audience. On the morning of Díaz Serrano's appearance, *El Universal* noted that the director would need to explain the missing 318 million barrels of crude oil, a discrepancy found in Pemex's own reports and publicized by Castillo less than two weeks earlier.[93] While Díaz Serrano blamed the scandal on "some erratic opinions spread by groups working against the national interest," a PRI representative began the questioning by citing the press as a credible source that could explain the barrels of oil missing from Pemex's balance sheet.[94]

The Pemex director denied the charges and blamed Castillo and *Proceso*'s editors for misleading public opinion. In his defense, Díaz Serrano asserted that the newsmagazine had failed to reach out for comment, suggesting that the scandal had emerged from shoddy journalistic practice. He elaborated that the published Pemex figures were consolidated to include only the most relevant ones, leaving out losses caused by inadvertent spills, evaporation, and volume eliminated by refining out salt and other contaminants. Citing *Huele a gas!* and Castillo's October 1977 *Proceso* article, Díaz Serrano explained, "If they had asked us, we would have resolved it; but instead, they turn it into negative publicity, before verifying whether the information is right or wrong."[95] If true, it is not surprising that *Proceso* would distrust Pemex statements on the matter. Castillo's and others' exposés consistently accused public officials of lying in the face of questioning. Díaz Serrano's explanation itself rested upon the occlusion of information: by aggregating all the losses into one opaque figure, it was easier to deflect criticism.

Díaz Serrano's oblique references to Castillo and Rius did not go unchallenged during his questioning. Pablo Gómez Álvarez, a representative of the leftist coalition, argued that "it is not right that you to use the space of Congress to accuse someone who cannot respond to you because they do not have the floor." Moreover, Gómez Álvarez underscored that Díaz Serrano had made a serious claim when he accused the authors of *Huele a gas!* of "working against the national interest." Challenging the political culture that refused to name names, the representative demanded greater accountability in the proceedings.[96]

*Novedades* declared Díaz Serrano's appearance a resounding victory for the ruling party. The newspaper also signaled "the pathetic ignorance of those communists and their accomplices regarding the reality of the country, our oil industry, and the quality of the great men of this constitutional and revolutionary regime."[97] One columnist warned against further criticism, asserting that "after that report and interrogation, the only ones who will have doubts about our oil wealth and the Pemex director's honesty will be those like Heberto [Castillo] who do not search for the truth but rather for opportunities for self-promotion that will strengthen his political group."[98] The columnist suggested that Castillo's political ambitions disqualified his claims. In this formulation, all politicians produced skewed information, and the truth was determined by whoever had the last word.

Denuncia journalists, however, claimed that the congressional appearance signaled tectonic shifts in Mexican politics. An *Unomásuno* opinion piece exclaimed that eight hours of televised questioning was a breath of fresh air in Mexico's "private, hermetic, and sectarian" public life.[99] Others conveyed a sense of awe at being able to watch a congressional hearing on television, which they saw as evidence that the PRI was losing its monopoly over public discourse.[100] These reactions suggested the understanding that the PRI maintained power by managing public opinion and that, once wrested away, political life could become democratized.

## THE POLITICAL DOWNFALL OF DÍAZ SERRANO

The Ixtoc 1 disaster and the televised questioning of the Pemex director began the downward spiral that ultimately ended Díaz Serrano's career. Deep cleavages had emerged within the government regarding the course of oil development, and fears mounted that Díaz Serrano would be the PRI's next presidential candidate, as the outgoing president always selected the party's nominee. One political insider referred to Díaz Serrano as a "combination of Shah and Khomeini; the former because of his greed and the latter because of his demagoguery and violence."[101]

These conflicts were soon aired in myriad documents leaked to *Proceso*. The most scandalous exposé appeared in May 1981. Based on a thirty-eight-page report from the Ministry of Programming and Budget, *Proceso* reporter Carlos Ramírez proclaimed, "Petróleos Mexicanos is a state company that practically does whatever it pleases, with no heed for the law, regulations, and norms of official control."[102] The document confirmed what Castillo had argued for years: Pemex provided unreliable data, acted without government approval, and had become "a State within a State." Ramírez concluded that instead of providing a solution to economic crisis, corruption within Pemex had aggravated it. The company, he argued, wasted massive amounts of public funds to fuel the self-interested activities of its director.[103] Just ten days later, on June 6, 1981, Díaz Serrano resigned.

Ramírez's article coincided with climaxing conflicts in López Portillo's cabinet. Economic officials had grown increasingly anxious about the country's reliance on oil exports. One leaked report, marked confidential, noted that between 1976 and 1979 oil had jumped from 16 percent of total exports to 44 percent. As oil production increased, manufacturing exports fell from 40 percent in 1976 to 29 percent in 1979. Even so, Díaz Serrano disregarded warnings and declared plans to raise the production limit to four million barrels per day by the end of 1982, leading officials to fear that he had grown too powerful.[104] Then, in May 1981, Díaz Serrano announced to the *New York Times* that he had reached an agreement with the United States to lower the price of oil. He did so without consulting the president, let alone the cabinet.[105] Combined with bad publicity, Díaz Serrano's rash move facilitated efforts to remove him.

That same year the price of oil plunged and global interest rates rose, auguring economic crisis. By 1982 Mexico's foreign debt had more than tripled, and hydrocarbons had grown to 72.5 percent of the country's total exports.[106] In August the finance minister announced that the country would not be able to make its foreign debt repayments, sending the economy into a tailspin. Meanwhile, Castillo's warnings seemed to be coming true. An agreement with the IMF delivered a loan in exchange for anticipated oil sales and placed various restrictions on Pemex's daily operations. Journalist Rafael Rodríguez Castañeda reproduced a copy of the loan letter and reported that Mexico's agreement for funding from the IMF "has opened the door to interventionism, has brought into question the sovereignty of the national political economy, and in practice makes Pemex a subordinate of the U.S. government."[107] Promises of abundance had turned to economic crisis.

Díaz Serrano did not face real consequences until the new president, Miguel de la Madrid, took office. Despite strong evidence of Díaz Serrano's role in the crisis, the PRI offered him a senate seat. In 1983, however, box after box of incriminating documents arrived at *Proceso*'s door. Allegedly sent by Carlos Salinas of the Ministry of Programming and Budget (and future president in 1988), the documents described an embezzlement scheme through which Díaz Serrano had earned $34 million as Pemex director.[108] *Proceso* broke the story on June 20, 1983.[109] Just a few weeks later, on July 15, Díaz Serrano appeared before the Congress, where representatives decided to remove his senatorial immunity.

By this point, Díaz Serrano's crimes were notorious and had garnered him widespread antipathy. Protesters waited outside the congressional chambers with signs that demanded "Jail Díaz Serrano for Being a Thief." They also taunted Pemex's ex-director, declaring that he was worse than the loathsome nineteenth-century caudillo Antonio López de Santa Anna, and demanded that López Portillo be punished next.[110] Díaz Serrano was arrested, though he maintained his innocence, and in 1983 he was sent to prison—an unprecedented punishment for an official of his rank. In the course of only seven years, the Pemex director had gone from being one of Mexico's most powerful public officials to an inmate at the Mexico City Reclusorio Sur penitentiary, where he would spend five years. By this point, Mexico's oil exportation was popularly associated with economic crisis, not abundance.

## CONCLUSION

Muckraking journalism around Pemex corruption began as one individual's efforts but evolved into a broader concern both within the press and the administration. Critical coverage was ironically facilitated by the highly publicized 1976 intervention in *Excélsior*, which spawned new publications that asserted their independence based on the experience of censorship. This self-presentation no doubt ignored the financial and interpersonal ties that continued to bind denuncia reporters and their publications to governing officials. Yet it became a powerful discursive tool to gain cultural clout.

Numerous individuals mobilized print media for different ends, whether it be to send each other cryptic messages, to undermine political rivals, to manage public opinion, or to openly denounce political wrongdoing. The oil boom generated intense debate about Mexico's development and corruption, and the Ixtoc 1 oil spill provided the dramatic event that ignited public outrage against the corruption of Pemex director Díaz Serrano. As was often the case, denuncia journalism fed on ruling party divisions while exacerbating internal regime conflicts. The punishment of such a high-ranking official signaled important shifts in political culture and expectations. The rash of new revelations and the evidence of elite in-fighting further revealed that the PRI could not effectively control public debate nor stave off scrutiny.

Overborrowing against future oil revenues and the global drop in oil prices precipitated an economic crisis, and disgruntled administration officials used the Pemex director as a scapegoat for a grim economic horizon. This and other scandals became central to how urban Mexicans narrated the economic crisis. Specifically, the Pemex scandal forged the now commonly understood association between Díaz Serrano and rampant PRI corruption and mismanagement. One 1993 Mexican documentary visually represented this connection by panning the Pemex logo and a portrait of Díaz Serrano across the screen as the narrator described economic crisis and corruption.[111] Castillo's coverage had particularly enduring relevance in shaping this narrative, and decades later, copies of *Huele a gas!* could still be found at sidewalk used book sales.[112] Encyclopedias, Mexican textbooks, and popular histories also continue to cite Díaz Serrano as a prime example of the corruption that plagued López Portillo's administration.[113] This public memory continues to provide a "horizon within which a public finds itself, constitutes itself, and deliberates its own existence."[114]

The Pemex case became a cautionary tale of the state's failures to redistribute wealth. Over the following years, committed Marxists and conservative opposition leaders alike cited Díaz Serrano's crimes to emphasize that corruption was one of the country's most pressing problems. The journalist-politician most committed to the oil case, Heberto Castillo, hoped that by exposing Díaz Serrano's illegal dealings with foreign petroleum corporations, the government would be forced to defend oil sovereignty. Others, however, used his exposés to make the opposite argument. Neoliberal cabinet members, for example, upheld the Pemex case to justify the deregulation and liberalization of state-owned enterprises. This chapter has contextualized how contemporary notions of corruption, particularly in important state-run industries, had their roots in press scandals.

Even while Castillo offered a nuanced argument for Mexican sovereignty, the popular takeaway of the scandal was that one man had single-handedly destroyed Pemex. While Díaz Serrano emerged as the primary scapegoat for oil corruption, a mysterious fire in the Pemex archives suggested that many more officials could be implicated.[115] Reducing the company's records to ashes, the fire cast a shadow over the unprecedented imprisonment of such a high-ranking official. Amid scandal, much more remained concealed than exposed.

CHAPTER 4

# THE SPECTACLE OF IMPUNITY

The underbelly of Mexico's rapid urbanization was apparent by the late 1970s; traffic congested capital city streets, air pollution strained lungs and endangered wildlife, and muggings and home invasions became more frequent. Transit cops were known to harass, extort, and intimidate unsuspecting bystanders, raising bitter outrage. While these issues were particularly acute in the Mexico City metropolitan area, residents of other cities—from Acapulco to Guadalajara—expressed similar frustrations. Of particular concern was the expanded power of the security forces, which tortured and disappeared suspected dissidents with impunity. Everyday encounters with violence dispelled lofty promises of democratic opening. With little faith in official channels of redress, ordinary residents wrote to well-positioned journalists to seek out justice.

Popular frustrations found catharsis with the publication of a tell-all book, *Lo negro del Negro Durazo*. The thin paperback hit newsstands in the fall of 1983 and became an instant hit. By 1984 the book had sold over one million copies, gone through sixteen printings, and inspired comic book series, ballads, and a film. The gripping firsthand account detailed José González González's experience working as a bodyguard for Arturo Durazo, Mexico City's former chief of police. González exposed Durazo's alleged crimes of embezzlement, torture, and even murder, all of which the author argued could explain the current economic crisis.[1]

While *denuncia* journalists had aired some of the first details about Durazo's crimes, the ensuing scandal soon escaped their control. Popular media imaginatively reinterpreted the details of investigative press exposés, allowing the sensational allegations to move between high and low outlets. Several serialized comic books used racialized and gendered discourses to stoke outrage. They framed Durazo's financial crimes as particularly egregious because the ex-chief was uneducated, dark-skinned, and (alternately) hypersexual or impotent. These narratives heightened the spectacle of impunity, demonstrating that scandals could expand contestatory publics and expose serious wrongdoing, while undergirding antidemocratic prejudices. By expanding the audience beyond the educated upper middle classes, these works threatened to politicize and unite the lower classes, raising concerned interest from intelligence agents and government officials. Since the scandal first surfaced, Durazo's notoriety has endured in national public memory of the economic crisis and state impunity.

## POLICE ABUSE AND NOTIONS OF (IN)JUSTICE

Durazo came from humble beginnings, but he rose through the ranks of Mexico's various security and police forces. Born in 1922 in Cumpas, an agricultural town in the northern state of Sonora, Durazo migrated as a boy to Mexico City, where he attended primary school with future presidents Luis Echeverría and José López Portillo. Durazo particularly endeared himself to López Portillo by defending him from schoolyard bullies.[2] Biographical details for Durazo's adolescence and early adulthood are thin, but we know that he dropped out of school and earned a living as a personal bodyguard and then transitioned to work in state police and security organizations.[3] In this capacity he reputedly tortured Ernesto (Ché) Guevara and Fidel Castro before they went on to lead the Cuban Revolution. Durazo later headed the Federal Judicial Police (Policía Federal Judicial, or PJF) unit at the Mexico City International Airport, where he shepherded contraband into the country. In January 1976 a Miami, Florida, grand jury indicted Durazo for drug trafficking, but Mexican authorities refused to extradite him. When López Portillo assumed the presidency in December of that year, he appointed his childhood friend as Mexico City's chief of police. In his new position Durazo operated with unprecedented impunity and formalized connections between drug trafficking organizations and the police department.[4] The long-standing rivalries between the federal and city police increased during these years, as they competed for a share of drug profits.[5]

Civilian complaints frequently surfaced that agents arrested, threatened, or beat bystanders without cause. In the postrevolutionary era, *nota roja* (a sensational style of crime news) detailed these abuses and impugned police corruption and incompetence.[6] Beginning in the late 1950s, student movements made police repression a central target of their protests. Most famously, the 1968 student movement demanded the dissolution of the *granaderos* (riot police) who were notorious for their violent invasions of university and high school campuses. In the early 1970s squatter and land rights groups in Nezahualcóyotl also protested the violent evictions and confiscations carried out by police. Popular frustrations with police impunity were only amplified during Durazo's tenure.[7]

Reporters often mediated denunciations of crimes, as few residents believed that a formal report would yield results. Manuel Buendía, the most widely read journalist in Mexico at the time, regularly received complaints from readers, acquaintances, and friends who hoped that he would intercede on their behalf. In one instance, Buendía wrote directly to Durazo to report that a UNAM student had been unfairly arrested by police. The columnist knew the victim personally; in 1973 Buendía had begun giving journalism classes at the nation's most prestigious public university. He recounted that "in the university, [the student] asked me if there really was nothing to do in this case, when two citizens are willing to present their complaint and support their accusations against those involved."[8] By referencing the UNAM, Buendía signaled the importance of a denunciation from an educated middle-class victim. The journalist also kept a record of the request, providing a paper trail in case of inaction.

Buendía's weekday column frequently commented on the gap between police rhetoric and action. He was fascinated with Mexico City's underworld and narrated his articles in the vernacular of a noir crime drama, inflected with Catholic references culled from his training to be a priest in adolescence. Buendía began his journalism career in the conservative PAN's newspaper, *La Nación*, before working as a crime reporter for the popular tabloid *La Prensa*. He ascended to the directorship of the newspaper but later transitioned to full-time column writing at *El Día*, where he explored connections between Mexico City police and drug trafficking gangs. By the late 1970s his "Red Privada" column had become required reading for the political class, appearing in the conservative national broadsheet *El Sol de México* and later *El Universal*. As Buendía grew bolder in his accusations against the Catholic Church, the CIA, the PAN, and other powerful interest groups, his editors declined to publish certain columns. To avoid censorship, Buendía took his column to *Excélsior* and also contracted with a new syndication service, the Mexican Information Agency (Agencia Mexicana de Información), which distributed his articles in dozens of regional newspapers beginning in 1979.[9] The fact that Buendía used regional publications to circumvent capital city censorship underscores how the denuncia press began and persisted in regional newspapers like *El Informador* (Guadalajara) and *El Norte* (Monterrey).

Buendía critically covered Durazo's performance, focusing on the police department's incompetence and criminality. In August 1979 the columnist argued that Mexico City police not only failed to safeguard public order but also actively participated in criminal activity, including bank robberies. The piece masterfully interwove ironic playfulness and serious critique, and it opened by mocking Durazo's recent initiative to rehabilitate two million stray dogs and train them as canine units "capable of detecting explosives, spies, and narcotic contraband."[10] Dripping sarcasm, Buendía noted that the announcement was "quickly becoming one of the most sensational news items of the year so far," and he predicted that the initiative could earn Durazo a Nobel Prize nomination. His hyperbolic language imitated lackey reporters who lauded the public health benefits of removing "mangy" and "rabid" dogs from the streets, a racialized reference to criminals as well as street dogs.[11] Buendía also mocked how the publicity stunt presumed that residents would welcome more policing efforts. He noted that "until now, Mexico City residents could not decide which was better (or less bad): to have a policeman nearby or not to see one for many surrounding blocks."[12] Invoking common knowledge, Buendía commented on the widespread expectation that police would harm, rather than protect, residents.

Many journalists personally observed or experienced police violence and focused their coverage accordingly. Indeed, on the night before his article was published, Buendía and his neighbors witnessed two officers violently assault a young man in their quiet Lindavista neighborhood, situated in the city's northern sector. With his wife and their three children at home, the columnist held a personal interest in keeping their street safe. Buendía's presence at the scene transformed an everyday experience of injustice into an opportunity for accountability and resolution. His neighbors requested his intervention, providing him with the pertinent details, such as the victim's name and the car's make, model, registration number, and license plate number. Left alone with this information, an ordinary eyewitness would need to register a formal report with the Office of the Public Prosecutor (Ministerio Público) that would likely go unresolved.[13] By contrast, Buendía was well connected and immediately wrote directly to Carlos Hank González, the mayor (jefe de gobierno) of the Distrito Federal (the administrative unit of Mexico City).

Buendía requested that the mayor, who oversaw the police department, take action, and the columnist promised "to publish the results, whatever they may be."[14] He testified that from his home window he had seen a patrol car stop a young man for drunk driving. While police encountered no resistance, one officer forcibly removed the driver from his car and brutally beat him, compelling bystanders to intervene and beg the police not to kill the man. Buendía's neighbors asked him to intercede, and when he asked for the name and badge number of the "psychopath" (the most violent policeman), "another uniformed maniac violently and with a torrent of insults threw me in the back of his patrol car #2448." The policeman soon thought better of arresting the nation's most famous journalist and dropped Buendía off a few blocks from his home. By carefully recounting the episode and providing precise details, like the number of the patrol car, Buendía expected the Distrito Federal mayor to take appropriate action.

Authorities promptly responded to the columnist's complaint, and Durazo himself oversaw the interrogation of the offenders, who were eventually removed from their posts. Two weeks later Buendía publicized the incident as confirming that the "problem with the police" was, alongside traffic and trash collection, the most pressing concern for Mexico City residents, according to a recent poll.[15] Yet Buendía also suggested that police accountability was within reach for the ordinary individual. While the case had required constant vigilance, he reported the episode as a civics lesson and highlighted his intervention by reproducing his original letter to Hank González. By referencing a document of his own creation, Buendía suggested that writing enjoyed greater authority than orality.[16] Referencing the common tendency to let crimes go unreported, he encouraged readers to learn from his encounter and present a complaint the next time they experienced police injustice. Buendía argued that there was no harm in denouncing a crime. "Why not file your report, *and sustain it with civic valor*? If they ignore you, then you can submit the complaint to your favorite columnist."[17] He framed this as a harmless, but potentially empowering, exercise. Even as he deployed a language of civic duty, Buendía recognized that most crime reports did not lead to investigations, let alone justice. By positioning himself as a mediator, he suggested that he could act as a more effective arm of civil society by circumventing the torpid bureaucracy and interceding with the highest-ranking officials. However, his direct intervention did not challenge established hierarchies, but instead undergirded them. Moreover, Buendía intervened on behalf of individuals rather than collectives and thus failed to deliver broader guarantees or structural change. In this formulation, accountability necessitated chance and personal ties with powerful figures.

Readers could challenge journalists' visions of democracy and rights. For example, Luz María responded to the column in a personal letter that argued for an alternative interpretation of the events: Buendía received justice because he himself was powerful. She accused the columnist of underplaying the dangers that Mexico City residents faced in their encounters with police. Luz María typed her correspondence on plain paper with no letterhead, suggesting that she lacked credentials or institutional affiliations to grant weight to her petitions. She lambasted Buendía for his naïveté, opening her letter by asserting that "in Mexico only an idiot or an insane person would submit and sign a police report against a particular authority and include their address to top of it all off."[18] She reasoned that even with proof and eyewitnesses "not only would [authorities] not respond to the complaint . . . but the person who filed it, along with his or her family, would become victims of repression." Evidence alone was not enough to deliver justice. Luz María highlighted a point that Buendía himself had alluded to but downplayed: without a powerful intercessor, a denunciation against the police would only invite more abuse. Readers asked journalists to take on this danger by writing on their behalf. Without guarantees of safety, Luz María argued, civic engagement and accountability were illusory. Her letter suggested that popular understandings of justice stemmed from everyday experience, and she challenged Buendía for discounting this knowledge.

## THE LIMITS OF TRANSPARENCY

One year later, Buendía's role as an intermediary became the object of public skepticism when his peers asked him to intercede in another police abuse case. On November 6, 1980, DFS agents attacked radio journalist Héctor Gama in broad daylight. Gama had left the UNAM's Radio Educación studio that afternoon to do a "flash poll" for his weekly program, *Derecho a la Información*, which was inspired by congressional hearings about guaranteeing access to government information. In a café in the middle-class Roma Norte neighborhood, Gama approached a table of conversing men, who turned out to be plainclothes DFS agents staking out the National Center for Social Communication (Centro Nacional de Comunicación Social, or CENCOS) across the street.[19] The agents threatened to arrest Gama and demanded to know "who [he] was to go around managing public opinion." When the reporter refused to show identification, the agents forcibly shut off his tape recorder and dragged him outside, where they brutally beat him.

Gama wrote an *El Universal* op-ed on the incident, which he described as a human rights abuse. He opened his piece by provocatively asserting that "in the face of police irrationality, the common citizen lives without rights." Without money or power, he added, "[the ordinary person] must shield himself from the blinding reflection of a metallic badge or resign himself to suffering all manner of abuses." Like Luz María, Gama saw his experience as unexceptional, but he connected quotidian police abuse to the persistence of the Dirty War, the brutal counterinsurgency campaign carried out by security forces against presumed leftists since the late 1960s. While President López Portillo had declared amnesty for armed leftist groups as part of the 1977 Political Reform, Gama asserted that "in Mexico there are still secret prisons, torture by electric cattle prod, water torture (*el pocito*), mock executions, and other well-known [practices]."[20] This, he noted, contradicted official claims that Mexico was the last Latin American defense against dictatorship.[21] Gama's reference to the widespread knowledge of clandestine prisons and torture highlights how open secrets created a web of complicity. While many possessed varying degrees of knowledge regarding the Dirty War, secrecy prevented accountability.

Until the late 1970s the Mexico City press largely turned a blind eye to government counterinsurgency campaigns and instead focused on "terrorist" activity by leftist guerrillas.[22] However, nongovernmental groups like the Mexican Front for Human Rights (Frente Mexicano por Derechos Humanos) had publicized the state's imprisonment, torture, and assassination of peasant leaders since the 1960s.[23] New organizations, like the Committee for the Defense of Prisoners, the Persecuted, the Disappeared and Political Exiles (Comité Pro-Defensa de Presos, Perseguidos, Desaparecidos y Exiliados Políticos), joined in 1977 to pressure the government to account for enforced disappearances. In 1978 such abuses also received attention from international human rights organizations when Amnesty International released a report accusing the DFS, PJF, and Federal Preventive Police (Policía Federal Preventiva) of torture, illegal imprisonment, and disappearances.[24] Mexico City print media also began interviewing survivors and discussing such practices more openly. In 1978, for example, *Unomásuno* asserted that "many of those who are arrested are not political militants but simply representatives of popular discontent."[25] Even so, reporters clearly feared the consequences of such reportage and articles often appeared without bylines.

Before publishing his piece, Gama sought support from fellow reporters, including Buendía, whom he asked to sign a petition to the secretary of the interior.[26] But Buendía only acted after Gama's article appeared in print. Though both journalists could be characterized as critical of public officials, they held distinct political allegiances. Gama's journalism had developed out of his active participation in the 1968 student movement, which Buendía had distrusted, if not reviled.[27] Moreover, Buendía's closest informants hailed from the very intelligence institutions responsible for the repression that Gama and others suffered. The columnist even carried an agency badge that granted him access to privileged spaces and allowed him to carry a gun for personal protection.[28] Gama, meanwhile, implied that the DFS badge was a symbol of corruption and violence.

Over the following week, *El Universal* and *Excélsior* engaged in an intertextual discussion of Gama's case and offered conflicting perspectives on the relationship between transparency and accountability. Buendía finally weighed in only to declare the case closed and to praise DFS director Miguel Nazar Haro for opening an investigation into the attack.[29] Buendía's relationship with the DFS became an object of public criticism when another opinion leader revisited the details of the incident. In his long-standing *El Universal* op-ed column, leftist leader Heberto Castillo commented on the silences in Buendía's "Red Privada." Castillo summarized the events leading to the investigation, beginning with Gama's correspondence to "various journalists with recognized vertical pull."[30] While Buendía's column omitted his own intermediary role, Castillo revealed that a well-placed request was what led to the investigation. At the same time, he avoided naming Buendía explicitly and thus limited the audience that would understand the oblique reference.

The printed exchange was more than an internecine squabble among big egos. It represented a public conversation about the prescribed parameters of democratic accountability and transparency. Castillo underscored the DFS's penchant for obstructing, rather than facilitating, justice and argued that negotiating with Nazar Haro underwrote the unbridled power of the intelligence agency. He reminded readers of the DFS director's "reputation for being a ferocious repressor." Castillo implicitly referenced his own harrowing experience as a political prisoner; Nazar Haro had tortured Castillo, leaving his face disfigured.[31] In addition to directing the DFS, Nazar Haro created and directed a clandestine counterinsurgency organization, the White Brigade (Brigada Blanca). Formed in 1976 with the mission of continuing illegal activity without the public's knowledge, the brigade comprised select members of the military, the DFS, the Office of the Attorney General of the

Republic (Procuraduría General de la República, or PGR), the Office of the District Attorney of the State of Mexico (Fiscalía General de Justicia del Estado de México), and the Federal Preventive Police.³² Nazar Haro's counterinsurgency strategies drew upon his previous training at the School of the Americas, a U.S. Army institute for Latin American soldiers. It was not until October 8, 1980, that the Ministry of National Defense (Secretaría de Defensa Nacional) finally confirmed the existence of the White Brigade.

Castillo also asserted that the DFS collaborated with criminal organizations and concluded that "the Federal Security Office should disappear" because it empowered thugs to commit atrocities with no accountability.³³ Accountability in the press, he suggested, was impossible without transparency about one's sources, and repression could not be resolved through behind-the-scenes mediations. The following year Nazar Hazar faced legal scrutiny that forced him to resign. In July 1981 a San Diego, California, grand jury indicted him for overseeing a criminal operation that resold stolen U.S. cars. Tellingly, Nazar Haro's resignation in January 1982 was the result of foreign pressure and was unrelated to his torture of political prisoners.³⁴

Gama's case highlights tensions within denuncia journalism. Reporters like Buendía frequently accused officials and security forces of wrongdoing while protecting some of the most repressive actors who provided him with valuable information. This was not an isolated incident; detailed analysis of Buendía's columns reveals his reticence to criticize the DFS. At the same time, Buendía's next exposé demonstrates that seemingly compromised reporters could still expand the boundaries of public debate.

## RÍO TULA AND THE SEEDS OF SCANDAL

Buendía's sources helped him identify the perpetrators of a multiple homicide committed about sixty miles north of Mexico City. On January 14, 1982, residents of Tula, Hidalgo, discovered nine bodies, all bearing signs of gruesome torture, floating in a sewage canal.³⁵ The Red Cross arrived first to the crime scene, followed by five different police agencies, predominantly from Mexico City, which soon initiated parallel investigations. Scuba divers searched for additional victims and pulled three more bodies from the sewer, bringing the total count to twelve. According to Manuel Camín, columnist and director of *Últimas Noticias*, *Excélsior*'s sister afternoon newspaper, the discovery signified "the crime of the century."³⁶ He spared no sensational detail, describing a grisly scene of bodies that had been "tortured, mutilated—one also decapitated—riddled with bullets, [and] slashed to pieces." With drug trafficking networks just beginning to shift to overland routes through Mexico, homicides of this magnitude had not yet become commonplace. The Río Tula murders marked the beginning of an investigation that would incriminate Durazo and the investigative unit that he oversaw, the Investigative Division for Crime Prevention (División de Investigaciones para la Prevención de la Delincuencia).

The Río Tula homicides garnered U.S. news coverage, with the *Los Angeles Times* reporting on the chaotic investigation.[37] As new details from coroners became available, police and federal organizations promoted competing theories about the suspected perpetrators. Initial hypotheses suggested that the victims were drug traffickers massacred by a rival gang. While weeks passed before authorities ascertained the victims' identities, their expensive clothing and South American "physical type" were enough to raise suspicions of illicit activity. Camín hinted that an escalating battle between Mexico state police and gangs had culminated in the homicides.[38] However, he himself had well-known connections with Mexico City police and was considered by some journalists to be a "thuggish reporter," perhaps a reference to being an extortionist. Capital city organizations soon came under scrutiny after detectives determined that the victims had been killed in Mexico City and their bodies discarded in a sewage drain and floated to Hidalgo.[39] To deflect blame, city police spread alternative theories, including one that implicated the PJF and another that blamed the violence spilling over the southern border from Guatemala as thousands fled a brutal counterinsurgency campaign there.[40] The conflicting investigations and theories are not surprising given that organizations like the DFS, the PJF, and the Mexico City police were competing for control over drug trafficking routes and criminal rackets.[41]

Nearly two weeks after the Río Tula murders came to light, Buendía laid the groundwork for his accusation against the Mexico City police chief, Durazo. The columnist conveyed a story of moral decay, relating the events in the style of a detective fiction writer. He described the "blood curdling" crime and its unproductive investigation as "infecting" those who read about it in the newspaper. Buendía further noted that society was "frightened by a simple and terrifying truth: this multiple homicide was committed in Mexico," referring to assumptions that the country remained safer than the rest of Latin America.[42] He argued that the multiple murders were unprecedented and damaging, even to those who only read about them. Yet Buendía only intimated who was responsible, suggestively asking, "Has police corruption surpassed what we thought possible?"

By March, investigators located two additional bodies in Río Tula, bringing the total homicide count to fourteen. Buendía had also grown bolder in his accusations that the Mexico City police had committed the murders. In a groundbreaking column he became the first reporter to blame Durazo, publishing information from five anonymous informants within police and intelligence organizations.[43] Buendía revealed that the homicide victims included three Mexicans and eleven Colombians who had belonged to a gang of bank robbers. When a special operations unit of the Mexico City police, the Jaguar Group, learned of a 140-million-peso robbery booty, Buendía argued, "they were tempted by greed." During a torture session to locate the stash, police inadvertently killed one of the captured, "sealing the others' fates."

Buendía accused a high-ranking police official of ordering and covering up the crime, but he stopped short of printing Durazo's name. Buendía instead reported that the riot police usually oversaw the Jaguar Group, and "only a chief of police could have ordered that the surveillance be removed at the precise moment when they discarded the fourteen bodies." As if this was not an explicit enough accusation, he divulged that "everyone knows the name of the public official whose interests established this series of cover-ups."[44] Buendía's refusal to print Durazo's name, however, offered plausible deniability against charges of defamation or worse. Despite continued international and national press coverage of the Río Tula murders, the police chief and the Jaguar Group members continued in their posts.[45] Absent a direct accusation, Durazo and the administration did not have to respond publicly. However political pressure was mounting against Durazo, and the PGR opened an investigation into his finances.[46] Buendía's intelligence contacts, acting in their own interest, had facilitated his exposé on the Río Tula murders, but the story soon acquired a distinct meaning for popular media consumers.

## "LA CRISIS"

As the country barreled toward economic disaster, it was Durazo's profligacy, not his alleged involvement in the homicides, that became the focus of multiple accusations. Shortly after the Río Tula case came to light, the Mexican peso underwent its second devaluation since 1976. The subsequent August 1982 debt default effectively froze all borrowing, aggravated already high inflation and unemployment, and catalyzed a region-wide crisis. In a last-ditch effort to salvage his legacy, López Portillo proclaimed on September 1 that all banks operating in Mexico would be nationalized and their accounts converted from dollars to pesos.[47] The president promised that the nationalization would protect against antipatriotic capital flight. Business elites, in turn, blamed the president for bankrupting the country. At a conference organized by the PAN, the keynote speaker described Durazo and López Portillo as representative of the "thieves that have not only stolen the people's wealth . . . but also their freedom."[48] These two figures, in addition to Pemex's ex-director Jorge Díaz Serrano and Carlos Hank González, the millionaire mayor of the Distrito Federal, became popular representatives of the corruption that had bankrupted the country.

The economic crisis turned even greater attention toward the extravagant wealth of a handful of public officials, including the outgoing president himself. Amid news of public sector budget cuts, *Proceso* published photographs of the "disturbing mansions" owned by powerful officials.[49] Among them was Durazo's so-called Parthenon, which towered above the bay in Zihuatanejo, Guerrero. *Proceso* reporter Ignacio Ramírez wrote an exposé on the property, creating a spectacle of the police chief's twenty-thousand-square-meter vacation home. Like an *Architectural Digest* spread, the article visually toured the lavish property, describing its cost (some 700 million pesos) and its decorative touches (Hellenic pillars and statues). Rather than cultivating admiration or jealousy, however, Ramírez described the estate as decadent and immoral. He channeled his criticism through the commentary of one Zihuatanejo resident who demanded to know, "Where did Durazo get so much money? . . . while we're so screwed here."[50] Contrasted against the falling wages and purchasing power of most Mexicans, the ostentatious wealth demanded explanation. While generating public outrage, the spectacle of profligate officials facilitated incoming president Miguel de la Madrid's efforts to blame the crisis on the previous administration.

The *Proceso* exposé prompted television host Jacobo Zabludovsky, famously loyal to the PRI, to interview Durazo about his allegedly ill-gotten gains. Though the chief of police dismissed the questions as mere jealousy, public demands for justice persisted.[51] Acapulco's leader of the United Socialist Party of Mexico (Partido Socialista Unificado de México), which united leftist parties in 1981, called on the Congress to investigate Durazo's mansion, which had been built on collectively owned and farmed *ejidal* land. A state representative further demanded the expropriation of Durazo's property and its conversion into a cultural center.[52]

While reporters sought to identify the responsible parties, cartoonists suggested that no single person or organization could carry the blame for "la crisis," a ubiquitous term that after 1982 referred not only to a specific eco-

Figure 4.1 Rius, "Listos con las listas!," *Proceso*, September 27, 1982, 31.

nomic disaster but, as Claudio Lomnitz notes, to the "situations, practices, and sentiments" of an era.[53] Cartoonists delivered some of the most incisive readings of Mexican politics; they faced fewer editorial pressures than reporters and embraced ambivalent interpretations of political life. Amid economic crisis, cartoonists including Helioflores, Naranjo, and Rius offered bottom-up readings of the economic disaster and mocked cynical government attempts to manipulate public opinion. Rius, for example, channeled popular sentiment toward the bank nationalization in his *Proceso* cartoon published on September 27 (see figure 4.1).

In the drawing, a list of state crimes, including the Tlatelolco Massacre and the Río Tula murders, are scribbled on the wall of a city street. As if to cover them up, someone has painted "Nationalized Bank" over them. Graffiti on the urban landscape stood in for popular opinion that could not find expression in print. A peasant stands looking thoughtfully at the wall and muses, "They shouldn't forget that we don't forget." Rius suggests that each of these wrongs, which correspond with distinct presidential terms, cannot be pinned on a single administration, nor can they be erased with popular initiatives. Instead, he argues that the regime still bears responsibility for repression, and even Río Tula cannot be singly blamed on Durazo.

On November 10, 1982, López Portillo signed a new agreement with the IMF. In exchange for deferred debt payments and loans, Mexico would

Figure 4.2 Rius, "Medio siglo de siglas," *Proceso*, November 29, 1982, 37.

implement the fund's structural adjustment recommendations, ushering in years of austerity. While investigative print media decried the agreement as evidence of U.S. exploitation, another Rius cartoon in *Proceso* portrayed the budget cuts as the culmination of the PRI's long-standing inability to deliver prosperity (see figure 4.2).

Under the title "A Half Century of Slogans," the cartoon pictures two indigent men panhandling on a city sidewalk.[54] Painted on the wall behind them is the PRI's logo, which would have been ubiquitous during an election year like 1982. Referring to the party acronym, one of the men comments to the other, "The *R* is for *rateros* (thieves), the *I* is for *ineptos* (the inept), and the *P* you cannot say," allowing readers to fill in the blank with their preferred expletive, *pendejos* (dumbasses) or *putos* (faggots).[55] Rius suggests that urban dwellers are not easily persuaded by PRI campaign publicity. Instead, they openly mock it and offer their own critical interpretation of the party's lackluster performance. The relationship between the poor and the urban landscape is distinct from the previous cartoon, in which ordinary people alter the landscape to project their own political views. Here they merely respond to PRI propaganda, but by putting these attitudes in print, Rius seeks to capture ephemeral urban acts and assign them the weight of public opinion.

Helioflores also canonized popular jokes by putting them into print. On López Portillo's last day in office, the cartoonist darkly suggested that the president's term had ended in such disaster that he might be driven to commit suicide. The *El Universal* cartoon, titled "At the End," pictured López Portillo with a rope around his neck attached to a heavy rock. Peering over a cliff edge, the lame-duck president stands poised to throw himself from his perch (a large bone, which referenced the material benefits of government work).[56] The image also referred to López Portillo's promise earlier that year to defend the peso "like a dog." When the peso was devalued only a few weeks later, he became the subject of many canine-related jokes, and bystanders even barked when the president appeared in public.[57] The discovery of the construction of five mansions for López Portillo's family in the exclusive Lomas de Vista Hermosa neighborhood brought him under further scrutiny, and the hill where the residences sat became popularly dubbed "la Colina del Perro" (the Dog's Hill). The cartoon modeled irreverent disdain for the highest officeholders and acted as an "equalizer" in an unequal society.[58]

President-elect de la Madrid faced a public relations challenge; popular outrage required that he acknowledge the role of individual corruption, while political survival dictated that he avoid indicting the entire regime. To assuage discontent he campaigned on an anticorruption platform of "moral renovation." De la Madrid promised to rationalize political culture and the economy, and his discourse of cultural and political austerity departed sharply from López Portillo's flamboyant personal style and promises of abundance. De la Madrid dramatically slashed the social safety net and sold or liquidated over 40 percent of public companies during his term. He was not merely following IMF dictates but rather pursuing policies that he had learned while earning his master's degree in public administration from Harvard University.[59]

The incoming administration framed corruption as a flawed cultural trait. The day after taking office, de la Madrid presented an austerity program before Congress to show that politicians would not be immune. He emphasized that widespread personalism required the transformation toward a more rational and disinterested political culture, beginning with the elimination of "the sale of influence."[60] Formerly considered perks of the job, some of the practices he identified included giving friends access to government vehicles, diverting public employees to act as one's personal assistants, using state funds to pay for private security details, and taking joy rides in government planes. In speeches after the inauguration, the new cabinet of technocrats, or foreign-trained policy experts, also downplayed large-scale corruption. Instead they focused on tightening household budgets and urged Mexicans to show their solidarity by cutting back.[61]

Select PRI officials joined in calling for an investigation into corrupt politicians, though they were careful to emphasize that offenders were isolated to the previous administration. By May 1983 the PGR began issuing warrants for the arrest of high-ranking officials. For example, the former director of the National Bank of Rural Credit (Banco Nacional de Crédito Rural), Miguel Lerma Candelaria, faced charges of fraud and bribery, including payments of up to 194,000 pesos to journalists. He fled the country to evade arrest, but the pursuit of high-profile figures like Lerma Candelaria and Díaz Serrano threatened that other officials might similarly be implicated. While many journalists supported the anticorruption measures, they accused government officials of much larger crimes, including collusion with criminals and involvement in drug trafficking. Scandals also easily escaped top-down control, and the press and protesters clamored for the PGR to bring similar charges against Durazo, Hank González, and even López Portillo.[62]

### THE REAL CRIMINALS

Frustrations with corruption were aggravated not only by financial hardship but also by physical insecurity. Popular tabloids blamed the government for hunger and the police for crime. Between 1982 and 1983 Mexico City experienced a nearly 50 percent jump in reported crimes, with an even greater increase in robberies.[63] A UNAM law professor, Luis de la Barreda Solórzano, observed a cognitive shift during these years. Prior to 1983, few middle-class Mexicans personally knew the victims of crimes, but two years later, he noted, "we all have an aunt that was robbed in her own apartment, a friend that was stripped in public view, a neighbor whose wallet was taken in a restaurant by a gang that entered peacefully."[64] The result, he wrote, was a feeling of impotence and "collective neurosis": "We all are afraid of being mugged."

As demonstrated by Stuart Hall, the perception of a "crime wave" often reveals more about contemporary social anxieties than it does about a significant increase in criminal activity. In the case of Mexico, overall crime, especially homicides, had decreased steadily since 1930, though urban dwellers continued to perceive violent crime to be a serious problem.[65] In the 1980s, robberies did increase from previous years, and press reports of a "wave of kidnappings" no doubt fueled and legitimated concerns. Yet unlike in Great Britain and the United States, where the "mugging crisis" generated demands for harsher law-and-order policies, Mexico City reporters did not call for greater policing but instead for justice.[66] They blamed the spike in robberies on economic need, and they called for a renewed government commitment to social security and welfare.

Working-class newspapers provided a rationale for economic crimes, ultimately holding the government accountable for austerity policies. For example, in January 1983, *La Prensa* printed a bolded headline, "The Wave of Kidnappings Increases," and warned that the city was witnessing a new type of crime that emerged from the economic crisis. This structural explanation contrasted sharply against de la Madrid's cultural one. The reporter editorialized that robberies stemmed from hunger, not greed, and described intruders as entering homes and stealing only food and alcohol. Similarly, a surge of kidnappings in supermarkets targeted homemakers whose credit cards and vehicles identified them as affluent. Kidnappers would hold a mother's child hostage until she handed over a ransom of basic foodstuffs. The reporter asserted that police were complicit or ineffectual, adding that the victims "do not file crime reports, fearing they will suffer additional retaliation."[67] If the impact of the economic crisis varied by class, the article suggested that no one was immune to police abuse. Thus, *La Prensa* reporters blamed the government for failing to combat poverty and the police for failing to stop crime.

The advertisements that accompanied the article give a sense of *La Prensa*'s readership. In contrast to the expensive products advertised in *El Universal* or *Excélsior*, *La Prensa*'s pages were peppered with announcements for cattle available on a ranch outside Mexico City, a garage offering reconstructed engines, and low-budget hernia treatments. On the opposite page were movie listings, a public service announcement for an educational television series for those without any formal schooling, and an advertisement for a training program for "field hands." *La Prensa* advertisers targeted low-income sectors, people who did manual labor for a living.

That month a *La Prensa* columnist reported that thieves increasingly robbed pharmacies, looking for scarce and expensive medicines. This was the government's fault, he argued, because it had raised the value-added tax on prescription drugs, limiting the supply. The reporter called on the Ministry of Commerce (Secretaría de Comercio) to intervene and prioritize the sick, who "may fall ill and even take to the city's streets to beg for a cent to pay for the prescriptions they carry."[68] The article explicitly identified the poor as victims of government austerity policies. Referencing a familiar stereotype, the columnist argued that begging for medication was not a trick.[69] He explained, "The misery is evident in these famished children who accompany their parents and grovel on the sidewalk or in the halls of the Metro." The reference to public transportation highlights how urban infrastructure brought the poor into contact with middle-class city dwellers. Empathizing with those who stole from pharmacies, the columnist blamed the government for dangerous streets and argued that "the price hike on medicines is criminal."[70]

While popular tabloids like *La Prensa* provided a structural explanation for crime, chronicles and letters from readers highlight the indignation that many felt when crimes went unpunished. In 1984, *Unomásuno* published a multipart series that explored the personal experiences of rape victims. In 1977 and 1978, two men robbed dozens of Mexico City residences and sexually assaulted many of the women who were home. In his six-part series, chronicler Ramón Márquez revealed that the public prosecutor had received over forty reports of robbery and that many of these denunciations included charges of rape. Years later, however, these violations remained unpunished.[71] Márquez included the reaction of one victim who was raped shortly after giving birth: "Is that what justice means in Mexico, sir? Can we accept that these bad actors—who act like animals, who are sick, who are so despicable, who are a danger to society—have been absolved of minimum sentences of four to six years?"[72]

Letters, protests, and crime news similarly illustrate the popular frustration with injustices perpetrated by politicians and the police. *Últimas Noticias* reported a strike organized by truck drivers to protest police extortion and robberies, and *La Prensa* published eyewitness accounts of police abuse, which included the murder of a civilian during a traffic incident.[73] Readers also wrote to Buendía with complaints when official channels failed to yield justice. For example, one Guadalajara reader wrote with a proposal that crime victims should pursue collective action. After suffering a mugging, he saw unionizing as the only logical path forward.[74] A self-described "modest housewife" and assiduous reader of "Red Privada" similarly wrote to Buendía to complain that a congressional representative had illegally squatted in her family's home eight years earlier. Though her husband worked as a waiter, they had saved enough money to build a home, which the representative had effectively expropriated. Years of failed legal battles to reclaim their property left her feeling "both indignant and totally disillusioned to see the type of political representatives imposed upon us and how our laws fall short of bringing justice."[75]

Readers also wrote to Buendía about abuses by police. An engineer who worked for the Federal Electricity Commission (Comisión Federal de Electricidad) in Mexico City described witnessing fifteen police descend "Gestapo style" from a city government truck and rob fruit from a street stand in the Roma neighborhood. The reader explained that the owners, "a couple of shopkeepers of humble origin," had no defense against such "gangster-like behavior."76 The witness described the police as criminals who terrorized the population without consequences. This led him to question the relationship between established legal protections and their practical application: "In practice, are there any individual rights for our people?" The letters highlighted that authorities not only failed to protect the population; police officers were themselves the perpetrators of crime. Generalized frustration with police abuse made Durazo an obvious target for opprobrium.

## THE SPECTACLE OF DURAZO

*Lo negro del Negro Durazo*, published in the fall of 1983, blamed the nation's financial crisis, Mexico City crime, and generalized corruption on Durazo's imperious reign over the city's police department. The author, José González, promised that he would give the "true" account of a case that had already fascinated and alarmed readers. The memoir's format emulated the direct participant accounts, *testimonio*, that had become popular in Latin America in the 1960s.77 González opened his book with the formulaic statement of testimonial literature, confessing that "I, Pepe González González, author of this work, began killing at age twenty-eight." He admitted to committing over fifty assassinations, many of them directly ordered by Durazo. The editor's prologue underscored how "above all, [this book] is a denunciation—which we hope the relevant authorities will take into account—against what a public official with total impunity can do in a country gravely beset by corruption."78 The editor emphasized that López Portillo was also a target of the denunciation, because the president, like Durazo, had benefited from a state of impunity.

González dedicated the book to Julio Scherer García, "without whose help and advice this work would never have seen the light of day."79 The *Proceso* director had played a key role in compiling and editing the narrative, and the meandering prose suggests that Scherer García recorded his conversations with González and later edited them into a book-length account. *Proceso*'s publishing house, Esfuerzo, agreed to publish the work after many others declined. González also noted that the PGR had refused to hear his voluntary testimony against Durazo, showing that printed denunciations offered a lever of justice when legal mechanisms failed.

*Proceso* promoted the book and promised that it would grant readers privileged insight into the inner workings of the city's police department. On September 26, 1983, the magazine's cover featured an image of a corpulent Durazo next to the headline, "The Criminal Biography of Durazo, Written by

His Head Assistant." Above it was a short list of Durazo's alleged crimes: "torture, narco-trafficking, the Tula assassinations." Reporter Ignacio Ramírez excerpted *Lo negro del Negro Durazo*'s most tantalizing details to build interest in the book's upcoming release. He described it as "a hallucinating history, which seems more like a story of a secret society, a no-holds-barred tale told with the blessing of the countries' highest authorities."[80] The book's exposé on the seedy underworld of corrupt cops, Ramírez teased, provided a firsthand account of the impunity that pervaded political power.

*Lo negro del Negro Durazo* made corruption legible through a discussion of Durazo's race and class, an explanation that was absent from previous reportage. González implied that authorities had erred in charging a working-class, dark-skinned man with the protection of the city. This not only confirmed readers' assumptions about the background of criminals—who were often presumed to be poor, dark-skinned urban dwellers—but also their expectations regarding who possessed the authority to rule. González depicted Durazo as a low-class hooligan who had no education but had nonetheless ascended the rungs of power because of his childhood friendship with López Portillo. According to González, Durazo was ashamed of his origins and had "practically lived in squalor" like "a common thug" before he entered public service.[81] To paint a picture of Durazo's working-class background, González reproduced his crude language and described how the chief of police frequented seedy cabarets and "low-class dance halls." Such details did not speak to any actual wrongdoing but rather scandalized readers with Durazo's unrefined personal style and provided a narrative for why Durazo had failed in his public duties.

González further distinguished himself from Durazo, whose dark skin earned him the nickname "El Negro" as a boy. Rather than referencing an Afro-Mexican heritage, which Durazo likely did not have, the nickname reflected the stigmatization of darker skin. Color-based nicknames are quite common in Mexico, but the meaning and usage is relational and situation specific. *Negro*, for example, can be a pejorative insult or a term of endearment (particularly within families), depending on the context.[82] Regardless of the intention, however, the nickname reflects the valorization of whiteness. Indeed, González repeatedly reminded readers of his own nickname, "El Güero" (Whitey), and referenced his Spanish background to undergird his respectability. Since the colonial era, Europeans had occupied the top of social hierarchy, while Indigenous peoples, the most common targets of racism, were at the bottom. Nicknames like El Negro did not directly reference indigeneity, but demonstrated the social stigma of darker skin.

González portrayed the draining of public coffers and the mismanagement of the police force as Durazo's most egregious transgressions, devoting little space to the practices of torture and murder that came to light with the Río Tula case. He instead detailed how the ex-chief of police had formalized drug trafficking ties with the police department and gave officers packages of cocaine for street distribution.[83] González further calculated fabulous earnings that depended directly on the abuse of Mexico City residents. Police department rackets, including a weekly quota of cars towed and drivers extorted, funded Durazo's lavish mansions and extensive personal staff. Durazo also diverted police resources for his own personal use: he mobilized squad cars and 650 officers for the construction of his southern Mexico City residence in Ajusco.[84] Upon completion, the mansion boasted a discotheque modeled as an exact replica of Studio 54, a casino, an indoor pool, a stable, sports courts, and a racetrack. According to González, Durazo used police helicopters to fly in guests to his cocaine-fueled parties, and he humiliated officers by making them serve as waitstaff while forbidding them from partaking of the banquet. Amplifying the image of high politics as spectacle, the book also included embarrassing details of Durazo's cocaine abuse and sexual impotence, meting out retribution through public humiliation.

The public response to the book was immediate. Castillo commented that morale was at an all-time low in Mexico, and noted that González's story showed "the arbitrary use of the Republic's resources and powers was given to a group of gangsters who basically had no limits."[85] Describing popular reactions, Buendía similarly argued that feelings of "terror, shame, and humiliation" were giving way to anger and demands for justice.[86] He reprinted his findings about the Río Tula murders from more than a year and a half earlier, but this time he mentioned Durazo by name. The host of a Radio UNAM program, *Palabras sin Reposo*, similarly discussed the case and called upon authorities to "rid our society of this evil."[87] With a legal case mounting against him, Durazo fled the country in November 1983.

While denuncia journalists emphasized how Durazo symbolized generalized state impunity, urban dwellers offered their own interpretations. González, who was now famous due to the book's success, appeared on talk radio programs to answer listeners' questions and elaborate on his book's revelations. Francisco Huerta, host of *Voz Pública*, describes how González phoned into his program to offer two thousand pesos to rural listeners who had called to describe their financial difficulties.[88] In addition to amplifying his own fame, then, González's appearances allowed him to assume the role of a benefactor. Residents also expressed their disdain for Durazo in public performances and hand-drawn signs that ridiculed Durazo as "a frivolous gangster." In a more festive interpretation, a street theater group parodied the ex-chief of police in a performance for three hundred attendees; the group's chosen name, Los Nacos, was itself a race-loaded, pejorative term that derided the uneducated, Indigenous urban poor.[89] Durazo's Ajusco property was even temporarily converted into a "Museum of Corruption" and became a popular weekend attraction for curious Mexico City residents.[90] Radio talk shows, posters, and performances allowed residents to register their outrage and offer their own commentaries on the case. Meanwhile, the museum provided a public space where residents could collectively consume the scandal.

On January 30, 1984, the PGR charged Durazo with tax evasion, seized his Ajusco property, and issued a warrant for his arrest. Two months later, the attorney general added charges of smuggling, extortion, and the illegal possession of weapons. In the meantime, the FBI warned Mexican authorities that Durazo had plans to assassinate President de la Madrid, perhaps in retaliation for the charges.[91]

Despite the promise of a legal case against him, Durazo's case continued to inspire creative depictions in films, theatrical parodies, and comic books, moving seamlessly between high and low media.[92] Broadcast networks produced popular television specials that visually toured Durazo's mansions, exposing national audiences to the drama, and radio programs kept listeners abreast on Durazo's criminal charges. In early 1984, new comic books further popularized the case. Weekly issues of the serialized dramas sold between fifty thousand and 150,000 copies on corner newsstands, and they ranged from the pricier 150 pesos to a very accessible thirty-five pesos.[93] The comic books were closely based on González's book, and some even lifted the book's chapter subheadings for the titles of their weekly issues. The serials ranged from serious to light in tone, but all included editor's notes that asserted that the comics were denunciations against Durazo's crimes.

The comic books relied on gendered, racialized, and classed story lines to generate outrage and scandal. One series, *El infierno del Negro Durazo* (The hell of Black Durazo), suggested that Durazo's dark skin was symptomatic of his bad character. The first issue depicted the Río Tula murders, which the author compared to the Holocaust. The author noted that when Durazo was finally detained, "he had a mustache, was thin, but he could never lighten his [skin] color nor lighten his black soul."[94] Drawn in a realist fashion, the series portrayed Durazo as an evil, criminal mastermind with scenes that depicted the various torture techniques that he and his men deployed and their involvement in drug trafficking. *El infierno del Negro Durazo* also frequently used the rape of beautiful white women to represent Durazo's cruelty and corruption and to allow readers to satisfy their morbid voyeurism. The comic books thus deployed narratives around race and hypersexuality to elucidate state violence and impunity.

The *Picardías del Negro Durazo* (Black Durazo's dirty tricks) series assumed a much lighter tone but deployed similar tropes to explain corruption and to mock Durazo. Rather than showing a hypermasculine and criminal mastermind, the *Picardías* series depicted Durazo as a childish, impotent, and blundering buffoon, deploying another racialized characterization historically linked to both Black and Indigenous peoples. This series was by far the more popular of the two comic books, circulating 150,000 copies per issue compared to *El infierno*'s 50,000.[95] *Picardías* was secretly edited by Editores Asociados Mexicanos and spearheaded by the administrative director of the *Excélsior* newspaper. Each issue gave readers the opportunity to mock the ex-chief of police, who appeared cartoonishly obese and often burst into tears or wet himself when things went awry. Scenes also depicted Durazo as an emasculated husband whose imperious wife routinely humiliated him. Like *El infierno*, such narratives used gendered language as a vehicle for critique. In *Picardías*, however, Durazo's childishness and impotence made him a source of ridicule. Here, too, Durazo's skin color stood in for his low moral character and his unfitness for office. Supporting characters employed a litany of terms to mock his dark skin, including "black sausage" and "Ethiopian god incarnate." One issue made the critique even more obvious with its mocking title: "This Black Guy Wants to Govern Us" (see figure 4.3).[96]

In the cover image, Durazo is clad like a Roman emperor and oversees the construction of classical sculptures presumably destined for one of his mansions. Meanwhile, his obsequious second-in-command, Francisco Sahagún Baca, oozes praise for the chief of police. The juxtaposition of the title and the imagery suggest that Durazo is a low-class impostor. Here the implication could not be clearer: Durazo's ineptitude and corruption are intimately tied to his skin color and class background, which the authors use to naturalize his unfitness for office. By mercilessly humiliating Durazo, the comic books provided a catharsis for popular anger against corrupt and abusive police. In the absence of official justice, mocking the former chief of police was the only means for ordinary residents to vent their anger.

The *Picardías* comics allowed readers to not only mock Durazo but also to laugh at their own misfortune. Drawing on González's allegations,

Figure 4.3 Cover of *Picardías del Negro Durazo* comic book.

one scene showed a man paying an exorbitant impound fee after his car was towed and stripped by police. Defeated by an intransigent bureaucracy, the man is forced to drive away in a car without wheels.[97] The comic book also treated the topic of sexual violence: In one episode, police officers try to rob a nearby pedestrian. When they discover that he is carrying nothing but a pizza, they gang-rape him in their vehicle. After he is thrown naked from the car, the victim only complains that his pizza has gotten cold.[98] Sexual violence by police officers had become a frequent source of denunciation in Mexico City, but this representation invited readers to laugh at how accustomed they had grown to humiliations by police.

On June 29, FBI agents arrested Durazo in Puerto Rico and removed him to Los Angeles, where he was imprisoned while he awaited trial. He remained there for one year and eight months before being extradited to Mexico. While the de la Madrid administration claimed the arrest was evidence of a successful anticorruption campaign, this chapter suggests that the scandal shaped calculations regarding how to proceed. Indeed, the government did not initially appear eager to indict Durazo and waited a full year after de la Madrid took office to pursue charges. Moreover, the administration monitored the publication of articles and comics about Durazo, displaying concerns that the case could spin out of control and spark popular protests. Comic book publishers were aware of this; they used fake addresses and pseudonyms, and their distributors drove in unmarked vehicles to avoid detection.[99]

In a Mexican Senate debate following Durazo's arrest, one senator described popular opinion as the catalyst for prosecution. Explicitly mentioning *Lo negro del Negro Durazo*, the senator emphasized that "Durazo's case has national interest and demands public satisfaction."[100] He even acknowledged official responsiveness to the press as a source of pride, noting that Mexico allowed denuncia journalism to thrive. He added that, based on what it reported, "the [office of the] Federal Attorney General pursues and punishes the guilty. If it did not, the government would be reprimanded." Durazo was imprisoned upon his arrival to Mexico and later sentenced to twenty-five years in prison, though he would ultimately serve fewer than eight years. But the case highlighted a key weakness of the justice system: institutional accountability and justice hinged on the persistent publicity provided by reporters and scandalous cultural production. Moreover, the senator's praise for denuncia journalism rang hollow after the recent murder of the country's most famous reporter.

## "THE JOURNALIST WHO KNEW TOO MUCH"

Just one month earlier, on May 30, 1984, Buendía was assassinated, realizing his long-standing predictions of his inevitable demise. He had left his office in Juárez, a downtown neighborhood crowded with office buildings, department stores, and hotels, at around 6:30 PM. As Buendía walked to the parking garage, a young man approached him from behind and shot him four times at point-blank range.[101] The murder of a journalist of Buendía's stature was unprecedented in Mexico and elicited shock and fear. Writing for *Nexos* magazine, Héctor Aguilar Camín reflected that "it would be difficult to select a better target than Buendía to fill Mexican society with a sense of dread, anarchy, and ominous change in public life."[102] Another journalist wondered "Who's next?"—voicing fears that none were safe if the most famous journalist could be murdered.

Criminal investigators and foreign correspondents speculated that the assassination was retaliation for Buendía's combative coverage. *Le Monde* reported the murder under the ominous headline, "The Journalist Who Knew Too Much."[103] The *New York Times* eulogized Buendía as a political insider whose "columns made enemies of dozens of powerful people. He received frequent death threats during his career, and he took them seriously. The columnist carried a pistol at all times."[104] Mexican intelligence officials, however, were interested in what Buendía had not yet published. Agents for the DFS were the first to arrive at the crime scene, and they ascended to the columnist's office and allegedly took folders containing his recent research, which promised to implicate the intelligence agency in the drug trade.[105]

Publicly, however, the DFS maintained that the perpetrator could be found in the text of "Red Privada" or in the myriad threats that Buendía received from right-wing groups. Agents reviewed his column and identified the number of times that Buendía had discussed an individual, group, or corporation since January 1983. Such aggregations assumed that all references were negative. The final tally showed that Jorge Díaz Serrano and the clergy received the highest mentions, each appearing in "Red Privada" twenty-seven times over the previous sixteen months. Durazo appeared ten times, and Coca-Cola and McDonald's collectively appeared seven times.[106] Notably absent from the initial list of suspects were any current officeholders.

Mexico City's political class and media workers turned out in force for Buendía's funeral, evidencing the columnist's far-ranging influence. His close ties with DFS and Ministry of the Interior officials had earned him criticism while making Buendía appear invulnerable to attack. Yet public commen-

Figure 4.4 "En el Ateneo de Angangueo, 1981," *Nexos*, July 1984, 7.

tary largely silenced these political relationships. In an article on the murder, *Nexos* portrayed the columnist as daring and brave, while including a photograph that suggested Buendía's more complex position vis-à-vis power brokers.[107] The photograph pictured prominent journalists at El Ateneo de Angangueo, a regular gathering of Mexico City intellectuals in the upscale Condesa neighborhood.

Seated around a table on a leafy patio are Fernando Benítez, Buendía, Elena Poniatowska, and Iván Restrepo; they flank President López Portillo, presumably the guest of honor. The men are dressed sharply in dark suits and ties, and Poniatowska is outfitted in a dazzling white dress with her blond hair feathered back. The snapshot conveys wealth, power, and security, but Buendía's murder disrupted this glossy image of a relationship among equals and reminded reporters that the threat of violence always lurked in their social relationships with powerholders.

Some commentators did challenge the depiction of Buendía as an innocent martyr. In a lengthy DFS memorandum, reporter Jorge Jóseph asserted that the columnist was not a truth teller but rather "a gangster journalist" who used his column as a weapon to extort the powerful.[108] A former colleague from *La Prensa*, Jóseph painted Buendía as morally bankrupt, alleging that the columnist had grown rich from his journalism. This alone would not distinguish Buendía from any other director of a popular newspaper, and Jóseph further portrayed the columnist as overly impressionable. He blamed the influence of colleagues like Elena Poniatowska and Enrique Ramírez y Ramírez for Buendía's ideological drift to the Left. Jóseph asserted that Buendía's assassination would serve the interests of the Soviet Union, which could blame the CIA. For Jóseph, the murder did not augur dangerous changes for press freedom but rather for communist incursion.

Fictionalized accounts of Buendía's murder linked the assassination to another scandal when film director Ismael Rodríguez Jr. released *Masacre en el Río Tula* in 1985.[109] The film told the story of Víctor, a Mexico City cab driver unwittingly drawn into a Colombian drug trafficking circle. Víctor's character was based upon Armando Magalléan Pérez, a Mexican taxi driver murdered in the Río Tula case. *Masacre* portrayed a villainous Mexico City police force that profited from the capital's surging criminal activity. The Colombian drug gang and Víctor appeared sympathetic in comparison, as the film ends with their torture and murder at the hands of the Mexican special forces.

While Durazo and his counterparts were not named in the film, the movie was still censored and prohibited from showing in Mexico City until 1991.[110] The press provided many possible explanations for the film's censorship, but most reporters framed it as a response to the film's depiction of a journalist whose murder police had inadvertently caused. The police commissioner in *Masacre* ominously warned, "It is more dangerous to kill a journalist than a drug boss."[111] The film reminded viewers not only of the Río Tula case but also of Buendía's murder and accusations of foul play. A film adaptation of González's book ran into similar problems and within one week of the movie's release, the General Cinematography Office (Dirección General de Cinematografía), overseen by the Ministry of the Interior, removed it from major theaters.[112]

Even with Durazo behind bars, the echoes of his scandal continued to preoccupy governing officials and outrage Mexican citizens. Just two months after the film's release, reports surfaced that DFS director José Zorrilla was involved in drug trafficking. Prosecutors also identified him as the intellectual author of Buendía's assassination, arguing that Zorrilla feared the columnist was going to reveal linkages between security organizations and drug-trafficking organizations.¹¹³ Yet it was not until January 16, 1993, that Zorrilla was convicted and sentenced to thirty-five years in prison. Buendía's murder, along with the revelation of DFS involvement, considerably dampened optimism regarding the opening of the press.

José González also did not weather the scandal well. He suffered a brutal attack from Durazo's hired thugs, who beat him bloody and permanently blinded him in one eye.¹¹⁴ Durazo also sued González for libel and won. In 1986 a judge ruled that González owed Durazo 100 million pesos for "moral damages." One *El Universal* columnist ominously linked this decision with Buendía's death, noting that "we now not only have to be careful that what happened to Buendía doesn't happen to us, but we also have to be prepared ... to defend ourselves against inept judges," referring to the magistrate who decided González's case.¹¹⁵ These cases, the columnist asserted, showed that journalists risked legal action or worse if they insisted on publishing denunciations.

## CONCLUSION

The case of Arturo "El Negro" Durazo became one of the most iconic scandals in twentieth-century Mexico. This chapter has traced the circuitous path by which denuncia coverage of economic mismanagement and police corruption electrified an audience that extended beyond Mexico City. While many residents might not read *Proceso*, which appealed to left-leaning members of the educated middle class, they encountered the scandal because print media informed a wider cultural matrix, including television, popular books, comics, and talk radio. *Proceso* journalists facilitated the popularization of print exposés by collaborating directly with González to shepherd the publication of his sensational tell-all account. The scandal thrived for years because it resonated with public resentment toward financial and physical insecurity and outrage at the impunity that reigned among the high-ranking officials. Escaping the control of any individual author, the case inspired myriad creative reinterpretation in films, comics, graffiti, and street performance. The scandal generated such popular pressure for justice that the administration had no choice but to respond.

Most scandals followed a similar trajectory, beginning first with exposure, then outrage, and finally the expiation that brought the case to a logical close. Durazo's punishment did not reduce popular interest in his case, however. One of the DFS's final reports described the proliferation of popular comic books in November 1985; the intelligence agent noted that by demonstrating acts of injustice and corruption, the comic books "smear the reputations of some current administration officials."[116] The report points to the government's efforts to censor popular depictions of Durazo's corruption even after his arrest. DFS agents aptly summarized the reasons for doing so by concluding that the magazines "make a mockery of officials and the very system of government." While the de la Madrid government claimed Durazo's indictment and imprisonment as part of the moral renovation's successes, the press and popular cultural products described his corruption as delegitimizing the whole regime and not simply the previous administration.

It is tempting to interpret the confrontational coverage of police abuse and economic mismanagement through the conceptual framework of a watchdog press that was gaining greater independence from the state. But this chapter emphasizes that denuncia reporters were engaged in a constant balancing act of concealment and revelation. For example, Buendía revealed the perpetrators of the Río Tula homicides without directly naming Durazo. In discussing the assault against Gama, Buendía also concealed his close connections with the very organization that attacked the Radio Educación reporter. Castillo, meanwhile, called out Buendía's dissimulation while only referring obliquely to the columnist. Finally, comics discussed the Durazo case while providing false publishing houses and addresses, preventing audiences (and, critically, intelligence agents) from identifying the authors. In short, revealing wrongdoing often rested upon the preservation of myriad other secrets. Moreover, this interplay of concealment, revelation, and dissimulation could fracture publics rather than bridging divides between them. With veiled references and silences, columnists disclosed their insider knowledge to particular audiences while excluding those who could not decode the layered messages. Finally, while the Mexican public sphere was becoming more robust in terms of the voices and issues represented, Buendía's murder augured increasing violence in later years as public officials and criminal organizations colluded in drug trafficking.

Cultural production around the Durazo scandal also mobilized existing gender and racial prejudices to generate outrage. Comic books and González's memoir became lightning rods for popular anger toward police. Years of experiencing unfair arrests, beatings, and extortion had generated deep-seated detestation for police. The growth of urban insecurity and crime further deepened anger toward the incompetence and inaction of the police department. Comic books and González's tell-all account provided cathartic outlets for ordinary people to ridicule Durazo, the highest representative of the police department. These publications mobilized tropes of dark-skinned men as either hypersexual or impotent; brutally evil or passively childlike. Racialized and gendered stereotypes thus provided a language for mocking and disqualifying Durazo. The tensions within the Durazo case underscore some of the weaknesses of thinking of press responsibility or freedom only in terms of independence from government restraint. In this case, widespread criticism of public officials created publics united around the idea that the darker classes were unfit to hold power.

CHAPTER 5

# A MEDIATED DISASTER

The imprisonment of high-profile figures like Arturo Durazo and Jorge Díaz Serrano signaled an important change in political culture. But making an example of select officials did not alter the everyday experience of corruption. When the most devastating earthquake in Mexico's recorded history struck the capital on September 19, 1985, political corruption acquired new significance. Evidence emerged that housing negligence, construction fraud, and illegal labor practices had resulted in thousands of deaths, sparking intense debates about the consequences of undemocratic governance.

As residents were heading to work, school, or just waking up, the tremors (measuring 7.8 on the Richter scale) toppled hundreds of buildings in the city's densely populated historic and commercial center. The twisted entrails of destroyed landmarks blocked major thoroughfares; chemical spills engulfed structures in conflagrations that blazed for days; pipelines erupted, flooding streets and buildings; and electricity and phone towers collapsed, cutting the city's telecommunications network off from the rest of the country. Most tragically, thousands of people remained trapped under wrecked buildings as emergency workers struggled to respond to the crisis. Within the first twenty-four hours, officials confirmed only 378 deaths, while newspapers reported up to four thousand fatalities and ten thousand wounded.[1] The earthquake also displaced up to eight hundred thousand residents, who were forced to sleep in the streets that night.[2] The following evening more buildings collapsed when an aftershock measuring 6.5 on the Richter scale hit, aggravating the population's panic.

This was a natural disaster with political consequences. Within ten days, Mexican opinion leaders argued that the earthquake signaled a definitive turning point for the country. One of the president's political advisers acknowledged that "the earthquakes have made society question the legitimacy of the political system and their confidence in our way of life."[3] The tremors disinterred evidence of illicit activity, including the bodies of tortured prisoners in the PGR basement; shoddy construction materials such as sand-filled columns; and clandestine sweatshops hidden in plain sight. Such powerful physical evidence, and the media exposés that publicized it, ignited popular outrage and placed governing officials on the defensive.

The onslaught of scandals, alongside broad-based protests, shaped the perception of a political rupture. Opinion writers held the government responsible for the lives that might have been saved if help had arrived during those critical first hours. Chroniclers explored intimate experiences of trauma and loss, as well as widespread fury at corruption and discrimination.[4] In the face of a state-imposed "information blockade," radio provided important, up-to-date news on the locations of shelters, the status of building inspections and demolitions, and the damage sites that still required rescue assistance.[5] Denunciations also featured a greater diversity of voices and perspectives. Neighborhood associations and labor organizations created bulletins that addressed community concerns. Academics organized press conferences to amplify the voices of rescue volunteers and mobilized residents. Newspapers with known alliances within the government, including *El Día*, *El Universal*, and *Excélsior*, also pursued investigations into official negligence.[6] Structural changes facilitated this uncommonly critical stance. The economic crisis had squeezed state budgets, reducing the funds available for bribes to journalists.[7] Long-standing advertising agreements also diminished with the mass privatization of public companies; over the following decades, the private sector would assume a more prominent role in shaping news coverage.

The earthquake was Mexico's first mediated natural disaster, meaning that exchanges across multiple platforms shaped the perceptions and consequences of the event. For weeks, broadcast and print media discussed little else, and governing officials and organized residents alike read the political possibilities through this coverage. Residents' subjectivities were shaped by the ways in which mainstream media covered their communities. Victims also contested depoliticized representations that made a spectacle of the tragedy; they produced their own press bulletins, insisted on videotaping political negotiations, or simply refused to give interviews or to appear on camera.

This chapter highlights how scandals emerging from the 1985 earthquake brought contests over public space and representation into sharp relief.

## THE MEDIATIZATION OF ORGANIZED RESIDENTS

Many people remained trapped under heavy rubble after apartment complexes and hospitals collapsed. The city government was notoriously slow to send rescue assistance, leading neighbors and students to mobilize their own rescue teams.[8] Volunteers tunneled through the wreckage with oxygen tanks and water, hoping to buy survivors a few more hours before the heavy concrete obstructions could be removed. These *topos* (moles), as they became known, soon figured prominently as central protagonists in media coverage. Broadcast and print media alternatively characterized volunteers as agents of democratization, self-interested publicity seekers, or anarchists who obstructed the legitimate efforts of the Mexican military and the Red Cross. These representations had real consequences; they could signify differential access to resources, and they shaped governing officials' disposition toward organized residents.

Four days after the earthquake, Carlos Monsiváis published a chronicle that became one of the most widely cited news items on the volunteer rescue efforts. In *Proceso*'s lead article, titled "The Solidarity of the Population Was Actually a Takeover of Power," he described how ordinary people assumed the responsibilities that normally fell to congressional representatives, traffic cops, and firefighters.[9] Weaving together eyewitness testimonies, Monsiváis vividly portrayed, for example, the youths who spent hours searching for survivors and the homemakers who made sandwiches to feed the volunteers. Taking a serious tone uncommon to his generally tongue-in-cheek writing, Monsiváis argued that "Mexico City experienced a takeover of power, among the most noble in its history, that went far beyond the limits of mere solidarity."[10] While he did not believe that rescue workers had literally displaced the state, his phrasing of a "takeover" rhetorically underscored the political and cultural significance of residents' self-organization. With his reference to "mere solidarity," he countered government attempts to frame volunteer efforts as apolitical manifestations of patriotism.

Monisváis challenged mass media attempts to minimize the physical and political impact of the disaster. He took particular issue with coverage by Televisa, the broadcast monopoly that owned seventy-eight out of the country's eighty-five television stations by the mid-1970s.[11] Three days after the earthquake Raúl Velasco had returned to host his popular variety show,

*Siempre en Domingo*, and reassured viewers that "everything is the same, minus a few buildings."[12] Ironically, the broadcast monopoly's infrastructure had been seriously affected by the earthquake, and eighty Televisa employees died when one of the company's buildings collapsed. Two other company buildings and one antenna were also severely damaged, cutting all transmission in the initial hours after the disaster. Other television programs further echoed the government's message that the city had "returned to normal," while urging residents not to leave their homes nor meddle in the state's clean up and rescue efforts.

Monsiváis, however, hoped that the civilian mobilization would succeed where other grassroots organizing had failed. The co-optation of the 1968 student movement had been one of his biggest disappointments. Like other antistatist leftists, Monsiváis rejected Leninist tactics of negotiating with PRI organizations. He instead idealized self-criticism, pluralism, and unmediated dialogue; he admired U.S. culture for demonstrating these qualities and wished to see them develop in Mexico.[13] With low voter turnout for newly formed leftist coalitions, Monsiváis was not optimistic that opposition parties would be successful. Instead he saw an independently mobilized civil society as the greatest hope for political change. His pronunciation of a "takeover" was a rhetorical strategy that suggested that ordinary people had rejected the PRI's corporatist model of governance. The article's accompanying photographs underscored the overwhelming civilian rescue efforts. One image, simply titled "Help" (see figure 5.1), invited viewers to imagine themselves as part of the effort.

In the foreground, facing away from the camera, young men stand waiting to receive orders. With the camera placed in the middle of the action, the viewer's gaze is drawn in the same direction, toward the volunteers who have scaled ladders, climbed the wreckage, and stand poised with shovels. One individual at the center of the image points to something outside the frame, seemingly instructing viewers to join in the urgent rescue efforts. The photograph's vantage point suggests that readers should look to civil society for direction.

As Mexico's premier cultural critic, Monsiváis's framework shaped how some neighborhood groups understood their own mobilization. His reputation for independence and his history of activism gave him the social capital that made his arbitration credible.[14] Print media and neighborhood bulletins liberally borrowed from Monsiváis's article to argue that Mexico City civil society had blossomed. One housing rights advocacy group quoted the "Takeover" article in its October 1 bulletin, *Dinámica Habitacional*. Invoking

Figure 5.1 "Ayuda," *Proceso*, September 23, 1985, 9.

the significance of residents' organizing, the bulletin echoed Monsiváis's declaration that "Mexico City experienced a takeover of power, among the most noble in its history, that went far beyond the limits of mere solidarity."[15] The bulletin did not attribute the statement, but included quotes, indicating that the *Proceso* article had achieved wide resonance only ten days after its publication. In adopting Monsiváis's language, the organization's leaders framed their demands as marking a fundamental shift in state-society relations that surpassed limited housing goals.[16]

This rhetorical framework also heightened government concerns that thousands of displaced residents would organize outside PRI structures. While governing officials publicly praised volunteer rescue efforts as evidence of Mexican patriotism and resilience, they privately worried that they were losing control over middle-class citizens. Fears of political anarchy were evident in negotiations between the Ministry of Urban Development and Ecology (Secretaría de Desarrollo Urbano y Ecología, or SEDUE) and city center residents whose housing had been damaged.

In the first meeting on September 27, SEDUE director Guillermo Carrillo Arena obliquely referenced Monsiváis's article. He asserted that the city government was regaining control and no longer required residents' help, taking literally Monsiváis's declaration that civil society had usurped state authority. As was common discursive practice, the SEDUE director only made veiled references to Monsiváis, not wishing to amplify the chronicler's fame. Carrillo Arena obliquely responded to the "Solidarity" article, however, by using the precise language of a "takeover" of power—a framework and title unique to Monsiváis's article. After a lengthy and tense exchange with community leaders, Carrillo Arena grew frustrated that the neighborhood groups remained unaffiliated with PRI institutions. He repeatedly demanded to know who made up the groups and emphasized that the government only knew how to work with PRI organizations, adding, "We cannot open a consultation office for 30 million Mexicans." Carrillo Arena worried that references to political rebellion, however rhetorical, would lead to chaos. He asserted that "the government does not accept, in any way, being overtaken, and the government does not accept, in any way, that you are going to take it over. And the government does not accept, in any way, negotiating with groups that will not be precise about who they are, where they are located, and whom they represent. We are extremely interested right now in an organized civil society."[17] He distinguished between "organized" civil society, which worked through state structures, and the anarchic independent civil society invoked by Monsiváis, highlighting how the term itself became contested after the earthquake.[18]

Displaced residents organized to demand housing reconstruction and transparent and timely building inspections, but they confronted persistent government efforts to deny responsibility for the extensive damage. Residents' mobilizations were mediated by radio, television, and print media, which sought to answer the questions central to these negotiations: Was an uncommonly strong tremor to blame for the collapsed apartment complexes, which were constructed just a few decades prior? Or did blame reside with the construction firms who used shoddy building materials to cut costs, city officials who issued building permits in exchange for bribes, or public housing authorities who had not properly maintained the buildings? Perhaps it was the residents who made unauthorized changes to their apartments, tearing down walls that might have better withstood the tremors. The answers to these questions had serious ramifications for displaced residents, resulting in fraught debates about the disaster.

These concerns were particularly acute in the Nonoalco-Tlatelolco public housing complex. Situated just north of the historic city center, the complex housed over one hundred thousand people and accounted for 40 percent of the residents affected by the disaster.[19] President Adolfo López Mateos had inaugurated Tlatelolco, as the housing development was commonly called, in the early 1960s and heralded the modernist complex as evidence of the state's democratic development. Yet in 1968 this neighborhood became the site of state repression; snipers positioned themselves in the high-rise buildings and targeted protesters who had gathered in the Plaza de las Tres Culturas below. In addition to a direct attack, the complex suffered from negligence; by the late 1970s the housing development had fallen into disrepair, with numerous outstanding tenant requests for updates and repairs. Tlatelolco residents were among the first to mobilize after the earthquake, and they blamed federal housing authorities for the loss of so many lives.[20]

Tlatelolco neighborhood groups complained that SEDUE officials failed to provide accurate information to residents and misrepresented their meetings to the broader public.[21] In response, residents organized marches to the president's residence and to the Congress. They also circulated their own bulletin, *El Tlatelolca*, and planned to videotape their second meeting with SEDUE officials. In the 1980s video technology became lighter (easier to carry) and more affordable, allowing artists, opposition parties, and labor unions to record and disseminate their organizing efforts.[22] On September 30, neighborhood leaders arrived to their meeting with UNAM television camera crews in tow. SEDUE officials insisted that the meeting was private, however, and that a government commission was solely "responsible for the diffusion of all issues related to the earthquake."[23] Housing officials underscored the state's total authority to convey the earthquake's ostensibly apolitical meaning. In a tense standoff, SEDUE camera crews filmed the residents as UNAM camera crews filmed the housing authorities.[24] Ultimately, neighborhood leaders were forced to remove their cameras if they wished the meeting to proceed. Even though the SEDUE planned to subsequently publicize the meeting's results, officials wished to conceal an uncontrolled dialogue that might make the organization vulnerable to criticism.

Public officials also mobilized experts to instruct residents in the proper way to understand the tragedy. To this end, the Ministry of the Interior produced a new radio program, *Los Expertos Colaboran* (*The Experts Weigh In*), which invoked scientific authority to undermine accusations of corrupt housing construction and negligent building maintenance. Broadcast by the state-owned Mexican Radio Institute (Instituto Mexicano de la Radio), the program's opening credits declared the disaster to be an "unforeseeable accident of nature" and praised Mexico City residents for banding together in a time of crisis.

In the third episode, which aired on September 30, the host invited a structural engineer and a seismologist to respond to accusations of corruption. He noted, "People are saying that government buildings were the hardest hit; is there any explanation for that?"[25] Residents and journalists alleged that officials had illegally sold construction licenses, which allowed private contractors to skirt regulations and use cheaper materials. This created unstable structures that quickly collapsed when the earthquake hit, while many colonial-era buildings remained standing. Newspapers like *Excélsior* had also reported long-standing demands for repairs by Tlatelolco residents, suggesting that the extensive damage could have been avoided.[26] In response to the radio host's question, Jorge Prince Alfaro of the Mexican Society of Seismic Engineering (Sociedad Mexicana de Ingeniería Sísmica) chuckled dismissively. He drew clear boundaries between public and private industry and argued that private companies constructed the buildings, while the government was simply a tenant and therefore not responsible for failures.[27] Prince Alfaro did not deny that public buildings were disproportionately affected, but instead tried to complicate ideas of who bore responsibility.

The careers of both guests suggest, however, that there was no clear dividing line between public and private construction. Both Prince Alfaro and civil engineer Fernando Lozoya sat on committees that established building codes and regulations in Mexico City; both belonged to public unions; and both consulted for organizations that established professional standards.

Meanwhile, their private construction work relied on partnerships with public fiduciaries and required close ties with city officials, who provided licenses.

The guest experts argued that blaming the damage on corruption was a misguided attempt to make sense of the earthquake's devastation. Civil engineer Lozoya declared that the population was seeking to find solace by blaming the government, but the reality was not so simple. He instead returned to a natural explanation and underscored the earthquake's unprecedented strength. Lozoya insisted that criticisms stemmed from the desire to find a culprit and thus to be able to comprehend the devastation.[28] His comment reflected broader tendencies by public radio and the Ministry of Health and Assistance (Secretaría de Salubridad y Asistencia) to use psychological prescriptions to undermine public criticism.

State-sponsored broadcast programs, neighborhood news bulletins, radio call-in shows, and extensive print reportage highlight the intertextual exchanges that pervaded news coverage after the earthquake. Public officials took to the airwaves to counter damaging articles, and influential writers like Monsiváis shaped popular and government outlooks on the volunteer mobilization. The SEDUE director, for example, misinterpreted Monsiváis's "Solidarity" article as a forecast of political anarchy and accordingly hardened his stance toward residents. In this sense, the volunteer efforts and negotiations with residents were shaped by media representations. Contests over political interpretation became particularly fraught when a viral scandal hit news media.

## THE SPECTACLE OF "THE POOR WOMEN"

The discovery of clandestine sweatshops just south of the bustling historic center became one of the most electrifying and enduring scandals after the earthquake. It offered a gripping narrative of young and underprivileged girls and women laboring under exploitative conditions in modern-day sweatshops run by Jewish-Mexican and Lebanese-Mexican owners. More than sixteen hundred garment workers died when the tremors reduced some two hundred workshops to rubble. Many of these unmarked eleven-story buildings were not zoned to support heavy sewing machinery and collapsed into piles only three stories tall, sending reams of fabric across the major thoroughfare of San Antonio Abad.[29] The garment workers' case soon became ubiquitous in broadsheets, tabloids, and comic books that dramatized the case. Many city dwellers would also encounter the scandal aurally or visually, as television and radio presenters interviewed garment workers and produced new programs to explore the case. Interpretations varied as PRI officials, investigative journalists, and garment workers themselves mobilized the scandal to distinct ends. Incapable of stemming the spectacle around the case, governing officials tried to limit the political fallout by reframing damaging news items in their favor.

*La Jornada*, a new tabloid-size daily, was among the first to break the garment workers' story.[30] Founded in September 1984, the newspaper's stated mission was to contribute to formal democratization and to "the needs and demands of workers in the countryside and the city, as well as the country's marginalized majority."[31] The acronym of *La Jornada*'s controlling company, DEMOS (Desarrollo de Medios, S.A.), underscored the founders' democratic aspirations. This society-centered focus was also reflected in the financial structure of the newspaper; reporters were primary and equal shareholders of the cooperative, which they believed would foster more democratic decision making. This model emerged from founders' previous experiences at *Unomásuno*. Left-leaning essayists, including Carlos Monsiváis and Iván Restrepo, and reporters, including Carmen Lira and Víctor Payán, had resigned from *Unomásuno* in 1983, frustrated by undemocratic management. The director, Manuel Becerra Acosta, had surreptitiously purchased the majority of the cooperative's shares to gain control of the periodical.[32] He was also frequently absent from the newsroom, allegedly due to his struggle with alcoholism. Some writers who resigned also believed that Becerra Acosta had aligned with the government of President Miguel de la Madrid, possibly to gain relief on an outstanding debt owed to the state financial lender, Nafinsa. The exodus of *Unomásuno* staff drained the newspaper of its significant talent and diminished the publication's reputation for independence. Yet the departed reporters overstated the extent to which *Unomásuno* was hamstrung by public officials, at least initially. Indeed, the newspaper continued to publish chronicles that were concerned with issues facing ordinary Mexicans, and its reporters also remained committed to investigative journalism. Even so, *Unomásuno*'s reputation never recovered after the schism.

*La Jornada* founders widely publicized their venture as the antithesis of *Unomásuno*. They created a cooperative ownership structure and made shares available to the public so that readers could participate. *La Jornada* quickly established itself as an investigative outlet and critically covered the November 1984 explosion of the San Juanico gas plant that killed at least five hundred people and left thousands wounded. *La Jornada*'s reportage on the

1985 earthquake further established the newspaper's credentials as an ally of social movements.

On September 28, journalists Andrea Becerril and Pascual Salanueva reported on the government's apparent indifference toward some six hundred garment workers who remained trapped in the wreckage of sweatshops.[33] The situation was brought to their attention by surviving garment workers and their families who blocked streets outside the factories to demand rescue aid. According to the reporters, it took city officials over a week to dispatch heavy machinery and experienced French and U.S. aid workers to the damage site. By the time emergency response teams arrived to the Topeka factory, nine days after the earthquake, they could only save twenty-five workers and recover one hundred bodies. The reporters described the rescue of one of the "fortunate" few, twenty-five-year-old Rosa Luz Hernández Rivero. They noted that the emaciated victim was so bruised that her mother could only identify her by the necklace that she wore. References to the rescued woman's youth and femininity signaled her vulnerability and her abandonment by government officials, who had failed to send critical assistance.

Initially little seemed to separate the garment workers' stories from many others after the earthquake, and there was minimal coverage of the clandestine sweatshops until October 3, when *La Jornada* reporter Sara Lovera published one of the most influential exposés on the matter. In her front-page investigative article, cowritten with Luis Alberto Rodríguez, she revealed that city labor officials and private factory owners had colluded first to conceal poor working conditions and later to fire employees without pay. Lovera got the story by sneaking into a dinner organized by the Garment Industry Association (Cámara de la Industria del Vestido). At an event packed with some one thousand industry representatives, she witnessed the association's legal council, Federico Anaya Sánchez, advise employers to suspend all labor without severance pay, which would leave approximately forty thousand workers without any safety net. For readers, the most scandalous detail of the article was Anaya Sánchez's recommendation "that [factory owners] should not worry about paying salaries or indemnities, except in cases where the managers 'really love their workers.'"[34] For many this cynical remark encapsulated the private sector's callousness toward its employees, even at a moment of extreme suffering. The quote anchored extensive coverage of the scandal, and journalists and politicians frequently repeated the statement as evidence of private-sector disregard.[35]

Lovera also exposed Anaya Sánchez's admission, made in the same speech, that city labor officials knowingly colluded to maintain the workers' poor labor conditions in factories. She reported that "the lawyer also informed the business community that they could count on the cooperation of 'my friend' Hugo Vladimiro López Pérez, Director of Labor and Social Welfare of the Department of the Federal District, 'who was going to come, but thought that his words could compromise the authorities.'"[36] Such collusion was an open secret, but the lawyer's frank admission scandalized readers, highlighting how knowledge acquired political significance when it became public. Anaya Sánchez's familiar references to "his friend" also undergirded widespread accusations that the earthquake's toll was directly tied to official corruption. Moreover, López Pérez's statement revealed half-hearted attempts to conceal the labor department's allegiances to bosses. In a personal interview, Lovera wryly recounted the article's reception: "Imagine! [Anaya Sánchez] didn't know that I was there. I wrote the piece and it became a scandal."[37]

The circumstances of the story's uncovering reveal that, at a fundamental level, Mexican investigative journalism thrived when personal relationships tied reporters to their stories. A few prominent *La Jornada* writers and editors, including Monsiváis and Aguilar Camín, respectively, had mothers who were garment workers. Lovera also had connections in the industry, as her mother owned a clothing shop. She gained access to the meeting through a close family friend who had been invited to the dinner and offered the reporter her ticket. As Lovera quipped, "I put on a silk dress and went as the owner of a clothing factory." In addition to requiring ingenuity and personal connections, Lovera's access to the meeting was contingent on her racial and class background. Light-skinned, upper middle class, and dressed in silk, she could easily pass as the wife of a factory owner.

Lovera's reporting united two of her long-standing political projects: workers' and women's rights. She had aligned with leftist movements from a young age. At fifteen, she joined the MLN, and one year later she became part of a Maoist group, the Communist Spartacus League (Liga Comunista Espártaco). In the 1970s she participated in the burgeoning feminist movement, joining liberal organizations including Women in Solidarity and Action (Mujeres en Acción Solidaria) and socialist associations like Feminist Struggle (Lucha Feminista). Unlike many reporters of her generation, Lovera studied journalism formally and graduated in 1968 from Mexico's oldest journalism school, the Carlos Septién García School of Journalism (Escuela de Periodismo Carlos Septién García). She joined early efforts to democratize media production by studying agricultural communication at the Chapingo National Agricultural School (Escuela Nacionale de Agricultura in Chapingo)—a rural setting distinct from her native Mexico City. In the 1970s Lovera reported for multiple organizations, including the Mexico City mayor's office, but she established her journalism career at *El Día*. In 1981 she moved to *Unomásuno*, and in 1984 she became a founding member of *La Jornada*, where she was assigned the labor beat.[38] Her peers referred to her—disparagingly according to one colleague—as "Sara la Obrera" (a play on her last name, Lovera, and the Spanish word for a female manual worker, *obrera*).[39]

Beginning in the late 1970s Mexico City news publications, especially *El Día* and *Unomásuno*, hired more women and university graduates. Even so, women's presence in newsrooms did not overturn the masculine sociability that nurtured state-press relations. Male reporters often met with their sources in cantinas and at late-night poker games; these social gatherings could be raucous, and they typically excluded women. *Unomásuno* reporters recall that the newspaper's director hosted wild parties where reporters and politicians partook of alcohol, drugs, and prostitutes.[40] Because female reporters did not participate in these social events, they may have been less likely to gain the confidences of inside sources. Lovera's use of disguise was an investigative technique that, while not limited to female reporters, was necessary to gain confidences.[41] Her bracing personal style transgressed norms of feminine docility and alienated some of her peers.[42] She acknowledged as much during an interview, noting, "I was always a woman, and I continue to be a woman, whom many people do not like because I have always been very blunt."[43] Being "blunt" could mean refusing to dissimulate or to mollify her colleagues, behaviors that were particularly expected of women.

Memorable quotes and episodes provided shared reference points as scandalous narratives circulated. As in Lovera's article, which furnished a quote from the garment industry's lawyer, Becerril provided another image that media associated with the garment workers' case. On October 5 the reporter revealed that Elías Serur, owner of the Dimensión Weld clothing company, had entered his factory to recover safes, primary materials, and sewing machinery, even while many of his workers remained trapped in the wreckage. Serur did so with the permission of the city government; an expedited permit allowed him to bypass military personnel guarding the building.[44] The story of factory owners removing their machinery before rescuing their workers went viral, and reporters and broadcasters recited the episode to introduce their audiences to the garment workers' case. For example, Radio Educación launched a program, *La Causa de las Mujeres*, that followed the garment workers' struggle. Accusing factory owners of acting like "real vultures," an anti-Semitic slur, each episode included a sound bite that described how the owners took out their machinery before rescuing survivors.[45] Such memorable quotes and episodes were essential to the circulation of scandals, as they created shared narratives and images while allowing for differing interpretations.

Diverse news outlets followed the story and discovered that similar practices had occurred at other sweatshops. In *El Día*, reporter Georgina Howard interviewed garment workers and their family members who were camped outside the Amal factory (whose name ironically means "hope" in Arabic). The camp occupants intended to block managers from entering the building, hoping to pressure their bosses to pay indemnities and outstanding wages. Howard conveyed the outrage that families felt after "owner José Asez Abad, knowing there were still signs of life last Thursday afternoon, cordoned off the building, but not without first taking out some machinery and money." She described a father, whose daughter remained trapped under the wreckage, screaming, "I accuse the owner of criminal negligence."[46] By ignoring cries for help, the father argued that the factory owner had left his workers to die. Howard included additional details that highlighted the owner's perversity. For example, family members had labored for hours alongside volunteers to clear pathways through the heavy rubble to reach survivors, only to see owners use their tunnels to remove fabric and sewing machinery.

Many reporters and public officials resorted to gendered depictions to convey the plight of garment workers, around 85 percent of whom were female. At times they simply referred to the workers as the "poor women," suggesting that factory owners had failed in their paternal duties.[47] Howard's *El Día* article headline described garment workers in similar terms, lamenting, "Squashed by Employer Ambition, Surviving Seamstresses Cry for Help from Authorities."[48] Until the economic crisis, working women were generally divorced or widowed, and cultural norms dictated that women should only work outside the home if they lacked a male provider.[49] Stressing the feminine and childlike qualities of the garment workers downplayed their organizing capacity and reflected the discursive feminization of poverty. Gendered narratives suggested the need for guidance and urged labor authorities to save "poor women" from greedy factory owners.

In their demands to labor and federal officials, Dimensión Weld's garment workers also invoked their motherly obligations. Rather than citing a liberal language of universal rights, they appealed to the state's paternal duty to protect unmarried women, asserting, "We are all single mothers and we don't have anything to eat."[50] While they invoked the state's patriarchal obligation, many of these workers were heads of households who had sustained their families for years. This was evident in an *Unomásuno* article that described the survivors of a collapsed factory on San Antonio Abad. Garment worker Hermelinda Martínez had improbably escaped the building by using a ream of fabric to shimmy out of a window. Martínez told journalist Saide Sesin that she worried about her lost wages, as she was responsible for her seven nieces and nephews. For another poor family from Tecamachalco, Puebla, the death of their seventeen-year-old daughter, María de Jesús Sánchez Azcona, signified a dire economic loss. María had started working at fourteen, and her family depended on her wages to survive. Her father remarked that "she was little, but every two weeks she'd send us a small allowance. Out there in our humble home we did not earn wages because we planted corn and everything was reinvested in the harvest."[51] Her father maintained that he had not wanted his young daughter to work, but "she was proud to help with the expenses. She had six siblings." The interviews testified to the fact that precarious sweatshop labor by women and girls kept many families afloat financially.

Although slower to address the story, the PRI's newspaper *El Nacional* highlighted garment workers' unpreparedness to organize without state tutelage. Articles emphasized that the women were single parents and earned less than the minimum wage, thus finding themselves unable to provide for their children. One piece reported that managers would not allow women time off, even when they needed to take their children to see a doctor.[52] In another *El Nacional* article, the reporter described the camps of family members and friends waiting outside the Amal, S.A., and Skilón factories to hear news about the location of their loved ones: "Fathers, brothers, husbands, and sons of the workers have waited day and night in makeshift tents since September 20."[53] Accompanied by a color photograph of listless family members resting on a makeshift bench, the article portrayed the absence of the garment workers as most acutely felt by the boys and men in their families, who needed their sisters and mothers at home.

*El Nacional* was founded in 1929 to project the views of the newly formed official party, but the newspaper never achieved the influence that its founders envisioned. Though it was circulated free of charge among state bureaucrats and politicians, by the 1970s it was deeply in debt and had a negligible readership. Manuel Buendía observed that the government behaved like a "stingy, ignorant stepmother" toward *El Nacional* and other state-run media outlets. Minimal funding and loose editorial oversight meant that government-funded outlets at times paradoxically worked at cross-purposes with the official party.[54] A 1981 report by the Ministry of Social Communication (Secretaría de Comunicación Social) concurred, describing the newspaper as an embarrassment. Reporters were poorly compensated—paid only two hundred pesos per article rather than given a regular salary—and churned out more low-quality pieces as a result.[55]

*El Nacional* nonetheless facilitated PRI efforts to mobilize the spectacle to their own ends. While the newspaper cannot be read as a direct expression of the party agenda, it offers a glimpse into one way in which the PRI's institutions represented the case. On October 9, the periodical finally weighed in and accused avaricious factory owners of exploiting garment workers. *El Nacional* emphasized the foreignness of the manufacturers—even though they were Mexican born—to deflect criticism away from the public-private collusion that had allowed factory owners to flout labor laws. One reporter discussed the scandal at damage sites, describing how owners "dedicated themselves to hurriedly taking out their machinery and clothing inventory. As of now they continue trying to do so. Why would they care for the lives of their workers? Cheap, plentiful labor."[56] Another journalist reported suspicions that factory owners had removed and disappeared cadavers to avoid paying indemnities to employees' families.[57] While denouncing the unfeeling treatment toward workers, these articles minimized the role that labor regulators had played in protecting factory owners. This reflected a broader government strategy as well. On October 10, the Office of the Federal Attorney General for Labor Protection (Procuraduría Federal de la Defensa del Trabajo, or PFDT) announced that it was suing factory owners on garment workers' behalf, and the organization established an information booth on San Antonio Abad to receive additional reports of abuses.[58] Governing officials mobilized *denuncia* journalism to serve their distinct political ends, demonstrating that scandals were sufficiently flexible to accommodate multiple interpretations.

Sensationalist coverage in *El Nacional* and elsewhere further depoliticized the case. Accounts of the ruined sweatshops read like scenes from a horror film. News articles described the overwhelming odor of decaying bodies that extended for an entire block. One included macabre details of "reams of fabric completely bloody with the remains of human flesh."[59] This imagery conveyed a truly horrifying situation and invited readers into the visual and olfactory experience of the sweatshops. One article even suggested that the workshops were haunted, describing how a psychic had entered one of the factories and heard the voice of a young girl crying.[60] But the fixation on the supernatural invited a distinctly apolitical engagement with the case, silencing urgent questions regarding why the buildings collapsed and how owners operated clandestine sweatshops with impunity. Consuming the spectacle could mean indulging morbid voyeurism rather than mobilizing righteous indignation.

Even so, many national broadsheets, television series, and magazines did detail the complicity between managers and labor authorities. *Excélsior* asserted that negligent government oversight allowed managers to pay garment workers less than minimum wage, to require long hours (often without breaks to use the bathroom or eat lunch), and to deny their workers medical and social security benefits.[61] Since the 1976 change of leadership, the newspaper had returned to its identity as a pro-government organ, but editors evidently felt empowered by the postearthquake public mood to publish more critical pieces. *Excélsior* even reproduced images of a pay slip to provide evidence of paltry wages. The newspaper also highlighted the scandalous comments by owners, who, according to garment workers, threatened, "You can do whatever you want, because I have a lot of money to buy off the authorities."[62] *Unomásuno* similarly reported denunciations that labor officials and PRI representatives were trying to manipulate the scandal rather than help workers.[63]

Pressure mounted for the relevant authorities to take action. On October 15, the minister of labor and social welfare, Arsenio Farell Cubillas, gave a dramatic televised statement in which he admitted that in the Local Labor Settlement and Arbitration Board (Junta Local de Conciliación y Arbitraje, or JLCA) "there is undeniably very serious collusion between labor inspectors, government officials, and unions. It is a monstrous collusion."[64] The uncommonly frank admission electrified public discussions, and *Excélsior* editors asserted that "this is not a 'small' case; it is an issue that polarizes national attention because of the flagrant violation of labor laws."[65] That same day the Ministry of Labor and Social Welfare (Secretaría del Trabajo y Previsión Social) shuttered eleven sweatshops after employers refused to give indemnities to their workers. The PFDT also warned that owners who failed to pay their workers minimum wage would face punishment, including prison sentences and steep fines.[66]

While it was an open secret that labor regulators and union leaders were complicit in maintaining poor working conditions, the open admission by the minister forced a degree of accountability and was followed by the swift punishment of select offenders. The following day, JLCA president Antonio Burelo and Hugo V. López Pérez, the labor official whose statements as reported by Sara Lovera sparked controversy, tendered their resignations.[67] Notably, these were officials operating at the city, and not federal, level. The official trade union confederation, the Revolutionary Confederation of Workers and Peasants (Confederación Revolucionaria de Obreros y Campesinos) also expelled five labor leaders for negligence and corruption, and in early November three factory owners received prison sentences for removing their machinery at the expense of possible survivors. The rapid response by labor authorities highlights the extent to which the media spectacle, combined with popular protests, pressured officials to make a public display of accountability and justice.

## ACTS OF REFUSAL

The scandal no doubt contributed to the punishment of labor officials, but many protesters remained wary of unsolicited press attention, fearing manipulation or deception. Some rescue efforts appeared to be mere publicity stunts, as one team, which included the son of a famous singer, arrived at a damage site with camera crews poised to capture their valiant efforts.[68] Outside another clothing factory, fights erupted as competing groups vied for camera time. Garment workers complained that this distracted from their concerns, and they resented their objectification by media.

A common criticism of televised coverage was that it depoliticized the disaster by focusing disproportionately on the heroism of the rescue efforts. Monsiváis delivered perhaps the most blistering critique in a chronicle for *Proceso*. In a parody of a popular Televisa newscast, Monsiváis portrayed the filming of survivors as exploitative and vulgar. He described camera crews standing idly by during rescue efforts and only jumping to action when a victim was located. Monsiváis relayed, for example, the tongue-in-cheek "tragedy" of a reporter unable to get the spectacular scoop he was hoping for after a successful rescue mission: "The television reporter is exasperated. The interviewee has the chance of a lifetime and it only occurs to him to ask for water. Trapped there for interminable hours of agony that he should have used to better polish his sentences so that when the ultimate opportunity arose, the camera, the microphone, the country, the international community . . . and he asks for water. How anticlimactic!"[69] The scene suggested that the government and its media allies staged rescue efforts to fit a narrative of solidarity and nationalism. With the ironic reference to the interviewee's "chance of a lifetime," Monsiváis accused mainstream reporters of failing to acknowledge the lives at stake in these critical moments. He included the testimonies of displaced residents whom broadcasters did not deem "television-worthy" (*televisibles*). Monsiváis quoted the residents of the working-class Morelos neighborhood stating that "the government and the mass media abandoned us to our fate." For some disenfranchised residents, media attention—however sensationalist—could mean access to critical resources.

Others, however, suggested that news coverage silenced their own voices. On October 16, an *El Día* journalist was flummoxed to find that garment workers declined to be interviewed. The reporter lamented that they had "even stopped believing in the efforts of journalists, refusing to cooperate and on a few occasions even hiding to avoid being photographed."[70] The journalist's frustration implied that the interviewees owed a debt of gratitude for supportive press coverage. Yet garment workers' refusal underscores the extent to which the story had escaped their control. The fact that they resorted to hiding from the camera further suggests that photographers had not respected workers' verbal requests. One individual, Cristina Peralta, who worked for the Dimensión Weld company, explained that the media attention had not translated into "action against the injustices being committed against [us]." Refusing to allow their pain to serve other interests, some garment workers avoided cooperating with media altogether.

Such episodes illustrate not only the power imbalance between reporters and marginalized workers but also the difference in their political goals. This was evident in a televised episode of *Aquí Nos Tocó Vivir*, which aired on Canal Once, a state-funded culture and education channel, four weeks after the earthquake. Journalist Cristina Pacheco interviewed four garment workers who had joined the collective organization efforts; as they spoke, the camera panned to the destroyed buildings behind them and took in the busy streets that surrounded their makeshift camps. Pacheco questioned the women about their working conditions (hours, rates, child care, health benefits), and the workers generally spoke positively about their jobs, indicating that they hoped to return to the factories soon. Pacheco seemed nonplussed; this was not the established story of the garment workers. When pressed, one interviewee admitted that she was reticent to elaborate because her boss might be watching. Pacheco seized on the comment, drawing a larger lesson for viewers: "What you just said concerns me, 'if he finds out.' . . . Do you think that it should be prohibited for people to state their opinion?"[71] The interviewee rejoined, "No, of course not," but she acknowledged that her employer "doesn't like it that people are out here," referring to the camps in front of collapsed factories. The exchange highlighted a tension that pervaded media interest. The moral outrage against factory owners fueled press coverage, while glossing over the lived realities of the garment workers themselves, whose livelihoods and families depended on their jobs. Even sympathetic journalists described the workers as both exploited and uncooperative; as helpless children and heads of households; as union pioneers and ignorant laborers. In these moments, the workers' acts of refusal registered their discontent with media coverage.

With the help of feminist organizations like the Organization for Initiatives on Latin American Development (Coordinación de Iniciativas para el Desarrollo de América Latina), garment workers began issuing their own news bulletins to better mobilize media coverage to their advantage. Lovera recalls visiting the garment workers' camps for months to provide training sessions in media literacy and labor laws.[72] The resulting bulletins were short and to the point; they frequently commented on recent sources of outrage ("The owner [of the Piamonte factory], Jacobo Fasja Dabbad... took out his sewing machines to avoid his responsibility to his workers"). They also publicized their material needs, which were less likely to appear in news coverage. An October 16 bulletin, for example, included the address where donations could be sent.[73] These appeals to "economic and moral support" highlighted how garment workers believed the media could best serve their interests.

On October 20, eight thousand garment workers won expedited registration of an independent union, the September 19 Seamstresses' Union (Sindicato de Costureras 19 de Septiembre). By this point, their reasons for insisting on independence were well known. As *Unomásuno* and other news outlets reported, the Confederation of Mexican Workers (Confederación de Trabajadores de México, or CTM)—the largest of the government-affiliated labor organizations—had "sold collective contracts, signed them behind workers' backs, and maintained illegal relationships with the bosses."[74] Garment workers were not even aware that they belonged to a union. Though governing officials tried to distance the PRI from blame, the party's beleaguered CTM had become a central target of denunciation.

The garment workers' case remains one of the most memorable and recognizable scandals of the 1985 earthquake. Initial coverage began in smaller publications oriented toward the middle classes, but television, radio, and other cultural outlets quickly picked up the story. It offered a neatly bounded morality tale: girls and women exploited at the hands of avaricious factory owners. In addition to drawing upon gendered assumptions about female vulnerability, the scandal connected with the discontent fueled by an economic crisis. Sweatshop conditions exemplified the precariousness with which ordinary Mexicans could identify. Moreover, many blamed foreign exploitation, and particularly by the IMF, for unemployment, inflation, and wage freezes. Blaming allegedly foreign factory owners thus fit within broader narratives that blamed foreign exploitation for the crisis. In the case of the earthquake, however, public officials could not absolve state labor institutions from blame, and public-private collusion became a central theme of denunciations.

## INFORMING FROM THE BOTTOM UP

While many reporters focused on high-level political convulsions, some explored the microlevel processes that augured political change. Chronicles became the defining genre of the earthquake and intervened in conflicts over voice and representation. The long-form genre decentered official and elite narratives by relying on the testimonies of ordinary people. Chroniclers registered a distinct type of denunciation: the everyday disrespect demonstrated by public officials, military personnel, and economic elites. They also traced the affective reactions to the earthquake, offering intimate, first-person narratives that allowed readers to identify with the victims or to imagine themselves as the volunteers. This style of voice democratized the experiences that could be explored and the issues that could be denounced while challenging notions of authority that were often couched in masculinist and purportedly rational terms.[75]

Among the most celebrated chroniclers was Monsiváis, who built on the Mexican literary genre of *crónica* that emerged in the nineteenth-century writings of Manuel Gutiérrez Nájera and Guillermo Prieto, among others.[76] Monsiváis particularly credited flâneur Salvador Novo with shaping his own use of humor, social critique, and "discursive fluidity."[77] By the 1970s new influences also shaped Mexican crónica—particularly New Journalism, the U.S. literary reporting style that privileged firsthand accounts from groups marginalized by mainstream media. Monsiváis was extremely well read, and he admired U.S. writers, including Truman Capote and Tom Wolfe, who had popularized the genre in the United States in the mid-1960s. Like his U.S. counterparts, Monsiváis assumed an ironic, often biting, sensibility to mock dominant power structures. But he adapted New Journalism by omitting the first-person narrator.[78] His chronicles often focused on attacking core values of Mexican culture, such as nationalism, Catholicism, and heteronormativity. This distinguished him from other denuncia journalists who focused almost exclusively on formal politics and rarely interrogated the values and practices that underpinned political culture. In the 1970s chronicles became a key feature of critical and investigative publications like *La Cultura en México*, *Proceso*, and *Unomásuno*.[79]

Novelist and journalist Elena Poniatowska wrote the largest volume of—and arguably the most influential—chronicles after the earthquake. Unlike Monsiváis, who interspersed his uniquely stylized observations with firsthand accounts from interviewees, Poniatowska rarely interjected her own voice. Instead she offered her chronicles as curated spaces for the uninterrupted testimonies of victims and volunteers. She initially submitted her pieces to *Novedades*, where she had contributed articles for twenty years. The editor, however, soon declined to publish more chronicles about the earthquake, saying that "they depressed the readers."[80] This decision, recalled by Poniatowska decades later, highlights how editors understood the difference between sensationalizing tragedy and probing the disaster's emotional consequences. While the former would entertain consumers and sell newspapers, the latter threatened to politicize readers or reduce their interest in the periodical. *La Jornada* expressed interest in Poniatowska's work, and on October 8, 1985, the periodical began the daily publication of Poniatowska's multipage chronicles. Her pieces enjoyed pride of place, occupying the entire back page, which in the tabloid-size paper served as a prominent space for long-form articles. Poniatowska stopped contributing chronicles in December because she, too, "became terribly depressed" by the subject matter.

The child of French and Polish nobility, Poniatowska and her family migrated from Paris to Mexico City during World War II.[81] She initially established her place within Mexican journalism by conducting interviews for the society pages, beginning auspiciously with the U.S. ambassador to Mexico, but she soon became interested in documenting the lives of ordinary people.[82] By the early 1960s reporters were interviewing her for cultural profiles, fascinated by the apparently innocent, blond-haired, blue-eyed woman who had become tangled up in a career dominated by alcoholic men and social climbers.[83] Her best-selling 1971 account of the 1968 student massacre, *La noche de Tlatelolco*, solidified her reputation as a chronicler committed to social justice.[84] Poniatowska moved in a social circle of Mexico City intellectuals that met periodically in the home of Iván Restrepo. She was one of only two women in the group, and was affectionately dubbed "La Princesa" by her male counterparts. She was always meticulously dressed and well coiffed, and her femininity and sophistication may have made her acceptable in the male-dominated field of journalism.

*La Jornada* was a natural fit for Poniatowska's chronicles. According to the editor in chief, Carlos Payán Velver, the periodical aimed to "record the real, everyday experiences that are not always reflected in the concerns and statements of the country's political and economic leaders."[85] Poniatowska's pieces after the earthquake explored issues such as public health services, housing reconstruction, and volunteer rescue efforts. While Monsiváis argued that the spontaneous organizing signified the rejection of an ineffective, corporatist government, Poniatowska mobilized her collected testimonies to identify the personal experiences that led to subtle shifts in political consciousness. After the earthquake her chronicles focused on feelings of outrage at the structural problems facing the country: high levels of inequality, bureaucratic inefficiency and corruption, classism and racism, and an undemocratic and unaccountable city government. The tone was often emotional and earnest, in contrast to Monsiváis's ironic and baroque flourishes.

One of Poniatowska's first chronicles after the earthquake underscored the injustice of the disaster through the testimony of UNAM professor Antonio Lazcano Araujo, who was tasked with spraying cadavers with formaldehyde. Lazcano volunteered at the Mexican Institute for Social Security (Instituto Mexicano del Seguro Social) baseball stadium in Colonia del Valle, a centrally located upper-middle-class neighborhood, where rescue workers deposited thousands of bodies for identification. He vividly portrayed his horror by describing his sensorial experience upon entering the stadium: the intense smell of formaldehyde, the clacking of typewriters as bureaucrats wrote death certificates, the cold sensation on his legs from carrying dry ice, and the visions of dead bodies lined neatly along the ground in hundreds of rows. He described one cadaver that grabbed his attention: "The first one I saw was a tall girl, lying on the ground, very white, her body covered with bruises, completely naked with shaved pubic hair and very large breasts heavy with milk. [The tag] read: 'No. 76, Gynecology-Obstetrics, Hospital Juárez.' I noticed that she had a half-moon shaped tear on her abdomen, and it made me really sad to realize that this woman had just had her baby; her abdomen had not even been sterilized yet."[86] The detail of Lazcano's recollection suggested the profound emotional impact it had on him. The cadaver's exposed body, open incision, and baby signified a heightened vulnerability and loss of innocence. Enraged at the injustice, Lazcano asserted, "It's not fair. It's not fair that in this country, hospitals, schools, government buildings, and public offices fall. It's not fair that it always hits those who are weakest." In conveying Lazcano's account to readers, Poniatowska allowed his observation about inequity to speak for itself; she, in contrast to Monsiváis, did not explicitly argue that there was a process of political awakening underway.

*La Jornada* photographers also captured the haunting experience of identifying the bodies. On September 23, the newspaper's front page featured an intimate portrait by photographer Pedro Valtierra (see figure 5.2). The

Figure 5.2 Pedro Valtierra, "Identificación de cadáveres en el Seguro Social," *La Jornada*, September 23, 1985, 1.

horror of the scene is conveyed in the face of the subject, who somberly covers her mouth to block the smell of rotting cadavers, as she walks slowly through rows of pine box caskets in the baseball stadium. In the background are the scoreboard, bleachers, and cheerful advertisements: the site of leisure and entertainment has been transformed into a massive morgue. Valtierra captures the individual experience through the tight-angled photograph and the sensory allusions, inviting an affective response to the tragedy.

Poniatowska's crónicas also built on civic efforts to produce and inform media coverage. On September 24, natural and social scientists founded the Center for Information and Analysis of the Effects of the Earthquake (Centro de Información y Análisis de los Efectos del Sismo, or CIASES) to combat "the deliberate concealment and confusion provoked by those who, in defense of powerful interests, do not hesitate to hide the truth."[87] The center aimed to democratize the process of information gathering and thereby counter state-aligned media. CIASES circulated flyers inviting Mexico City residents to weekly press conferences where they could share their experiences. The founders also wrote their own analyses of the earthquake's damage, which they attributed to "social, economic, and political conditions."

From October 11 through November 8, *Excélsior* dedicated a full section of the newspaper to publishing CIASES-generated articles.[88]

Poniatowska and Monsiváis were present at nearly every CIASES press conference, and they used testimonies shared there to source their chronicles. For example, Poniatowska's article on October 18 was based on an account that she heard at a CIASES press conference three days earlier. She dedicated most of the resulting article to the uninterrupted account by Xavier González, a mathematics instructor who organized a rescue brigade of Metropolitan Autonomous University (Universidad Autónoma Metropolitana) students. In his original testimony, transcribed by CIASES, González related the construction failures that volunteers found during their efforts to remove wreckage. For example, he recounted his shock when his team discovered that some of the supporting columns were filled with sand instead of concrete; rescuers would spend hours breaking down columns so that they could be removed without the assistance of heavy machinery, while other columns would fall apart right away because they were filled with sand. Rescue volunteers also found numerous free-hanging concrete slabs unattached to any columns. This was a powerful image when juxtaposed with the many accounts of people who had literally been crushed and buried beneath these tombstones (the Spanish construction term for stone slab, *losa*, also means "tombstone"). González noted that "anyone who knows construction realizes the significance of this failure."[89] In her chronicle, Poniatowska reproduced the statement, but added the word *criminal* ("the *criminal* significance of this failure") to make explicit that the construction failures resulted from intentional actions by contractors, aided by city officials.[90]

Like many others, González's testimony highlighted how the rescue efforts were both emotionally and physically taxing, and he expressed concern for the mental health of the volunteers.[91] Poniatowska captured these individual experiences and opened her chronicle by narrating them in the first person: "'The only possibility of peace is to lock myself in a room with my children.' 'I can't sleep.' 'I see visions.' 'I hear voices.' 'I'm disgusted by food.' 'I will never eat meat again.' 'I am obsessed.' Many rescuers are in crisis." Drawing upon González's testimony, Poniatowska addressed how Mexico City residents might manage the earthquake's psychological toll and even mobilize it politically. She quoted the volunteer's argument that "the rescue experiences must be collected; made into a memory that serves for the future; we have never had a similar experience. How will the social unrest be expressed?"[92] Her chronicle directly quoted González's testimony but rearranged his sentences to produce a cohesive narrative that argued that the emotional effects of the earthquake were not apolitical but instead directly connected to broader issues of social concern.

In so doing, Poniatowska challenged the numerous public service announcements that responded to depression and fear and urged residents to visit a psychologist. Discussions of psychological well-being removed the stigma of seeing a mental health professional but often defined political criticism as incompatible with the healing process.[93] This argument not only appeared in government-sponsored programming but also in outlets conventionally known for critical coverage. On Radio Educación, for example, the *Participación Ciudadana* program conspicuously avoided any discussion of formal politics or corruption. The show aired between noon and 1:00 PM and targeted housewives, presumably charged with their families' emotional well-being. The program emphasized that "reconstruction must begin with the family," and women constituted the majority of listeners who called in with questions.[94] Psychologists on the program offered advice that addressed feelings of survivors' guilt; they focused on the individual, rather than collective, resolution to the tragedy and discouraged listeners from transforming their individual feelings into broader social action. Mental health services addressed a serious need, but programs like *Participación Ciudadana* suggested that seeking structural change would only slow the recovery process. By contrast, González's testimony underscored the notion that psychological struggles were in fact a collective experience, and Poniatowska's chronicles began the collective memory work that González called for.

Poniatowska also explored testimonies by disenfranchised people to demonstrate that grievances stemmed not only from the high-level corruption but also from individual experiences of discrimination. She recounted the testimony of Alonso Mixteco Pastor, a self-identified Indigenous man who had miraculously escaped his collapsed building in the working-class neighborhood of Tepito with no rescue assistance. Mixteco Pastor dug a thirty-meter tunnel through the wreckage and "became known as 'the man who got out alone.'" Poniatowska included Mixteco Pastor's account of trying to return to the wreckage and rescue his friends. Referring to the military standing guard outside, he explained, "They wouldn't let me: 'No. You don't know how, you can't.' I was the only one who knew where [my friends] were, given that I had saved myself. But according to them, I couldn't butt in because I wasn't part of the rescue crew. . . . What right did they have to treat me like that? Had they been trapped under the wreckage? Did they know how it felt?"[95] Mixteco Pastor's testimony underscored the relevance of experiential knowledge and the indignation at being dismissed. Readers might interpret his question "Had they been trapped under the wreckage?" as a broader denunciation that public officials did not suffer the consequences of their own impunity. While authorities did not value his knowledge, he asserted that ordinary citizens best understood how to govern and provide for their communities.

Mixteco Pastor also critiqued government discrimination against Indigenous and poor people. He recounted listening to radio broadcasters announce the president's visit to damage sites. While he heard that the president would visit hard-hit middle-class neighborhoods such as Colonia Roma, he complained that politicians did not bother visiting his neighborhood: "That made me a little uncomfortable. It made me feel bad because we marginalized people will always be marginalized." His political subjectivity thus emerged from his individual experience and from his critical reading of media. The radio silenced the needs of his community, and he saw this as evidence of political marginalization. Poniatowska concluded with Mixteco Pastor's rejection of state assistance: "That's why, *compañeros*, I got tired of chewing so much dust to climb through the tunnel and make it out of a hole; like a worm I dug, like a worm. Now I'm rebelling. I don't want dust or nitre, nor a house filled with holes anymore. I want all Mexicans to receive fair treatment."[96] Poniatowska recorded Mixteco Pastor's politicization, born not only out of the state's negligence but also out of racism and discrimination, and she suggested that an empowered civil society required not only solidarity but also individual transformations in consciousness.

Monsiváis also explored how quotidian experiences of discrimination became lightning rods for politicization. In one chronicle he interviewed garment workers who remained at the encampments. To explain why they continued to mobilize, even after winning their union registration, one worker described a confrontation with an older woman outside a damaged sweatshop. Suggesting that the workers were wasting time, the older woman said, "What are you waiting for? Go off and sell quesadillas." The disparaging comment referred to an alternative occupation for someone of the garment workers' class and racial background. The interviewee had rejoined, "The problem is that many women died.... We can't make quesadillas so long as they aren't given justice."[97] The interaction lingered with the garment worker who viewed it as evidence of why she and others must continue their struggle for fair and just treatment.

Chronicles demonstrate that the voices that made up denuncia journalism had diversified. The most popular and well-known journalists, Monsiváis and Poniatowska, deployed intimate and identifying narratives to denounce structural problems of discrimination, paternalism, and neglect. By harnessing the voices of volunteers and survivors, Monsiváis and Poniatowska looked to civil society to narrate the meaning and consequences of the earthquake. These chronicles would later be anthologized and become required reading for those interested in Mexico's democratization, further cementing both writers' authority as the narrators of the earthquake.[98]

## CONCLUSION

In the aftermath of the 1985 earthquake Mexico City residents witnessed and participated in protracted contests over public space and representation. The extensive damage transformed the urban landscape, pushing thousands of residents into the streets. Residents repurposed sidewalks and medians into makeshift shelters, took over major thoroughfares with protests, and camped in front of hospitals and public administration buildings. The city government converted spaces of leisure, like the baseball stadium, into massive morgues. Next of kin, waiting to identify and collect their loved ones, formed long lines that stretched into the street, disrupting the flow of traffic. Meanwhile, collapsed factories, hospitals, and apartment buildings provided a visual reminder of the tragedy and became sites of intense political conflict.

With government agencies too disorganized to effectively manage print media coverage, major broadsheets and tabloid-size dailies investigated the corruption and negligence that costs thousands of lives. The tremors ruptured several open secrets: that modernist public housing was unsafe, that labor officials failed to ensure fair working conditions, and that illegal practices of torture continued. Many residents and laborers had denounced these realities, but scandals—and the unearthing of physical evidence—disrupted government officials' ability to dissimulate their knowledge. A diversity of voices also found expression in print, expanding the boundaries of the public sphere. Chronicles furnished spaces in which Indigenous people, women, and students could describe their experiences with everyday injustices and record the fatal consequences of corruption and impunity. Notably, chronicles phrased denunciation in affective language, decentering the masculinist mode of accusation that was typical of investigative journalism.

The 1985 earthquake represented a mediated disaster, as press coverage was central to how residents experienced and understood the event. Indeed, victims suggested that media was central to the formation of their political subjectivity. They saw coverage of their neighborhoods or workplaces as evidence of their own inclusion or exclusion from the national imaginary. Yet organized residents asserted their perspectives into these debates, producing bulletins or videos or simply refusing to become the protagonists of apolitical spectacles. Interpretations of the disaster were not fixed, and conflicts emerged over representation. The following year, similarly charged contests surfaced when the right-leaning PAN stood poised to mobilize middle-class dissent into an historic electoral victory.

CHAPTER 6

# THE WEAPONIZATION OF SCANDAL

In July 1985 Chihuahua City resident María del Pilar Treviño invited Mexico's most famous writer, Octavio Paz, to visit her northern borderland city. She urged him to "turn your eyes to Chihuahua, come meet us, and then write about what is happening here." For Treviño, who was chairperson for her local Social Civic Action (Acción Cívica Social) department, "what was happening" was a powerful movement for democracy spearheaded by the PAN. The conservative party had swept Chihuahua's midterm elections in 1983, winning the state's seven most important mayoralties. Two years later, the PAN handily won five out of ten federal congressional seats in contention. But Treviño worried that "few know or care what happens here."[1] While many northern residents heralded an insurgent movement for democracy, the country's political and cultural center appeared impervious, and Treviño lamented that "the national press has pushed us aside." To be invisible to Mexico City media, she suggested, was to remain politically marginalized and irrelevant. Treviño continued to send letters to Paz, and though he never replied, national attention soon fixated on the northern border state.

One year after Treviño penned her first letter, Chihuahua became the subject of national and international headlines. The state's elections were the most anticipated contests of the summer of 1986, and opposition leaders predicted that the PRI would lose a governorship for the first time. The ruling party dedicated considerable resources toward preventing this from happening, and despite the presence of international and national electoral observers, the races ended with credible accusations of fraud. Numerous eyewitness accounts reported that ballot boxes had disappeared from polling stations or arrived already full, and electoral observers witnessed familiar methods of voter manipulation including *el carrusel* (in which the same person votes multiple times), the intimidation of opposition party observers, and falsified vote counts. While electoral fraud was not new, the scale and visibility of denunciations was unprecedented. The PAN's sympathizers carried out acts of civil disobedience for over a month, and U.S. print and broadcast media offered critical coverage of the events.

While *denuncia* journalists acknowledged evidence of fraud, the Chihuahuan elections raised thorny questions about politicizing the case. Reporters and intellectuals recognized that most instances of fraud did not gain national, let alone international, attention, and they explicitly questioned whose interests would be served by making a scandal of Chihuahua's state elections. Concerns surfaced that ill-intentioned groups could use scandals as weapons against their political opponents. Staking out distinct ideological positions, some leftist journalists worried that the scandal provided the justification for U.S. military intervention and legitimated illegitimate actors—the conservative opposition and its illiberal allies in the church and in business lobbies. Liberal and conservative writers and Chihuahuan activists, meanwhile, believed that muted electoral coverage in mainstream newspapers and television programs evidenced government censorship or Mexico City discrimination. These conflicts were not limited to published intellectual debate. Chihuahuan readers weighed in with angry phone calls to newsrooms, accusing editors of co-optation and self-censorship. Disputes over journalistic ethics and biases also escalated into shouting matches between national and foreign correspondents. These confrontations reveal expectations that the press was an advocate that could not (and should not) be objective.

For social movement activists, the 1985 Mexico City earthquake had raised hopes that media could support, rather than hinder, grassroots organizing. The 1986 elections, by contrast, revealed the regional imbalances, international influences, and patchwork censorship that shaped Mexico's media landscape. Transnational broadcasting agreements and satellite and video technologies facilitated transborder news exchange, amplifying the relevance of U.S. media coverage to Mexican politics. Meanwhile, residents living in the Mexican-U.S. borderlands began to challenge their marginalization by the Mexico City press, which disproportionately set the terms of national debate. Their frustrations revealed how national media could at once bring together and fracture publics. Finally, censorship persisted in uneven and unpredictable ways, as newspapers publicized their intimidation by soldiers and *pistoleros* (guns for hire). For some journalists, this panorama seemingly undermined the democratic possibilities of media access.

## "FEW KNOW OR CARE WHAT HAPPENS HERE"

Treviño suggested that Mexico City reporters could not witness important political change because they were looking in the wrong direction. National news circulation was generally unidirectional, traveling outward from the capital. Mexican wire services like Notimex sold articles to broadcast and print media subscribers across the country, but most news agencies lacked the resources to provide consistent coverage of regional issues. In fact, Notimex maintained only four bare-bones regional offices in Cuernavaca, Guadalajara, Mérida, and Monterrey and could not afford to hire a full-time reporting staff.[2] Instead Notimex and upstart wire services like *Proceso*'s Comunicación e Información, S.A. de C.V. (CISA) hired stringers who were working full-time at local news outlets. CISA offices were also poorly equipped, lacking teletype machines; and reporters had to dictate stories by telephone or send them by mail, considerably slowing operations. Unsurprisingly, many regional newspapers found it most cost-effective to subscribe to international news services like the Associated Press from the United States or Great Britain's Reuters, which produced a larger volume of articles. These realities made it challenging for local and regional concerns to garner national attention.

Treviño was not alone in her belief that Mexico City media ignored many of the issues that affected those living outside the capital. Readers sometimes wrote to well-known Mexico City columnists requesting publicity for a local issue, and they often accompanied their requests with newspaper clippings, indicating that local media outlets were already covering such topics.[3] This was evident in a 1986 handwritten letter from Sinaloa resident Jorge Sepúlveda to Miguel Ángel Granados Chapa, a *La Jornada* columnist and editor. Sepúlveda's letter described a climate of growing insecurity and gun violence in his hometown of Culiacán and he expressed his hope that "those of you who are held in high esteem and enjoy national prestige will help us with articles."[4] Underlying—but unspoken in—these personal appeals was the belief that local accountability required pressure from Mexico City.

Urban readers across Mexico could find many capital city newspapers on local newsstands, but they were accustomed to uneven and slow distribution. One reader in Hermosillo, Sonora, complained that delivery delays often meant that his copy of *La Jornada* did not arrive until 6:00 PM. Another from Tamaulipas grumbled that some days the same newspaper did not arrive at all.[5] Local radio reporters, operating on shoestring budgets, at times used popular Mexico City columns to fill out their broadcasts. For example, a Guadalajara reporter for Radio Universidad read Manuel Buendía's columns aloud for seven years on his program.[6] Meanwhile, the major broadcaster Televisa knit together a national viewership with popular programs such as *24 Horas*, *Hoy Mismo*, and *Siempre en Domingo*. Locally produced television and radio programs rarely made their way to capital-city consumers, however.[7]

Information flows reflected the centralization of political power and resources, and the president's communication office focused its energies on cultivating relationships with Mexico City media outlets. In September 1982, the Social Communication Office of the Presidency (Oficina de Comunicación Social de la Presidencia, or CSP) took the rare initiative to convene television and radio broadcasters from all over the country. The ministry hoped to unify national coverage of a recent and controversial decision to nationalize the central bank. But local media producers reporting from the northern borderlands used the meeting to gather critical information and challenge the ministry's Mexico City–centric focus. They also contested the ways in which commercial television and radio sidelined the concerns of residents outside Mexico City.[8]

In the meeting with CSP officials, reporters asserted that a vacuum of information had heightened the uncertainty and anxiety resulting from the economic crisis. Mario Enrique Mayares, a radio host in Baja California Norte, heard rumors that maquiladora workers would be given special permission to open bank accounts in dollars, and he asked the CSP minister, Francisco Galindo Ochoa, to confirm whether this was true.[9] Since the Border Industrialization Program began in 1965, U.S.-owned manufacturing plants (maquiladoras) in Mexico had expanded and employed tens of thousands of workers who were paid in U.S. dollars. After the economic crisis, however, the Mexican federal government prohibited the circulation of foreign currency.[10] Mayares noted that sporadic communication from the federal government further exacerbated an already confusing situation.

Salvador Ajoux, a radio host from Monclova, Coahuila, felt similarly ill prepared to answer his listeners' questions. Municipal authorities were no help, and he noted that "we are in a vicious circle in which the lack of information produces more uncertainty and leaves us in the media not knowing how to respond."[11] One of the meeting's organizers, Luis Cueto, admitted that the federal government's communication strategy targeted Mexico City media with "more or less broad, national coverage, but the local and very important programs that you broadcast daily have not been reached."[12] In effect, communication officials expected national media to convey government information to the entire country and authors of press bulletins imagined their audience to be capital city dwellers. The national media's marginalization of local issues thus reflected the federal marginalization of regional political concerns.

Francisco King, a news anchor and radio host in La Paz, Baja California Sur, blamed national news programs for failing to inform viewers. He argued that popular Televisa broadcasts like Guillermo Ochoa's *Hoy Mismo* only covered the concerns of greater Mexico City residents. Moreover, he accused officials in attendance of giving "political answers" without actually responding to reporters' questions. King emphasized, "Believe me that we are more worried about the economic situation that has leveled Mexico than about the decision on the bank nationalization," thus challenging the ministry's assumption that media primarily served to promote government programs.[13] Significantly, King expressed this directly to public officials, criticizing not only government-aligned news broadcasts but also the stated purpose of the meeting.

Distance from federal oversight did have its advantages. In the 1980s regional newspapers like Monterrey's *El Norte* and *El Porvenir* gained greater autonomy and frequently criticized the central government. Alejandro Junco, the conservative founder of *El Norte*, had studied journalism at the University of Texas–Austin, and in 1970 he established a summer workshop to train his reporters in U.S. journalistic practices.[14] Muckraking publications like *Diario de Irapuato* and *Zeta* also appeared in the 1980s in Irapuato and Tijuana, respectively, attacking corrupt officials.[15] Isolation from the political center also allowed media to reflect the perspectives of rural and Indigenous peoples, as evidenced by the spread of community radio. Living in the Mexican-U.S. borderlands further fostered a distinctive sense of political geography and community. The *San Diego Union Tribune* and *Los Angeles Times*, alongside local radio and television programming, frequently covered Baja Californian social and political issues, and media in Texas similarly reported on developments across the border. Mexican reporters also used the border to circumvent censorship. Jesús Blancornelas and Héctor "El Gato" Félix, who codirected *Zeta*, used printing presses in San Diego to produce their muckraking newspaper before they distributed it across the border in Tijuana.[16] At the same time, regional reporters were vulnerable to violence.

Reporters at the *Diario de Irapuato*, for example, suffered threats, physical attacks, and even murder in the 1980s.[17]

Marginalization by national media no doubt contributed to the sense among northerners that they shared more culturally with the United States than with Mexico City. In the early 1980s the PAN channeled the complaint that "few know or care about what happens here" into significant electoral victories. By spring 1986 conservative opposition leaders in Chihuahua declared that the PAN enjoyed broad enough support to win the governorship.[18] Frustrated by having their political struggles silenced by Mexico City media, PAN activists cultivated the interest of U.S. reporters, raising suspicions regarding foreign interests in the election.

## A THREAT TO MEXICAN SOVEREIGNTY

Heightened U.S. government and media attention complicated the stakes of the 1986 Chihuahuan elections. Reporters from prominent U.S. news outlets, including the Public Broadcasting Service (PBS), *Los Angeles Times*, *New York Times*, and *Washington Post*, forecast the likelihood of fraud and loudly warned that Mexico's democracy was in jeopardy. The PAN actively courted foreign media, and Mexico City journalists and federal government officials worried that negative U.S. attention foreshadowed election meddling or worse. With dwindling popular support, the PRI capitalized on the specter of U.S. intervention to warn that the PAN would undermine Mexican sovereignty. The fears of hidden motives behind U.S. coverage shaped subsequent interpretations of the scandal.

Months before the Chihuahuan elections, PBS forecast that the gubernatorial race would serve as a barometer of Mexico's democracy. In April the service aired a *Frontline* documentary episode, "Standoff in Mexico," that warned that the PRI might manipulate the results in its favor. In the introduction, the narrator intoned, "Fixed elections and violence right across the border. Mexico claims to be a democracy. We wait to see if that is true."[19] The documentary followed the 1985 congressional and local elections in Chihuahua and the gubernatorial elections in Sonora, focusing particularly on the PAN's protests against fraud and corruption. The special devoted significant camera time to Francisco Barrio, a local business owner who had wrested the Ciudad Juárez mayoral seat from the PRI in 1983 and was the PAN's candidate for the upcoming gubernatorial race.

The documentary argued that the PRI was deaf to popular demands and could only win through fraud. Aerial shots captured a plaza brimming with cheering PAN supporters, and interviews with working-class Chihuahua City residents underscored how ordinary people were "tired of the system." This contrasted against a scene of President Miguel de la Madrid's visit to Ciudad Juárez, which depicted an intransigent president insisting that "Mexico does not need lessons in democracy from abroad."[20] Explicitly contesting this claim was a quieter scene that followed Barrio and his wife leading a strike in the city square under a banner that read "Lesson in Democracy." Posted by PAN protesters, the sign challenged de la Madrid's assertion that exogenous forces motivated opposition movements. Ironically, however, the sign was written in English and thus explicitly addressed a U.S. audience. PAN leaders certainly saw the *Frontline* documentary as legitimating their warnings of fraud, and they widely publicized the program, mailing home-recorded videocassettes to their networks across the country.[21]

Leftist Mexican reporters and PRI leaders were wary of the PAN's attempts to cultivate sympathy abroad. Rumors swirled that the Committee for the Struggle for Democracy (Comité de Lucha por la Democracia), a PAN-allied business group, had not only financed the PBS documentary but also poured some 20 million pesos into paid U.S. newspaper advertisements, an assertion that improbably suggested that the party's allies had grown so powerful that they could sway U.S. media coverage. Publications like *La Jornada*, *Proceso*, and *Unomásuno* saw U.S. media as a proxy for the government, which they worried might intervene in Mexico's political affairs. Raising the specter of foreign election meddling, *Proceso* described the documentary as "proof of U.S. aspirations for the blue and white party," a reference to the PAN's colors.[22] Journalists also repeatedly underscored the economic and ideological affinities between the PAN and the U.S. Republican Party, highlighting shared preferences for free trade and socially conservative policies. For Mexican leftists, U.S. warnings of fraud rang false; instead of genuine concern, such publicity appeared to be an effort to manipulate the election results.[23]

The Mexican left and the PRI had long used the United States as a foil for nationalist rhetoric. While the ruling party had maintained close and collaborative relations with the United States since 1940, Mexican officials often blamed unpopular domestic policies on "Yankee imperialism."[24] Moreover, in the 1960s and 1970s, PRI officials tried to discredit opposition movements with accusations that they were funded by foreign interests, whether from the United States, Cuba, or the Soviet Union. While such accusations were primarily rhetorical, by the early 1980s, new developments made U.S. support for Mexico's ruling party appear much more tenuous. First, the economic crisis had placed the PRI in a politically precarious position; the party had to satisfy U.S. government and IMF lenders while addressing domestic discontent with austerity measures. Political commentators like Jorge G. Castañeda hypothesized that the United States aimed to bring an acceptable opposition party to power, believing that the PRI was losing political control.[25] U.S. backing for right-wing groups in Nicaragua and El Salvador also seemingly provided a blueprint for foreign intervention in Mexico.[26] In short, some political commentators believed that the United States was willing to intervene in Mexican elections to ensure the continuity of economic agreements.

On May 9 Porfirio Muñoz Ledo, former PRI party president and UN ambassador, warned de la Madrid that a U.S. smear campaign was underway against Mexico. Muñoz Ledo worried that U.S. government and CIA officials were using news media "to damage the credibility of the country in general and its political system in particular."[27] The goal of this campaign, he believed, was "to create a favorable environment for U.S. political and economic intervention in Mexico." Cognizant that the United States had indirectly intervened in Central America, most recently to support right-wing counterinsurgencies, Muñoz Ledo worried that U.S. officials harbored similar designs for Mexico. In his view, negative U.S. media coverage provided the discursive justification for another intervention.

Recent developments did indicate a strained relationship between the two governments. After the February 1985 murder of U.S. Drug Enforcement Agency operative Enrique Camarena in Mexico, major U.S. media outlets highlighted instability and corruption south of the border. According to Castañeda, heightened U.S. criticism of the PRI led ordinary Mexicans and political leaders alike to believe that "Mexico is the target of a U.S. campaign to destabilize the Miguel de la Madrid government."[28] Another dip in global oil prices also left Mexico unable to make its foreign debt payments, prompting an impending debt renegotiation. In May 1986 the *New York Times* cited CIA reports that warned "Mexico could become one of this nation's most important foreign policy problems."[29] That same month, U.S. representatives raised concerns about electoral fraud, breaking with the long-standing toleration of the PRI's political dominance. On May 13, the U.S. Senate Committee on Foreign Relations began its hearings on the "situation in Mexico." Chaired by Republican senator Jesse Helms, the committee highlighted problems of drug trafficking, migration, economic stagnation, and widespread government corruption and fraud. In his opening remarks, Helms asserted, "These events are affecting the United States deeply. We can no longer sit back passively."[30] Representatives proposed that the U.S. government send observers to monitor the Chihuahuan elections, and Helms even called for de la Madrid to resign.

In his report to the president, Muñoz Ledo proposed that Televisa counterbalance such negative images abroad. While U.S.-based wire services had long shaped Mexican media coverage, it was only in the 1970s that satellite technology and an expanded microwave system allowed Mexican media to significantly inform U.S. Spanish-language programming. Telesistema Mexicano (the predecessor to Televisa) created the Spanish Information Network (SIN) in 1962 to deliver content, primarily telenovelas, to Spanish speakers in the United States. By the 1970s, SIN distributed around one thousand hours of programming each month to U.S. viewers.[31] Muñoz Ledo suggested that positive SIN coverage could reframe the conversation around Chihuahua's elections. He also recommended that Mexican opinion leaders from both the Left and the Right unite to project a more positive image of the PRI abroad, urging that commentators withhold criticism in the interest of national sovereignty. Muñoz Ledo seemingly implied that by projecting a positive image, the Mexican government could prevent U.S. subversion.

Televisa did cover the Senate hearings and reported that Helms's "insults" and accusations of electoral fraud had no basis in fact.[32] The de la Madrid government also turned the hearings into a rallying cry for Mexican autonomy and organized a march "in defense of national sovereignty" on May 22.[33] Unlike most state-sponsored rallies, which enticed participants with small handouts, this one mobilized independent leftist participants as well. But the march sidestepped the fact that the PRI had already ceded significant economic sovereignty to international lending institutions—specifically, the IMF and the World Bank. Even longtime PRI loyalists recognized this contradiction. At the party's national assembly, Julio Zamora Batiz, a former Mexico state senator, declared that "the imposition of austerity on salaried workers, small businessmen, peasants, and professionals to pay more on the foreign debt is incongruent with the PRI's responsibility and historical tradition."[34] Yet PRI leaders were unwilling to publicly acknowledge the reasons for popular discontent. The party's gubernatorial candidate in Chihuahua, Fernando Baeza, insisted that the PRI remained committed to social democracy.[35]

The anticipatory coverage of the Chihuahua state elections raised the specter not only of fraud but also of scandal. Ominous warnings that the United States would be monitoring the elections sparked accusations of foreign meddling. Mexican federal government officials and left-leaning journalists assessed the hidden motives lurking behind U.S. interests, suggesting that it was not the truth of the accusations that was important but the motives that undergirded them. Mexico City opinion writers and essayists soon joined U.S. reporters in forecasting the stakes of the Chihuahuan elections.

They went beyond the *Frontline* documentary's prognostications and emphasized that Chihuahua's elections would catalyze Mexico's democratization. Presenting PAN victory as inevitable, bold pronouncements sparked deep-seated disagreements about political culture, democracy, and citizenship in Mexico City opinion pages.

## "THE CRADLE FOR CHANGE"

Months before the elections commenced, predictions overwhelmed Mexico City opinion pages, anticipating and thereby shaping the scandal. Over the previous decade, analysis articles and essays had become a more prominent feature of Mexico City news, and publications like the monthly magazine *Nexos* provided a forum for academics to debate ideas for a wider audience. Editorials in national broadsheets also featured blistering denunciations of human rights abuses, at times contradicting muted front-page reportage in the same publication. In anticipation of the Chihuahuan gubernatorial elections, essays, columns, and features in *Nexos* and *La Jornada* identified Chihuahua's history and regional character as well suited for democratic change.

Opinion writers framed the significance of electoral fraud even before it happened. After their celebrated coverage of the 1985 earthquake, *La Jornada* editors were cognizant of the influence their newspaper enjoyed. When they convened in February 1986, Carlos Tello, an economist and former government minister, asserted that the newspaper should "anticipate [issues] to such a degree that what *La Jornada* says will influence the decisions that are about to be made."[36] Rather than responding to official bulletins and speeches, editors would project their own priorities into the public sphere. Forecasting the major issues of the year, they placed Mexico City's democratization, pollution, energy, higher education, earthquake victims, torture, and "the situation in Chihuahua" on the editorial agenda. Added to the list by public intellectual Héctor Aguilar Camín, the state election was among the few issues that turned the editors' gaze away from the nation's capital.

Leftist news publications were not alone in placing the Chihuahuan elections on the editorial agenda. Neoliberal intellectuals and conservative journalists similarly declared Chihuahua a historic and future site of Mexican democracy. Among them was magazine director Enrique Krauze, who became one of the most influential voices on the elections. He argued that that state's history and frontier geography made it a "the cradle for the new era."[37] Krauze first articulated this idea in an essay for *Vuelta* magazine, but his argument garnered broader interest when it was published as part of the 1986 revised edition of his popular book *Por una democracia sin adjetivos*. In the new chapter Krauze cited Chihuahua's catalyzing role in the Mexican Revolution as evidence of the state's inclination toward rebellion. Echoing Frederick Jackson Turner's famous "frontier thesis," which argued that pioneers eschewed old institutions, aristocracies, and hierarchies as they moved west, Krauze romanticized Mexican northerners as rugged individualists whose autonomous spirits were inherently opposed to the PRI's ailing corporatism.[38] Unsurprisingly, Krauze's book was wildly popular among PAN activists in Chihuahua, who frequently referenced it to legitimate their movement.[39]

Krauze's idealized citizen was racialized as white. He implicitly contrasted Chihuahuans against central (read: Indigenous) Mexicans, who were presumably trapped in baroque patron-client relationships. Krauze characterized *norteños* (northern Mexicans) as possessing "a violent tradition, a deep sense of isolation; the view of life as a challenge; a basically creole, secular, and liberal culture; an ancestral autonomy, a fidelity to Spanish cultural roots ... which by its very nature and durability permits business with the Anglo Saxon without implying the loss of one's soul; a long-standing resentment toward centralized power that easily translates into an almost racial hatred for everything that arrives from the south."[40] The implicit contrast to this masculine, white citizen was Indigenous peoples, whom towering Mexican intellectuals like Krauze's mentor Octavio Paz had described as ideologically rigid, personalist, feminized, and overly deferential political subjects.[41]

Krauze's chapter further echoed northerners' own self-fashioning as autonomous innovators. Since the 1910 revolution, Monterrey industrialists contrasted the urbanity and modernity of their city, a hub for factories and railroads, against Mexico's predominantly rural agrarian society. As Michael Snodgrass argues, "This regional identity built on the *norteños'* critical view of central and southern Mexico: lethargic, submissive, and economically backward societies weighed down by an oppressive colonial heritage."[42] This image of central Mexico contrasted racialized ideas of sloth and passivity against the depiction of lighter-skinned, masculine virility in the north. Krauze's characterization of Chihuahuans drew on these historic associations to argue that norteños possessed the modern qualities necessary to usher in democracy.

Krauze's idealized notion of citizenship underscored his belief that the PRI's corruption, bureaucracy, inefficacy, and paternalism were the primary impediments to modernization. He supported the government's neoliberal austerity policies and cheekily praised Chihuahuans for recognizing that they could trade with the United States "without implying the loss of one's soul." If the embrace of free trade was a sign of open-mindedness, Krauze implied that the rejection of market-oriented policies was evidence of stubbornness or xenophobia. That summer Mexico was poised to enter a free trade agreement, the General Agreement on Tariffs and Trade, which would further break down economic protections. Krauze saw this as a necessary step for the country's political and economic progress.

Krauze had entered Mexico City's intellectual scene in the late 1970s when he joined Paz's literary magazine, *Vuelta*. In 1981 Krauze became deputy director of the publication, and he sought to distinguish the magazine's literary criticism from the publicly engaged writings of Marxist and leftist intellectuals, whom he accused of kowtowing to governing officials.[43] In making this criticism, he followed his PhD adviser, Daniel Cosío Villegas, who had similarly accused intellectuals of relinquishing their critical functions after the revolution.[44] By the late 1980s Krauze had established himself as a prominent public intellectual, and he frequently published in English, appointing himself as a Mexican spokesperson for an international audience. He was also one of the few writers to benefit from the privatization of cultural activity and the defunding of Mexican universities. In 1987 Krauze would work as a consultant for Televisa to create historical soap operas based on his presidential biographies.[45]

Krauze suggested that his arguments about Mexican democracy were grounded in empirical, apolitical, and thus unassailable facts. He received his doctorate in history from the prestigious Colegio de México, and he positioned himself as a gatekeeper of historical writing. For example, his 1983 book of essays *Caras de la historia* distinguished between those who wrote "history for power" and those who wrote "history for knowledge."[46] Yet his essay on Chihuahua's 1986 elections mobilized a selective version of revolutionary history that advanced his argument. Krauze highlighted northerners' proclivity for revolution by focusing on Francisco Madero's 1910 uprising, which called for the overthrow of dictator Porfirio Díaz but not for overturning structures of inequality. Meanwhile, Krauze contrasted rebellious northerners against supposedly passive southerners, silencing the revolutionary peasant movements for land and social justice that had erupted in the south.

This analysis did not escape criticism. Adolfo Gilly, a leftist UNAM history professor and former political prisoner, rebuked Krauze's political uses of history. In a blistering *La Jornada* review of *Por una democracia sin adjetivos*, Gilly accused Krauze of silencing rural people to rewrite history in favor of the PAN. To explain the delegitimation of the PRI, Krauze's book referenced, among other things, state violence against people in the countryside. Yet Gilly argued that "it appears completely unfair and biased to me, in the context of a book where thousands of peasants never appear, to only speak of them when they are dead, imprisoned, [and] tortured, their dwellings and fields burned, their wives and daughters raped.... [These were] peasants whose cause and defense was not the PAN, but rather precisely the left that daily and stubbornly has taken up their plight."[47] Gilly argued that Krauze had cynically written revisionist history to claim that the PAN represented a popular, rather than an elite, political project.

Debates about the political uses of history illustrate a heightened awareness of and disagreement about the roles that intellectuals should play in shaping public debate. While Krauze argued against politically motivated historiography, he undoubtedly hoped that his public writing would shape broader understandings about democratic possibilities. Gilly was not the only historian critical of Krauze. Aguilar Camín, who also held a doctorate in history from the Colegio de México, had cofounded *Nexos* monthly magazine in 1978 to counterbalance *Vuelta*, which he saw as a hermetic project. By contrast, *Nexos*'s founders underscored their mission of making academic work legible to the broader public.[48] Moreover, they saw their role as Gramscian intellectuals who would serve the interests of society by discussing pressing political issues such as economic inequality. The rivalry with *Vuelta* continued when Krauze included Aguilar Camín among his list of historians who wrote "for politics," not knowledge.[49] Opinion and analysis pieces contained layers of insider knowledge that shaped their significance for distinct audiences. Many academics would read exchanges between essayists for the coded (or direct) barbs that betrayed mutual animosity between these elite men. Others, like Chihuahuan activists, may have encountered Krauze for the first time and read his book as inspiration for their struggle.

Despite their mutual animosity and distinct understandings of the role of the intellectual, Aguilar Camín and Krauze drew strikingly similar portraits of democratic change in Chihuahua. Both saw the frontier as an historic site of rebellion.[50] In an April 1986 *Nexos* essay, Aguilar Camín argued that the PAN's opposition continued the work of 1968 protesters. He explained that "the subversion that animates them, as in '68, does not seek to break the law, but to comply with it. It does not promote violence or revolutionary change, but more simply, respect for the established laws for parties and free elections."[51] Drawing parallels with the 1968 student movement highlighted the educated, middle-class, and urban composition of the activists. Aguilar

Camín's emphasis on their shared legal methods and reformist demands further distinguished the PAN activists from the radical peasant and guerrilla groups that had mobilized in the 1960s and 1970s. He asserted that the constitutional demand to vote made it "impossible to discredit [the PAN], but it also is impossible to satisfy it without a profound change in political culture." DFS spies offered a savvy reading of Aguilar Camín's politics, noting that while he sat on the editorial board at the left-leaning newspaper *La Jornada*, he did not share the leadership's "radical agenda."[52] They observed that he was more interested in making money, referring to the payments Aguilar Camín received as an adviser for various government ministries.

Like Krauze, Aguilar Camín underscored the legitimacy and democratic nature of the PAN by emphasizing the respectability of its membership. Similar analyses also appeared in reported pieces, which framed PAN activists as uniquely suited to democratic engagement. In early May *Proceso*'s veteran reporter, Francisco Ortiz Pinchetti, flew to Chihuahua City, where he remained for a number of months. The practice of sending correspondents for such lengthy stints was uncommon for Mexican newspapers with limited budgets. Given Ortiz Pinchetti's sympathies with the PAN, he likely was instrumental in advocating for on-the-ground coverage leading up to the elections.[53] His first article from the field appeared in *Proceso*'s May 5 issue. Entitled, "Chihuahuans Want Democracy and Repudiate the PRI," the piece equated political opening with free elections and the PRI's removal from power. As Ortiz Pinchetti proclaimed, "Today Chihuahua is, without exaggeration, an emergency zone for the Mexican political system."[54]

Ortiz Pinchetti contrasted PAN voters' fervent rejection of the PRI with the lukewarm support that the ruling party drew in Chihuahua. The reporter described slipping unnoticed into a PRI campaign rally in Chihuahua City, where he witnessed a disappointing turnout that he attributed to waning loyalty to PRI corporative organizations. The article's corresponding image pictured the national PRI president, Adolfo Lugo Verduzco, speaking at the rally. Photographed from behind, Lugo Verduzco's dark silhouette contrasted with the well-lit rows of empty bleachers before him. Rather than the effusive masses that the PRI boasted, *Proceso* showed the party leader orating to a half-filled auditorium, an offstage perspective that challenged ruling party claims of broad popular support.[55]

Everyone knew that the rallies were performances, rather than genuine, popular mobilizations, but *Proceso* editors implied that the photograph had broken with an open secret. The image's composition subverted party propaganda that would have been familiar to readers: the PRI not only bused in supporters to rallies but also published photographs that memorialized these events. Indeed, prior to the Chihuahuan elections, progovernment newspapers like *El Heraldo de México* printed images of crowds cheering "as one" for PRI gubernatorial candidate Baeza.[56] Banners were raised to signal the allegiance of corporative groups, including the CNOP and the CTM. The image captured the quintessential crowd, with its many bodies clearly represented, yet indistinguishable, from one another. Only the signs with Baeza's name differentiated the picture from the hundreds of others that official photographers snapped to document popular support. *Proceso*, by contrast, presented a realist image that depicted the abandonment of the party. The representation of ailing corporatist structures echoed criticisms voiced for decades by independent union leaders, student movements, and other opposition groups. However valid such critiques of clientelism were, they were overstated given the harsh realities of the public sector's dismantlement, which had significantly weakened corporatist organizations and diminished whatever political power that labor retained.

Ortiz Pinchetti's characterization of the crowd also subtly commented on the undesired qualities of a modern citizen. He described PRI voters as childlike, rural, and unproductive. He reported that to draw a crowd, the ruling party had distributed free food rations to over two thousand peasants; mobilized half of Chihuahua City's bus fleet to transport supporters to rallies, leaving many residents without rides to work; and had local presses publish circulars obligating union members to attend. Despite these efforts, Ortiz Pinchetti noted, the crowd was lackluster and included seven hundred school girls who were not even eligible voters. Attendance also plummeted after the (literal) pork was distributed; this characterization of the crowd suggested that peasants were motivated by small handouts rather than ideology. Ortiz Pinchetti also implied that the PRI voter was unproductive, as they were either unemployed or missed work to attend the rally. He contrasted these individuals against the industrious PAN supporters who were inconvenienced as they missed their buses en route to work or school. The juxtaposition of peasants with the schoolchildren in the crowd further suggested that the party infantilized its voters. By contrast, Ortiz Pinchetti argued that PAN supporters were rejecting paternalistic culture by rejecting the PRI. These depictions reinforced ideas that linked modern citizenship with urbanity and connected undemocratic ignorance with the peasantry.[57]

Sympathetic observers framed the election results as inevitable by describing northern PAN voters as destined for democracy. In their estimations, northerners shared the best aspects of U.S. culture—independent thinking, individualism, and an entrepreneurial spirit—and this presumably made them ideally suited for political democracy. Meanwhile, these descriptions downplayed Indigenous organizing, most notably in Juchitán, Oaxaca. There a Zapotec political movement, spearheaded by the Coalition of Workers, Peasants, and Students of the Isthmus (Coalición Obrera, Campesina, Estudiantil del Istmo), had swept local elections in 1981 only to be forcibly evicted by corrupt PRI officials in 1983. Three years later, the coalition was mounting a renewed challenge to the local PRI government. By underscoring the supposedly illiberal political traditions of southern Mexico, however, capital city writers projected which moments of fraud were considered most egregious.

## PUBLICIZING CENSORSHIP

Debates over Chihuahua's democratic character began in left-leaning and liberal magazines, but the state elections soon elicited unprecedented national and international interest. Days before the polls opened, prominent Chihuahua City leaders, including PAN mayor Luis H. Álvarez, declared a hunger strike and installed themselves in the central plaza to demand a clean election.[58] Mexican organizations, such as the National Women's Civic Association (Asociación Nacional Cívica Femenina), sent 360 observers from eight states to Chihuahua.[59] Fifty Mexico City correspondents, who typically did not venture outside the capital, also flooded Chihuahua City and Ciudad Juárez a few days prior to the July 6 elections. The *Los Angeles Times* predicted a referendum on the political system and referred to the elections as "Mexico's most hotly contested political race in 60 years."[60] Mexican denuncia journalists also predicted that repeating common practices of vote buying, intimidation, and obstruction would now have serious political consequences. Regional publications like *El Porvenir* ominously warned that if fraud occurred, "the message will be that the government is de facto carrying out a self-coup d'état."[61]

Such forecasts of fraud contrasted against evident censorship and self-censorship in local newspapers and national television. Televisa and state-owned Channel 13 judiciously ignored the Chihuahua elections and PAN protests, eliciting angry criticism of "information manipulation" from Krauze and local civic organizations.[62] Ciudad Juárez editors also had to answer to "persistent readers" who complained that the newspaper was silencing the concerns of PAN activists. Local readers expected critical coverage, and select Chihuahua's publications had developed strong ties with civil society, contributing to a pluralistic and combative public sphere.[63] When Chihuahuan newspapers silenced evidence of fraud, readers were quick to complain. On July 5, *Diario de Juárez* published a testy editorial defending itself against accusations that "Chihuahuan newspapers, at least the most important ones, have been the victims of a series of government intimidations which have forced them to renounce their independence." The editors minimized these complaints, which they said lacked "proof or concrete facts." But responding in print to ephemeral phone calls amplified and legitimated readers' claims. Against accusations that the newspaper unfairly covered the PAN, *Diario de Juárez* editors invoked journalistic norms of objectivity, emphasizing, "We are not with the PAN. We are not with the PRI. We simply examine the facts without any ideological framework."[64] Readers were likely unconvinced by this appeal to journalistic disinterest. While their complaints drew stark lines between independence and co-optation, they did not suggest that media coverage should be unideological. In fact, Ciudad Juárez residents wanted the press to serve an advocate of civil society, not as a neutral arbiter of differing positions.

While *Diario de Juárez* editors vigorously denied accusations of self-censorship, other articles contradicted that claim. Just three days earlier, the same newspaper reported that soldiers had confronted two photojournalists and seized their undeveloped film.[65] The *Diario de Juárez* photographers were documenting the arrival of military planes to Ciudad Juárez when the soldiers intercepted them. With their film confiscated, the journalists could only report on the incident of censorship. Reading these two *Diario de Juárez* articles together highlights the pressures that local newspapers face and their conflicting attempts to both deny and publicize this reality.

Contests over press freedom extended beyond questions of government interference. On election day, national and foreign correspondents clashed over issues of ideological allegiance, relative journalistic power, and profit seeking. Some Mexican reporters were wary of the dozens of U.S. correspondents who suddenly showed an interest in a Mexican state election. After the polls closed with few incidents, one *Unomásuno* reporter mocked the "disappointment of foreign correspondents, particularly from the United States, who expected violent elections." According to the anonymous reporter, U.S. correspondents were searching for a sensational story to sell to their readers. *Unomásuno* noted that a U.S. television journalist had even complained that "my bosses in New York called me and said that I'm sending total crap... that they want articles on the violence. But what the hell can I do? There isn't any."[66] *Unomásuno* suggested that greedy editors saw Chihuahua's elections as newsworthy only if they devolved into violence.

*Unomásuno* editors, who had aligned more closely with the de la Madrid administration, may have found the story of U.S. media sensationalism a useful distraction from evidence of electoral fraud. However, the criticism nonetheless drew upon genuine arguments for a New International Information Order (NIIO), which had appealed to leftist Latin American journalists in the 1970s. In advocating for an NIIO, Global South intellectuals accused North Atlantic media, particularly wire services, of selectively and disproportionately highlighting violence and natural disasters in their coverage of the Third World. This reportage, sometimes referred to as "coups and earthquakes" journalism, portrayed countries in the Global South as perennially chaotic, which critics argued bolstered U.S. interventionist aims. Mexico City had hosted multiple regional and United Nations Educational, Scientific and Cultural Organization conferences on the NIIO and thus became a key site where these debates unfolded. By the late 1980s NIIO advocacy had retreated, but educated Mexico City journalists were familiar with the continued criticism of imperialism and media.[67]

At the same time, accusations of foreign meddling offered PRI officials a convenient means to deflect scrutiny. This was evident in a confrontation between foreign correspondents and Mexican reporters. Summarizing the incident, *Unomásuno* described foreign reporters as overly aggressive; they had "cornered" PRI municipal delegate Mario Niebla and peppered him with questions. The delegate responded by accusing correspondents of wanting to see "a Roman circus, a bloody spectacle," implying that foreign interest in the election was by its very nature sensationalist.[68] Mexican journalists came to Niebla's defense, and *Unomásuno* described a tense scene that escalated into a shouting match. The reporter observed that "when the foreigners asked questions, national [reporters] made faces, smirked, or rebuked [them]. When Mexican journalists posed questions, the mocking came from the foreigners." By vividly conveying this confrontation, *Unomásuno* gave lie to *El Diario de Juárez*'s claims that journalism was an unideological pursuit. Instead, on-the-ground conflict highlighted that a journalist's nationality, publication, and presumed partisan allegiance took on charged significance as correspondents reported on the election proceedings. Moreover, *Unomásuno*'s criticisms of U.S. reportage more subtly deflected news of fraud than the practice of ignoring the elections entirely. Indeed, the PAN's complaints against Televisa had prompted Secretary of the Interior Manuel Bartlett to ask owner Emilio Azcárraga to make his alliance with the government "less obvious."[69]

Federal- and state-level censorship limited front-page coverage of the electoral fraud in all but a few newspapers. After the polls closed, *La Jornada* detailed numerous irregularities, including the burning of ballot boxes after citizens had already cast their votes and the removal or intimidation of PAN electoral observers.[70] The newspaper also denounced the circulation of apocryphal PAN flyers, which urged sympathizers to abstain from voting. *El Porvenir* similarly offered in-depth coverage of the corrupt practices that impeded fair elections. Reporters detailed wide discrepancies between the number of registered voters and the final tallies at numerous polling stations. *El Porvenir* correspondents observed poll workers engaging in *tortuguismo*, or intentional slowness, to discourage or prevent voting.[71] Yet the PRI appeared impervious to these denunciations and announced that it had won nearly every contest in the state of Chihuahua—the governorship, fourteen legislative seats, and all but one municipality. Tens of thousands of protesters flooded the streets of Chihuahua City and Ciudad Juárez, and local newspaper and radio offices became targets of angry protesters, who resented that the media silenced their demands.[72]

Many Mexico City broadsheets published dissonant information on the elections. For example, *El Universal*'s front pages juxtaposed interviews with PRI and PAN representatives, implying that views on fraud boiled down to partisanship. *El Universal*'s longtime director and publisher, Juan Francisco Ealy Ortiz, appeared keen to avoid the topic altogether and dedicated minimal front-page space to the postelection protests. By contrast, *El Universal* columnists introduced eyewitness accounts that confirmed that the PRI had tampered with ballots and voter rolls and had intimidated journalists and poll observers. Opinion writer Alejandro Avilés, for example, obliquely criticized the newspaper director for parroting the federal government line, lamenting, "It is so difficult to defend the truth! It always has been, but even more so when communication media (all TV and most of the radio and the press) are manipulated by a regime of lies and deceit." Avilés noted the evident "truth" of a "gigantic [electoral] fraud," and his refusal to name names suggested that *El Universal* was included in his denunciation.[73]

Evidence of intimidation also appeared in *El Universal*'s opinion pages. One article testified that "reporters were beaten" when they tried to photograph unmarked trucks that had exchanged empty ballot boxes with ones that were already stuffed full of votes.[74] Employing the passive voice left readers to speculate who, exactly, had attacked the journalists and who the drivers were. Finally, foreign correspondents were not exempt from intimidation, and they denounced the Ministry of the Interior for tapping the foreign press office telephones.[75] Publishing evidence of aggressive actions against journalists established the risks and stakes of postelection coverage but nonetheless betrayed the PRI's successful efforts to prevent the publication of visual evidence.

For nearly four decades it had been an open secret that how one voted did not matter; the PRI would always emerge the victor. Elections functioned as predetermined "rites of appointment," and dissimulating knowledge of the fixed outcome allowed electoral contests to legitimate the winners.[76] Popular jokes and ballads cynically mocked this dynamic, observing that even the deceased turned out to vote for the PRI (a reference to the use of outdated voter registries).[77] Similarly, it was common knowledge that governing officials manipulated media. Reading about censorship left readers to wonder what journalists might have reported had officials not intervened.

By 1986, however, access to a diverse array of media made it impossible for the federal government to entirely silence reports of electoral fraud. International and national news already penetrated urban Chihuahuan households, and residents in the Mexican-U.S. borderlands consumed U.S. television and radio programs, which reported on the elections. Activists for PAN, anticipating censorship, also produced flyers and bulletins that gave their own perspective on fraud. Readers' and protesters' complaints to newspaper directors further asserted that self-censorship was both obvious and scandalous. Televisa officials even acknowledged that their lack of coverage in Chihuahua had diminished the broadcaster's reputation with viewers.[78] The publicity of censorship thus became an additional source of delegitimation for the PRI.

## "A DANGEROUS OBSESSION WITH UNANIMITY"

Denuncia journalists agreed that the fraud was uniquely egregious because it had been so widely anticipated and publicized and yet so clumsily executed and denied. Mexico City leftist intellectuals nonetheless questioned whether the scandal would empower illegitimate actors. These writers saw the PAN's platforms of lowered trade barriers and closer relations with the United States as fundamentally opposed to socioeconomic democracy. Other opinion writers worried that the electoral fraud distracted from more troubling issues, like violence against Indigenous peoples. These debates occupied Mexico City opinion pages for weeks as PAN activists continued their protests along the Mexican-U.S. border.

Some opinion leaders saw PAN sympathizers as illegitimate actors who cynically manufactured the electoral fraud to undermine Mexico's secularism and sovereignty. Media scholar Raúl Trejo Delarbe described the PAN-led protests, which blocked major intersections and boycotted commercial activity, as *cacerolismo*, recalling how a similar demographic in Chile had demonstrated their support for President Salvador Allende's removal by banging pots (*cacerolas*) in 1973.[79] For Trejo Delarbe, the mere presence of conservative middle-class protesters in the streets could portend a U.S.-sponsored coup. What to Krauze appeared to be a democratic uprising looked to Trejo Delarbe like the masses that would vote for fascism or invite U.S. intervention. He warned journalists not to laud every challenger to the PRI, regardless of its ideology.

Cartoonists similarly characterized PAN protesters as motivated by outside interests. One cartoon, printed in *Unomásuno*'s monthly cultural supplement *Página Uno*, referenced the participation of the Catholic Church in the postelection protests. In the spring of 1986, Chihuahuan bishops had published warnings of fraud, and over the summer clergy joined the protests by refusing to celebrate Mass.[80] The *Página Uno* cartoon depicted the PAN as a puppet of both the Catholic Church and the United States.[81] In the image, a priest controls a puppet, dressed as a PAN protester, who cries "Fraud." The priest smiles sinisterly, unaware that he himself is being manipulated by a larger hand (with "USA" printed on the cuff sleeve). The cartoon collapsed multiple concerns into one image by suggesting that church and U.S. interests neatly aligned in support of the PAN. Accusations of foreign and religious meddling highlighted fears that unknown figures used the outcry against electoral fraud to undermine national ideals of sovereignty and secularism.

Other opinion leaders worried about the silencing of more scandalous atrocities. Laura Bolaños, a longtime opinion writer for *El Universal*, noted that while a presumably stolen election generated international attention and outrage, the disappearance of some five hundred peasants in the Dirty War did not. She offered her own explanation for why the PAN was able to freely organize while peasants were not: "Could it be that the Government is afraid of white people [*los güeros*]? Could it be that among white people, at the end of the day, there are no substantive differences?"[82] By identifying a greater source of outrage, Bolaños highlighted the inequities of scandal. She went beyond commenting on the contingent nature of reporting and public outrage, which made some exposés garner more public attention than others. Instead, Bolaños hinted that in the national consciousness, not all deaths could be grieved, and thus could not become the object of scandal.[83]

For other Mexico City columnists these explanations wrongly justified fraud. José Agustín Ortiz Pinchetti (brother of Francisco), a lawyer who represented *La Jornada*, contrasted the straightforward sensibility of Chihuahuans against the "venality" of Mexico City journalists, whom he accused of minimizing or qualifying the electoral fraud. Referring to northerners' desire for clean elections, he reasoned that "the simplicity of their goal is perhaps due to this pragmatic and frank people's unique way of thinking and speaking."[84] For Chihuahuans, he argued, fraud was an uncomplicated matter, while Mexico City residents participated in a baroque political culture that disinclined them toward democracy.

While these debates largely circulated in the elite sphere of print media, *Proceso* reporter Francisco Ortiz Pinchetti believed that the PAN would suffer real world consequences. He worried that if national media abandoned the protesters, the federal government would refuse to annul the election results. On August 3 he penned a letter to Heberto Castillo, the influential PMT leader who had recently visited Chihuahua City. Castillo had urged the hunger strikers to end their fast, but Francisco begged him to reconsider his position. Francisco accused Mexico City leftists of defending electoral fraud—and, by extension the PRI, simply because they distrusted the PAN's "supposed invocations abroad." He defended the PAN's decision to solicit foreign coverage, reasoning that "we just want foreigners to realize what type of democracy is practiced in Mexico." Francisco argued that nationalists like Castillo should be more concerned that such a strategy was necessary in the first place. Protesters sought U.S. sympathy, he argued, because the Mexican government would not otherwise respond. "The government doesn't give a damn because we don't count for them. So long as it is only Mexicans . . . who demonstrate [and] protest, and only the Mexican press that speaks about it, the government and its party don't care." Francisco highlighted the continued weakness of accountability, asserting that only outside pressure would bring justice. His letter underscored the thorny issue of taking sides in the Chihuahuan election. For many, unseating the PRI was the first and crucial step toward democracy; for others the PAN's loss, while not justifiable, was acceptable. Responding to Castillo's claims that the opposition was anti-nationalist, Ortiz Pinchetti demanded to know "Do you also believe that the PRI is our FATHERLAND?"[85] In effect, he saw the acceptance of fraud as a defense of the PRI.

Ortiz Pinchetti's reasoning was complicated a few days later when five U.S. senators called for President de la Madrid to nullify the Chihuahuan elections.[86] Mexico City reporters and intellectuals had difficulty discerning the stakes of electoral fraud when U.S. lawmakers tried to steer the results in the PAN's favor. Union leader Antonio Gershenson addressed these concerns directly by arguing that democracy could not exist without national sovereignty. In a *La Jornada* opinion article the following day, he reasoned that "it would be futile to wait for democratization to arrive from the outside. If decisions are made outside Mexico, we Mexicans might as well elect a viceroy."[87] The reference to a viceroy recalled conservatives' historical preferences for foreign rule, including their willingness to invite a French monarch to govern in the mid-nineteenth century. Gershenson's vision of national sovereignty required not only control over political decisions but also over economic ones. He, alongside other leftists, acknowledged the fraud but denied that it was scandalous by asserting that elections alone would not deliver democracy.

Despite these differences, conservatives and leftists agreed that the PRI needed to adapt to the demands of its citizenry. Intellectuals signed a petition, which appeared in national news publications on July 28. Héctor Aguilar Camín, Enrique Krauze, Lorenzo Meyer, Carlos Monsiváis, and Octavio Paz, among others, asserted that the PRI's claims to victory in 98 percent of Chihuahua's races "reveal a dangerous obsession with unanimity."[88] *El Porvenir* columnists concurred, noting, "When a regime has to resort to its maximum force, the military, to win elections, it is because all of its resources of persuasion have run out."[89]

This "obsession with unanimity" had serious effects for some journalists. While some Mexico City intellectuals debated the interests behind the scandal, others highlighted the growing threats to their profession. In August 1986 the Union of Democratic Journalists (Unión de Periodistas Democráticas, or UPD) warned that Mexican reporters faced an increasingly dangerous landscape; thirty-seven journalists had been assassinated in Mexico since 1976.[90] In July 1986, as debates raged about the Chihuahuan elections, two journalists in Matamoros were shot and killed. Among them was Norma Moreno Figueroa, who had reported on connections between the Tamaulipas governor and drug traffickers. Beyond physical vulnerability, the UPD also highlighted a shifting dynamic in which "private corporations exert greater and greater influence in the realm of information."[91] While eliciting little attention, these warnings foreshadowed changes in the landscape of denuncia journalism, which could easily be missed in the debates surrounding the elections.

## CONCLUSION

The scandal concerning Chihuahua's elections took place before a single vote was cast. Anticipatory U.S. coverage and congressional oversight warned of the dire consequences of fraud. Opinion leaders like Aguilar Camín and Krauze provided a framework for understanding Chihuahua's critical place within Mexican democratic change. Sympathetic reporters like Francisco Ortiz Pinchetti similarly claimed that the PAN's victory was inevitable. The confluence of media coverage, civic mobilization, and U.S. government interest threatened a scandal long before the results were tallied. The growing imbrication with transnational media also raised questions of how U.S. media might set the agenda or even spark scandals in Mexico, possibly with goals that were contrary to the national interest.

Unsurprisingly, when the federal government announced that the PRI had swept the 1986 elections, protesters and oppositional media loudly challenged the results. But the significance of the elections became a thorny subject of public debate, particularly in the opinion pages of Mexico City newspapers. Left-leaning journalists warned that sinister interests lurked behind the scandal, suggesting that it was not the truth of the accusations that was important but the motives that lay behind them. Conservative and neoliberal writers, in turn, accused leftists of justifying fraud and defending the PRI. Conflicts also erupted on the ground, as Mexican and U.S. correspondents accused their counterparts of being imperialist plotters or co-opted hacks. These debates highlight the intersubjective processes that determined the significance of scandals and underscored that scandal was not only a vehicle for accountability but also for manipulation.

Media coverage of the 1986 Chihuahuan elections raised the political stakes for the upcoming 1988 presidential elections. In May 1987 a disaffected faction of the PRI announced that it would present Cuauhtémoc Cárdenas, son of former president Lázaro Cárdenas, as an opposition candidate. The faction, which later formed the National Democratic Front (Frente Democrático Nacional) party, opposed austerity measures and the undemocratic selection of the PRI's presidential candidate.[92] Cárdenas mobilized broad-based support, signaling the end to decades of uncompetitive presidential elections. Organizations like Civic Alliance (Alianza Cívica) were formed to monitor the fairness of the elections. Significantly, they not only observed the voting process but also denounced biased media coverage in over seventy outlets.[93] When Televisa ignored the opposition candidates and tried to steer attention away from the elections, civic organizations like the Active and Peaceful Civic Resistance (Resistencia Civil Activa y Pacífica, or RECAP) organized a boycott against the broadcast monopoly.[94]

Despite high expectations, the 1988 race ended with the PRI's victory and well-founded claims of fraud. Before the elections, the PRI manipulated the voter registry, purging names and adding inaccurate information that disqualified registered voters while making it possible for illegitimate voters to cast ballots. On election day, opposition parties denounced that ballot boxes were robbed at gunpoint or later stuffed with ballots that did not match those counted at the polling station. But the most notorious and memorable sign of fraud that night was a suspicious "computer crash" that disrupted the newly implemented electronic vote tally. When the PRI announced that its candidate, Carlos Salinas, had won by a historically narrow margin of the vote (just over 50 percent), massive protests flooded Mexico City's streets, and they continued for months.[95] As with the 1986 Chihuahuan elections, media helped establish the stakes of this fraud.

# EPILOGUE

On the eve of the October 1987 *destape* (the sitting president's naming of his successor), a sensational book sparked conflicts within President Miguel de la Madrid's administration. Provocatively titled *Un asesino en la presidencia?*, the short book (some called it a pamphlet) delivered a stunning denunciation against Carlos Salinas, a prominent member of the cabinet and a front runner to be the incumbent's handpicked candidate (*tapado*). Governing officials suspected that the auspiciously timed denunciation served a hidden, and thus pernicious, agenda. Political elites had long accused *denuncia* journalists of delivering baseless accusations for pay, and the PRI's splintering in 1987 only aggravated fears of conspiracy. Rumors swirled that the book was ghostwritten by one of Salinas's rivals in the administration, while others blamed a Mexico City official. The mysterious interests behind the book amplified its perceived political significance.

*Un asesino en la presidencia?* unearthed a disturbing episode from Salinas's childhood, long buried from public view.[1] In December 1951 Carlos (age three), his brother Raúl (age five), and their friend Gustavo (age eight) were playing in the Salinas family's country vacation home when the brothers discovered their father's loaded rifle in a closet. Playing a game of "assassin," one of the boys pointed the rifle at the family's twelve-year-old domestic servant, Manuela. The boy pulled the trigger and hit the girl beneath her left eye, killing her immediately. When the housekeeper discovered Manuela lying in a pool of blood, the boys nonchalantly explained, "We just killed her." The murder of a poor, Indigenous girl at the hands of three wealthy boys soon made national news. Mexico City newspapers chided the family patriarch, Raúl Salinas Lozano, for failing to safely stow his weapon and described the murder as a tragic accident. The courts agreed, mandating counseling for the boys while avoiding further punishment. With the publication of *Un asesino en la presidencia?*, the case once again became the subject of public attention. Though original newspaper accounts did not name which boy pulled the trigger, the book suggested that it was the group's youngest member, presidential hopeful Carlos Salinas.

The authors, lawyer José Luis González Meza and *Por Esto!* reporter Walter López Koehl, introduced their short book by arguing that "Mexico's rulers evade the legal and political responsibility that they deserve."[2] They rattled off a laundry list of corrupt Salinas family dealings, all beginning with Manuela's murder. Among other crimes, the authors alleged that the elder Raúl Salinas had been involved in a multimillion-dollar fraud in the henequen industry and reminded readers of Mario Menéndez Rodríguez's 1963 denunciations against agrarian officials, including then Secretary of Industry and Commerce Salinas Lozano. *Un asesino* argued that acts of murder and embezzlement were not unrelated, but rather evidence of the impunity with which the nation's rich and powerful acted, often at the expense of the most marginalized and vulnerable.

The book caused a sensation and sparked buoyant press coverage that focused not only on state impunity but also on journalistic ethics. These discussions touched upon the long-standing ambiguities that surrounded denuncia journalism. *Proceso* journalist Enrique Maza, for example, tried to distinguish his newsmagazine's independent reporting from the "propagandist" (*panfletario*) content of *Un asesino*.[3] In an editorial he discredited the book by discussing various conflicts of interest, suggesting that González Meza and López were motivated by personal vendetta. Two recent lawsuits had pitted them both against high-ranking political officials, including Salinas, and Maza intimated that the authors used their "shameless insults" as extortion. Yet *Proceso* glossed over the fine line that separated substantiated denunciations from baseless attacks. Indeed, *Un asesino* did not reveal new or unfounded information, but simply provided a different interpretative framework for evaluating wrongdoing and demanding justice. Even so, the scandal soon centered on the hidden motives behind the book.

Despite the accusations in *Un asesino*, Salinas narrowly won the 1988 presidential election, but he did not easily forget the smear campaign against him. His intelligence sources identified the powerful Pemex union leader, Joaquín "La Quina" Hernández Galicia, as the mastermind behind the book. This confirmed Salinas's suspicions that Hernández Galicia, historically a staunch PRI ally, had secretly supported the National Democratic Front (Frente Democrático Nacional) and thereby siphoned crucial votes away from the ruling party. Having faced an unprecedented electoral challenge, Salinas did not easily forgive Hernández Galicia's betrayal, and the president-elect wasted little time in retaliating. On January 10, 1989, barely one month after Salinas took office, federal police raided La Quina's home in Ciudad Madero, Tamaulipas, where they discovered two hundred Uzi machine guns and the dead body of a federal agent. Police promptly arrested the union leader, who was charged with murder and arms trafficking. Hernández Galicia confessed and later received a prison sentence of thirty-five years.

The Quinazo, as the spectacle became known, was welcomed both at home and abroad as a victory over corruption. Spanish newspaper *El País* celebrated the move as evidence of Mexico's democratization, and the *Wall Street Journal* enthused that Salinas had "quickly transformed his image from milquetoast to macho man."[4] But La Quina's dramatic downfall also illuminated the contradictions of justice and accountability. Reflecting on the government response, reporter Maza asserted that "La Quina's story is not new nor is it hidden, even if it has just been 'uncovered' in recent days."[5] Since 1983, *Proceso* had exposed the union boss's misdeeds, including his illicit enrichment, arms trafficking, and likely participation in the mysterious murders of regional Pemex union leaders. Yet neither the de la Madrid government nor the PGR had responded to these exposés. Maza suggested that Salinas only acted against the union leader to satisfy his own personal vendetta. Indeed, it later emerged that police had facilitated La Quina's arrest by forcing a confession and planting a dead body at the union leader's home.[6] Subsequent investigations into the case revealed additional motives; Hernández Galicia's imprisonment facilitated the government's defanging of Mexico's largest and most powerful union, which the leader had controlled for decades. La Quina's removal enabled the Salinas government to impose austerity measures and force the union to cut 120,000 jobs.[7] Salinas thus used the Quinazo to enact his program of rationalizing the Mexican economy while claiming to have served democratic ends. For some the political machinations undermined celebrations that justice had been served.

Television programs further challenged the president's anticorruption narrative. The Salinas administration arranged for La Quina to read his signed confession via live television broadcast—a standard performance of justice being served. But when the time came, La Quina went off script and denounced that his admission of guilt had been coerced. The union boss made an emotional appeal to viewers' sympathies, claiming that interrogators had threatened that he would never see his family again if he did not sign the statement. It was common knowledge that police tortured prisoners to extract confessions, but the high-profile live event made Hernández Galicia's disruption particularly subversive. The broadcaster abruptly cut the transmission, but censorship only amplified the spectacle.[8]

The Quinazo was only the first of many stranger-than-fiction scandals that punctuated Salinas's presidency and led to unprecedented accusations against a sitting president and his family. On March 23, 1994, the PRI's presidential candidate, Luis Donaldo Colosio, was assassinated while campaigning in Baja California. Such a high-profile homicide had not occurred since the 1928 assassination of President Álvaro Obregón.[9] Televised news broadcasts replayed scenes of terror for shocked Mexican viewers, and presenters tried to get live statements from Colosio's devastated wife in the hospital. Soon after Colosio's assassination, on September 28, 1994, the secretary general of the PRI, José Francisco Ruiz Massieu, was murdered on the street in Mexico City. Despite numerous cover-up attempts, news publications like *El Economista*, *La Jornada*, *Proceso*, and *Reforma* revealed a dense web of baroque corruption and family intrigue that implicated the Salinas family. The scandal peaked with the February 1995 arrest of the ex-president's brother, Raúl, whom the PGR charged with masterminding Ruiz Massieu's murder. Carlos Salinas promptly went into exile after his brother's arrest, further inflaming speculation regarding the ex-president's involvement.[10]

Scholars point to the rash of political scandals in the 1990s as a turning point in the history of the Mexican press. According to these accounts, national print media finally assumed the role of an independent watchdog that would hold government accountable. Sallie Hughes notes that Colosio's shocking assassination led publisher Juan Francisco Ealy Ortiz (a personal friend of the murdered presidential candidate) to break with the PRI and adopt a more critical stance in his *El Universal* newspaper.[11] Chappell Lawson further argues that a steady drumbeat of scandals undermined the legitimacy of the political system and demonstrated that corrupt practices would be exposed to public scrutiny.[12] This book has shown, however, that these scandals were the culmination of much longer trends in Mexico City journalism. The density of critical outlets, divisions among public officials, and evolving norms of journalism all facilitated the exposure of electrifying denunciations. Celebratory narratives of a steady march toward press freedom are also complicated by the fact that critical journalists suffered setbacks under Salinas's presidency. Radio programs, including Francisco Huerta's *Voz Pública* and Miguel Ángel Granados Chapa's *Radio Mil*, were canceled; *Excélsior* journalist Manú Dornbierer was also fired after writing a denunciatory article about the president's brother.[13] New threats from organized crime also made reporting more precarious.

As suggested by the Quinazo, scandals could conceal the interests and manipulations that led to the publicity of wrongdoing. Scandals sensationalized the revelation of crimes but obscured the difference between knowing and reckoning. Neither *Un asesino en la presidencia?* nor the Quinazo revealed new information about either Salinas or Hernández Galicia. While print media had implicated both individuals in various crimes, these denunciations were met with government inaction. Indeed, La Quina's arrest was sensational precisely because his corruption and impunity were already so well known. While scandals often included some form of secrecy and deceit, governing officials used them as opportunities for high-profile performances of justice being served. The 1990s marked the culmination of a growing trend in which public officials embraced scandal as a defining mechanism of politics.

CONCLUSION

This book has shown that scandal was a critical, but episodic and inequitable, vehicle for justice in late twentieth-century Mexico. Hard-hitting exposés, tell-all books, and scandalously frank interviews forced issues into the public sphere. Popular pressure, combined with intraelite divisions, could lead to the resignation or even imprisonment of offenders. Ordinary Mexicans regularly encountered corruption, bureaucracy, and violence, and they grumbled about official lies and bald-faced electoral fraud. But this knowledge did not always lead to a collective reckoning with wrongdoing. If denunciations did not necessarily expose unknown information, they did force accusations into the open. This book has thus been concerned with what happened when commonplace complaints became the object of public discussion and scrutiny.

Print media's close relationship with the government had conditioned the possibilities of denunciations since the postrevolutionary period. As the one-party state consolidated its power in the late 1930s, leaders recognized that mass media furnished a critical tool for managing dissent. President Lázaro Cárdenas created the newsprint producer and distributor, PIPSA, which subsidized compliant print media while bankrupting dissident periodicals. Broadcast media, however, soon became the government's preferred medium of communication, and regulations mandated that all radio stations air the official program, *La Hora Nacional*, which projected a homogenized vision of Mexican national culture through carefully selected music and dramas. As of 1950, television offered another tool for communicating official views. As labor strikes and student movements soon proliferated in Guadalajara, Mérida, Mexico City, Monterrey, Morelia, and Puebla, television news programs silenced or villainized protesters. In short, ruling party officials mobilized media to control political discourse in the capital city and to project that vision to other parts of the country.[1]

While national broadsheets toed the government line, technological change disrupted state efforts to carefully orchestrate coverage. In the 1960s the availability of the mimeograph enabled the rapid and affordable reproduction of neighborhood bulletins, flyers, and song sheets. Handbills informed city residents of strikes and student protests, drawing more participants to the streets. Megaphones offered an even more basic tool for diffusing alternative news. In the 1970s state officials photocopied and circulated internal reports, and news editors reproduced images of leaked documents that they placed alongside investigative articles. While readers could not access the full documents, these visual aids underscored the fact that the denunciations were grounded in evidence. The decade also witnessed a flourishing of community radio, which decentered mainstream commercial news production. By the 1980s video technology was more affordable, and activists recorded their events or relevant programs and distributed the videotapes via mail.

While new technologies facilitated the diffusion and reproduction of alternative viewpoints, they also generated greater confusion regarding authorship, authenticity, and motive. Political groups frequently published apocryphal bulletins under the names of rival organizations. This long-standing practice was accelerated by the accessibility and affordability of photocopying. Voice recording technology also offered a possibility for the faithful reproduction of new views or for surreptitious fabrication. Facsimiles of leaked documents raised questions regarding how journalists accessed their sources and who benefited from their exposés. The popularity of television similarly coincided with suspicions that camera crews staged or manipulated scenes to serve government interests. Finally, the circulation of U.S. media in Mexico raised questions of how outside groups might weaponize scandal. In short, the mobilization of new technologies presented the possibility for both transparency and manipulation.

Processes of revelation, concealment, and dissimulation constituted the Mexico City public sphere in the late twentieth century. Governing officials stridently denied accusations in speeches and press bulletins while privately pressuring reporters to keep quiet. Rival politicians leaked salacious tips to divert attention from more damaging information. Meanwhile, journalists selectively aired leaked documents while withholding other secrets to maintain good relationships with their informants. Ordinary media consumers understood that political interests and manipulations were part of news production. But secrecy created knowledge hierarchies that kept most people from knowing what agenda undergirded a given news story.[2] For this reason, denunciations in Mexico City media were often met with public ambivalence. By the 1990s the pace of scandals became dizzying, and ordinary people alternatively responded with outrage or apathy.

This book has charted the development of a mediated urban citizenship. From the mid-twentieth century on, a dense news and culture landscape shaped political sensibilities and behaviors. Newsstands hawked diverse scandals, from bared breasts and gory crime scenes to political misdeeds. Televisions played in bars and barbershops, radios blared music and *novelas* in tenements and subdivisions, and movie theaters were packed with spectators on weekends. In the 1960s nearly every urban home had a radio set from which viewers could access programming from Cuba, Russia, and the United States. Saturated media diets also reshaped the ways in which urban residents understood themselves as citizens. Ordinary people registered their views by transforming the public landscape with graffiti, protest signs, effigies, and street performances. They wrote letters to journalists and news publications, or authored their own news by circulating flyers and bulletins. And they commented on scandals with cynical jokes that amended or subverted elite interpretations.

Journalists' coverage of scandalous misdeeds provided the language and images that continue to shape public memory, and this was not particular to the late twentieth century. Perhaps one of Mexico's most famous scandals occurred in 1901 when Mexico City police raided a private party and arrested forty-one men, half of whom were cross-dressing. The incident inspired sensationalized press coverage, engravings, and a novel. Reporters fueled moral panic, fixating on the erosion of the social fabric, and the governor responded by summarily sentencing the men to hard labor. One of the longer-lasting legacies of the scandal was the new discourse around homosexuality.[3] In the 1920s the *nota roja* genre of crime journalism similarly delivered emotional portraits of high-profile murderers, transforming criminals into celebrities with lasting public resonance. As Pablo Piccato notes, these narratives furnished distinct visions of justice and truth.[4] Similarly, in the later part of the century, the imbrication of print and broadcast media allowed scandalous narratives to circulate from print journalism to radio, television, and comic books, forging shared narratives around corruption.

Over the late twentieth century, the cross-pollination of radio, television, and print media content expanded the national appetite for sensational narratives. The 1968 creation of the national wire service, Notimex, stitched together regional and capital city news, as did the AMI, which syndicated critical Mexico City columns in dozens of news publications across the country. By the 1980s television, print media, and radio picked up stories from niche publications, and *denuncia* journalists reported on portrayals and reinterpretations that appeared in broadcast media and films. Comic books, novels, and movies provided creative reinterpretations of high-profile stories, solidifying their relevance for new generations that had not lived through the events.

Like those of any narrative, the meanings of scandals were never fixed and they could be easily appropriated and mobilized for distinct ends. For example, during the economic crisis, journalistic exposés revealed a massive embezzlement in the state-owned and -operated oil company Pemex. After uncovering this case in the early 1980s, Heberto Castillo and *Proceso* reporter Carlos Ramírez urged the government to defend national sovereignty and uproot corruption so that oil wealth could be redistributed. By contrast, technocratic and conservative commentators referenced the Pemex corruption case to argue for the liberalization and deregulation of the economy. For some, the Pemex case became a justification for the austerity measures and budget cutting that followed Mexico's debt default. Critical press articles thus easily escaped the control of their authors.

Similarly, after the devastating 1985 Mexico City earthquake, the public was disgusted by revelations that private factory owners had rushed to the damage sites to remove their sewing machinery while abandoning the young female employees who remained trapped in the wreckage. References to "the rescue of machinery" circulated widely through media and invoked criticisms of corporate greed—and not without a little anti-Semitism. While *denuncia* reporters argued that private-public collusion made buildings more unsafe and unstable, governing officials mobilized the sensational narrative to argue that private, not public, actors were responsible for the deaths of so many garment workers. Changing political, social, and economic conditions continue to shift interpretations of these cases. Even so, many of these media-driven scandals remain central in narratives of late twentieth-century political change. Print media headlines, chronicles, and exposés have furnished scholars with enduring arguments about the watershed moments in Mexico's transition to democracy. By demonstrating how these narratives were created, this book has underscored that the idea of watershed moments was itself a creation of the press, as journalists tried to make sense of the events in real time.

As Mexico City writers pressed to open a closed political system, they did not see all voices as equally deserving of amplification. For this reason, Jürgen Habermas's normative vision of democratic and horizontal debate does not capture the dynamics of the Mexican public sphere. Denunciations could naturalize racial and class inequalities, as in the case of Arturo "El Negro" Durazo, which revealed the sensational violence and corruption of the Mexico City police. As discussed in chapter 4, popular reinterpretations of the scandal underscored how Durazo's lower-class roots, coarse mannerisms, and presumed racial background disqualified him for public office. Comic books and films explained Durazo's violence and corruption by emphasizing his dark skin and aberrant masculinity (either impotent or hypersexual). Mexico City commentary on the Chihuahuan state elections, examined in chapter 6, similarly racialized the ideal citizen: in praising the industriousness, innovation, and whiteness of northerners, many conservative writers suggested that central (Indigenous) Mexicans were less inclined toward democracy and thus less desirable citizens. These discussions subtly affirmed readers' assumptions about whose knowledge and activism should be praised and whose should be feared or avoided.

Many reporters also made gendered claims to authority. Since the nineteenth century, combat journalists and printers had presented themselves as honorable men crusading for justice.[5] This practice continued in the twentieth century and was further shaped by New Journalism trends, which situated the reporter as a key protagonist in his story. Mexican reporters like Manuel Buendía, Heberto Castillo, Julio Scherer García, and Mario Menéndez Rodríguez frequently detailed their encounters with state violence and their heroic willingness to speak truth to power. Their narrations suggested that their exposés carried greater weight because of their sacrifice. The glorification of the daring male investigative reporter was also shaped by the Watergate scandal, which Mexican news outlets closely followed. The *Washington Post*'s Carl Bernstein and Bob Woodward served as models of courageous reporters willing to take down the world's most powerful leader. Finally, many journalists (men and women alike) and public officials described rational speech as male and irrational speech as female, discounting women's knowledge by feminizing subversive narratives.

The figure of the denuncia journalist changed over the course of the late twentieth century. As the Mexican and U.S. economies became increasingly integrated, U.S. journalists played a more prominent role in the Mexican public sphere. Major U.S. newspapers sent correspondents to cover contested state elections, heightening national and international expectations of the results. The U.S. government also invested more money in training foreign journalists—an effort to inculcate reporters in the Western values of democracy and a free press. In addition to enrolling in these programs, Mexico City reporters increasingly pursued university training in their fields, receiving a theoretical education in communications studies and ethics training in investigative methods. By the 1980s denuncia journalists also expanded their targets of investigation, taking aim at the U.S. government, the CIA, the conservative opposition, and even each other.

These journalists did not contribute to a single, unified opposition movement for democracy. *La Jornada* amplified the voices of displaced residents who mobilized after the earthquake and later of the Zapatistas who took up arms in Chiapas in 1994. Right-leaning outlets like *El Norte*, *El Porvenir*, and *Reforma* followed PAN and Catholic activists, and *El Día* supported the peasant and workers' struggles to reform PRI organizations from within. All were critical news outlets, but their visions for political change varied significantly. Denuncia publications were also riddled with internal conflicts due to ideological and interpersonal differences. Big personalities and bruised egos led journalists to frequently tender resignations and join new publications. While reporters shared criticisms of the PRI, they often disagreed on the best path forward, leading to acrimonious public debates between towering figures such as Julio Scherer García and Octavio Paz or Adolfo Gilly and Enrique Krauze, among others. Presumably independent journalists could differ on issues of major importance, including the significance of electoral fraud and the type of democracy that Mexico should aspire to implement.

Mexico was not alone in witnessing the proliferation of political scandals in the 1980s and 1990s. In Latin America, where many countries were transitioning from authoritarianism to democracy, media took advantage of newfound freedoms. After years of censorship, major news outlets in Argentina, Brazil, and Peru exposed human rights abuses and corporate malfeasance. Corruption scandals even led to the impeachment of Brazilian president Fernando Collor de Mello in 1992 and to the resignations of Argentina's finance minister Antonio Erman González, among others, in 1991. Mexico formed part of a regional trend that witnessed the confluence of political transitions and press scandals.

Scholars of Latin America have assumed a positive relationship between journalism and democracy, asserting that an investigative press improves the quality of democratic institutions and enforces accountability between elections.[6] Yet they have also struggled to square worsening conditions for the press with the prevalence of scandals. While Silvio Waisbord notes that liberal democracy is an essential condition for scandals to emerge, he finds that the Argentine press suffered retaliation, including cuts in state advertising and lawsuits, for its coverage in the 1990s.[7] Some journalists even received threats and faced violence. Since then, the situation in Mexico has been even more deadly for reporters. Murders of journalists have increased significantly since 2006, when President Felipe Calderón declared a militarized war on drugs. Reporters have been caught in the crosshairs of an increasingly violent drug trade and become the targets of complicit politicians.[8] In effect, transition from one-party rule has only made reporting more dangerous.

Even the country's most prominent reporter, Carmen Aristegui, was not immune to reprisals. After exposing the Casa Blanca scandal, which revealed a conflict of interest between the wife of President Enrique Peña Nieto and a state contractor, three MVS Noticias reporters, including Aristegui, were fired in March 2015. Aristegui only resumed reporting in January 2017 via an online program, *Aristegui en Vivo*, and she later joined Radio Centro in October 2018.[9] Thus, even as the electoral field has become more competitive and civil society more robust, reporters can face serious repercussions for what they write. Instead of witnessing a gradual move toward more press freedom, we have instead seen an unpredictable rhythm of tightening and loosening. Moreover, different actors, including drug trafficking organizations and private enterprises, have assumed a greater role in regulating public expression. Private advertising accounts for a far greater proportion of media revenue than government publicity, leading reporters and directors to consider business interests in their coverage.[10]

In the past forty years, Mexico's political system has become more pluralistic, more competitive, and more representative of different groups of people. The public sphere is diverse, and civil society is engaged and vibrant. At the same time, economic inequality has increased significantly, and violence against journalists has also increased. Denuncia journalism did not deliver a universal or rational accountability or even necessarily justice. For every prominent political scandal in the late twentieth century, there were multiple instances of bad behavior that never appeared in the press or were reported but received little notice. The accident of timing, a particularly resonate image or narrative, the commitment of a tenacious reporter, or the collaboration of disaffected political elites are only a few of the factors that help explain what created a scandal. Reckoning with injustice thus rested precariously on the ability to make a scandal.

# NOTES

## INTRODUCTION

1. Unless otherwise noted, all translations are the author's own. Manuel Buendía, "Red Privada," *Excélsior*, July 27, 1979, 1.
2. Andrew Sackett, "Fun in Acapulco? The Politics of Development on the Mexican Riviera," in *Holiday in Mexico: Critical Reflections on Tourism and Tourist Encounters*, ed. Dina Berger and Andrew Grant Wood (Durham, NC: Duke University Press, 2010), 161, 170.
3. Buendía, "Red Privada."
4. Daniel Rodríguez to Manuel Buendía, August 2, 1979, Fundación Manuel Buendía (hereafter FMB), Datos Personales, Binder 3.
5. With the exception of *Siempre!* magazine, such critical reporting was limited to niche or local publications prior to the 1960s.
6. See, for example, Joe Foweraker and Ann L. Craig, *Popular Movements and Political Change in Mexico* (Boulder, CO: Lynne Rienner Publishers, 1990); Alonso Lujambio, *Federalismo y congreso en el cambio político de México* (México: Universidad Nacional Autónoma de México, 1995); Carlos Elizondo Mayer-Serra and Benito Nacif Hernández, eds., *Lecturas sobre el cambio político en México* (México: Fondo de Cultura Económica, 2002); Todd A. Eisenstadt, *Courting Democracy in Mexico: Party Strategies and Electoral Institutions* (New York: Cambridge University Press, 2004); Beatriz Magaloni, *Voting for Autocracy: Hegemonic Party Survival and Its Demise in Mexico* (New York: Cambridge University Press, 2006); Kenneth Greene, *Why Dominant Parties Lose: Mexico's Democratization in Comparative Perspective* (New York: Cambridge University Press, 2007); Louise E. Walker, *Waking from the Dream: Mexico's Middle Classes after 1968* (Stanford, CA: Stanford University Press, 2013).
7. Heather Levi, *The World of Lucha Libre: Secrets, Revelations, and Mexican National Identity* (Durham, NC: Duke University Press, 2008), 46.
8. Natalia Roudakova, *Losing Pravda: Ethics and the Press in Post-truth Russia* (New York: Cambridge University Press, 2017), 26. See also Ari Adut, *On Scandal: Moral Disturbances in Society, Politics, and Art* (New York: Cambridge University Press, 2008), 19, 21.
9. Brodwyn M. Fischer, *A Poverty of Rights: Citizenship and Inequality in Twentieth-Century Rio de Janeiro* (Stanford, CA: Stanford University Press, 2008), 6; James

Holston, *Insurgent Citizenship: Disjunctions of Democracy and Modernity in Brazil* (Princeton, NJ: Princeton University Press, 2008), 7.

10 Evelina Dagnino, "Citizenship in Latin America: An Introduction," *Latin American Perspectives* 30, no. 2 (2003): 211–12. See also Sonia E. Álvarez, Evelina Dagnino, and Arturo Escobar, eds., *Cultures of Politics / Politics of Cultures: Revisioning Latin American Social Movements* (Boulder, CO: Westview, 1998).

11 Silvio Waisbord, *Watchdog Journalism in South America: News, Accountability, and Democracy* (New York: Columbia University Press, 2000), has also found this to be the case in South America.

12 Alan Knight, "Historical Continuities in Social Movements," in *Popular Movements and Political Change in Mexico*, ed. Joe Foweraker and Ann L. Craig (Boulder, CO: Lynne Rienner, 1990), 96.

13 See, for example, Stanley Ross, "Mexico: The Preferred Revolution," in *Politics of Change in Latin America*, ed. Joseph Maier and Richard W. Weatherhead (New York: Frederick A. Praeger, 1964), 140–54.

14 Karin Wahl-Jorgensen, "Mediated Citizenship(s): An Introduction," *Social Semiotics* 16, no. 2 (2006): 197–203.

15 Leonor's last name is illegible in her signature, which is why I have not included it in the citation. Leonor to Miguel Ángel Granados Chapa, Colección Particular Miguel Ángel Granados Chapa. I was the first researcher to access Granados Chapa's private collection, which at the time was unorganized and in the care of his son, Luis Fernando Granados. The family has since donated the collection to the Universidad Autónoma de México–Cuajimalpa, where it is currently being archived.

16 Daniel Lerner, *The Passing of Traditional Society: Modernizing the Middle East* (Glencoe, IL: Free Press, 1958); Nils Gilman, *Mandarins of the Future: Modernization Theory in Cold War America* (Baltimore: Johns Hopkins University Press, 2004), 5.

17 Vanessa Freije, "'The Emancipation of Media': Latin American Advocacy for a New International Information Order in the 1970s," *Journal of Global History* 14, no. 2 (2019): 301–20.

18 Anne Rubenstein, *Bad Language, Naked Ladies, and Other Threats to the Nation: A Political History of Comic Books in Mexico* (Durham, NC: Duke University Press, 1998); Julia Tuñón, *Mujeres de luz y sombra en el cine mexicano: La construcción de una imagen (1939–1952)* (México: Colegio de México, 1998); Joy Elizabeth Hayes, *Radio Nation: Communication, Popular Culture, and Nationalism in Mexico, 1920–1950* (Tucson: University of Arizona Press, 2000); Gilbert M. Joseph, Anne Rubenstein, and Eric Zolov, eds., *Fragments of a Golden Age: The Politics of Culture in Mexico since 1940* (Durham, NC: Duke University Press, 2001); Mary Kay Vaughan and Stephen E. Lewis, eds., *The Eagle and the Virgin: Nation and Cultural Revolution in Mexico, 1920–1940* (Durham, NC: Duke University Press, 2006).

19 For example, Mexico was the sixth nation in the world to air a televised broadcast. Celeste González de Bustamante, *"Muy buenas noches": Mexico, Television, and the Cold War* (Lincoln: University of Nebraska Press, 2012), 4.

20 Benjamin T. Smith, *The Mexican Press and Civil Society, 1940–1976: Stories from the Newsroom, Stories from the Street* (Chapel Hill: University of North Carolina Press, 2018), 27.

21 Instituto Nacional de Estadística y Geografía, *Sexto censo de población 1940* (México: Instituto Nacional de Estadística y Geografía, 1940), https://www.inegi.org.mx/programas/ccpv/1940/; Instituto Nacional de Estadística y Geografía, *IX censo general de población 1970* (México: Instituto Nacional de Estadística y Geografía, 1970), https://www.inegi.org.mx/programas/ccpv/1970/default.html#Tabulados; Rubenstein, *Bad Language, Naked Ladies*, 14; Smith, *The Mexican Press*, 14.

22 Oscar Lewis, *Los hijos de Sánchez: Autobiografía de una familia mexicana* (México: Fondo de Cultura Económica, 1964); Carlos G. Vélez-Ibañez, *Rituals of Marginality: Politics, Process, and Culture Change in Urban Central Mexico, 1969–1974* (Berkeley: University of California Press, 1983).

23 International Research Associates, S.A. de C.V., *The Readership of* Suplemento Semanal *in Mexican Cities and Towns*, vol. 1, 1966, U.S. National Archives and Record Administration (hereafter NARA), RG 306, A1 1018, Box 9, 3, 13. Of those surveyed, 44 percent had more than a primary education.

24 Anne Rubenstein, "Theaters of Masculinity: Moviegoing and Male Roles in Mexico before 1960," in *Masculinity and Sexuality in Modern Mexico*, ed. Víctor M. Macías-González and Anne Rubenstein (Albuquerque: University of New Mexico Press, 2012), 132–54; Andrew Paxman, "Cooling to Cinema and Warming to Television: State Mass Media Policy, 1940–1964," in *Dictablanda: Politics, Work, and Culture in Mexico, 1938–1968*, ed. Paul Gillingham and Benjamin T. Smith (Durham, NC: Duke University Press, 2014), 310.

25 *Variety*, June 1, 1966, 21. Thank you to Andrew Paxman for providing me with the *Variety* reference. International Public Opinion Research, Inc., *A Survey of Political Opinion and Communications Behavior in Mexico: A Preliminary Report*, December 31, 1952, NARA, RG 306, P 78, Box 15, 11. The sample size was 4,776 people.

26 Arthur F. Corwin, *Contemporary Mexican Attitudes toward Population, Poverty, and Public Opinion* (Gainesville: University of Florida Press, 1963), 22; González de Bustamante, "Muy buenas noches," 9–10.

27 I took the average of data available from these three cities. Television ownership was lower (23 percent) in midsize cities such as Ciudad Juárez, Hermosillo, Jalapa, and Matamoros, but radio ownership remained high (74 percent). International Research Associates, S.A. de C.V., *The Ownership of Radio and Television Sets in Various Mexican Cities*, April 1965, NARA, RG 306, A1 1018, Box 9, 1–3, 5–9.

28 The total population was 50,695,000. Banco de México, *México social: Noventa indicadores seleccionados* (México: Banco Nacional de México, 1982), 4. See also Larissa Adler Lomnitz, *Networks and Marginality: Life in a Mexican Shantytown*, trans. Cinna Lomnitz (New York: Academic Press, 1977); Wayne Cornelius, *Politics and the Migrant Poor in Mexico City* (Stanford, CA: Stanford University

Press, 1975), 16–17, 27; and Ariel Rodríguez Kuri, "Secretos de la idiosincrasia: Urbanización y cambio cultural en México, 1950–1970," in *Ciudades mexicanas del siglo XX: Siete estudios históricos*, ed. Carlos Lira Vásquez and Ariel Rodríguez Kuri (México: SEP-CONACYT / Colmex / UAM Azcapotzalco, 2009), 29.

29 The Servicio de Información de *Excélsior* distributed its news stories to regional subscribers in the 1960s. Additional news agencies appeared in the 1970s, including Comunicación e Información, S.A. de C.V.; Lemus; and Notimex. Coordinación General de Comunicación Social, "Bases estratégicas para la construcción de un Sistema Nacional de Comunicación Social," vol. 3, Archivo Particular Luis Javier Solana.

30 Jürgen Habermas, *The Structural Transformation of the Public Sphere: An Inquiry into a Category of Bourgeois Society*, trans. Thomas Burger (Cambridge: Cambridge University Press, 1989), 25–26.

31 Habermas, *The Structural Transformation*, 169.

32 Nancy Fraser, "Rethinking the Public Sphere: A Contribution to the Critique of Actually Existing Democracy," *Social Text* 25–26 (1990): 56–80.

33 Mary Roldán, "Popular Cultural Action, Catholic Transnationalism, and Development in Colombia before Vatican II," in *Local Church, Global Church: Catholic Activism in Latin America from Rerum Novarum to Vatican II*, ed. Stephen J. C. Andes and Julia G. Young (Washington, DC: Catholic University of America Press, 2016), 245–74; Benjamin T. Smith, "The Paradoxes of the Public Sphere: Journalism, Gender, and Corruption in Mexico, 1940–70," *Journal of Social History* 52, no. 4 (2019): 1330–54; Pablo Piccato, *A History of Infamy: Crime, Truth, and Justice in Mexico* (Oakland: University of California Press, 2017); Naomi Schiller, *Channeling the State: Community Media and Popular Politics in Venezuela* (Durham, NC: Duke University Press, 2018).

34 Hilda Sábato, *The Many and the Few: Political Participation in Republican Buenos Aires* (Stanford, CA: Stanford University Press, 2001); Camilo D. Trumper, *Ephemeral Histories: Public Art, Politics, and the Struggle for the Streets in Chile* (Oakland: University of California Press, 2016).

35 Pablo Piccato, *The Tyranny of Opinion: Honor in the Construction of the Mexican Public Sphere* (Durham, NC: Duke University Press, 2010), 17.

36 On the Colombian case see, for example, Líbera Guzzi, "Medios y democracia: Reflexiones acerca del periodismo público en Colombia," *Chasqui* 122 (2013): 9.

37 Julio Scherer García and Carlos Monsiváis, *Tiempo de saber: Prensa y poder en México* (México: Aguilar, 2003); Enrique Condés Lara, *Represión y rebelión en México (1959–1985): La guerra fría en México. El discurso de la represión*, vol. 2 (México: Miguel Ángel Porrúa, 2007), 70–77; Chappell Lawson, *Building the Fourth Estate: Democratization and the Rise of a Free Press in Mexico* (Berkeley: University of California Press, 2002), 26–27, 65; Jacinto Rodríguez Munguía, *La otra guerra secreta: Los archivos prohibidos de la prensa y el poder* (México: Random House Mondadori, 2007); Rodolfo Gamiño Muñoz, *Guerrilla, represión y prensa en la década de los setenta en México: Invisibilidad y olvido* (México: Instituto Mora, 2011), 102–5.

38 Sallie Hughes, *Newsrooms in Conflict: Journalism and the Democratization of Mexico* (Pittsburgh: University of Pittsburgh Press, 2006); Lawson, *Building the Fourth Estate*.

39 Mary Kay Vaughan, *Portrait of a Young Painter: Pepe Zúñiga and Mexico City's Rebel Generation* (Durham, NC: Duke University Press, 2014); Piccato, *A History of Infamy*; Smith, *The Mexican Press*.

40 See, for example, Gilbert M. Joseph and Daniel Nugent, eds., *Everyday Forms of State Formation: Revolution and the Negotiation of Rule in Modern Mexico* (Durham, NC: Duke University Press, 1994); Mary Kay Vaughan, *Cultural Politics in Revolution: Teachers, Peasants, and Schools in Mexico, 1930–1940* (Tucson: University of Arizona Press, 1997).

41 Paul Gillingham and Benjamin T. Smith, "Introduction: The Paradoxes of Revolution," in *Dictablanda*, 20.

42 See, for example, Rogelio Hernández Rodríguez, *El centro dividido: La nueva autonomía de los gobernadores* (México: Colegio de México, 2008); Elisa Servín, "Reclaiming Revolution in Light of the 'Mexican Miracle': Celestino Gasca and the Federacionistas Leales Insurrection of 1961," *The Americas* 66, no. 4 (April 2010): 527–57; and Gillingham and Smith, *Dictablanda*.

43 Condés Lara, *Represión y rebelión*, vols. 1 and 2; Alan Knight, "The Myth of the Mexican Revolution," *Past and Present* 209, no. 1 (2010): 266; Walker, *Waking from the Dream*. Notable exceptions are Diane Davis, *Urban Leviathan Mexico City in the Twentieth Century* (Philadelphia: Temple University Press, 1994); Jeffrey W. Rubin, *Decentering the Regime: Ethnicity, Radicalism, and Democracy in Juchitán, Mexico* (Durham, NC: Duke University Press, 1997); and A. S. Dillingham, "Indigenismo Occupied: Indigenous Youth and Mexico's Democratic Opening (1968–1975)," *The Americas* 72, no. 4 (2015): 549–82.

44 Sergio Aguayo Quezada, *La charola: Una historia de los servicios de inteligencia en México* (México: Grijalbo, 2001); Tanalís Padilla, *Rural Resistance in the Land of Zapata: The Jaramillista Movement and the Myth of the Pax-Priísta, 1940–1962* (Durham, NC: Duke University Press, 2008); Alexander Aviña, *Specters of Revolution: Peasant Guerrillas in the Cold War Mexican Countryside* (New York: Oxford University Press, 2014); and Gladys McCormick, *The Logic of Compromise in Mexico: How the Countryside Was Key to the Emergence of Authoritarianism* (Chapel Hill: University of North Carolina Press, 2016).

45 Walker, *Waking from the Dream*; María L. O. Muñoz, *Stand Up and Fight: Participatory Indigenismo, Populism, and Mobilization in Mexico, 1970–1984* (Tucson: University of Arizona Press, 2016); Sandra C. Mendiola García, *Street Democracy: Vendors, Violence, and Public Space in Late Twentieth-Century Mexico* (Lincoln: University of Nebraska Press, 2017).

46 Roderic A. Camp, *Intellectuals and the State in Twentieth-Century Mexico* (Austin: University of Texas Press, 1985), 19.

47 Michael Taussig, *Defacement: Public Secrecy and the Labor of the Negative* (Stanford, CA: Stanford University Press, 1999), 5.

48 Condés Lara, *Represión y rebelión*, vol. 2, 72–73.

49 Ieva Jusionyte, "Crimecraft: Journalists, Police, and News Publics in an Argentine Town," *American Ethnologist* 43, no. 3 (2016): 453, emphasis in the original.
50 Quotes respectively from Joanna Davidson, "Cultivating Knowledge: Development, Dissemblance, and Discursive Contradictions among the Diola of Guinea-Bissau," *American Ethnologist* 37, no. 2 (2010): 221; and Thomas O. Beidelman, "Secrecy and Society: The Paradox of Knowing and the Knowing of Paradox," *Passages* 5 (1993): 6.
51 Waisbord, *Watchdog Journalism*, 104. On the negative connotation associated with denuncia journalism, see also Alberto Dines, *O papel do jornal* (São Paolo: Summus Editorial, 1986); Carlos Soria, "Fundamentos éticos de la presunción de inocencia o la legitimidad del periodismo de denuncia," *Comunicación y Sociedad* 9, nos. 1–2 (1996): 99–219; and José María Desantes Guanter, "Naturaleza y deontología del periodismo de denuncia," *Comunicación y Sociedad* 10, no. 2 (1997): 49.
52 Fausta Gantús, *Caricatura y poder político: Crítica, censura y represión en la Ciudad de México, 1876–1888* (México: Colegio de México / Instituto Mora, 2009), 125–45; Claudio Lomnitz, *The Return of Comrade Flores Magón* (New York: Zone Books, 2014), 83; Ana María Serna, "Prensa y sociedad en las décadas revolucionarias (1910–1940)," *Secuencia* 88 (2014): 127.
53 Rebeca Monroy Nasr, "De disparos fotográficos: Ezequiel Carrasco, reportero gráfico de la Revolución," in *Los hados de febrero: Visiones artísticas de la decena trágica*, ed. Rafael Olea Franco (México: Colegio de México, 2015); Piccato, *A History of Infamy*.
54 Jorge Volpi Escalante, *La imaginación y el poder: Una historia intelectual de 1968* (México: Ediciones Era, 1998); Patricia Cabrera López, *Una inquietud de amanecer: Literatura y política en México, 1962–1987* (México: Universidad Nacional Autónoma de México, 2006), chap. 3.
55 Manuel Becerra Acosta, *Dos poderes* (México: Grijalbo, 1984), 67.
56 Paul Gillingham, "Who Killed Crispín Aguilar? Violence and Order in the Postrevolutionary Countryside," in *Violence, Coercion, and State-Making in Twentieth-Century Mexico*, ed. Wil G. Pansters (Stanford, CA: Stanford University Press, 2012), 93; Carlos Moncada, *Oficio de muerte: Periodistas asesinados en el país de la impunidad* (México: Random House Mondadori, 2012); Smith, *The Mexican Press*.
57 José Luis Martínez, *La vieja guardia: Protagonistas del periodismo mexicano* (México: Random House Mondadori, 2005). Prior to the 1980s, most reporters learned their trade in newsrooms. See, for example, Ana María Serna, "*Se solicitan reporteros*": *Historia oral del periodismo mexicano en la segunda mitad del siglo XX* (México: Instituto Mora, 2015), 41.
58 Gabriela Polit Dueñas, "Chronicles of Everyday Life in Culiacán, Sinaloa," in *Meanings of Violence in Latin America*, ed. Gabriela Polit Dueñas and Maria Helena Rueda (New York: Palgrave Macmillan, 2011), 155–56.
59 Ramón Márquez, "Víctimas acosadas," *Unomásuno*, September 14, 1984, 23; Carlos Monsiváis, *Entrada libre: Crónicas de la sociedad que se organiza* (México: Ediciones Era, 1987).

60 "Planes de estudio, Ciencias Políticas y Sociales," 1979, Biblioteca Nacional, Archivo Histórico de la Universidad Nacional Autónoma de México, Fondo Consejo Universitario, Comisión Permanente, Caja 6, Exp. 6a; and Daniel C. Hallin and Paolo Mancini, *Comparing Media Systems: Three Models of Media and Politics* (New York: Cambridge University Press, 2004), 254.
61 See for example, Rodríguez Munguía, *La otra guerra secreta*, 326–27, 330.
62 Blanco Moheno, *Memorias de un reportero*, 3rd ed. (México: Editorial V Siglos, 1979), 79; and Condés Lara, *Represión y rebelión*, vol. 2, 91–94; Manuel Mejido, *Con la máquina al hombro* (México: Siglo XXI Editores, 2011), 22, 26.
63 Blanco Moheno, *Memorias de un reportero*, 65.
64 Thanks to Mary Roldán for providing me with these comparative references.
65 Mario Menéndez Rodríguez, "La complicidad del silencio: El caso de los dieciocho millones," *El Diario de Yucatán*, February 21, 1963; Miguel Ángel Granados Chapa, "Un deporte de moda: La cacería de periodistas," *Siempre!*, September 21, 1977, 12, 69.
66 Miguel Cabildo, "Hizo delincuentes a sus subordinados: Durazo obligaba a su personal a entregarle el producto de sus mordidas," *Proceso*, March 26, 1984, 16–17; and Carlos Fazio, "La embestida de Washington, porque 'México se alinea con Nicaragua': Se implicó a la familia de la Madrid en el narcotráfico," *Proceso*, May 17, 1986, 6–9.
67 For earlier scandals, see Everard Meade, "From Sex Strangler to Model Citizen: Mexico's Most Famous Murderer and the Defeat of the Death Penalty," *Mexican Studies / Estudios Mexicanos* 26, no. 2 (2010): 323–77; Claudio Lomnitz, "Mexico's First Lynching: Sovereignty, Criminality, Moral Panic," *Critical Historical Studies* 1, no. 1 (2014): 85–123; Edward Wright-Ríos, *Searching for La Madre Matiana: Prophecy and Popular Culture in Modern Mexico* (Albuquerque: University of New Mexico Press, 2014); and Piccato, *A History of Infamy*.
68 Luise White, *Speaking with Vampires: Rumor and History in Colonial Africa* (Berkeley: University of California Press, 2000), 58; and Adut, *On Scandal*, 3.
69 Don Kulick and Charles H. Klein, "Scandalous Acts: The Politics of Shame among Brazilian Travesti Prostitutes," in *Recognition Struggles and Social Movements: Contested Identities, Agency, and Power*, ed. Barbara Meil Hobson (New York: Cambridge University Press, 2003), 217, emphasis in original.
70 Rubén Uriza Castro, "Artificioso conflicto en Acapulco en torno a placas de taxis," *Excélsior*, July 28, 1979, 18.
71 Manuel Buendía to Minister of the Interior Enrique Olivares Santana, August 31, 1979, FMB, Correspondencia, Binder 9.
72 Miguel Ángel Granados Chapa, *Buendía: El primer asesinato de la narcopolítica en México* (México: Grijalbo, 2012), 155.
73 James C. Scott, *Weapons of the Weak: Everyday Forms of Peasant Resistance* (New Haven, CT: Yale University Press, 1985), 27, 29–30, 282.
74 See, for example, Robert M. Entman, *Scandal and Silence: Media Responses to Presidential Misconduct* (Cambridge: Polity Press, 2012), 4–6; Brendan Nyhan, "Media Scandals Are Political Events: How Contextual Factors Affect Public

Controversies over Alleged Misconduct by U.S. Governors," *Political Research Quarterly* 70, no. 1 (March 2017): 223–36.
75  Adut, *On Scandal*, 74.
76  Jean K. Chalaby, "Scandal and the Rise of Investigative Reporting in France," *American Behavioral Scientist* 47, no. 9 (2004): 1194–1207.
77  Rodríguez Munguía, *La otra guerra*, 159–66.
78  Reuters, "Mexico Sheds a Little Light on Its Secrets," *New York Times*, June 13, 2003, A13; Padilla, *Rural Resistance*; Gillingham and Smith, *Dictablanda*; Walker, *Waking from the Dream*.
79  Aguayo Quezada, *La charola*, 230; and Tanalís Padilla and Louise E. Walker, "In the Archives: History and Politics," *Journal of Iberian and Latin American Research* 19, no. 1 (2013): 1–10.
80  There is some disagreement regarding the strength and importance of the DFS at midcentury. McCormick argues that the agency played a key role in identifying rural political threats in the 1950s even while the DFS itself was not responsible for the repression. On the other hand, Aguayo Quezada argues that the agency only became powerful in the 1970s when its capacity, autonomy, and budget expanded; he notes, for example, that the DFS grew from 120 agents in 1965 to 3,000 by 1981. See, McCormick, *The Logic of Compromise*, 138–39; and Aguayo Quezada, *La charola*, 124.
81  Ann Laura Stoler, *Along the Archival Grain: Epistemic Anxieties and Colonial Common Sense* (Princeton, NJ: Princeton University Press, 2009), 26; Taussig, *Defacement*, 57.
82  Paul Christopher Johnson, *Secrets, Gossip, and Gods: The Transformation of Brazilian Candomblé* (New York: Oxford University Press, 2002), 7.

## CHAPTER 1. RECKONING WITH THE REVOLUTION

1  "La revolución y el México de hoy," *Siempre!*, November 23, 1966, 16–17.
2  "La revolución," 17.
3  Benjamin T. Smith, *The Mexican Press and Civil Society, 1940–1976: Stories from the Newsroom, Stories from the Street* (Chapel Hill: University of North Carolina Press, 2018), 56–57, 67.
4  Smith, *The Mexican Press*, 76.
5  Blanco Moheno, *Memorias de un reportero*, 83, 106.
6  Mario Menéndez Rodríguez, "Escándalo agrario," *El Diario de Yucatán* (Mérida), January 22, 1963, reprinted in Mario Menéndez Rodríguez, *Yucatán o el genocidio* (México: Fondo de Cultura Popular, 1964), 51–54.
7  Smith, *The Mexican Press*, 119. With 42,705 copies in circulation each day, *El Diario de Yucatán* was the regional newspaper with the third-highest circulation in the country, following *El Norte* (Monterrey) and *El Occidental* (Guadalajara). In 1960 the total population of Yucatán was 614,049. Dirección General de Estadística, *VIII censo general de población 1960, estado de Yucatán* (México: Secretaría de Industria y Comercio, 1963), http://internet.contenidos.inegi.org

.mx/contenidos/Productos/prod_serv/contenidos/espanol/bvinegi/productos/historicos/1290/702825413095/702825413095_1.pdf.

8 Roberto Blanco Moheno, *Memorias de un reportero*, 3rd ed. (México: Editorial V Siglos, 1979), 109.

9 "Candidate Finds Mexicans Angry: Presidential Nominee Hears Criticism on Land Reform," *New York Times*, April 12, 1964, 2.

10 Ariel Rodríguez Kuri, "Secretos de la idiosincrasia: Urbanización y cambio cultural en México, 1950–1970," in *Ciudades mexicanas del siglo XX: Siete estudios históricos*, ed. Carlos Lira Vásquez and Ariel Rodríguez Kuri, 19–51 (México: SEP-CONACYT / Colmex / UAM Azcapotzalco, 2009), 28–29.

11 Paul Kennedy, "Díaz Is Sworn in as Mexico's Head; Stresses Farm Problems— Ties to Cuba to Continue," *New York Times*, December 2, 1964, 16.

12 Menéndez Rodríguez, *Yucatán o el genocidio*, 137–38.

13 Ben Fallaw, "Cárdenas and the Caste War that Wasn't: State Power and Indigenismo in Post-Revolutionary Yucatán," *The Americas* 53, no. 4 (1997): 552; Sterling Evans, "King Henequen: Order, Progress, and Ecological Change in Yucatán, 1850–1950," in *A Land Between Waters: Environmental Histories of Modern Mexico*, ed. Christopher R. Boyer (Tucson: University of Arizona Press, 2012), 150–51, 53.

14 Menéndez Rodríguez, *Yucatán o el genocidio*, 160–61, 53–54.

15 For a fuller biographical portrait of Menéndez Rodríguez, see Smith, *The Mexican Press*, 118–23.

16 Mario Menéndez Rodríguez, "Sr. Presidente López Mateos: Sólo usted puede decir la última palabra," *El Diario de Yucatán*, February 11, 1963, reprinted in Menéndez Rodríguez, *Yucatán o el genocidio*, 73–74, emphasis in the original.

17 Ben Fallaw, *Cárdenas Compromised: The Failures of Reform in Postrevolutionary Yucatán* (Durham, NC: Duke University Press, 2001), 90–95.

18 Menéndez Rodríguez, *Yucatán o el genocidio*, 73–74, emphasis in the original. The Judas metaphor was also employed by radical rural schoolteachers. See, for example, Alexander Aviña, *Specters of Revolution: Peasant Guerrillas in the Cold War Mexican Countryside* (New York: Oxford University Press, 2014), 98.

19 Fallaw, *Cárdenas Compromised*, 134–37; Raúl Cázares Ponce, "Exhortan a la Unión a los henequeneros," *Excélsior*, February 22, 1963, 10. These findings appeared in Mario Menéndez Rodríguez, "La complicidad del silencio," *El Diario de Yucatán*, February 21, 1963.

20 In 1960, overall literacy was around 56.29 percent for men and 51.9 percent for women in Yucatán state. These figures likely reflected urban readers, who accounted for a similar proportion, 63 percent, of the overall population. Secretaría de Industria y Comercio, *VIII censo general de población 1960*.

21 Cázares Ponce, "Exhortan a la Unión," 10.

22 Alberto Carrillo Suárez to Adolfo López Mateos, July 5, 1963, Archivo General de la Nación (hereafter AGN), Fondo Presidencial Adolfo López Mateos, Caja 280, Exp. 404.1/98, 3.

23 Diane Nelson, *Who Counts? The Mathematics of Death and Life after Genocide* (Durham, NC: Duke University Press, 2015), 11.

24 Raúl Cázares Ponce, "Fraude en Yucatán a los henequeneros," *Excélsior*, March 1, 1963, 1, 10.
25 "Defraudaciones a los ejidatarios," *Excélsior*, March 7, 1963, 6.
26 John Kenneth Turner, *Barbarous Mexico: An Indictment of a Cruel and Corrupt System* (New York: Cassell, 1911).
27 In so doing they attempted to appease the demands associated with the Zapatista and even Villista revolutionary forces. See John Womack, *Zapata and the Mexican Revolution* (New York: Alfred A. Knopf, 1968); and Emilio H. Kourí, "Interpreting the Expropriation of Indian Pueblo Lands in Porfirian Mexico: The Unexamined Legacies of Andrés Molina Enríquez," *Hispanic American Historical Review* 82, no. 1 (2002): 106.
28 Fallaw, *Cárdenas Compromised*, 126.
29 Luis Alfonso Ramírez, "Corrupción, empresariado y desarrollo regional en México: El caso yucateco," in *Vicios públicos, virtudes privadas*, ed. Claudio Lomnitz (México: CIESAS, 2000), 151–53.
30 "Defraudaciones a los ejidatarios."
31 The first was Gustavo Martínez Mejía, an ejidal representative in the National Bank of Ejido Credit (Banco Nacional de Crédito Ejidal). Mendoza would be followed in May by Franco Ledesma Ramírez, deputy director of the National Bank of Exterior Commerce (Banco Nacional de Comercio Exterior) and the National Bank of Ejido Credit. Menéndez Rodríguez, *Yucatán o el genocidio*, 137.
32 "El problema henequenero en el estado de Yucatán," April 17, 1963, AGN, Dirección Federal de Seguridad (hereafter DFS), Versión Pública Mario Menéndez Rodríguez, Legajo 1, 8, 3, 7.
33 "El problema henequenero," 5.
34 Renata Keller, *Mexico's Cold War: Cuba, the United States, and the Legacy of the Mexican Revolution* (New York: Cambridge University Press, 2015), 112–19.
35 U.S. consulate, Mérida, to U.S. Department of State, "Alleged Bankruptcy and Economic Paralysis in Yucatan," May 24, 1963, U.S. National Archives and Records Administration (hereafter NARA), RG 59, Box 3984, POL 18 MEX, 2.
36 "Memorandum," AGN, DFS, Versión Pública Jacobo Zabludovsky, March 15, 1963, 1; Celeste González de Bustamante, *"Muy buenas noches": Mexico, Television, and the Cold War* (Lincoln: University of Nebraska Press, 2012), 60–61.
37 Menéndez Rodríguez, *Yucatán o el genocidio*, 19.
38 Menéndez Rodríguez, *Yucatán o el genocidio*, 5.
39 Menéndez Rodríguez, *Yucatán o el genocidio*, 165–67, 174; Smith, *The Mexican Press*, 123.
40 U.S. embassy, Mexico City, to U.S. Department of State, "A Description of the Mexican Magazine *Siempre!*," May 31, 1963, NARA, RG 59, Central Foreign Policy Files (hereafter CFPF), INF 10 MEX, Box 3271, 2. It is worth noting that circulation figures vary widely depending on the source. Smith, *The Mexican Press*, 28, cites other sources, for example, that listed the circulation of *Siempre!* at just twenty-five thousand in 1967.
41 Blanco Moheno, *Memorias de un reportero*, 13–14.

42 Mary Kay Vaughan, *Portrait of a Young Painter: Pepe Zúñiga and Mexico City's Rebel Generation* (Durham, NC: Duke University Press, 2014), 189–90.
43 Thanks to Andrew Paxman for pointing this out to me.
44 Rius, "En este pueblo no hay ladrones," *Siempre!*, October 20, 1965, 11.
45 Elena Garro, "El problema agrario," *La Cultura en México*, September 1, 1965, 2.
46 Rebecca E. Biron, *Elena Garro and Mexico's Modern Dreams* (Lewisburg, PA: Bucknell University Press, 2013), 55–57.
47 John Mraz, *Looking for Mexico: Modern Visual Culture and National Identity* (Durham, NC: Duke University Press, 2009), 185, 171.
48 Roland Barthes, "The Photographic Message," in *Image, Music, Text*, trans. Stephen Heath (New York: Hill and Wang, 1977), 15–31; and Deborah Poole, "'An Image of 'Our Indian': Type Photographs and Racial Sentiments in Oaxaca, 1920–1940," *Hispanic American Historical Review* 84, no. 1 (2004): 38–39.
49 Mraz, *Looking for Mexico*, 162–66.
50 Garro, "El problema agrario," 5, 2.
51 Garro, "El problema agrario," 5.
52 Samuel Ramos, *El perfil del hombre y la cultura en México* (México: P. Robredo, 1938); Carlos Monsiváis, *Mexican Postcards*, trans. John Kraniauskas (London: Verso Books, 1997), 98–99. On the presumed linkage between criminality and urban indigeneity, see Robert Buffington, *Criminal and Citizen in Modern Mexico* (Lincoln: University of Nebraska Press, 2000), 145, 164.
53 "Confederación Nacional de Organizaciones Populares," June 21, 1965, AGN, DFS, 30-24-965, Legajo 6.
54 Oscar Lewis, *Los hijos de Sánchez: Autobiografía de una familia mexicana* (México: Fondo de Cultura Económica, 1964).
55 Oscar Lewis, "Preface," in *The Children of Sánchez: Autobiography of a Mexican Family*, 2nd ed. (New York: Vintage Books, 1963). On the other hand, Jean Franco underscores that the life stories in *The Children of Sánchez* "often undermine the very culture of poverty thesis they are supposed to illustrate." See Jean Franco, *Plotting Women: Gender and Representation in Mexico* (New York: Columbia University Press, 1989), 160.
56 Karin Alejandra Rosemblatt, "Other Americas: Transnationalism, Scholarship, and the Culture of Poverty in Mexico and the United States," *Hispanic American Historical Review* 89, no. 4 (2009): 617.
57 Ariel Rodríguez Kuri, "Ganar la sede: La política internacional de los juegos olímpicos de 1968," *Historia Mexicana* 64, no. 1 (2014): 243–89.
58 George F. Flaherty, *Hotel Mexico: Dwelling on the '68 Movement* (Oakland: University of California Press, 2016), 83.
59 Luis Cataño Morlet, "'Los hijos de Sánchez,' libro obsceno, subversivo y antimexicano," February 1965, Archivo Histórico del Fondo de Cultura Económica (hereafter AH-FCE), Colección Oscar Lewis, Legajo 2.1, 3.
60 Cataño Morlet, "'Los hijos de Sánchez,'" 1.
61 Luis Cataño Morlet, "Comentarios al libro Los Hijos de Sánchez," *El Día*, February 17, 1965, 4.

62 Rachel Kram Villarreal, "Gladiolas for the Children of Sánchez: Ernesto P. Uruchurtu's Mexico City, 1950–1968" (PhD diss., University of Arizona, 2008), 222; Rosemblatt, "Other Americas," 619–22.

63 Universidad Nacional Autónoma de México, *Anuario estadístico*, 1959, Archivo Histórico de la Universidad Nacional Autónoma de México (hereafter AH-UNAM), 12; Universidad Nacional Autónoma de México, *Anuario estadístico*, 1961, AH-UNAM, 10.

64 "Planes de estudio: Ciencias políticas y sociales," vol. 1, 1976, AH-UNAM, Fondo Consejo Universitario, Comisión Permanente, Caja 5, Exp. 2.

65 *Editor and Publisher International Yearbook, 1966* (New York: Editor and Publisher, 1966), 495.

66 "Nuevas opiniones en torno a la denuncia de la SMGE contra Lewis," *El Día*, February 14, 1965, 3.

67 "Hablan Flores Olea y Fuentes sobre la denuncia contra Oscar Lewis," *El Día*, February 15, 1965, 3.

68 Antonio Elizondo, "Pero, estamos en jauja! La prensa dice una cosa, pero la realidad es otra," *Siempre!*, January 1, 1964, 24–25.

69 "Cartas y Opiniones: Sale en defensa de Oscar Lewis," *El Día*, February 19, 1965, 2.

70 "Cartas y Opiniones: Opinión de la JES-UGOCM sobre el libro Los hijos de Sánchez, de Oscar Lewis," *El Día*, March 12, 1965, 2.

71 "Cartas y Opiniones: Considera que el libro de Lewis no es un trabajo científico," *El Día*, February 23, 1965, 2.

72 René Arteaga, "Agria disputa en la mesa redonda sobre la obra Los Hijos de Sánchez," *El Día*, March 5, 1965, 3.

73 For an analysis of how the subjectivity of another Sánchez family member, Consuelo, was altered by her interactions with Lewis, see Franco, *Plotting Women*, 163.

74 Arnaldo Orfila confirmed in a letter to Lewis that Manuel was indeed the voice in the recording. He also noted that the presentation of the tape "made quite an impression" on attendees. Arnaldo Orfila to Oscar Lewis, March 13, 1965, AH-FCE, Colección Oscar Lewis, Legajo 2.1, 2.

75 Orfila to Lewis, March 13, 1965, 3.

76 Oscar Castañeda Batres, "La verdad sobre una denuncia contra Lewis," AH-FCE, Colección Oscar Lewis, Legajo 2.1.

77 The FCE initiated a complaint of copyright violation but worried that this would just delight the *Diario de México* editors by attracting more attention from readers.

78 Program scripts, *La ciudad y la cultura*, April 1965, AH-UNAM, Fondo Dirección General de Difusión Cultural, Dirección de los Servicios Coordinados de Radio, Televisión y Grabaciones, Caja 15, Exp. 85, 4; Víctor Urquidi, *Los hijos de Jones* (Austin: Institute of Latin American Studies, University of Texas, 1963); Alberto Quiroz, *Historias para Oscar Lewis: El reverso de "Los hijos de Sánchez"* (México: B. Costa / Amic Editores, 1966); Salvador Díaz Garay, *Los hijos de Smith* (México: Meridiano, 1969).

79 Oscar Lewis to Arnaldo Orfila, June 18, 1965, AH-FCE, Colección Oscar Lewis, Legajo 2.1.
80 Others believed that his firing was retaliation against the publication of C. Wright Mills's book *Listen, Yankee*. Carlos Fuentes to Arnaldo Orfila Reynal, November 16, 1965, Princeton University Library (hereafter PUL), Special Collections (hereafter SC), Carlos Fuentes Papers (hereafter CFP), Box 125, Folder 2.
81 Elena Poniatowska to Carlos Fuentes, December 6, 1965, PUL, SC, CFP, Box 120, Folder 28; Fernando Benítez to Carlos Fuentes, December 29, 1965, PUL, SC, CFP, Box 89, Folder 11.
82 "Anuncia Orfila la creación de la empresa Siglo XXI Editores, S.A.," *El Día*, November 19, 1965, 3.
83 "Estado de Yucatán," January 27, 1966, AGN, DFS, Versión Pública Mario Menéndez Rodríguez, Legajo 1, 2.
84 Smith, *The Mexican Press*, 126.
85 "Sucesos Para Todos," June 14, 1966, AGN, DFS, Versión Pública Mario Menéndez Rodríguez, Legajo 1.
86 Menéndez Rodríguez, *Yucatán o el genocidio*, 246; U.S. consulate, Mérida, to U.S. Department of State, "Hunger Strike in Mérida," January 28, 1965, NARA, RG 59, Box 2474, POL 13-1; "Información de Mérida: Situación económica de los cultivadores del henequén," March 26, 1966, AGN, Dirección General de Investigaciones Políticas y Sociales (hereafter DGIPS), Caja 453, Exp. 1; "Información de Mérida," December 13, 1966, AGN, DGIPS, Caja 825, Exp. 7.
87 U.S. consulate, Mérida, to U.S. Department of State, "'A New Impulse': Informe of Governor of Yucatan," February 25, 1966, NARA, RG 59, Box 2477, POL 18, 2.
88 Víctor Rico Galán, "La mafia del henequén arroja lastre," *Siempre!*, September 29, 1965, 27.
89 See "Manifestación del Sindicato de Cordeleros," May 29, 1966, AGN, DGIPS, Caja 454, Exp. 2.
90 Mario Menéndez Rodríguez, "Yucatán: Estado sin gobierno," *Sucesos para Todos*, January 14, 1967, 14.
91 See "Denuncia presentada por Menéndez Rodríguez," May 30, 1966, Versión Pública Mario Menéndez Rodríguez, AGN, DFS, Legajo 1, 1.
92 Menéndez Rodríguez, "Yucatán: Estado sin gobierno," 14.
93 Menéndez Rodríguez, "Yucatán: Estado sin gobierno," 16.
94 U.S. consulate, Mérida, to U.S. Department of State, "A Short Sociology of Yucatecan Politics," NARA, RG 59, Box 2342, 5.
95 U.S. embassy, Mexico City, to U.S. Department of State, "Menéndez Resigns from Sucesos," December 22, 1967, NARA, RG 59, Box 2338, 4.
96 U.S. Information Agency, Office of Research, "Media Usage by Latin American University Students," 1964, NARA, P 160, Box 21, 9, 11; Renata Keller, "Testing the Limits of Censorship? *Política* Magazine and the 'Perfect Dictatorship,' 1960–1967," in *Journalism, Censorship and Satire in Mexico*, ed. Paul Gillingham, Michael Lettieri, and Benjamin Smith (Albuquerque: University of New Mexico Press, 2019), 221–35.

97 U.S. embassy, Mexico City, to U.S. Department of State, "Sucesos Criticizes Castro," February 1, 1968, NARA, RG 59, PPB MEX, Box 389.

## CHAPTER 2. "VEHICLES OF SCANDAL"

An earlier version of this chapter was originally published in the *Hispanic American Historical Review* under the title "Speaking of Sterilization: Rumors, the Urban Poor, and the Public Sphere in Greater Mexico City" (2019): 303–36, © 2019, Duke University Press.

1 Enrique Condés Lara, *Represión y rebelión en México (1959–1985)*, vol. 2 (México: Miguel Ángel Porrúa, 2007), 144–45.
2 Gabriela Aceves Sepúlveda, *Women Made Visible: Feminist Art and Media in Post-1968 Mexico City* (Lincoln: University of Nebraska Press, 2019), 75.
3 Arno Burkholder de la Rosa, "El olimpo fracturado: La dirección de Julio Scherer García en *Excélsior* (1968–1976)," *Historia Mexicana* 59, no. 4 (2010): 1369.
4 This finding challenges the assertion that rumors thrive amid state secrecy and a tightly controlled press. See Luise White, *Speaking with Vampires: Rumor and History in Colonial Africa* (Berkeley: University of California Press, 2000), 57; S. A. Smith, "Talking Toads and Chinless Ghosts: The Politics of 'Superstitious' Rumors in the People's Republic of China, 1961–1965," *American Historical Review* 111, no. 2 (2006): 408; and Lauren Derby, "Imperial Secrets: Vampires and Nationhood in Puerto Rico," *Past and Present* 199 (2008): 294, 303.
5 Louise E. Walker, *Waking from the Dream: Mexico's Middle Classes after 1968* (Stanford, CA: Stanford University Press, 2013), 52. See also Héctor Aguilar Camín, "Ante la industria del rumor," *La Cultura en México*, January 1, 1975, 8; and Sara Moirón, "A falta de información, el rumor," *Proceso*, November 27, 1976, 16–18.
6 Rodolfo Gamiño Muñoz, *Guerrilla, represión y prensa en la década de los setenta en México. Invisibilidad y olvido* (México: Instituto Mora, 2011), 103, 111–14.
7 "La ignorancia, barrera en contra de la vacunación en Ciudad Netzahualcóyotl," *Excélsior*, December 7, 1974, 16. Reporters regularly utilized two different spellings of the municipality. I have opted to employ the traditional spelling, Nezahualcóyotl, but I preserve the alternative spelling when it was used by reporters and state spies.
8 Carlos Pereyra, "El rumor, arma ideológica de la derecha," *La Cultura en México*, January 1, 1975, 7; Arturo Acuña, "Llorando los niños, llorando todos los niños," *La Cultura en México*, January 1, 1975, 2.
9 See for example, Soledad Loaeza, "La política del rumor: México, noviembre-diciembre de 1976," *Foro Internacional* 17, no. 4 (1977): 585; and José Agustín, *Tragicomedia mexicana 2: La vida en México de 1970 a 1982* (México: Editorial Planeta Mexicana, 1992), 100–101.
10 White, *Speaking with Vampires*, 5; Derby, "Imperial Secrets," 293.
11 Similarly, John Jackson makes the case that conspiracy theories are not just untruths but ways of bonding communities of color. See John Jackson, *Real Black: Adventures in Racial Sincerity* (Chicago: University of Chicago Press, 2005).

12 "Estado de México," December 11, 1974, Archivo Histórico de la Secretaría de Salud (hereafter AHSS), Secretaria Particular, Secretaría de Salubridad y Asistencia (hereafter SSA), Caja 268, Exp. 2.

13 "La ignorancia"; "Alarma en Nezahualcóyotl por una vacuna que aplican," *El Universal*, December 6, 1974, 11.

14 Ley General de la Población, January 7, 1974, http://imumi.org/attachments/Ley_General_de_Poblacion_1974.pdf; Gerardo Cornejo, et al., "Law and Population in Mexico" (monograph, Fletcher School of Law and Diplomacy, Tufts University, Medford, MA, 1975), 8–9.

15 Gabriela Soto Laveaga, "'Let's Become Fewer': Soap Operas, Contraception, and Nationalizing the Mexican Family in an Overpopulated World," *Sexuality Research and Social Policy* 4, no. 3 (2007): 23–25. On earlier attitudes of demographers and Mexican officials, see Arthur F. Corwin, *Contemporary Mexican Attitudes toward Population, Poverty, and Public Opinion* (Gainesville: University of Florida Press, 1963), 6–7; and Frederick C. Turner, *Responsible Parenthood: The Politics of Mexico's New Population Policies* (Washington, DC: American Enterprise Institute for Public Policy Research, 1974), 1–3.

16 Aceves Sepúlveda, *Women Made Visible*, 60.

17 George F. Flaherty, *Hotel Mexico: Dwelling on the '68 Movement* (Oakland: University of California Press, 2016), 83–84; José Revueltas, "TV y cultura en los juegos deportivos de la XIX Olimpiada," *México 68: Reseña Gráfica* 1, no. 33 (1968): 14.

18 Claudia Fernández and Andrew Paxman, *El Tigre: Emilio Azcárraga y su imperio Televisa*, 3rd ed. (México: Grijalbo / Raya en el Agua, 2013), 78, 127; Soto Laveaga, "'Let's Become Fewer.'"

19 "Información de Ciudad Netzahualcóyotl," December 10, 1974, Archivo General de la Nación (hereafter AGN), Dirección General de Investigaciones Políticas y Sociales (hereafter DGIPS), Caja 1714A, Exp. 2, 1.

20 "Información de Ciudad Netzahualcóyotl," 2.

21 Larissa Adler Lomnitz, *Networks and Marginality: Life in a Mexican Shantytown*, trans. Cinna Lomnitz (New York: Academic Press, 1977), 8; Wayne Cornelius, *Politics and the Migrant Poor in Mexico City* (Stanford, CA: Stanford University Press, 1975), 27.

22 The total population was 50,695,000. Banco de México, *México social: Noventa indicadores seleccionados* (México: Banco Nacional de México, 1982), 4. Population figures for the contiguous areas in Mexico state come from Cornelius, *Politics and the Migrant Poor*, 48.

23 The 1970 census reported that 83.2 percent of Nezahualcóyotl residents were literate, placing them above the national average (76.5 percent) and below the average for Mexico City (90.9 percent). Ethnographic research supports high literacy figures for the municipality. Carlos G. Vélez-Ibañez, *Rituals of Marginality: Politics, Process, and Culture Change in Urban Central Mexico, 1969–1974* (Berkeley: University of California Press, 1983), 46, 58–59, 63, 71.

24 Jean Meyer, "Disidencia jesuita: Entre la cruz y la espada," *Nexos*, December 1981, 18–19; Luis G. Del Valle, "Teología de la Liberación en México," in *El pensam-*

*iento social de los católicos mexicanos*, ed. Roberto J. Blancarte (México: Fondo de Cultura Económica, 1996), 248–51.

25 "Información de Ciudad Netzahualcóyotl."
26 "Estado de México."
27 "Secretaría de Educación Pública," December 10, 1974, AHSS, Secretaría Particular, SSA, Caja 268, Exp. 2; Celeste González de Bustamante, *"Muy buenas noches": Mexico, Television, and the Cold War* (Lincoln: University of Nebraska Press, 2012), 41.
28 Claudia Agostoni, "Médicos rurales y brigadas de vacunación en la lucha contra la viruela en el México posrevolucionario, 1920–1940," *Canadian Journal of Latin American and Caribbean Studies* 35, no. 69 (2010): 71.
29 "El falso rumor sobre la vacunación distrajo la atención de la policía," *El Universal*, December 11, 1974, 17.
30 Miguel López Saucedo, "Sicosis en el Vaso de Texcoco," *Excélsior*, December 10, 1974, 4, 19.
31 Report on rumors in Mexico City primary schools, December 9, 1974, AGN, DGIPS, Caja 1714A, Exp. 2.
32 "Nezahualcóyotl: Desde enero, legalización de zonas urbano-ejidales," *El Día*, December 8, 1974, 13.
33 Juan Manuel Ramírez Saiz, *El movimiento urbano popular en México*, 2nd ed. (México: Siglo XXI, 1999), 51–52.
34 Alejandra Massolo, *Por el amor y coraje: Mujeres en movimientos urbanos de la ciudad de México* (México: El Colegio de México, 1992), 162–63.
35 Report on assembly at CCH Oriente, December 9, 1974, AGN, DGIPS, Caja 1714A, Exp. 2, 1.
36 Report on assembly at CCH Oriente; Report on parents' protest in Iztapalapa, December 10, 1974, AGN, DGIPS, Caja 1714A, Exp. 2, 3.
37 Report on parents' protest in Iztapalapa, 4–5.
38 Molly Geidel, "'Sowing Death in Our Women's Wombs': Modernization and Indigenous Nationalism in the 1960s Peace Corps and Jorge Sanjinés' *Yawar Mallku*," *American Quarterly* 62, no. 3 (2010): 764.
39 It is worth noting that Mexican leftist critiques of family planning did underscore imperialist aims prior to the Mexican government's rollout of its own family planning initiative. See "Students Protest Violence at UNAM Prep Schools," July 21, 1971, U.S. National Archives and Records Administration (hereafter NARA), RG 59, Box 2473; and "Second Year of the Echeverría Administration," January 22, 1973, NARA, RG 59, Box 2472, 17.
40 Laura Briggs, *Reproducing Empire: Race, Sex, Science, and U.S. Imperialism in Puerto Rico* (Berkeley: University of California Press, 2003), 146–47. Between 1966 and 1968, aid agencies infamously made famine assistance to India conditional upon meeting population goals. See Matthew James Connelly, *Fatal Misconception: The Struggle to Control World Population* (Cambridge, MA: Harvard University Press, 2008), 217, 222–25.
41 Victoria Langland, "Birth Control Pills and Molotov Cocktails: Reading Sex and Revolution in 1968 Brazil," in *In from the Cold: Latin America's New Encounter*

*with the Cold War*, ed. Gilbert M. Joseph and Daniela Spenser (Durham, NC: Duke University Press, 2008), 320–21.

42 Richard D. Lyons, "Doctors Scored on Sterilization," *New York Times*, October 31, 1973, 7; Nancy Hicks, "Sterilization of Black Mother of 3 Stirs Aiken, S.C," *New York Times*, August 1, 1973, 27; Briggs, *Reproducing Empire*, 146.

43 "Las divergencias dificultan un acuerdo mundial sobre población," *El Día*, August 28, 1974, 3; Raúl Necochea López, *A History of Family Planning in Twentieth-Century Peru* (Chapel Hill: University of North Carolina Press, 2014), 114, 116, 149; Jadwiga E. Pieper Mooney, *The Politics of Motherhood: Maternity and Women's Rights in Twentieth-Century Chile* (Pittsburgh: University of Pittsburgh Press, 2009), 106, 124.

44 "Second Year of the Echeverría Administration," 9; Jocelyn Olcott, *International Women's Year: The Greatest Consciousness-Raising Event in History* (New York: Oxford University Press, 2017), 54.

45 Graciela M. Castro, "La superpoblación propicia muchas y serias manifestaciones de malestar y decadencia," *El Día*, September 18, 1974, 14; Turner, *Responsible Parenthood*, 18–19; Soto Laveaga, "'Let's Become Fewer,'" 21.

46 Miriam Ticktin, "A World without Innocence," *American Ethnologist* 44, no. 4 (2017): 578.

47 Report on assembly at CCH Oriente, 1.

48 Cornejo et al., "Law and Population in Mexico," 18. Cornejo and colleagues extrapolated from hospital data to estimate that there was one "illegally induced abortion" for every five births in Mexico City hospitals. A 1965 USIA survey found that 70 percent of Mexico City residents surveyed approved the use of birth control to limit family size. "Summary of Some World-wide Research on Population and Family Planning Attitudes," 1967, NARA, RG 306, P 160, Box 24, 2.

49 "Información del distrito de Chalco," December 10, 1974, AGN, DGIPS, Caja 1714A, Exp. 2.

50 Lynn Stephen, *Women and Social Movements in Latin America: Power from Below* (Austin: University of Texas Press, 1997), 128–29.

51 Miguel Díaz-Barriga, "Beyond the Domestic and the Public: *Colonas* Participation in Urban Movements in Mexico City," in *Cultures of Politics / Politics of Cultures: Re-visioning Latin American Social Movements*, ed. Sonia Alvarez, Evelina Dagnino, and Arturo Escobar (Boulder, CO: Westview, 1998), 267–69.

52 Corwin, *Contemporary Mexican Attitudes*, 22–23.

53 Roberto Legorreta, "El rumor sobre la irreal vacuna, grave provocación," *El Día*, December 11, 1974, 11.

54 See, for example, "Información de Ciudad Netzahualcóyotl"; and Report on parents' protest in Iztapalapa.

55 Legorreta, "El rumor sobre la irreal vacuna."

56 See, for example, Mary Kay Vaughan, *Cultural Politics in Revolution: Teachers, Peasants, and Schools in Mexico, 1930–1940* (Tucson: University of Arizona Press, 1997), 34–35, 122; and Matthew Butler, *Popular Piety and Political Identity in*

*Mexico's Cristero Rebellion: Michoacán, 1927–29* (New York: Oxford University Press, 2004), 90–93.

57 Paul Ramírez, "'Like Herod's Massacre': Quarantines, Bourbon Reform, and Popular Protest in Oaxaca's Smallpox Epidemic, 1796–1797," *The Americas* 69, no. 2 (2012): 203–35.

58 See, for example, Stephanie Baker Opperman, "Modernization and Rural Health in Mexico: The Case of the Tepalcatepec Commission," *Endeavour* 37, no. 1 (2012): 53.

59 "La ignorancia."

60 Susana Sosenski, *Niños en acción. El trabajo infantil en la ciudad de México 1920–1934* (México: Colegio de México, 2010), 43; Pieper, *The Politics of Motherhood*, 21.

61 Miguel Canton Zetina, "No hay esterilización: Criminal rumor contra las vacunas de la SSA," *La Prensa*, December 8, 1974, 16.

62 "Falsos rumores sobre la vacunación," *El Universal*, December 11, 1974, 28.

63 Sosenski, *Niños en acción*, 39–42; Susana Sosenski Correa, "El niño consumidor: Una construcción publicitaria de la prensa Mexicana en la década de 1950," in *Ciudadanos inesperados: Espacios de formación de la ciudadanía ayer y hoy*, ed. Ariadna Acevedo Rodrigo and Paula López Caballero (México: Colegio de México, 2012), 191.

64 "SSA: Falsos rumores," *La Prensa*, December 11, 1974, 28.

65 Jorge Ramos and Benito Olivares, "Pánico y violencia en varias colonias," *La Prensa*, December 10, 1974, 41.

66 "Campaña de vacunación a nivel nacional," *El Universal*, December 7, 1974, 16.

67 "Vacuna esterilizadora," December 12, 1974, AHSS, Secretaria Particular, SSA, Caja 268, Exp. 2, 2.

68 Ramos and Olivares, "Pánico y violencia," 41.

69 Raúl Álvarez Garín, *La estela de Tlatelolco: Una reconstrucción histórica del movimiento estudiantil del 68* (México: Grijalbo, 1998), 99; Julia L. Sloan, "Talking of Tlatelolco: The Power of Collective Memory Suppressed but Not Surrendered," in *Projections of Power in the Americas*, ed. Niels Bjerre-Poulsen, Helene Balslev Clausen, and Jan Gustafsson (New York: Routledge, 2012), 81.

70 Laura Castellanos, *México armado 1943–1981* (México: Ediciones Era, 2007), 160–63; Alexander Aviña, *Specters of Revolution: Peasant Guerrillas in the Cold War Mexican Countryside* (New York: Oxford University Press, 2014), 13.

71 "Información del distrito de Chalco," 1.

72 In 1972 the Mexican Congress amended Article 10 of the Constitution to impose additional restrictions on legal access to guns. Ley Federal de Armas de Fuego y Explosivos, January 11, 1972, http://www.diputados.gob.mx/LeyesBiblio/ref/lfafe/LFAFE_orig_11ene72_ima.pdf.

73 Loaeza, "La política del rumor," 562; Sergio Zermeño, *México, una democracia utópica: El movimiento estudiantil del 68* (México: Siglo XXI Editores, 1978), 171.

74 Juan Manuel Juárez Cortes, "Colaboran estudiantes a descubrir a los criminales," *La Prensa*, December 11, 1974.

75 This movement built upon earlier organizing efforts against free government-issued textbooks. Soledad Loaeza, *Clases medias y política en México: La querella escolar, 1959–1963* (México: El Colegio de México, 1988); Derek Bentley, "Democratic Openings: Conservative Protest and Political-Economic Transformation in Mexico, 1970–1986" (PhD diss., University of Georgia, 2017), 117–18.

76 "Información de Monterrey," October 11, 1974, AGN, DGIPS, Caja 1758-B, Exp. 10.

77 "Un verdadero crimen," *La Prensa*, December 11, 1974, 8; Javier Zamora, "Fuerzas retrógradas buscan, mediante el rumor, torcer el camino de México," *El Día*, December 12, 1974, 6; Mario Ezcurdia, "Las cuentas claras: ¿Cómo defendernos del 'cacerolismo'?," *El Universal*, December 13, 1974, 1, 13.

78 Fernández and Paxman, *El Tigre*, 195.

79 Walker, *Waking from the Dream*, 54.

80 For journalists' and academics' responses to the Chilean coup, see, for example, "Problema estudiantil," November 2, 1973, AGN, Dirección Federal de Seguridad, Versión Pública Froylán López Narváez, Legajo 1.

81 While Carlos Fuentes popularized this statement, Fernando Benítez coined it. Carlos Fuentes to Fernando Benítez, September 15, 1973, Princeton University Library, Special Collections, Carlos Fuentes Papers, Box 89, Folder 11. Over the summer of 1972, literary figures debated the role of the intellectual in political life. See, for example, "Fuentes de la polémica," *Plural*, July 1972, 38–39; Carlos Fuentes, "Opiniones críticas en el verano de nuestro descontento," *Plural*, August 1972, 3–9; Gabriel Zaid, "Carta a Carlos Fuentes," *Plural*, September 1972, 53.

82 Julio Scherer García, *Vivir* (México: Grijalbo, 2012), 66–67.

83 "Los rumores," n.d., AGN, Archivo Particular Porfirio Muñoz Ledo (hereafter AP-PML), Caja 65, Exp. 63; Carlos Arriola Woog, *Los empresarios y el estado: 1970–1982*, 2nd ed. (México: Universidad Nacional Autónoma de México / Miguel Ángel Porrúa, 1988), chap. 2.

84 See, for example, Kate Doyle, "The Nixon Tapes: Secret Recordings from the Nixon White House on Luis Echeverría and Much Much More," August 18, 2003, National Security Archive, https://nsarchive2.gwu.edu/NSAEBB/NSAEBB95/.

85 "Provocación cobarde, fines aviesos," *El Día*, December 11, 1974, 5.

86 Buendía wrote the column under a pseudonym; see J. M. Tellezgirón, "Para Control de Usted: Cacerolismo en acción," *El Día*, December 12, 1974, 3. See also Juan Nieto Martínez, "Política nacional," *La Prensa*, December 12, 1974, 10.

87 "La revista del PAN se hace eco de los rumores sobre la vacuna," *El Día*, December 12, 1974, 6.

88 See, for example, Vicente Leñero, *Los periodistas* (México: Joaquín Mortiz, 1978), 42–43; Manuel Mejido, *Con la máquina al hombro* (México: Siglo XXI Editores, 2011), 143; Rodríguez Munguía, *La otra guerra secreta*, 141, 143.

89 Benjamin T. Smith, *The Mexican Press and Civil Society, 1940–1976: Stories from the Newsroom, Stories from the Street* (Chapel Hill: University of North Carolina Press, 2018), 24, 30, 70, 72.

90 Froylán López Narváez, "Esterilizar niños, agitación rumoreada," *Excélsior*, December 11, 1974, 7.

91 Antonio Rodríguez, "Provocación contra México," *El Universal*, December 16, 1974, 5; Aquiles Fuentes, "De los rumores se intentará pasar a la acción frontal y abiertamente subversiva," *El Día*, December 17, 1974, 2.
92 "Un verdadero crimen."
93 See, for example, Iracheta, "Rumoreando," *El Universal*, December 12, 1974, 4.
94 Moisés González Navarro, *Población y sociedad en México (1900–1970)* (México: Universidad Nacional Autónoma de México, 1974), 138–39; Corwin, "Contemporary Mexican Attitudes," 22–23.
95 "Secretaría de Educación Pública," 4.
96 María Luisa Mendoza, "La A por la mañana," *El Universal*, December 21, 1974, 4.
97 Sergio Pitol, "Con Monsiváis, el joven," in *El Arte de la ironía: Carlos Monsiváis ante la crítica*, ed. Mabel Moraña and Ignacio M. Sánchez Prado (México: Universidad Nacional Autónoma de México / Ediciones Era, 2007), 343, 354.
98 Carlos Monsiváis, "Campañas de odio: Las calidades del rumor," *Excélsior*, December 17, 1974, 7–8.
99 Monsiváis, "Campañas de odio," 7–8.
100 Carlos Monsiváis, *Carlos Monsiváis* (México: Empresas Editoriales, 1966), 13–15, 18–19.
101 Genoveva Flores Quintero, *Unomásuno: Victorias perdidas del periodismo mexicano (1977–1989)* (México: Universidad Iberoamericana, 2014), 94.
102 Loaeza, "La política del rumor," 585.
103 U.S. embassy to U.S. secretary of state, "Exorcizing Demon—Mexico Passes through a Mini-crisis of Confidence," December 19, 1974, WikiLeaks, https://search.wikileaks.org/plusd/cables/1974MEXICO10599_b.html.
104 "Rumor sobre la esterilización en el niño," n.d, AGN, AP-PML, Caja 65, Exp. 63.
105 "Estado de Puebla," January 22, 1975, AHSS, Secretaria Particular, SSA, Caja 268, Exp. 2; "Información de Tuxtla Gutiérrez," January 26, 1975, AGN, DGIPS, Caja 1714A, Exp. 2.
106 Carlos Monsiváis, "El coleccionista de rumores," *Proceso*, November 27, 1976, 19.

## CHAPTER 3. MUCKRAKING AND THE OIL BOOM AND BUST

1 Heberto Castillo, "Pemex, fuente de contaminación," *Proceso*, July 16, 1979, 33.
2 See, for example, Heberto Castillo, "La corrupción revolucionaria institucional," *Proceso*, February 19, 1977, 40–41; José Reveles, "Ineficiencia y corrupción, plagas de la industria azucarera," *Proceso*, May 9, 1977, 6–9; Gastón García Cantú, "La escala móvil de la corrupción," *Proceso*, June 27, 1977, 30–31; and Juan José Hinojosa, "El macartismo, insuficiente contra la corrupción," *Proceso*, August 29, 1977, 36–37.
3 It is difficult to find exact circulation figures for *Proceso*, and the Ministry of Social Communication (Secretaría de Comunicación Social) even complained in a comprehensive 1981 study of communications in Mexico that the newsmagazine refused to share circulation or subscription figures. *Unomásuno*, an investigative daily with a comparable target demographic, reported a circulation of seventy

thousand copies per day. Self-reported figures should be taken with a grain of salt, however, as directors often padded the numbers to attract advertising. See Coordinación General de Comunicación Social, "Bases estratégicas para la construcción de un Sistema Nacional de Comunicación Social," Archivo Particular Luis Javier Solana (hereafter AP-LJS), vol. 3, 406; "Bases estratégicas," vol. 11, 2051.

4  Ignacio Millán, "Un mar de petróleo," *Proceso*, December 3, 1977, 44–45.
5  Paul Kershaw, "Averting a Global Financial Crisis: The US, the IMF, and the Mexican Debt Crisis of 1976," *International History Review* 40, no. 2 (2018): 292–93.
6  José López Portillo, *Mis tiempos: Biografía y testimonio político*, vol. 1 (México: Fernández Editores, 1988), 481–82; Rodolfo González Guevara, "Organización y articulación del PRI," October 1976, Archivo General de la Nación (hereafter AGN), Archivo Particular Porfirio Muñoz Ledo (hereafter AP-PML), Caja 386, Exp. 11; Elisa Servín, *La oposición política: Otra cara del siglo XX mexicano* (México: CIDE, 2006), 65.
7  "Distrito Federal," August 2, 1977, AGN, Dirección General de Investigaciones Políticas y Sociales (hereafter DGIPS), Caja 1595-D, Exp. 13, 3.
8  "Petróleos Mexicanos," in *Mexico: An Encyclopedia of Contemporary Culture and History*, ed. Don M. Coerver, Suzanne B. Pasztor, and Robert Buffington (Santa Barbara, CA: ABC-CLIO, 2004), 382–83.
9  José Andrés Oteyza, the secretary of patrimony and industrial development, quoted in Pedro Rosales C., "Petróleo, vía a la unidad americana," *Novedades*, August 2, 1977, 15.
10  Sadot Fábila Alva, "Explosiva expansión de Pemex," *El Día*, August 3, 1977, 1.
11  Francisco Salinas Ríos, "'Enormes yacimientos' de petróleo y gas en 3 estados: Pemex," *Excélsior*, August 31, 1977, 9.
12  "Al explotar nuevas fuentes: Pemex creará un buen número de empleos en varios estados," *El Día*, September 9, 1977, 2.
13  "Distrito Federal," July 15, 1976, AGN, DGIPS, Versión Pública Julio Scherer García.
14  Arno Burkholder, *La red de los espejos: Una historia del diario Excélsior* (México: Fondo de Cultura Económica, 2016), 162–67.
15  Manuel Mejido, *Con la máquina al hombro* (México: Siglo XXI Editores, 2011), 139.
16  "Periódico Excélsior," July 8, 1976, AGN, Dirección Federal de Seguridad (hereafter DFS), Versión Pública Scherer García, Legajo 1, 1.
17  See for example, Alan Riding, "Mexican Editor Ousted by Rebels," *New York Times*, July 9, 1976, 5; and Alan Riding, "Paper in Mexico Ends Liberal Tone," *New York Times*, July 10, 1976, 8.
18  Fundraisers drew between four hundred and two thousand attendees. See "Excélsior Compañía Editorial, S.C.L.," July 19, 1976, AGN, DFS, Versión Pública Manuel Becerra Acosta; "Problema estudiantil," July 29, 1976, AGN, DFS, Versión Pública Scherer García, Legajo 1; "Estado de Oaxaca," August 6, 1976, AGN, DFS,

Versión Pública *Excélsior*, Legajo 3; and Julio Scherer García to federal attorney general, October 25, 1976, AGN, DGIPS, Versión Pública Scherer García.

19 Vicente Leñero, *Los periodistas* (México: Joaquín Mortiz, 1978), 313–14.
20 Eric Zolov, "Expanding our Conceptual Horizons: The Shift from an Old to a New Left in Latin America," *A Contracorriente* 5, no. 2 (2008): 47–73.
21 Among the twenty-three prisoners was José Revueltas. See Emilio Valle, "Heberto Castillo escribirá historia," *Ultimas Noticias*, May 14, 1971, 1; and Guillermo Jordan, "Usar la libertad para ser libres," *Excélsior*, May 15, 1971, 6, 8.
22 "Estado de Baja California," April 25, 1972, AGN, DFS, Versión Pública Heberto Castillo; "Comité Nacional de Auscultación y Organización," May 28, 1974, AGN, DFS, Versión Pública Heberto Castillo.
23 Carlos B. Gil, *Hope and Frustration: Interviews with Leaders of Mexico's Political Opposition* (Wilmington, DE: SR Books, 1992), 246–49.
24 "Total independencia en el manejo de la producción de petróleo," *El Nacional*, June 3, 1977, 1.
25 Jesús Puente Leyva, "The Natural Gas Controversy," *Proceedings of the Academy of Political Science* 34, no. 1 (1981): 159.
26 See, for example, Heberto Castillo, "Comprometer el petróleo es comprometer a México," *Proceso*, June 20, 1977, 29.
27 Castillo's suspicions were correct. Adrián Lajous maintains that the Pemex administration, U.S. contracting companies, and foreign lenders knew that the Mexican reserve figures were inflated. Díaz Serrano had contracted one of the best-known Texas consulting firms, DeGolyer and MacNaughton, to conduct a study of Mexico's oil reserves. In the resulting report the company calculated reserves that were proven (95 percent certainty), probable (50 percent certainty), and possible (10 percent). Díaz Serrano converted all of these figures into the "proven reserves" figures that he touted regularly. Adrián Lajous, interview with the author, Mexico City, March 22, 2012.
28 Heberto Castillo, "El gasoducto a Texas: ¿Opción patriótica?," *Proceso*, September 12, 1977, 34.
29 Officials felt compelled to respond to Castillo's suggestion, but quickly dismissed the idea of transporting gas via tanker as being too costly. Liquid gas, according to one Pemex engineer, would need to be stored at −170°C at both the ports of departure and entry. Furthermore, transporting liquid gas would require special tankers, and the gas would need to be vaporized for clients upon arrival. This process was both complicated and costly. César O. Baptista, "¿Porqué el gasoducto a Texas y no al Golfo?," *Siempre!*, August 10, 1977, 22–23.
30 Manuel Camacho Solís, interview with the author, Mexico City, January 10, 2012. Beginning in 1977, Camacho Solís worked under future president Carlos Salinas in the Ministry of Programming and Budget (Secretaría de Programación y Presupuesto). According to Camacho Solís, what Castillo and others published on oil in *Proceso* set the terms of the debate. On Castillo's agenda-setting role, see also Puente Leyva, "The Natural Gas Controversy"; and Elena Poniatowska, "El derroche pondría en peligro nuestro petróleo," *Novedades*, November 14, 1977, 1, 14.

31 This process had begun with the August 1965 creation of the Instituto Mexicano de Petróleo at the behest of President Gustavo Díaz Ordaz. The institute conducted hydrocarbon research and provided training and technical expertise for Pemex employees. George Grayson, *The Politics of Mexican Oil* (Pittsburgh: University of Pittsburgh Press, 1980), 42; Lajous interview. Beginning in 1977, Lajous worked under Oteyza in the Ministry of Patrimony and Industrial Development (Secretaría de Patrimonio y Fomento Industrial), which later became the Ministry of Energy (Secretaría de Energía). There he was charged with learning the ins and outs of the oil industry. Lajous described the difficulties he and others experienced trying to make and evaluate policy because Pemex would not cede the necessary data. Lajous became Pemex director in 1994. Gustavo Carvajal, president of the PRI between 1979 and 1981, similarly recounted the challenges the administration faced to get information from Pemex, and he explained that the president did not have the facts necessary to make the appropriate policy decisions. Gustavo Carvajal, interview with the author, Mexico City, March 1, 2012.

32 Héctor Rivera Gallo, "Palabra del Lector: En favor del gasoducto," *Proceso*, September 19, 1977, 64. See also "Mexican Gas Pipeline to Go Ahead Despite Strategic Fears," *Latin America Economic Report* 5, no. 41 (1977): 180–81.

33 Heberto Castillo, "Cómo deseo estar equivocado," *Proceso*, October 3, 1977, 9; Heberto Castillo, "Teme Pemex la polémica?," *Proceso*, October 10, 1977, 35–36.

34 Francisco Huerta, *Crónica del periodismo civil: La voz del ciudadano* (México: Grijalbo, 1997), 17, 28, 74, 77.

35 Castillo, "Cómo deseo estar equivocado," 6.

36 Castillo, "Cómo deseo estar equivocado," 8.

37 For a broader discussion of writing and reading between the lines, see Leo Strauss, *Persecution and the Art of Writing* (Westport, CT: Greenwood, 1973).

38 "Distrito Federal," October 26, 1977, AGN, DGIPS, Caja 1553-A, Exp. 3, 12, 2, 4–5, 11.

39 Buro de Investigación Política, December 5, 1977, Centro de Estudios de Historia de México CARSO (hereafter CEHM CARSO), Fondo Jesús Reyes Heroles, DCXIX.71.60, Legajo 60, Carpeta 71.

40 *Diario de los Debates*, Legislatura L, Año II, Período Ordinario, October 26, 1977.

41 *Diario de los Debates*, October 26, 1977.

42 Petróleos Mexicanos, "Por qué construye el gasoducto?," October 1977, Fundación Heberto Castillo (hereafter FHC), Caja 60, Exp. 292.

43 Heberto Castillo, "Petróleo y gas, ¿vender más para perder más?," *Proceso*, November 14, 1977, 33; Poniatowska, "El derroche."

44 See for example, Manuel Buendía, "La Red Privada que no se publicó," *Proceso*, November 6, 1978, 26–27.

45 Alan Riding, "Ousted Mexican Journalists Start a Liberal Paper," *New York Times*, November 24, 1977, 7; "Problema estudiantil," February 13, 1978, AGN, DFS, 11-4-78, Legajo 437; Genoveva Flores Quintero, *Unomásuno: Victorias perdidas del periodismo mexicano (1977–1989)* (México: Universidad Iberoamericana, 2014), 175.

46 Nafinsa also lent funds to newspapers like *El Universal* and the *Sol* chain in the 1960s. Benjamin T. Smith, *The Mexican Press and Civil Society, 1940–1976: Stories from the Newsroom, Stories from the Street* (Chapel Hill: University of North Carolina Press, 2018), 71.
47 See, for example, Rafael Cardona, "La Selva Lacandona, foco de tensión cercano al estallido incontrolable," *Unomásuno*, November 1, 1977.
48 "Problema estudiantil," February 13, 1978, 2.
49 "Bases estratégicas," vol. 3, 478; Flores Quintero, *Unomásuno*, 73–74.
50 "Asunto: Periódico *Unomásuno*," December 17, 1977, AGN, DFS, 65-247-77, Legajo 1.
51 José Reveles, "La discusión interna sobre el gasoducto," *Proceso*, October 31, 1977, 6-9.
52 Mexico's first professional journalism school was the Carlos Septién García Escuela de Periodismo, founded by Acción Católica Mexicana in 1949. It was followed soon by programs at UNAM in 1951 and Veracruz University (Universidad Veracruzana) in 1954. See Leonardo Ferreira, *Centuries of Silence: The Story of Latin American Journalism* (Westport, CT: Praeger, 2006), 194–95; and Coordinación General de Comunicación Social, "Bases estratégicas," vol. 14, 2756–65.
53 Vanessa Freije, "'The Emancipation of Media': Latin American Advocacy for a New International Information Order in the 1970s," *Journal of Global History* 14, no. 2 (2019): 301–20.
54 Central Intelligence Agency, "The International Energy Situation: Outlook to 1985," April 1977, FHC, Caja 60, Exp. 292.
55 Heberto Castillo, "La CIA informa: México proveerá hasta 4.5 millones de barriles diarios de petróleo en 1985," *Proceso*, October 31, 1977, 12–17.
56 Castillo, "La CIA informa," 13.
57 Heberto Castillo, "Sobre el documento de la CIA," *Proceso*, November 7, 1977, 33.
58 Heberto Castillo, Article draft of "Sobre el documento de la CIA," November 7, 1977, FHC, Caja 100, Exp. 491.
59 Heberto Castillo to María Teresa Juárez de Castillo, August 1969, FHC, Caja 49, Exp. 240; Gil, *Hope and Frustration*, 254.
60 Castillo, "Sobre el documento de la CIA."
61 "Distrito Federal," October 28, 1977, AGN, DGIPS, Caja 1595-D, Exp. 15.
62 Camilo D. Trumper, *Ephemeral Histories: Public Art, Politics, and the Struggle for the Streets in Chile* (Oakland: University of California Press, 2016), 96.
63 "Distrito Federal," November 15, 1977, AGN, DGIPS, Caja 1595-D, Exp. 16.
64 To retain the rhyme, I have translated "shit" as "ass." The original term was "cacaducto." "Estado de Chihuahua," November 23, 1978, AGN, DFS, Versión Pública Heberto Castillo, 1.
65 "Estado de Chihuahua," 2.
66 Heberto Castillo and Rius, *Huele a gas! Los misterios del gasoducto*, 6th ed. (México: Editorial Posada, 1979), 22.
67 "Comité Nacional de Auscultación y Organización: PMT," August 7, 1973, AGN, DFS, Versión Pública Heberto Castillo, 3.

68 Ley Federal de Organizaciones Políticas y Procesos Electorales, December 30, 1977, http://dof.gob.mx/nota_to_imagen_fs.php?codnota=4672344&fecha=30/12/1977&cod_diario=201306; Barry Carr, *Marxism and Communism in Twentieth-Century Mexico* (Lincoln: University of Nebraska Press, 1992), 280, 302.
69 Linda Garmon, "Autopsy of an Oil Spill," *Science News* 118, no. 17 (1980): 267.
70 Petróleos Mexicanos, Boletín de prensa, June 11, 1979, AGN, AP-PML, Caja 58, Exp. 16, 3.
71 Enrique Aranda Pedroza, "No afectará a la industria el accidente del 'Ixtoc' 1," *Unomásuno*, June 17, 1979, 1.
72 "¿Qué pasa en el Ixtoc?," *Unomásuno*, June 17, 1979, 3.
73 Manuel Buendía, "Red Privada," *Excélsior*, January 11, 1979, 1.
74 José Ángel Conchello, "Incendios en Pemex: ¡Creo que eso no tiene perdón de dios!," *El Universal*, June 14, 1979, 4, 12. See also Luis González de Alba, "Ixtoc 1: Las culpas y las disculpas," *Unomásuno*, June 23, 1979, 6.
75 Conchello, "Incendios en Pemex," 12; Heberto Castillo, "Pemex, fuente de contaminación," *Proceso*, July 16, 1979, 33–34. Castillo referred to Díaz Serrano's founding and ownership of shares of the Permargo company, which subcontracted drilling of the Ixtoc 1 well to the U.S. company Sedco International.
76 See for example, Miguel Ángel Granados Chapa, "El derecho a la información, esa vacilada," *Siempre!*, November 9, 1977, 24–25; Alberto Pérez Leyva, "JLP: El derecho a la información complementa a libertad de expresión," *El Nacional*, January 5, 1978, 1; and Heberto Castillo, "El estado es a informar," *Personas*, January 8, 1979, 8–9.
77 Fernando González Gortázar, "Ixtoc 1: Algo flota sobre el agua," *Unomásuno*, June 29, 1979, 4.
78 "Ocultan información sobre los daños por el derrame en Campeche," *El Día*, June 14, 1979, 3; Víctor Alfonso Maldonado, "El accidente del Ixtoc 1," *Unomásuno*, June 17, 1979, 3.
79 Carlos Sánchez Cárdenas, "¡Pemex pagará!," *El Universal*, July 12, 1979, 4.
80 "Inició Pemex la explotación en la Sonda de Campeche," *El Nacional*, June 27, 1979, 6.
81 Isabel Morales, "Desprecia Pemex los daños que causa su contaminación," *Proceso*, July 2, 1979, 12–14.
82 Enrique Maza, "Pemex despoja, contamina y quiebra un modo de vida," *Proceso*, July 9, 1979, 11–13.
83 See, for example, Secretaría de Programación y Presupuesto, "El impacto petrolero en la política de gasto público," July 1979, FHC, Caja 61, Exp. 296.
84 Enrique del Val Blanco to the director of Petróleos Mexicanos Supplies and Warehousing, Raúl Cisneros Jiménez, June 21, 1979, Fundación Manuel Buendía (hereafter FMB), Datos Personales, Binder 3. The letter was copied to the minister of patrimony and industrial development, the undersecretary of commerce, and the Pemex director.
85 Manuel Buendía, "Red Privada," *Excélsior*, July 30, 1979, 1.
86 Buendía, "Red Privada," July 30, 1979, 8.

87  Jorge Díaz Serrano to Manuel Buendía, n.d., FMB, Correspondencia, Binder 9; Manuel Buendía to Reynaldo Jáuregui Zentella, director of Pemex public relations, September 6, 1979, FMB, Correspondencia, Binder 9.
88  In the anthology of essays published to honor Buendía after his death, nearly every contributor mentioned his wardrobe choices. Elena Poniatowska, for example, admitted that Buendía's apparel colored her first impression of him. A former student also described Buendía as sticking out in the UNAM: "In a department of jeans, backpacks, and t-shirts, of theorists who hate the bourgeoisie, he drew attention, passing elegantly through the halls with those well-cut suits." Héctor Aguilar Camín et al., *Los días de Manuel Buendía* (México: Océano / Fundación Manuel Buendía, 1984), 27, 63, 125. On *guayaberismo*, see Nicolás Salazar-Sutil, "What's in Your Wardrobe, Mr. Morales? A Study in Political Dress," *Popular Communication* 7, no. 2 (2009): 75; Marilyn Miller, "*Guayaberismo* and the Essence of Cool," in *The Latin American Fashion Reader*, ed. Regina A. Root (Oxford: Berg, 2005), 216, 221–22. Castillo later accused Buendía of trying to undermine the PMT. See "Foro de Excélsior: Campaña de Buendía contra el PMT, H. Castillo," *Excélsior*, July 23, 1982, 4, 37.
89  III Informe, *La República*, September 1979, PRI Centro Nacional de Información Documental Adolfo López Mateos.
90  Enrique Condés Lara, *Represión y rebelión en México (1959–1985)*, vol. 2 (México: Miguel Ángel Porrúa, 2007), 77; Smith, *The Mexican Press*, 109.
91  "Heberto Castillo: México entrega su riqueza petrolera," *El Universal*, August 10, 1979, 12; López Portillo, *Mis tiempos*, vol. 2, 866.
92  López Portillo, *Mis tiempos*, vol. 1, 649; López Portillo, *Mis tiempos*, vol. 2, 776.
93  Gregorio Meraz, "Heberto Castillo propone preguntas a Díaz Serrano," *El Universal*, September 20, 1979, 1, 7; Heberto Castillo, "Tercer informe, preguntas sin respuesta," *Ovaciones*, September 5, 1979, FHC, Box 105, Exp. 520.
94  *Diario de los Debates* 22, September 20, 1979, Legislatura LI, Año I, Período Ordinario, http://cronica.diputados.gob.mx/. The representative was Carlos Piñera Rueda.
95  *Diario de los Debates* 22.
96  *Diario de los Debates* 22.
97  "Díaz Serrano: Una victoria sin triunfialismos," *Novedades*, September 23, 1979, IV:1.
98  Alfredo Kawage Ramia, "Fama Pública," *Novedades*, September 23, 1979, IV:1.
99  Luis González de Alba, "Díaz Serrano en la Cámara, revisión del presente," *Unomásuno*, September 22, 1979, 7.
100 "Comparecencia de JDS: Ensayo para una sociedad crítica," *Unomásuno*, September 22, 1979, 1, 4.
101 Antonio Acevedo Gutiérrez to Jesús Reyes Heroles, April 23, 1979, CEHM CARSO, Fondo Jesús Reyes Heroles, DCXIX.10.7, Legajo 7.
102 Carlos Ramírez, "Las finanzas de Pemex a punto de estallar, por corrupción e incapacidad," *Proceso*, May 25, 1981, 6.

103 Ramírez, "Las finanzas de Pemex," 7. This report is also in Castillo's archive; see Secretaría de Programación y Presupuesto, Report on Pemex finances and administrative processes, 1981, FHC, Caja 60, Exp. 292.
104 Manuel Buendía, "Red Privada," *Excélsior*, February 4, 1980, 1, 8.
105 Lajous interview. See also Alan Riding, "The Political Background of Resignation at Pemex," *New York Times*, June 8, 1981, D:1.
106 The debt grew from $27.5 billion in 1976 to $92.4 billion in 1982. Louise E. Walker, *Waking from the Dream: Mexico's Middle Classes after 1968* (Stanford, CA: Stanford University Press, 2013), 78.
107 Rafael Rodríguez Castañeda, "Petróleo y soberanía económica, pignorados un año por mil millones de dólares," *Proceso*, November 15, 1982, 6.
108 Miguel Ángel Rivera, interview with author, Mexico City, July 17, 2013.
109 Fernando Ortega, "Un 'pobre' manejo administrativo, causa de la vulnerabilidad de Pemex," *Proceso*, June 20, 1983, 6–11.
110 The posters read, "Díaz Serrano a la Cárcel por Ladrón"; "Díaz Serrano le Ganaste a Sant Anna"; and "Y López Portillo Cuándo?" Elías Chávez, "Entre tumultos se inició el proceso," *Proceso*, July 18, 1983, 6–7.
111 "Ya nos saquearon," 1993, dir. Fernando Fuentes, *La vida en México en el siglo XX*, vol. 4 (México: Compañia Eurolatinoamericana de Comunicación Educativa, 2005), DVD.
112 Anne Rubenstein shared this observation with me.
113 José Agustín, *Tragicomedia mexicana 3: La vida en México de 1982 a 1994* (México: Editorial Planeta Mexicana, 1992), 25–28; "Corruption," in Coerver, Pasztor, and Buffington, *Mexico: An Encyclopedia*, 128; Gloria M. Delegado de Cantú, *Historia de México: De la era revolucionaria al sexenio del cambio*, vol. 2, 5th ed. (México City: Pearson Educación de Mexico, 2007), 432; "Corruption," in *Mexico Today: An Encyclopedia of Life in the Republic*, vol. 1, ed. Alex M. Saragoza, Ana Paula Ambrosi, and Silvia D. Zárate (Santa Barbara, CA: ABC-CLIO, 2012), 153.
114 Kendall R. Phillips, "Introduction," in *Framing Public Memory*, ed. Stephen Howard Browne, Barbara Biesecker, Barbie Zelizer, Charles E. Morris III, and Kendall R. Phillips (Tuscaloosa: University of Alabama Press, 2004), 4.
115 "Pemex: Incendio en los archivos," *Proceso*, September 13, 1982, 32.

## CHAPTER 4. THE SPECTACLE OF IMPUNITY

1 José González González, *Lo negro del Negro Durazo*, 7th ed. (México: Editorial Posada, 1983), 17.
2 As a child, López Portillo had been small and weak, tormented by illness. He devoted considerable space (over one hundred pages) in the first of his two-volume presidential memoir to his childhood, suggesting that he viewed this period as critical to his development as the future president of Mexico. José López Portillo, *Mis tiempos: Biografía y testimonio político*, vol. 1 (México: Fernández Editores, 1988).
3 González González, *Lo negro del Negro Durazo*, 41, 45–46.

4 Héctor Castillo Berthier and Wil Pansters, "Violencia e inseguridad en la Ciudad de México: Entre la fragmentación y la politización," *Foro Internacional* 47, no. 3 (2007): 594.
5 See, for example, Rafael Rodríguez Castañeda, *El policía: Perseguía, torturaba, mataba* (México: Grijalbo, 2013), 85.
6 Robert Buffington, "Institutional Memories: The Curious Genesis of the Mexican Police Museum," *Radical History Review* 113 (Spring 2012): 156; Pablo Piccato, "Murders of Nota Roja: Truth and Justice in Mexican Crime News," *Past and Present* 223 (May 2014): 227.
7 Jaime Pensado, *Rebel Mexico: Student Unrest and Authoritarian Political Culture during the Long Sixties* (Stanford, CA: Stanford University Press, 2013); Pedro Ocotitla Saucedo, "Movimientos de colonos en Ciudad Nezahualcóyotl: Acción colectiva y política popular, 1945–1975" (master's thesis, Universidad Autónoma Metropolitana-Itzapalapa, 2000), 177–80.
8 Manuel Buendía to Arturo Durazo, November 29, 1977, Fundación Manuel Buendía (hereafter FMB), Correspondencia, Binder 9.
9 Vanessa Freije, "Exposing Scandals, Guarding Secrets: Manuel Buendía, Columnismo, and the Unraveling of One-Party Rule in Mexico, 1965–1984," *The Americas* 72, no. 3 (2015): 383.
10 Manuel Buendía, "Red Privada," *Excélsior*, August 21, 1979, 1, 19.
11 See, for example, Gustavo Durán de Huerta, "Desde el Café," *Últimas Noticias*, August 16, 1979, 4.
12 Buendía, "Red Privada," August 21, 1979, 19.
13 On the process of registering a crime report with the public prosecutor, see Guillermo Raúl Zepeda Lecuona, *Crimen sin castigo: Procuración de justicia penal y ministerio público en México* (México: Centro de Investigación para el Desarrollo, Fondo de Cultura Económica, 2004), 108.
14 Manuel Buendía to Carlos Hank González, August 21, 1979, FMB, Correspondencia, Binder 9, 1.
15 Manuel Buendía, "Red Privada," *Excélsior*, September 11, 1979, 1. Buendía thanked Hank González for his speedy response; see Manuel Buendía to Carlos Hank González, August 27, 1979, FMB, Correspondencia, Binder 9.
16 On the "truth effect," see John Beverley, *Testimonio: On the Politics of Truth* (Minneapolis: University of Minnesota Press, 2004), 33.
17 Buendía, "Red Privada," September 11, 1979, 12, emphasis in the original.
18 Luz María to Manuel Buendía, September 12, 1979, FMB, Datos Personales, Binder 3.
19 Gama speculated that this was why DFS agents were in the café. DFS spies had broken into CENCOS and stolen portions of its archive on multiple occasions. See "Boletín de Prensa," July 9, 1977, Escuela Nacional de Antropología e Historia, Centro de Información y Documentación Guillermo Bonfil Batalla, Centro Nacional de Comunicación Social, Caja 7, Legajo 15; Héctor Gama, "Ciudadanos sin garantía," *El Universal*, November 12, 1980, 4, 8.

20  Gama, "Ciudadanos sin garantía"; Gladys McCormick, "The Last Door: Political Prisoners and the Use of Torture in Mexico's Dirty War," *The Americas* 72, no. 1 (Jan. 2017): 57–81.
21  On this presumed exceptionalism see, Enrique Condés Lara, *Represión y rebelión en México (1959–1985)*, vol. 1 (México: Miguel Ángel Porrúa, 2007), 21; and Gilbert M. Joseph and Daniela Spenser, eds., *In from the Cold: Latin America's New Encounter with the Cold War* (Durham, NC: Duke University Press, 2008).
22  Rodolfo Gamiño Muñoz, *Guerrilla, represión y prensa en la década de los setenta en México: Invisibilidad y olvido* (México: Instituto Mora, 2011), 106, 111. A notable exception was Mario Menéndez Rodríguez's *Por Qué?*
23  Andrea Radilla Martínez and Claudia E. G. Rangel Lozano, eds., *Desaparición forzada y terrorismo de estado en México: Memorias de la represión de Atoyac, Guerrero durante la década de los setenta* (México: Plaza y Valdés Editores, 2012).
24  Rodríguez Castañeda, *El policía*, 125.
25  "387 desaparecidos en Chilpancingo, por motivos políticos: La USCUAG," *Unomásuno*, March 12, 1978, 4.
26  Héctor Gama to Manuel Buendía, November 9, 1980, FMB, Correspondencia, Binder 2.
27  Paco Ignacio Taibo II, *'68* (México: Joaquín Mortiz, 1991), 68, 84. For Buendía's views, see, for example, J. M. Tellezgirón, "Para Control de Usted," *El Día*, March 15, 1968, 3. When writing his *El Día* column in the late 1960s, Buendía's used the pseudonym J. M. Tellezgirón.
28  Sergio Aguayo Quezada, *"La charola": Una historia de los servicios de inteligencia en México* (México: Grijalbo, 2001), 80.
29  Manuel Buendía, "Red Privada," *Excélsior*, November 14, 1980, 37.
30  Heberto Castillo, "'Cooperación': ¿De periodista agredido a policía?," *El Universal*, November 19, 1980, 5. Castillo reported that Buendía had written to the secretary of the interior, Enrique Olivares Santana, who then sent DFS director Miguel Nazar Haro instructions to locate the perpetrators. A copy of the letter preserved in Buendía's private archive confirms this account; Manuel Buendía to Secretary of the Interior Enrique Olivares Santana, November 12, 1980, FMB, Correspondencia, Binder 2.
31  Castillo, "'Cooperación'"; Julio Scherer García, *Vivir* (México: Grijalbo, 2012), 31. Some of Nazar Haro's former prisoners described him as taking sadistic pleasure in torture. See Rodríguez Castañeda, *El policía*, 27, 45–48; McCormick, "The Last Door," 77–78.
32  Rodríguez Castañeda, *El policía*, 81, 87–91.
33  Castillo, "'Cooperación.'"
34  Rodríguez Castañeda, *El policía*, 94–99.
35  "Aún buscan dos cadáveres en la Presa Veinte Arcos," *Últimas Noticias*, January 15, 1982, 2.
36  Manuel Camín, "Desde el Café," *Últimas Noticias*, January 16, 1982, 4.

37 Juan M. Vasquez, "Mexico Police Still Puzzled by Mass Murder of 12 Men," *Los Angeles Times*, January 22, 1982, 8.

38 Camín, "Desde el Café," January 16, 1982, 4. On Camín's reputation, see Manuel Becerra Acosta, *Dos poderes* (México: Grijalbo, 1984), 143; and Julio Scherer García, *Los presidentes* (México: Grijalbo, 1986), 227.

39 Rafael Medina Cruz, "Asesinadas en el DF las víctimas del Gran Canal: El MP de Tula," *Últimas Noticias*, January 20, 1982, 1.

40 Arturo Ríos Ruiz, "Culpan a la PJF de los asesinatos del Gran Canal," *Últimas Noticias*, January 19, 1982, 1, 9; Miguel Ángel Velázquez, "Se refugian en México miles de Guatemaltecos," *Unomásuno*, January 19, 1982, 1, 4.

41 Aguayo Quezada, *"La charola,"* 222–23.

42 Manuel Buendía, "Red Privada," *Excélsior*, January 28, 1982, 1, 13.

43 Manuel Buendía, "Red Privada," *Excélsior*, March 9, 1982, 13.

44 Buendía, "Red Privada," March 9, 1982, 8.

45 Miguel Ángel Granados Chapa, "No al gobierno de los policías," *Siempre!*, March 17, 1982, 10; "Latin Blotter," *Latin America Weekly Report*, March 19, 1982, 3.

46 "Actividades de Arturo Martínez Nateras," February 10, 1982, Archivo General de la Nación (hereafter AGN), Dirección Federal de Seguridad (hereafter DFS), Versión Pública Arturo Durazo Moreno; Report on activities of Arturo Durazo, April 26, 1982, AGN, DFS, Versión Pública Arturo Durazo Moreno.

47 VI Informe de Gobierno, *La República*, August 1982, PRI Centro Nacional de Información Documental Adolfo López Mateos.

48 "Conferencia sustentada por el Lic. José Ángel Conchello," September 8, 1982, AGN, DFS, Versión Pública Arturo Durazo Moreno, 3.

49 See, for example, Guillermo Correa, "En una colina con una fortaleza al centro, casas para los López Portillo," *Proceso*, September 13, 1982, 20–21; and Rafael Rodríguez Castañeda, "Tres hectáreas llenas de lujo, cerca de una empresa del Regente," *Proceso*, September 13, 1982, 22–23.

50 Ignacio Ramírez, "El Partenón de Durazo, en tierras ejidales," *Proceso*, September 13, 1982, 23–25.

51 Oscar Hinojosa, "Sólo Durazo habló: Es millonario, dijo, aunque gana $39,000 al mes," *Proceso*, September 27, 1982, 27–28.

52 "La UAG exigirá al Congreso del Estado investigue la propiedad de Arturo Durazo Moreno en Zihuatanejo, Guerrero," October 9, 1982, AGN, DFS, Versión Pública Arturo Durazo Moreno; "Para casa de la cultura la residencia de Durazo en Zihuatanejo sugieren," November 4, 1982, AGN, DFS, Versión Pública Arturo Durazo Moreno.

53 Claudio Lomnitz, "Times of Crisis: Historicity, Sacrifice, and the Spectacle of Debacle in Mexico City," *Public Culture* 15, no. 1 (2003): 131.

54 The title in Spanish is "Medio siglo de siglas." The word *siglas* actually refers to the initials in an acronym, but "slogan" is the best translation because the title and the cartoon are referring to each initial standing in for a broader trait attributed to the party.

55 The Spanish word *rateros* carries connotations than the English translation to "thieves" does not. A ratero is someone who pilfers or steals things, often of little value, through deception. Unlike a thief, the ratero is vile and despicable because of the ways in which he or she goes about stealing. For this reason, the term is often used to describe corrupt officials who grew rich from public coffers.
56 Helioflores, "Al final," *El Universal*, November 30, 1982, 5.
57 Another joke was that the new peso would bear the inscription "In Dog We Trust." Louise E. Walker, *Waking from the Dream: Mexico's Middle Classes after 1968* (Stanford, CA: Stanford University Press, 2013), 144, 159; Correa, "En una colina."
58 Samuel Schmidt, *Humor en serio: Análisis del chiste político en México* (México: Aguilar, 1996), 22.
59 Sarah Babb, *Managing Mexico: Economists from Nationalism to Neoliberalism* (Princeton, NJ: Princeton University Press, 2001), 171–74; Walker, *Waking from the Dream*, 152.
60 *Diario de los Debates* 46, December 3, 1982, Legislatura LII, Año I Período Ordinario, http://cronica.diputados.gob.mx/; Oficina de la Presidencia, "Boletín de prensa," December 14, 1982, AGN, Fondo Presidencial Miguel de la Madrid Hurtado (hereafter MMH), PR 02.03.02.00, Caja 1, Exp. 3, 2–3.
61 Carlos Salinas, speech at public service workers meeting, December 6, 1982, AGN, MMH, PR 02.03.02.00, Caja 1, Exp. 2, 4; Juan D. Lindau, "Technocrats and Mexico's Political Elite," *Political Science Quarterly* 111, no. 2 (1996): 295.
62 "Declaraciones del Sen. Filiberto Vigueras Lázaro," August 2, 1983, AGN, DFS, Versión Pública Arturo Durazo Moreno; Emilio Hernández, "Durazo quitó tierras, se apoderó del agua y corrompió al pueblo del Ajusco," *Proceso*, August 15, 1983; Julio Scherer García, *El poder: Historias de familia* (México: Grijalbo, 1990), 33–34.
63 Pablo Piccato, "Homicide as Politics in Modern Mexico," *Bulletin of Latin American Research* 32, no. S1 (2013): 106–7.
64 Luis de la Barreda Solórzano, "La crisis y la criminalidad," in *México ante la crisis*, vol. 2, ed. Pablo González Casanova and Héctor Aguilar Camín (México: Siglo Veintiuno Editores, 1985), 117–19.
65 Piccato, "Homicide as Politics," 107, 110.
66 Stuart Hall et al., *Policing the Crisis: Mugging, the State, and Law and Order* (New York: Holmes and Meier, 1978), 11, 20–21. On the reticence to demand greater policing, see Paul Chevigny, "The Populism of Fear," *Punishment and Society* 5, no. 1 (2003): 84.
67 Javier Rodríguez Lozano, "Aumenta la ola de secuestros," *La Prensa*, January 6, 1983, 25, 35. See also Jorge Adalberto Luna, "Prospectivas," *La Prensa*, January 10, 1983, 10.
68 Rafael Pérez and Martín del Campo, "Lo que el Pueblo Quiere," *La Prensa*, January 10, 1983, 10.
69 See, for example, José Joaquín Blanco, "Tacubaya, 1978," in *The Mexico City Reader*, ed. Rubén Gallo Fox, trans. Lorna Scott (Madison: University of Wisconsin Press, 2004), 200.

70 Pérez and Campo, "Lo que el Pueblo Quiere."
71 See for example, Ramón Márquez, "Tres días de trámites y desapareció el délito," *Unomásuno*, September 20, 1984, 22.
72 Ramón Márquez, "Víctimas acosadas," *Unomásuno*, September 14, 1984, 23.
73 Javier Rodríguez Lozano, "Asesinó un policía a un automovilista," *La Prensa*, January 6, 1983, 25; Manuel Lino B., "Por extorsión policiaca paran transportistas," *Últimas Noticias*, January 14, 1982, 1; Francisco Salinas Ríos, "Transportistas se quejan en la Cámara contra la DGPT," *Últimas Noticias*, January 15, 1982, 1, 2.
74 Carlos Cortes to Manuel Buendía, April 30, 1983, FMB, Datos Personales, unnumbered binder.
75 María Luisa Salcedo Cabrera to Manuel Buendía, FMB, Datos Personales, unnumbered binder.
76 Luis Héctor Valdez to Manuel Buendía, February 9, 1981, FMB, Correspondencia, Binder 2.
77 Beverley, *Testimonio*, chap. 1.
78 González González, *Lo negro del Negro Durazo*, 17, 11.
79 Scherer García, *Los presidentes*, 101–2; Scherer García, *Vivir*, 131.
80 Ignacio Ramírez, "Durazo hizo de la policía una organización criminal," *Proceso*, September 26, 1983, 7.
81 González González, *Lo negro del Negro Durazo*, 39.
82 Christina A. Sue, *Land of the Cosmic Race: Race Mixture, Racism, and Blackness in Mexico* (New York: Oxford University Press, 2013), 25, 30; Susana Vargas, "México: la pigmentocracia perfecta," *Horizontal*, June 2, 2015, accessed November 2, 2019, https://horizontal.mx/mexico-la-pigmentocracia-perfecta/.
83 González González, *Lo negro del Negro Durazo*, 123–24, 160–61.
84 González González, *Lo negro del Negro Durazo*, 71, 74, 79–83. *Proceso* had also published a few articles on Durazo's Ajusco residence before González's book came out. Hernández, "Durazo quitó tierras."
85 Heberto Castillo, "La náusea," *Proceso*, October 3, 1983, 36.
86 Manuel Buendía, "Red Privada," *Excélsior*, October 10, 1983, 1.
87 *Palabras sin Reposo*, Radio UNAM, September 22, 1983, Fonoteca Nacional de México (hereafter Fonoteca).
88 Francisco Huerta, *Crónica del periodismo civil: La voz del ciudadano* (México: Grijalbo, 1997), 97–98.
89 "Desplegado en la Escuela Normal Superior del Estado y la Escuela de Policía y Tránsito," February 22, 1984, AGN, DFS, Versión Pública Arturo Durazo Moreno; "Casa del Lago," September 2, 1984, AGN, DFS, Versión Pública Arturo Durazo Moreno.
90 Alan Riding, *Distant Neighbors: A Portrait of the Mexicans* (New York: Vintage Books, 1985), 132; Armando Bonilla, "¿Cómo es que el "Partenón a la corrupción" se convirtió en sede de la AMC?," *Ciencia MX*, http://www.cienciamx.com/index.php/anecdotas-cientificas/19178-como-es-que-el-partenon-a-la-corrupcion-se-convirtio-en-sede-de-la-amc.

91 Legal attache, Mexico City, to FBI director, "Arturo Durazo," February 24, 1984, AZCentral, http://archive.azcentral.com/persistent/icimages/news/2910_001_A.pdf.
92 Even in 1986, new articles and radio programs appeared about Durazo's case. See, for example, Carlos Marín, "El juicio a Durazo parece montado en su beneficio," *Proceso*, June 16, 1986, 16–20; *La Opinión de los Sucesos*, Radio UNAM, April 10, 1986, Fonoteca.
93 As a point of comparison, *Proceso*'s price in late 1984 was 120 pesos; the price rose considerably with inflation over the following two years.
94 *El infierno del Negro Durazo*, no. 1, Princeton University Library (hereafter PUL), Latin American Ephemera Collection (hereafter LAEC), Supplement 2, Politics in Mexico, Reel 1, 5.
95 Report to director Pablo González Ruelas, November 15, 1985, AGN, DFS, Versión Pública Arturo Durazo Moreno, 2.
96 *Picardías del Negro Durazo*, no. 42, PUL, LAEC, Supplement 2, Politics in Mexico, Reel 1.
97 *Picardías del Negro Durazo*, no. 14, PUL, LAEC, Supplement 2, Politics in Mexico, Reel 1, 30–32.
98 *Picardías del Negro Durazo*, no. 68, PUL, LAEC, Supplement 2, Politics in Mexico, Reel 1, 20–21.
99 Report to director Pablo González Ruelas.
100 "Declaraciones del Senador Faustino Alba Zavala," July 2, 1984, AGN, DFS, Versión Pública Arturo Durazo Moreno, 1.
101 "Investigación sobre el asesinato del periodista Manuel Buendía Tellezgirón," June 12, 1984, AGN, DFS, Versión Pública Manuel Buendía, Legajo 2, 1.
102 Héctor Aguilar Camín, "Buendia y los idus de mayo," *Nexos*, July 1984, 5.
103 Jean Claude Buhrer, "Le journaliste qui en savait trop," *Le Monde*, July 8, 1984, 6.
104 Richard J. Meislin, "Noted Mexican Journalist Shot Dead," *New York Times*, June 1, 1984, 3.
105 "Investigación sobre el asesinato," 3; Buendía began publishing his investigations into drug trafficking on May 4, 1984. See Aguayo Quezada, *"La Charola,"* 239.
106 "Investigación sobre el asesinato," 7.
107 Aguilar Camín, "Los idus de mayo," 7.
108 Jorge Jóseph, "Manuel Buendía: Errores de investigación y pistas posibles," June 19, 1984, AGN, DFS, Versión Pública Manuel Buendía Tellezgirón, Legajo 2, 1–2.
109 Jorge Manrique and Ismael Rodríguez Jr., *Masacre en el Río Tula*, dir. Ismael Rodríguez Jr. (México: Películas Rodríguez, 1985), DVD.
110 David Wilt, "Based on a True Story: Reality-Based Exploitation Cinema in Mexico," in *Latsploitation, Exploitation Cinemas, and Latin America*, ed. Victoria Ruétalo and Dolores Tierney (New York: Routledge, 2009), 165.
111 Manrique and Rodríguez, *Masacre en el Río Tula*.
112 Manuel Robles, "La película 'Lo negro del Negro,' ante el obstáculo mayor: El permiso oficial," *Proceso*, April 15, 1985, 22–26; Manuel Robles, "A cinematografía, la película sobre Durazo, para autorización," *Proceso*, April 22, 1985, 58.

113 Fernando Ortega Pizarro, "Para la DEA, Zorrilla es clave para descifrar el narcotráfico en México," *Proceso*, June 3, 1985, 6–9; Miguel Ángel Granados Chapa, *Buendía: El primer asesinato de la narcopolítica en México* (México: Grijalbo, 2012), 20–22. Russell H. Bartley and Sylvia Erickson Bartley, *Eclipse of the Assassins: The CIA, Imperial Politics, and the Slaying of Mexican Journalist Manuel Buendía* (Madison: University of Wisconsin Press, 2015), suggests that the web of complicity in Buendía's murder spread far beyond Zorrilla.

114 Huerta, *Crónica del periodismo civil*, 98.

115 Baltazar Ignacio Valadez, "Periodismo en peligro," *El Universal*, July 14, 1986, 5.

116 Report to director Pablo González Ruelas, 1, 4.

## CHAPTER 5. A MEDIATED DISASTER

1 *Unomásuno* reported one thousand missing and five thousand wounded, while *La Jornada* reported four thousand dead and ten thousand wounded. See "Mil desaparecidos; cinco mil heridos," *Unomásuno*, September 20, 1985, 1, 16; and "Cuatro mil muertos, 10 mil heridos y 500 construcciones destruidas," *La Jornada*, September 20, 1985, 3.

2 Rosa Rojas, "A la intemperie cientos de familias de Tlatelolco," *La Jornada*, September 22, 1985, 5; Diane Davis, "Reverberations: Mexico City's 1985 Earthquake and the Transformation of the Capital," in *The Resilient City: How Modern Cities Recover from Disaster*, ed. Lawrence J. Vale and Thomas J. Campanella (New York: Oxford University Press, 2005), 255–57.

3 I follow scholars and contemporary writers by referring to a singular "earthquake" when discussing the events and debates that followed the earthquakes on September 19–20, 1985. José Francisco Ruiz Massieu, "Reconstrucción y política," *La Jornada*, October 8, 1985, 5. On the earthquake as a turning point, see Fernando Solana Olivares, "Novedad de la patria: Las réplicas," *La Jornada*, September 30, 1985, 11.

4 Chroniclers have emphasized that the genre allows them to explore human experience that traditional reporting does not. See, for example, Juanita León, *Country of Bullets: Chronicles of War*, trans. Guillermo Bleichmar (Albuquerque: University of New Mexico Press, 2009), 1–3.

5 "Situación que prevalece con motivo de los movimientos telúricos," September 27, 1985, Archivo General de la Nación (hereafter AGN), Dirección Federal de Seguridad (hereafter DFS), 009-031-003, 3.

6 See, for example, Rogelio Hernández, "Incredulidad en el desolado Tlatelolco," *Excélsior*, October 12, 1985, 1, 10. *El Universal* also was the first newspaper to reveal that the body of Saúl Ocampo, a lawyer who had gone missing eight days prior to the earthquake, had been found gagged and bound in the trunk of a car. The car was discovered under the wreckage of the District Attorney General of the Federal District building. Humberto Musacchio, *Ciudad quebrada* (México: Ediciones Océano, S.A., 1985), 37–38.

7   Sallie Hughes, *Newsrooms in Conflict: Journalism and the Democratization of Mexico* (Pittsburgh: University of Pittsburgh Press, 2006), 40.
8   Jaime Avilés, "El salvamento nunca iniciado en el inmueble de San Camilito," *La Jornada*, September 21, 1985, 20; Francisco Ortiz Pinchetti, "Trabajos de rescate simulados, simple escenografía para una visita presidencial," *Proceso*, October 7, 1985, 28–29.
9   Carlos Monsiváis, "La solidaridad de la población en realidad fue toma de poder," *Proceso*, September 23, 1985, 6–15. On the influence of Monsiváis's articles, see Ignacio L. Marván and J. Aurelio Cuevas, "El movimiento de damnificados de Tlatelolco (septiembre de 1985–marzo de 1986)," *Revista Mexicana de Sociología* 49, no. 4 (1987): 111; Elena Poniatowska, "The Earthquake: To Carlos Monsiváis," *Oral History Review* 16, no. 1 (1988): 16; Dan La Botz, *Democracy in Mexico: Peasant Rebellion and Political Reform* (Cambridge, MA: South End Press, 1995), 66; and Ligia Tavera-Fenollosa, "Social Movements and Civil Society: The Mexico City 1985 Earthquake Victim Movement" (PhD diss., Yale University, 2008), chap. 4.
10  Monsiváis, "La solidaridad," 10.
11  Celeste González de Bustamante, *"Muy buenas noches": Mexico, Television, and the Cold War* (Lincoln: University of Nebraska Press, 2012), 22.
12  Claudia Fernández and Andrew Paxman, *El Tigre: Emilio Azcárraga y su imperio Televisa* (México: Grijalbo / Mondadori, 2001), 261–63.
13  Few book-length works have made Monsiváis the subject of analysis. Notable exceptions are Linda Egan, *Carlos Monsiváis: Culture and Chronicle in Contemporary Mexico* (Tucson: University of Arizona Press, 2001); and Jezreel Salazar, *La ciudad como texto: La crónica urbana de Carlos Monsiváis* (Monterrey, Mexico: Universidad Autónoma de Nuevo León, 2006); Mabel Moraña and Ignacio M. Sánchez Prado, eds., *El arte de la ironía: Carlos Monsiváis ante la crítica* (México: UNAM / Ediciones Era, 2007). Carlos Monsiváis, *Carlos Monsiváis* (México: Empresas Editoriales, 1966), 18–20; Carlos Monsiváis, *Días de guardar* (México: Ediciones Era, 1970), 28–44, 65–77; Barry Carr, *Marxism and Communism in Twentieth-Century Mexico* (Lincoln: University of Nebraska Press, 1992), 296–97; Egan, *Carlos Monsiváis*, 15, 38.
14  Monsiváis, *Carlos Monsiváis*, 41; Elena Poniatowska, *El tren pasa primero* (México: Alfaguara, 2005); Claire Brewster, *Responding to Crisis in Contemporary Mexico: The Political Writings of Paz, Fuentes, Monsiváis, and Poniatowska* (Tucson: University of Arizona Press, 2005), 40–47; Carlos Monsiváis, *Entrada libre: Crónicas de la sociedad que se organiza* (México: Ediciones Era, 1987), 13, 36.
15  Monsiváis, "La solidaridad," 10; *Dinámica Habitacional*, October 1, 1985, AGN, Fondo Presidencial Miguel de la Madrid Hurtado (hereafter MMH), 32.01.00.00, Caja 4, Exp. 17. *Dinámica Habitacional* was the bulletin of the Operational Center for Housing and Settlement (Centro Operacional de Vivienda y Poblamiento), an organization that young professionals founded in 1965 to improve living conditions for the urban poor. Priscilla Connelly, "The Mexican National Popular Housing Fund," in *Empowering Squatter Citizen: Local Government,*

*Civil Society, and Urban Poverty Reduction*, ed. Diana Mitlin and David Satterthswaite (London: Earthscan, 2004), 85.

16  See, for example, María Fernanda Somuano, "The Role of NGOs in the Process of Democratization: The Case of Mexico" (PhD diss., University of Iowa, 2003).

17  Minutes of a meeting between the SEDUE director and representatives of city center residents, September 27, 1985, AGN, MMH, 20.00.00.00, Caja 3, Exp. 3, 1401, 1410–11.

18  Alejandra Leal Martínez "De pueblo a sociedad civil: El discurso político después del sismo de 1985 / From People to Civil Society: Political Discourse after the 1985 Earthquake," *Revista Mexicana de Sociología* 76, no. 3 (2014): 441–69.

19  Combined with the second-largest housing complex, Multifamiliar Juárez, residents from the two complexes represented 65 percent of the total victims. Louise E. Walker, "Economic Fault Lines and Middle-Class Fears: Tlatelolco, Mexico City, 1985," in *Aftershocks: Earthquakes and Popular Politics in Latin America*, ed. Jürgen Buchenau and Lyman L. Johnson (Albuquerque: University of New Mexico Press, 2003), 192.

20  Many journalists domiciled in Tlatelolco, including Carlos Marín, making coverage of the damage that much more personal. See Norberto Hernández Montiel, "Demandan una investigación los colonos de Tlatelolco," *La Jornada*, September 24, 1985, 14; "Habitantes de Tlatelolco exigen indemnización," *La Jornada*, September 28, 1985, 11; Carlos Marín, "Los sobrevivientes del Nuevo León en pleito por sus derechos," *Proceso*, September 30, 1985, 32–36; and Monsiváis, *Entrada libre*, 45.

21  See, for example, the minutes of a meeting between the SEDUE and the Nuevo León Building Residents Association, October 7, 1985, AGN, MMH, 20.00.00.00, Caja 3, Exp. 2, 1–2.

22  Leticia Picazo Sánchez, *Una década de video en México 1980–1989: Dependencia extranjera y monopolios nacionales* (México: Editorial Trillas, 1994), 36–37.

23  Minutes of a meeting between the SEDUE and Nonoalco-Tlatelolco residents, September 30, 1985, AGN, MMH, 20.00.00.00, Caja 3, Exp. 3, 2.

24  Monsiváis, *Entrada libre*, 58.

25  Tape recording of radio program *Los Expertos Colaboran*, episode 3, September 30, 1985, AGN, MMH, 04.00.00.00, Caja 3, Exp. 4. On these accusations see, for example, Luis Javier Garrido, "El destino de la ciudad," *La Jornada*, September 20, 1985, back page; Fernando González Gortázar, "Los reclamos del temblor," *La Jornada*, September 24, 1985, 1; and Musacchio, *Ciudad quebrada*, 105.

26  Rogelio Hernández, "El miedo se hizo furia en Tlatelolco," *Excélsior*, September 24, 1985, 1.

27  The host returned to this question in the following episode. Tape recording of radio program *Los Expertos Colaboran*, episode 4, October 1, 1985, AGN, MMH, 04.00.00.00, Caja 3, Exp. 4.

28  Tape recording of radio program *Los Expertos Colaboran*, episode 3, September 30, 1985.

29 These mortality figures come from Fiona Wilson, *De la casa al taller: Mujeres, trabajo y clase social en la industria textil y del vestido, Santiago Tangamandapio* (Zamora, México: Colegio de Michoacán, 1990), 27. Reporter Sara Lovera described the reams of fabric as the first clue regarding the nature of the collapsed buildings. Sara Lovera, interview with the author, Mexico City, July 4, 2012.
30 For the first articles on the garment workers, see Luis García Rojas, "En las ruinas de las fábricas de ropa en la Calzada de Tlalpan quedaron sepultadas humildes costureras," *Unomásuno*, September 20, 1985, 13; and Arturo García Hernández, "En el segundo día, en busca de esperanza," *La Jornada*, September 21, 1985, 10.
31 "Origen, organización e integrantes del diario La Jornada," August 15, 1984, AGN, DFS, 009-042-089, Legajo 2, 5.
32 Report on resignations from *Unomásuno*, December 19, 1983, AGN, DFS, Versión Pública Elena Poniatowska, 1; Genoveva Flores Quintero, *Unomásuno: Victorias perdidas del periodismo mexicano (1977–1989)* (México: Universidad Iberoamericana, 2014), 89–90; Ana María Serna, *"Se solicitan reporteros": Historia oral del periodismo mexicano en la segunda mitad del siglo XX* (México: Instituto Mora, 2015), 70.
33 Pascual Salanueva and Andrea Becerril, "Rescatan a otra sobreviviente en el edificio de Topeka," *La Jornada*, September 28, 1985, 14.
34 Sara Lovera and Luis Alberto Rodríguez, "Sin empleo, 40 mil costureras," *La Jornada*, October 3, 1985, 1.
35 Though the article was cowritten, Monsiváis and others credited Lovera with the scoop. See, for example, Carlos Monsiváis, "¿Cuántos funcionarios caben en un aplazamiento de respuesta?," *Proceso*, October 28, 1985, 12.
36 Lovera and Rodríguez, "Sin empleo," 8.
37 Lovera interview.
38 Flores Quintero, *Unomásuno*, 161, 245–46.
39 Anonymous, conversation with the author, Mexico City, summer 2018.
40 Flores Quintero, *Unomásuno*, 129, 133, 140–41, 153, 164, 166–67.
41 Manuel Mejido describes dressing as a bartender and a waiter on separate occasions to access information. See Manuel Mejido, *Con la máquina al hombro* (México: Siglo XXI Editores, 2011), 72, 178–79.
42 Gabriel Aceves Sepúlveda notes that audiences often perceived women presenters on television as being "pushy." See Gabriel Aceves Sepúlveda, *Women Made Visible: Feminist Art and Media in Post-1968 Mexico City* (Lincoln: University of Nebraska Press, 2019), 61–62.
43 Lovera interview.
44 Andrea Becerril, "Pretenden dueños retirar maquinaria: Se unen costureras para exigir indemnización," *La Jornada*, October 5, 1985, 9.
45 Tape recording of radio program *La Causa de las Mujeres*, Radio Educación, October 1985, AGN, MMH, 11.00.00.00, Caja 2, Exp. 11. See also Salvador Corro, "Los derrumbes, pretexto para suprimir empleos," *Proceso*, October 7, 1985,

10–11; Humberto Aranda, "Incierto futuro de 3,400 costureras," *Excélsior*, October 12, 1985, 5; Carlos Velasco Molina, "Aún hay 1,600 cadáveres de costureras bajo los escombros," *Excélsior*, October 14, 1985, 19; Efraín Santos C., "Recurren costureras de San Antonio Abad al auxilio del Presidente de la República," *El Día*, October 15, 1985, 7; and Musacchio, *Ciudad quebrada*, 98.

46 Georgina Howard, "Aplastadas por la ambición patronal, costureras sobrevivientes claman auxilio a las autoridades," *El Día*, October 7, 1985, 2.

47 See, for example, Víctor Juárez, "Es monstruosa la colusión contra costureras: Farell," *Unomásuno*, October 16, 1985, 1.

48 Howard, "Aplastadas por la ambición patronal."

49 Women made up 32 percent of the economically active population by 1990. Julia Tuñón, *Women in Mexico: A Past Unveiled*, trans. Alan Hynds (Austin: University of Texas Press, 1999), 108–9.

50 Howard, "Aplastadas por la ambición patronal," 2.

51 Saide Sesin, "Clausuró la Delegación Cuauhtémoc una fábrica de ropa, laboraban dos mil costureras en 7 pisos," *Unomásuno*, October 11, 1985, 10.

52 Isabel Mayoral Jimenez, "Salen a relucir explotaciones a costureras," *El Nacional*, October 10, 1985, II, 3.

53 Nancy Rodríguez R., "Faltan por rescatarse 60 cuerpos en SAA," *El Nacional*, October 13, 1985, 2.

54 Manuel Buendía, "Notas de comunicación social," 1982, Fundación Manuel Buendía, Ponencias, 14–15.

55 Coordinación General de Comunicación Social, "Bases estratégicas para la construcción de un sistema nacional de comunicación social," 1981, vol. 3, Archivo Particular Luis Javier Solana, 478, 491.

56 Manuel Blanco, "Ciudad en el Alba: Las costureras," *El Nacional*, October 9, 1985, II, 1; See also "Penoso rescate de cuerpos en fábricas de ropa; los patrones tras sus pertenencias," *El Nacional*, October 12, 1985, 2.

57 Lázaro Serranía Álvarez, "Se complica el rescate de más cuerpos en fábricas de ropa y telas de San Antonio Abad," *El Nacional*, October 13, 1985, II, 3.

58 Cámara de Diputados, "Boletín de prensa," October 10, 1985, Archivo Particular Sara Lovera (hereafter APSL).

59 Serranía Álvarez, "Se complica el rescate."

60 Monsiváis, *Entrada libre*, 51.

61 See, for example, Aranda, "Incierto futuro," 5; and Velasco Molina, "Aún hay 1,600 cadáveres," 35.

62 Humberto Aranda, "Se coluden autoridades del DDF con patrones para reducir indemnizaciones," *Excélsior*, October 11, 1985, 43.

63 "Sobrevivientes de diversas fábricas de ropa constituyeron la Unión de Costureras en Lucha," *Unomásuno*, October 12, 1985, 8.

64 Miguel Ángel Ramírez, "Graves complicidades en la explotación de las costureras," *El Día*, October 16, 1985, 1.

65 "Sevicia y costureras," *Excélsior*, October 16, 1985, 6. See also Monsiváis, *Entrada libre*, 99.

66 Alfredo Marrón B., "Acción federal a favor de costureras: Comienzan a embargar," *Últimas Noticias*, October 15, 1985, 1, 10.
67 Raúl Trejo Delarbe, *Crónica del sindicalismo en México, 1976–1988* (México: Siglo XXI Editores, 1990), 255.
68 Saide Sesin, "Obligan a costureras a trabajar en edificios dañados," *Unomásuno*, October 9, 1985, 11; Mercedes Castro, "Entorpece el rescate de cuerpos la inexperiencia de voluntarios," *Metrópoli*, October 22, 1985, 5.
69 Carlos Monsiváis, "Los poderes contratacan ante una sociedad civil que rechaza la sumisión," *Proceso*, September 30, 1985, 11.
70 "Denuncian las costureras: La Procuraduría de Defensa del Trabajo, sólo se instaló para cubrir apariencias," *Metrópoli*, October 16, 1985, 4.
71 Once TV Mexico, "Grupo de costureras afectadas en el sismo de 1985," *Aquí Nos Tocó Vivir*, YouTube, https://www.youtube.com/watch?v=oL38c3mi3I4.
72 Lovera interview.
73 "Boletín de prensa," October 16, 1985, APSL.
74 Saide Sesin and Mario Alberto Reyes, "Integraron las costureras un sindicato libre," *Unomásuno*, October 20, 1985, 1.
75 Tuñón notes that the historical concept of the "feminine" has been associated with emotion, instinct, and nature, while the masculine has been associated with rationality. Tuñón, *Women in Mexico*, xiii–xiv.
76 Ignacio Sánchez Prado, "Carlos Monsiváis: Crónica, nación y liberalismo," in *El arte de la ironía: Carlos Monsiváis ante la crítica*, ed. Mabel Moraña and Ignacio Sánchez Prado (México: Ediciones Era, 2007), 309, 311–12.
77 Viviane Mahieux, *Urban Chroniclers in Modern Latin America: The Shared Intimacy of Everyday Life* (Austin: University of Texas Press, 2011), 4, 187–88.
78 Carlos Monsiváis, *A ustedes les consta: Antología de la crónica en México* (México: Ediciones Era, 1980), 75; Linda Egan, "Carlos Monsiváis 'Translates' Tom Wolfe," in *Mexico Reading the United States*, ed. Linda Egan and Mary K. Long (Nashville: Vanderbilt University Press, 2009), 109–10. On New Journalism, see Jason Mosser, *The Participatory Journalism of Michael Herr, Norman Mailer, Hunter S. Thompson, and Joan Didion: Creating New Reporting Styles* (Lewiston, NY: Edwin Mellen, 2012), 1–62.
79 Flores Quintero, *Unomásuno*, 239–44.
80 Elena Poniatowska, interview with the author, Mexico City, April 10, 2012.
81 The following biographical sketch comes from Michael K. Schuessler, *Elena Poniatowska: An Intimate Biography* (Tucson: University of Arizona Press, 2007), 45–93.
82 Most notably, she wrote a series of ethnographic articles for *Novedades* in 1957 on popular Mexican tradition and culture that were published as a collected volume of essays; see Elena Poniatowska, *Todo empezó el domingo* (México: Fondo de Cultura Económica, 1963).
83 On this reaction to Poniatowska's journalism career, see Schuessler, *Elena Poniatowska*, 118–20.
84 Elena Poniatowska, *La noche de Tlatelolco: Testimonios de historia oral* (México: Ediciones Era, 1971).

85 "Origen, organización e integrantes del diario La Jornada," 5.
86 Elena Poniatowska, "¿Cómo está lo de las cajas?," *La Jornada*, October 12, 1985, 23.
87 CIASES circular, November 6, 1985, AGN, MMH, 32.01.00.00, Caja 1, Exp. 8, 1.
88 CIASES series in *Excélsior*, AGN, MMH, 32.01.00.00, Caja 1, Exp. 7.
89 "CIASES Conferencia de prensa, sesión 3," October 15, 1985, AGN, MMH, 32.01.00.00, Caja 1, Exp. 3, 5, 4. This finding also became the subject of dark jokes. One, for example, made fun of SEDUE director Carrillo Arena, who was the contractor that built the wing of Hospital Juárez that collapsed during the earthquake. Playing on his second last name (*arena*, "sand"), people joked that the hospital collapsed because it was built with "Carrillo Arena" instead of cement. Humberto Musacchio, *Ciudad quebrada* (México: Ediciones Océano, 1985), 123.
90 Elena Poniatowska, "La incógnita es ahora cómo va a expresarse el malestar social," *La Jornada*, October 18, 1985, 23, emphasis in the original.
91 "CIASES Conferencia de prensa," 6.
92 Poniatowska, "La incógnita."
93 "A la población," AGN, MMH, 12.00.00.00, Caja 1, Exp. 11.
94 Tape recording of *Participación Ciudadana*, Radio Educación, AGN, MMH, 11.00.00.00, Caja 2, Exp. 10.
95 Elena Poniatowska, "Pido un buen trato para todos los mexicanos: Alonso Mixteco," *La Jornada*, October 22, 1985, backpage.
96 Poniatowska, "Pido un buen trato."
97 Carlos Monsiváis, "Al mes del temblor: Imágenes, estados de ánimo, afirmaciones, negaciones," *Proceso*, October 21, 1985, 23–24.
98 Elena Poniatowska, *Nada, nadie: Las voces del temblor* (México: Ediciones Era, 1988).

## CHAPTER 6. THE WEAPONIZATION OF SCANDAL

1 María del Pilar Treviño de González, *Enhorabuena, Chihuahua!* (Juárez, México: n.p., 1986), 39, 37.
2 The SCS estimated that CISA had thirty subscribers outside Mexico City. Coordinación General de Comunicación Social, "Bases estratégicas para la construcción de un Sistema Nacional de Comunicación Social," 1981, vol. 11, Archivo Particular Luis Javier Solana, 2065, 2080, 2083, 2110.
3 See, for example, José Chávez Morado to Miguel Ángel Granados Chapa, May 6, 1985, Colección Particular Miguel Ángel Granados Chapa (hereafter CP-MAGC); Leopoldo Graujos to Miguel Ángel Granados Chapa, March 30, 1987, CP-MAGC.
4 Jorge Selpúlveda to Miguel Ángel Granados Chapa, January 15, 1986, CP-MAGC, 2.
5 Antonio Ponce to Miguel Ángel Granados Chapa, December 22, 1985, CP-MAGC; Graujos to Granados Chapa.
6 Álvaro González to Manuel Buendía, April 26, 1983, Fundación Manuel Buendía, unnumbered binder, 1.

7  Sallie Hughes finds that 80 percent of Mexican television stations reproduced the programming of Mexico City's two major broadcasting networks. See Sallie Hughes, *Newsrooms in Conflict: Journalism and the Democratization of Mexico* (Pittsburgh: University of Pittsburgh Press, 2006), 165.
8  Minutes of a meeting between media representatives and the Social Communication Office of the Presidency (Oficina de Comunicación Social de la Presidencia), September 6, 1982, AGN, Fondo Presidencial José López Portillo, Comunicación Social de la Presidencia, Caja 272, Exp. 1, part 2.
9  Minutes of a meeting between media representatives, 3–4.
10 See for example, Abelardo Villegas, "México en sus fronteras," *Proceso*, October 11, 1982, 14–15; and Francisco Ortiz Pinchetti, "La frontera, hambrienta, en un asilamiento que es jauja de especuladores," *Proceso*, October 11, 1982, 6–15.
11 Minutes of a meeting between media representatives, part 4, 8.
12 Minutes of a meeting between media representatives, part 3, 2.
13 Minutes of a meeting between media representatives, part 4, 2.
14 Hughes, *Newsrooms in Conflict*, 114.
15 Rafael Loret de Mola, *Denuncia: Presidente sin palabra* (México: Grijalbo, 1995).
16 Vanessa Freije, "Censorship in the Headlines: National News and the Contradictions of Mexico City's Press Opening in the 1970s," in *Journalism, Censorship and Satire in Mexico*, ed. Paul Gillingham, Michael Lettieri, and Benjamin T. Smith (Albuquerque: University of New Mexico Press, 2018), 251.
17 Loret de Mola, *Denuncia*, 83–94.
18 Carlos Sirvent, *Encuesta electoral en Chihuahua, 1986* (México: Universidad Nacional Autónoma de México, 1987).
19 Héctor Galán, "Standoff in Mexico," *Frontline*, Public Broadcasting Service, aired April 1, 1986 (Boston: WGBH Educational Foundation, 1986), VHS, 58 mins.
20 Galán, "Standoff in Mexico."
21 Olga Leticia Moreno, *Qué pasó en Chihuahua?* (México: Editores Asociados Mexicanos, 1986), 121–22.
22 Manuel Robles, "La TV oficial de Estados Unidos, propagandista del PAN," *Proceso*, April 14, 1986, 14.
23 Enrique Maza, "La oposición, sólo respuesta visceral a la crisis: Baeza," *Proceso*, May 26, 1986, 10; "Fraudulentas, las elecciones presidenciales en 82: Helms," *La Jornada*, June 16, 1986, 8.
24 See, for example, Renata Keller, *Mexico's Cold War: Cuba, the United States, and the Legacy of the Mexican Revolution* (New York: Cambridge University Press, 2015); Jaime Pensado, *Rebel Mexico: Student Unrest and Authoritarian Political Culture during the Long Sixties* (Stanford: Stanford University Press, 2013), 219.
25 Jorge G. Castañeda, *México: El futuro en juego* (México: Joaquín Mortíz / Planeta, 1987), 35.
26 Nicaraguan Embassy to *Proceso* magazine, November 13, 1981, AGN, DFS, Versión Pública Julio Scherer García, Legajo 2; Porfirio Muñoz Ledo to Miguel de la Madrid, August 26, 1982, AGN, Archivo Particular Porfirio Muñoz Ledo (hereafter AP-PML) Caja 162, Exp. 27.

27 Porfirio Muñoz Ledo to Miguel de la Madrid, May 9, 1986, AGN, AP-PML, Caja 163, Exp. 55, 1.
28 Castañeda, *México: El futuro en juego*, 29.
29 See, for example, Joel Brinkley, "Concern Growing among U.S. Aides on Mexico Future," *New York Times*, May 26, 1986, 1.
30 *Situation in Mexico: Hearings before the Subcommittee on Western Hemisphere Affairs of the Committee on Foreign Relations*, 99th Cong., 2nd session (1986), 2, 6.
31 Raúl Trejo Delarbe, ed., *Televisa, el quinto poder*, 2nd ed. (México: Claves Latinoamericanas, 1985), 35, 185, 5, 7, 9; Claudia Fernández and Andrew Paxman, *El Tigre: Emilio Azcárraga y su imperio Televisa*, 3rd ed. (México: Grijalbo / Raya en el Agua 2013), 167.
32 For example, *24 Horas de la Tarde con Abraham Zabludovsky* (1986), https://www.youtube.com/watch?v=AKRHVPveM4Y.
33 Randal Sheppard, *A Persistent Revolution: History, Nationalism, and Politics since 1968* (Albuquerque: University of New Mexico Press, 2016), 84.
34 Julio Zamora Batiz, "Por la unidad priísta," May 22, 1986, AGN, AP-PML, Caja 383, Exp. 67, 4.
35 Maza, "La oposición," 9.
36 Minutes from the *La Jornada* editorial board meeting, February 4, 1986, CP-MAGC, unnumbered box, 2.
37 Enrique Krauze, *Por una democracia sin adjetivos* (México: Joaquín Mortíz / Planeta, 1986), 142. Much serious historiography underscores the relationship between the frontier and political change. See, for example, Héctor Aguilar Camín, *Frontera nómada: Sonora y la revolución mexicana* (México: Siglo Veintiuno Editores, 1977); Daniel Nugent, *Spent Cartridges of Revolution: An Anthropological History of Namiquipa, Chihuahua* (Chicago: University of Chicago Press, 1993); Friedrich Katz, *The Life and Times of Pancho Villa* (Stanford, CA: Stanford University Press, 1998); and Paul Vanderwood, *The Power of God against the Guns of Government: Religious Upheaval in Mexico at the Turn of the Nineteenth Century* (Stanford, CA: Stanford University Press, 1998).
38 Frederick Jackson Turner, *The Frontier in American History* (New York: Henry Holt, 1920).
39 Eduardo Valle, "Democracia sin adjetivos," *El Universal*, July 17, 1986, 4. Krauze's intervention also shaped academic works. See, for example, Alberto Aziz Nassif, *Chihuahua: Historia de una alternativa* (México: Centro de Investigaciones y Estudios Superiores en Antropología Social / Desarrollo de los Medios, S.A., 1994), 29. Democracy was a key topic of academic debate in the 1980s. See, for example, Pablo González Casanova, "Cuando hablamos de democracia, de qué hablamos?" *Revista Mexicana de Sociología* 48, no. 3 (July–Sept. 1986): 3–6.
40 Krauze, *Por una democracia*, 120.
41 Social science research of the 1950s and 1960s was instrumental in outlining this political culture. For a good summary, see Soledad Loaeza, "El laberinto de la pasividad," *Nexos*, December 1, 1981, 10–13.

42 Michael Snodgrass, 'We Are All Mexicans Here': Workers, Patriotism, and Union Struggles in Monterrey," in *The Eagle and the Virgin: Nation and Cultural Revolution in Mexico, 1920–1940*, ed. Mary Kay Vaughan and Stephen E. Lewis (Durham, NC: Duke University Press, 2008), 315, 316.

43 Maarten van Delden, "Conjunciones y disyunciones: La rivalidad entre *Vuelta* y *Nexos*," in *El laberinto de la solidaridad: Cultura y política en México (1910–2000)*, ed. Kristine Vanden Berghe and Maarten van Delden (Amsterdam: Rodopi, 2002), 107. On debates between journalists see Adolfo Gilly, "El amor a la verdad," *Sábado: Suplemento de Unomásuno*, March 7, 1981, 8; and Rafael Rodríguez Castañeda, "Sólo el presidente puede limitar el poder presidencial: Krauze," *Proceso*, October 18, 1982, 6–14.

44 Victoria E. Campos, "Toward a New History: Twentieth-Century Debates in Mexico on Narrating the National Past," in *A Twice Told Tale: Reinventing the Encounter in Iberian/Iberian American Literature and Film*, ed. Santiago Juan-Navarro and Theodore Robert Young (Newark: University of Delaware Press, 2001), 59.

45 Jorge Hernández Campos et al., "A Forum on Mexico's Survival," *Washington Quarterly* 9, no. 1 (1986): 169–84; Claudio Lomnitz, "An Intellectual's Stock in the Factory of Mexico's Ruins," *American Journal of Sociology* 103, no. 4 (1998): 1057–58; Melanie Huska, "Entertaining Education: Teaching National History in Mexican State-Sponsored Comic Books and Telenovelas, 1963–1996" (PhD diss., University of Minnesota, 2013).

46 Rodolfo Pastor, "Más *Caras de la historia*," *Historia Mexicana* 33, no. 4 (1984): 540.

47 Adolfo Gilly, "La modesta utopía de Enrique Krauze," *La Jornada Libros*, August 9, 1986, 4.

48 Van Delden, "Conjunciones y disyunciones," 107–9.

49 Enrique Krauze, *Caras de la historia* (México: Planeta, 1983).

50 Aguilar Camín, *Frontera nómada*.

51 Héctor Aguilar Camín, "El canto del futuro," *Nexos*, April 1986, 26.

52 "Quién es quien," March 6, 1984, AGN, Dirección Federal de Seguridad, Versión Pública Héctor Aguilar Camín.

53 José Agustín Ortiz Pinchetti, interview with the author, Mexico City, February 17, 2018.

54 Francisco Ortiz Pinchetti, "Los chihuahuenses quieren democracia y repudian al PRI," *Proceso*, May 5, 1986, 17.

55 Ortiz Pinchetti, "Los chihuahuenses," 16.

56 *El Heraldo de México*, July 3, 1986, 2.

57 Ortiz Pinchetti, "Los chihuahuenses," 19.

58 The other two protesters on a hunger strike were Víctor Manuel Oropeza, a member of the Mexican Workers' Party (Partido Mexicano de Trabajadores) and journalist for the *El Diario de Juárez*, and Francisco Villareal, a businessman. Miguel Ángel Granados Chapa, "Plaza Pública," *La Jornada*, July 5, 1986, 2.

59 U.S. television coverage of Mexican politics also increased in the days prior to the election. Julio Hernández López, "PAN: Miles de vigilantes impedirán el

fraude electoral," *La Jornada*, July 5, 1986, 11; Pablo Hiriart, "Asustó al gobierno su apertura política: Barrio," *La Jornada*, July 4, 1986, 11.

60 Dan Williams, "Ruling Mexican Party Faces Tough Battle in Chihuahua State Balloting," *Los Angeles Times*, July 5, 1986, 4. The *New York Times* similarly highlighted the possibility of "the sharpest electoral challenge to the 57-year dominance of the ruling Institutional Revolutionary Party"; William Stockton, "Significant Vote Looms for Mexico," *New York Times*, June 8, 1986, 15.

61 Alejandro Páez Aragón, "Julio 6, parteaguas para México," *El Porvenir*, July 1, 1986, 6. See also Pablo Hiriart, "Indicios de que habrá fraude en Chihuahua: Monseñor Almeyda," *La Jornada*, July 5, 1986, 8.

62 Fernández and Paxman, *El Tigre*, 315–16.

63 Benjamin T. Smith, *The Mexican Press and Civil Society, 1940–1976: Stories from the Newsroom, Stories from the Street* (Chapel Hill: University of North Carolina Press, 2018), 255–58.

64 "Prensa y elecciones: el papel de *Diario de Juárez*," *Diario de Juárez*, July 5, 1986, 1.

65 "Arribaron anoche tres aviones con soldados: Decomisaron rollos a fotógrafos," *Diario de Juárez*, July 2, 1986, 2.

66 "PRI y PAN se dicen triunfadores en Chihuahua; bajó el abstencionismo," *Unomásuno*, July 7, 1986, 1.

67 Vanessa Freije, "'The Emancipation of Media': Latin American Advocacy for a New International Information Order in the 1970s," *Journal of Global History* 14, no. 2 (2019): 301–20.

68 Mario Alberto Reyes and Juan Antonio Torres, "Ante presiones del PAN, el gobierno dará marcha atrás en el fraude electoral: Gustavo Elizondo," *Unomásuno*, July 8, 1986, 6.

69 Fernández and Paxman, *El Tigre*, 293.

70 New legislation paved the way for the removal of electoral observers. In December 1985 the Chihuahua State Electoral Commission (Comisión Estatal Electoral de Chihuahua) rejected opposition parties' requests to monitor the polls, citing new regulations passed by the state legislature. The reform limited the number of opposition party representatives at the polls; imposed prohibitive residency requirements for electoral observers; granted the poll president the authority to remove observers; and increased the power of district, municipal, and state electoral authorities. Pablo Hiriart, "Anomalías durante los comicios empañaron el proceso," *La Jornada*, July 7, 1986, 1, 11; "La reforma obligada," *La Jornada*, July 7, 1986, 1, 3.

71 Nelly O. Martínez, Juana María López, and Diana Cisneros, "PRI dice arrollar en Chihuahua, callan candidatos; El PAN cauto," *El Porvenir*, July 7, 1986, 1.

72 Pablo Hiriart, "Anuncia Gurría que su partido recuperó varias alcaldías," *La Jornada*, July 8, 1986, 1; Julio Hernández López, "Realizará marchas y tomará caminos y oficinas públicas," *La Jornada*, July 8, 1986, 1, 3; and Nelly O. Martínez, Juana María López, and Diana Cisneros, "Paro exitoso; Crece tensión en Chihuahua," *El Porvenir*, July 11, 1986, 1.

73 Alejandro Avilés, "Frente a la mentira y el engaño," *El Universal*, July 9, 1986, 5. See also José Conchello, "Urnas, deudas, bayonetas y plegarias," *El Universal*, July 10, 1986, 4, 8.
74 David Orozco Romo, "Que las marrullerías os acompañen," *El Universal*, July 10, 1986, 5.
75 Nelly O. Martínez, "Extreman en Ciudad Juárez la vigilancia," *El Porvenir*, July 8, 1986, 1; Nelly O. Martínez, "Acusan de intervención a la prensa extranjera," *El Porvenir*, July 8, 1986, 3.
76 Electoral primaries allowed for popular input in the 1940s but these were abolished by 1950. See Paul Gillingham, "'We Don't Have Arms, but We Do Have Balls': Fraud, Violence, and Popular Agency in Elections," in *Dictablanda: Politics, Work, and Culture in Mexico, 1938–1968*, ed. Paul Gillingham and Benjamin T. Smith (Durham, NC: Duke University Press, 2014), 151.
77 Adolfo Gilly and Rhina Roux, *Cartas a Cuauhtémoc Cárdenas* (México: Ediciones Era, 1989), 105–10.
78 Fernández and Paxman, *El Tigre*, 315–16.
79 Raúl Trejo Delarbe, "Acción Nacional en Chihuahua," *La Jornada*, July 8, 1986, 9.
80 Teresa Gurza, "Lo prohibe el derecho canónico: Jerónimo Prigione," *La Jornada*, July 20, 1986, 1, 4.
81 "Fraude en Chihuahua," *Página Uno*, July 20, 1986, I.
82 Laura Bolaños, "Los que no tienen derechos," *El Universal*, July 10, 1986, 5.
83 Judith Butler, *Precarious Life: The Powers of Mourning and Violence* (New York: Verso, 2004), xiv–xv.
84 José Agustín Ortiz Pinchetti, "Un fraude sin adjetivos," *La Jornada*, July 12, 1986, 7.
85 Francisco Ortiz Pinchetti to Heberto Castillo, August 3, 1986, Fundación Heberto Castillo, Caja 180, Exp. 882, 1, 3.
86 "Maños extranjeras pretenden interferir en Chihuahua," *El Universal*, August 9, 1986, 6.
87 Antonio Gershenson, "No hay democracia sin independencia nacional," *La Jornada*, August 10, 1986, 6. Gershenson sat on the executive committee for the Nuclear Industry Workers Union (Sindicato Único de Trabajadores de la Industria Nuclear).
88 "El caso Chihuahua," *Proceso*, July 28, 1986, 4. The signatories were Héctor Aguilar Camín, Huberto Batis, Fernando Benítez, José Luis Cuevas, Juan García Ponce, Luis González y González, Hugo Hiriart, David Huerta, Enrique Krauze, Teresa Losada, Lorenzo Meyer, Carlos Monsiváis, Carlos Montemayor, Marco Antonio Montes de Oca, Octavio Paz, Elena Poniatowska, Ignacio Solares, Abelardo Villegas, Ramón Xirau, Isabel Turrent, and Gabriel Zaid.
89 Irma Salinas Rocha, "Chihuahua," *El Porvenir*, July 18, 1986, 7.
90 "No permitiremos que sean acalladas las voces periodísticas dignas," *El Universal*, August 16, 1986, 5.
91 Gonzalo Martre, "El periodista ante el estado," *El Universal*, August 19, 1986, 5; Loret de Mola, *Denuncia sin palabra*, 31.

92 Luis Javier Garrido, *La ruptura: La corriente democrática del PRI* (México: Grijalbo, 1993), 76–77.
93 Sergio Aguayo Quezada, "A Mexican Milestone," *Journal of Democracy* 6, no. 2 (1995): 164.
94 Fernández and Paxman, *El Tigre*, 319–20, 324.
95 Kathleen Bruhn, *Taking on Goliath: The Emergence of a New Left Party and the Struggle for Democracy in Mexico* (University Park: Pennsylvania State University Press, 1997), 140–42; Pedro Arredondo, Gilberto Fregoso Peralta, and Raúl Trejo Delarbre, *Así se calló el sistema: Comunicación y elecciones en 1988* (Guadalajara, México: Universidad de Guadalajara, 1991).

## EPILOGUE

1 José Luis González Meza and Walter López Koehl, *Un asesino en la presidencia?* (México: Ediciones Universo, 1987), 9–11.
2 González Meza and López Koehl, *Un asesino*, 5, 9.
3 Enrique Maza, "Ante la sucesión, se acaba la tolerancia para el gobierno de un solo hombre," *Proceso*, May 18, 1987, 23.
4 Antonio Caso, "El 'caso La Quina' confirma la voluntad de Salinas para democratizar México," *El País*, January 13, 1989, https://elpais.com/diario/1989/01/13/internacional/600649213_850215.html; Matt Moffett, "Macho Image: Mexico's New President Takes a Tough Stance, Gains Wide Approval," *Wall Street Journal*, March 16, 1989, 1.
5 Enrique Maza, "El de La Quina, un imperio construido a golpes de corrupción," *Proceso*, January 16, 1989, 8.
6 Alexander S. Dawson, *First World Dreams: Mexico since 1989* (New York: Zed Books, 2006), 27–28.
7 Marjorie Miller, "Antipathy Marked Relations between Salinas, Oil Workers' Boss: Politics Seen behind Jailing of Mexico Unionist," *Los Angeles Times*, January 13, 1989, 8; Blanche Petrich, "Zedillo anuncia inversion en México," *La Opinión*, October 19, 1995, 1.
8 Dick Reavis, "How Do You Say 'Perestroika' in Spanish?," *Texas Monthly*, October 1989, 184.
9 José Luis Trueba Lara, *El derrumbe: Crónica audaz de los acontecimientos que han sacudido nuestro e scenario político actual* (México: Planeta, 1995), 64.
10 Blanche Petrich, "Crece escándalo Salinas: Investigan a esposa y hermana del ex presidente," *La Opinión*, December 1, 1995, 1; Rogelio Hernández Rodríguez, *Historia mínima del PRI* (México: Colegio de México, 2016), 218–19.
11 Sallie Hughes, *Newsrooms in Conflict: Journalism and the Democratization of Mexico* (Pittsburgh: University of Pittsburgh Press, 2006), 83; 140–44.
12 Chappell Lawson, *Building the Fourth Estate: Democratization and the Rise of a Free Press in Mexico* (Berkeley: University of California Press, 2002), 151.
13 El Fisgón and Helguera, *El sexenio me da risa: La historieta no oficial* (México: Grijalbo, 1994), 101, 125.

## CONCLUSION

1 Joy Elizabeth Hayes, *Radio Nation: Communication, Popular Culture, and Nationalism in Mexico, 1920–1950* (Tucson: University of Arizona Press, 2000); Celeste González de Bustamante, *"Muy buenas noches": Mexico, Television, and the Cold War* (Lincoln: University of Nebraska Press, 2012).
2 Joanna Davidson, "Cultivating Knowledge: Development, Dissemblance, and Discursive Contradictions among the Diola of Guinea-Bissau," *American Ethnologist* 37, no. 2 (2010): 221. See also Paul Christopher Johnson, *Secrets, Gossip, and Gods: The Transformation of Brazilian Candomblé* (New York: Oxford University Press, 2002), 4, 8.
3 Robert McKee Irwin, Edward J. McCaughan, and Michelle Rocío Nasser, "Introduction: Sexuality and Social Control in Mexico, 1901," in *The Famous 41: Sexuality and Social Control in Mexico, 1901*, ed. Robert McKee Irwin, Edward J. McCaughan, and Michelle Rocío Nasser (New York: Palgrave Macmillan, 2003), 4.
4 Pablo Piccato, *A History of Infamy: Crime, Truth, and Justice in Mexico* (Oakland: University of California Press, 2017).
5 Pablo Piccato, *The Tyranny of Opinion: Honor in the Construction of the Mexican Public Sphere* (Durham, NC: Duke University Press, 2010); Corinna Zeltsman, *Ink under the Fingernails: Printing and the Materiality of Politics in Nineteenth-Century Mexico* (Oakland: University of California Press, forthcoming), chap. 7.
6 See, for example, Silvio Waisbord, *Watchdog Journalism in South America: News, Accountability, and Democracy* (New York: Columbia University Press, 2000), xv, xvii; and Catalina Smulovitz and Enrique Peruzzotti, "Societal Accountability in Latin America," *Journal of Democracy* 11, no. 4 (2000): 147–58.
7 Silvio Waisbord, "Knocking on Newsroom Doors: The Press and Political Scandals in Argentina," *Political Communication* 11, no. 1 (1994): 23, 27–28.
8 Committee to Project Journalists, "Mexico" (webpage), https://cpj.org/americas/mexico/; Clare Ribando Seelke, *Violence against Journalists in Mexico: In Brief* (Washington, DC: Congressional Research Service, 2018), 6.
9 Gabriel Sosa Plata, *Días de radio: Historias de la radio en México* (México: Secretaría de Cultura, 2016); Silvia Higuera, "Mexican Federal Court Confirms Dismissal of Journalist Carmen Aristegui Was Illegal," *Journalism in the Americas* (blog), Knight Center for Journalism in the Americas, June 26, 2018, https://knightcenter.utexas.edu/blog/00-19886-mexican-federal-court-confirms-dismissal-journalist-carmen-aristegui-was-illegal.
10 Hughes, *Newsrooms in Conflict*, 98, 116.

# BIBLIOGRAPHY

## ARCHIVAL COLLECTIONS

Archivo General de la Nación, Mexico City
    Archivo Particular Porfirio Muñoz Ledo
    Dirección Federal de Seguridad
    Dirección General de Investigaciones Políticas y Sociales
    Fondo Presidencial Adolfo López Mateos
    Fondo Presidencial José López Portillo
    Fondo Presidencial Miguel de la Madrid Hurtado
Archivo Histórico del Fondo de Cultura Económica, Mexico City
Archivo Histórico de la Secretaría de Salud, Mexico City
Archivo Histórico de la Universidad Nacional Autónoma de México, Mexico City
Archivo Particular Luis Javier Solana, Mexico City
Archivo Particular Sara Lovera, Mexico City
Centro de Estudios de Historia de México, Mexico City
Centro Nacional de Información Documental Adolfo López Mateos, Mexico City
Colección Particular Miguel Ángel Granados Chapa, Mexico City
Escuela Nacional de Antropología e Historia, Mexico City
    Centro de Información y Documentación Guillermo Bonfil Batalla
        Fondo Centro Nacional de Comunicación Social, A.C.
Fundación Heberto Castillo, Mexico City
Fundación Manuel Buendía, Mexico City
National Archives and Record Administration, College Park, MD
    Central Foreign Policy Files
    U.S. Information Agency
Princeton University Library Special Collections, Princeton, NJ
    Carlos Fuentes Papers

## INTERVIEWS

Rafael Barajas (el Fisgón)
Manuel Camacho Solís
Gustavo Carvajal
Sergio González Rodríguez
Luis Hernández Navarro

Adrián Lajous Vargas
Froylán López Narváez
Sara Lovera
Omar Raúl Martínez
Enrique Mayoral Gil
Lorenzo Meyer
Humberto Musacchio
Carlos Olmos
Gregorio Ortega Molina
José Agustín Ortiz Pinchetti
Elena Poniatowska
Alan Riding
Raymundo Riva Palacio
Miguel Ángel Rivera
Gustavo Robles
Miguel Ángel Sánchez de Armas
Miguel Ángel Romero
Luís Javier Solana
Raúl Trejo Delarbe

## PUBLISHED PRIMARY AND SECONDARY SOURCES

Aceves Sepúlveda, Gabriela. *Women Made Visible: Feminist Art and Media in Post-1968 Mexico City.* Lincoln: University of Nebraska Press, 2019.

Adler Lomnitz, Larissa. *Networks and Marginality: Life in a Mexican Shantytown.* Translated by Cinna Lomnitz. New York: Academic Press, 1977.

Adut, Ari. *On Scandal: Moral Disturbances in Society, Politics, and Art.* New York: Cambridge University Press, 2008.

Agostoni, Claudia. "Médicos rurales y brigadas de vacunación en la lucha contra la viruela en el México posrevolucionario, 1920–1940." *Canadian Journal of Latin American and Caribbean Studies* 35, no. 69 (2010): 67–91.

Aguayo Quezada, Sergio. *La charola: Una historia de los servicios de inteligencia en México.* México: Grijalbo, 2001.

———. "A Mexican Milestone." *Journal of Democracy* 6, no. 2 (1995): 157–67.

Aguilar Camín, Héctor. *Frontera nómada: Sonora y la revolución mexicana.* México: Siglo Veintiuno Editores, 1977.

Aguilar Camín, Héctor, et al. *Los días de Manuel Buendía.* México: Océano / Fundación Manuel Buendía, 1984.

Aguilar Zinser, Adolfo, Cesáreo Morales, and Rodolfo F. Peña, eds. *Aún tiembla: Sociedad política y cambio social; el terremoto del 19 de septiembre de 1985.* México: Grijalbo, 1986.

Agustín, José. *Tragicomedia mexicana 2: La vida en México de 1970 a 1982.* México: Editorial Planeta Mexicana, 1992.

———. *Tragicomedia mexicana 3: La vida en México de 1982 a 1994*. México: Editorial Planeta Mexicana, 1998.

Alvarez, Sonia E., Evelina Dagnino, and Arturo Escobar, eds. *Cultures of Politics / Politics of Cultures: Re-visioning Latin American Social Movements*. Boulder, CO: Westview, 1998.

Álvarez Garín, Raúl. *La estela de Tlatelolco: Una reconstrucción histórica del movimiento estudiantil del 68*. México: Grijalbo, 1998.

Aricó, José. *La cola del diablo: Itinerario de Gramsci en América Latina*. Buenos Aires: Puntosur, 1988.

Arredondo, Pedro, Gilberto Fregoso Peralta, and Raúl Trejo Delarbre. *Así se calló el sistema: Comunicación y elecciones en 1988*. Guadalajara, México: Universidad de Guadalajara, 1991.

Arriola Woog, Carlos. *Los empresarios y el estado: 1970–1982*. 2nd ed. México: Universidad Nacional Autónoma de México / Miguel Ángel Porrúa, 1988.

Aviña, Alexander. *Specters of Revolution: Peasant Guerrillas in the Cold War Mexican Countryside*. New York: Oxford University Press, 2014.

Aziz Nassif, Alberto. *Chihuahua: Historia de una alternativa*. México: CIESAS / Desarrollo de los Medios, S.A., 1994.

Babb, Sarah. *Managing Mexico: Economists from Nationalism to Neoliberalism*. Princeton, NJ: Princeton University Press, 2001.

Banco de México. *México social: Noventa indicadores seleccionados*. México: Banco Nacional de México, 1982.

Barreda Solórzano, Luis de la. "La crisis y la criminalidad." In *México ante la crisis*, vol. 2, edited by Pablo González Casanova and Héctor Aguilar Camín, 117–26. México: Siglo Veintiuno Editores, 1985.

Barthes, Roland. "The Photographic Message." In *Image, Music, Text*, translated by Stephen Heath, 15–31. New York: Hill and Wang, 1977.

Bartley, Russell H., and Sylvia Erickson Bartley. *Eclipse of the Assassins: The CIA, Imperial Politics, and the Slaying of Mexican Journalist Manuel Buendía*. Madison: University of Wisconsin Press, 2015.

Becerra Acosta, Manuel. *Dos poderes*. México: Grijalbo, 1984.

Beidelman, Thomas O. "Secrecy and Society: The Paradox of Knowing and the Knowing of Paradox." *Passages* 5 (1993): 6–7.

Bennett, Vivienne. "The Evolution of Urban Popular Movements in Mexico between 1968 and 1988." In *The Making of Social Movements in Latin America: Identity, Strategy, and Democracy*, edited by Arturo Escobar and Sonia Alvarez, 240–59. Boulder, CO: Westview, 1992.

Bentley, Derek. "Democratic Openings: Conservative Protest and Political-Economic Transformation in Mexico, 1970–1986." PhD diss., University of Georgia, 2017.

Beverley, John. *Testimonio: On the Politics of Truth*. Minneapolis: University of Minnesota Press, 2004.

Biron, Rebecca E. *Elena Garro and Mexico's Modern Dreams*. Lewisburg, PA: Bucknell University Press, 2013.

Blanco, José Joaquín. "Tacubaya, 1978." In *The Mexico City Reader*, edited by Rubén Gallo, translated by Lorna Scott Fox and Rubén Gallo, 198–201. Madison: University of Wisconsin Press, 2004.

Blanco Moheno, Roberto. *Memorias de un reportero*. 3rd ed. México: Editorial V Siglos, 1979.

Brewster, Claire. *Responding to Crisis in Contemporary Mexico: The Political Writings of Paz, Fuentes, Monsiváis, and Poniatowska*. Tucson: University of Arizona Press, 2005.

Briggs, Laura. *Reproducing Empire: Race, Sex, Science, and U.S. Imperialism in Puerto Rico*. Berkeley: University of California Press, 2002.

Bruhn, Kathleen. *Taking on Goliath: The Emergence of a New Left Party and the Struggle for Democracy in Mexico*. University Park: Pennsylvania State University Press, 1997.

Buffington, Robert. *Criminal and Citizen in Modern Mexico*. Lincoln: University of Nebraska Press, 2000.

———. "Institutional Memories: The Curious Genesis of the Mexican Police Museum." *Radical History Review* 113 (Spring 2012): 155–69.

Burkholder de la Rosa, Arno. "El olimpo fracturado: La dirección de Julio Scherer García en *Excélsior* (1968–1976)." *Historia Mexicana* 59, no. 4 (2010): 1339–99.

———. *La red de los espejos: Una historia del diario Excélsior*. México: Fondo de Cultura Económica, 2016.

Butler, Judith. *Precarious Life: The Powers of Mourning and Violence*. New York: Verso, 2004.

Butler, Matthew. *Popular Piety and Political Identity in Mexico's Cristero Rebellion: Michoacán, 1927–29*. New York: Oxford University Press, 2004.

Cabrera López, Patricia. *Una inquietud de amanecer: Literatura y política en México, 1962–1987*. México: Universidad Nacional Autónoma de México, 2006.

Camp, Roderic A. *Intellectuals and the State in Twentieth-Century Mexico*. Austin: University of Texas Press, 1985.

Campos, Victoria E. "Toward a New History: Twentieth-Century Debates in Mexico on Narrating the National Past." In *A Twice-Told Tale: Reinventing the Encounter in Iberian / Iberian American Literature and Film*, edited by Santiago Juan-Navarro and Theodore Robert Young, 47–64. Newark: University of Delaware Press, 2001.

Carr, Barry. *Marxism and Communism in Twentieth-Century Mexico*. Lincoln: University of Nebraska Press, 1992.

Castañeda, Jorge G. *México: El futuro en juego*. México: Joaquín Mortiz / Planeta, 1987.

Castellanos, Laura. *México armado: 1943–1981*. México: Ediciones Era, 2007.

Castillo, Heberto, and Rius. *Huele a gas! Los misterios del gasoducto*. 6th ed. México: Editorial Posada, 1979.

Chalaby, Jean K. "Scandal and the Rise of Investigative Reporting in France." *American Behavioral Scientist* 47, no. 9 (May 2004): 1194–1207.

Chevigny, Paul. "The Populism of Fear: Politics of Crime in the Americas." *Punishment and Society* 5, no. 1 (2003): 77–96.

Coerver, Don M., Suzanne B. Pasztor, and Robert Buffington, eds. *Mexico: An Encyclopedia of Contemporary Culture and History.* Santa Barbara, CA: ABC-CLIO, 2004.

Condés Lara, Enrique. *Represión y rebelión en México (1959–1985): La guerra fría en México. El discurso de la represión,* vols. 1 and 2. México: Miguel Ángel Porrúa, 2007.

Connelly, Matthew. *Fatal Misconception: The Struggle to Control World Population.* Cambridge, MA: Harvard University Press, 2008.

Connelly, Priscilla. "The Mexican National Popular Housing Fund." In *Empowering Squatter Citizen: Local Government, Civil Society, and Urban Poverty Reduction,* ed. Diana Mitlin and David Satterthwaite, 82–111. London: Earthscan, 2004.

Cornejo, Gerardo, Alan Keller, Susana Lerner, and Leandro Azuara. "Law and Population in Mexico." Fletcher School of Law and Diplomacy, Tufts University, Medford, MA, 1975.

Cornelius, Wayne. *Politics and the Migrant Poor in Mexico City.* Stanford, CA: Stanford University Press, 1975.

Corwin, Arthur F. *Contemporary Mexican Attitudes toward Population, Poverty, and Public Opinion.* Gainesville: University of Florida Press, 1963.

Dagnino, Evelina. "Citizenship in Latin America: An Introduction." *Latin American Perspectives* 30, no. 2 (March 2003): 211–25.

Davidson, Joanna. "Cultivating Knowledge: Development, Dissemblance, and Discursive Contradictions among the Diola of Guinea-Bissau." *American Ethnologist* 37, no. 2 (2010): 212–26.

Davis, Diane. "Reverberations: Mexico City's 1985 Earthquake and the Transformation of the Capital." In *The Resilient City: How Modern Cities Recover from Disaster,* edited by Lawrence J. Vale and Thomas J. Campanella, 255–80. New York: Oxford University Press, 2005.

———. *Urban Leviathan: Mexico City in the Twentieth Century.* Philadelphia: Temple University Press, 1994.

Dawson, Alexander S. *First World Dreams: Mexico since 1989.* New York: Zed Books, 2006.

Delegado de Cantú, Gloria M. *Historia de México: De la era revolucionaria al sexenio del cambio.* Vol. 2. 5th ed. México: Pearson Educación de Mexico, 2007.

Derby, Lauren. "Imperial Secrets: Vampires and Nationhood in Puerto Rico." *Past and Present* 199, supplement 3 (2008): 290–312.

Desantes-Guanter, José María. "Naturaleza y deontología del periodismo de denuncia." *Comunicación y Sociedad* 10, no. 2 (1997): 47–77.

Díaz-Barriga, Miguel. "Beyond the Domestic and the Public: Colonas Participation in Urban Movements in Mexico City." In *Cultures of Politics / Politics of Cultures: Re-visioning Latin American Social Movements,* edited by Sonia Alvarez, Evelina Dagnino, and Arturo Escobar, 252–77. Boulder, CO: Westview, 1998.

Díaz Garay, Salvador. *Los hijos de Smith.* México: Meridiano, 1969.

Dillingham, A. S. "Indigenismo Occupied: Indigenous Youth and Mexico's Democratic Opening (1968–1975)." *The Americas* 72, no. 4 (2015): 549–82.

Dines, Alberto. *O papel do jornal e a profissão de jornalista.* 9th ed. São Paolo: Summus Editorial, 1986.

Eckstein, Susan, "Poor People versus the State and Capital: Anatomy of a Successful Community Mobilization for Housing in Mexico City." In *Power and Popular Protest: Latin American Social Movements*, edited by Susan Eckstein, 329–50. Berkeley: University of California Press, 2001.

*Editor and Publisher International Yearbook.* New York: Editor and Publisher, 1966.

Egan, Linda. *Carlos Monsiváis: Culture and Chronicle in Contemporary Mexico.* Tucson: University of Arizona Press, 2001.

———. "Carlos Monsiváis 'Translates' Tom Wolfe." In *Mexico Reading the United States*, edited by Linda Egan and Mary K. Long, 99–115. Nashville: Vanderbilt University Press, 2009.

Eisenstadt, Todd A. *Courting Democracy in Mexico: Party Strategies and Electoral Institutions.* New York: Cambridge University Press, 2004.

Elizondo Mayer-Serra, Carlos, and Benito Nacif Hernández, eds. *Lecturas sobre el cambio político en México.* México: Fondo de Cultura Económica, 2002.

Entman, Robert M. *Scandal and Silence: Media Responses to Presidential Misconduct.* Cambridge: Polity Press, 2012.

Evans, Sterling. "King Henequen: Order, Progress, and Ecological Change in Yucatán, 1850–1950." In *A Land between Waters: Environmental Histories of Modern Mexico*, edited by Christopher R. Boyer, 150–72. Tucson: University of Arizona Press, 2012.

Fallaw, Ben W. "Cárdenas and the Caste War That Wasn't: State Power and Indigenismo in Post-revolutionary Yucatán." *The Americas* 53, no. 4 (1997): 551–77.

———. *Cárdenas Compromised: The Failures of Reform in Postrevolutionary Yucatán.* Durham, NC: Duke University Press, 2001.

Fernández, Claudia, and Andrew Paxman. *El Tigre: Emilio Azcárraga y su imperio Televisa.* 3rd ed. México: Grijalbo / Raya en el Agua, 2013.

Ferreira, Leonardo. *Centuries of Silence: The Story of Latin American Journalism.* Westport, CT: Praeger, 2006.

Fischer, Brodwyn M. *A Poverty of Rights: Citizenship and Inequality in Twentieth-Century Rio de Janeiro.* Stanford, CA: Stanford University Press, 2008.

El Fisgón and Helguera. *El sexenio me da risa: La historieta no oficial.* México: Grijalbo, 1994.

Flaherty, George F. *Hotel Mexico: Dwelling on the '68 Movement.* Oakland: University of California Press, 2016.

Flores Quintero, Genoveva. *Unomásuno: Victorias perdidas del periodismo mexicano (1977–1989).* México: Universidad Iberoamericana, 2014.

Foweraker, Joe, and Ann L. Craig, eds. *Popular Movements and Political Change in Mexico.* Boulder, CO: Lynne Rienner, 1990.

Franco, Jean. *Plotting Women: Gender and Representation in Mexico.* New York: Columbia University Press, 1989.

Fraser, Nancy. "Rethinking the Public Sphere: A Contribution to the Critique of Actually Existing Democracy." *Social Text* 25–26 (1990): 56–80.

Freije, Vanessa. "Censorship in the Headlines: National News and the Contradictions of Mexico City's Press Opening in the 1970s." In *Journalism, Censorship and Satire in Mexico*, edited by Paul Gillingham, Michael Lettieri, and Benjamin T. Smith, 237–62. Albuquerque: University of New Mexico Press, 2018.

———. "'The Emancipation of Media': Latin American Advocacy for a New International Information Order in the 1970s." *Journal of Global History* 14, no. 2 (2019): 301–20.

———. "Exposing Scandals, Guarding Secrets: Manuel Buendía, Columnismo, and the Unraveling of One-Party Rule in Mexico, 1965–1984." *The Americas* 72, no. 3 (July 2015): 377–409.

Galán, Héctor. "Standoff in Mexico." *Frontline*, Public Broadcasting Service. Aired April 1, 1986. Boston: WGBH Educational Foundation, 1986. VHS. 58 mins.

Gamiño Muñoz, Rodolfo. *Guerrilla, represión y prensa en la década de los setenta en México: Invisibilidad y olvido*. México: Instituto Mora, 2011.

Gantús, Fausta. *Caricatura y poder político: Crítica, censura y represión en la Ciudad de México, 1876–1888*. México: Colegio de México / Instituto Mora, 2009.

Garmon, Linda. "Autopsy of an Oil Spill." *Science News* 118, no. 17 (1980): 267–70.

Garrido, Luis Javier. *La ruptura: La Corriente Democrática del PRI*. México: Grijalbo, 1993.

Geidel, Molly. "'Sowing Death in Our Women's Wombs': Modernization and Indigenous Nationalism in the 1960s Peace Corps and Jorge Sanjinés' *Yawar Mallku*." *American Quarterly* 62, no. 3 (2010): 763–86.

Gil, Carlos B., ed. *Hope and Frustration: Interviews with Leaders of Mexico's Political Opposition*. Wilmington, DE: SR Books, 1992.

Gillingham, Paul. "'We Don't Have Arms, but We Do Have Balls': Fraud, Violence, and Popular Agency in Elections." In *Dictablanda: Politics, Work, and Culture in Mexico, 1938–1968*, edited by Paul Gillingham and Benjamin T. Smith, 149–72. Durham, NC: Duke University Press, 2014.

———. "Who Killed Crispín Aguilar? Violence and Order in the Postrevolutionary Countryside." In *Violence, Coercion, and State-Making in Twentieth-Century Mexico*, edited by Wil G. Pansters, 91–111. Stanford, CA: Stanford University Press, 2012.

Gillingham, Paul, and Benjamin T. Smith, eds. *Dictablanda: Politics, Work, and Culture in Mexico, 1938–1968*. Durham, NC: Duke University Press, 2014.

Gilly, Adolfo, and Rhina Roux. *Cartas a Cuauhtémoc Cárdenas*. México: Ediciones Era, 1989.

Gilman, Nils. *Mandarins of the Future: Modernization Theory in Cold War America*. Baltimore: Johns Hopkins University Press, 2004.

González de Bustamante, Celeste. *"Muy buenas noches": Mexico, Television, and the Cold War*. Lincoln: University of Nebraska Press, 2012.

González Casanova, Pablo. "Cuando hablamos de democracia, de qué hablamos?" *Revista Mexicana de Sociología* 48, no. 3 (1986): 3–6.

———. *La democracia en México*. México: Ediciones Era, 1965.

González González, José. *Lo negro del Negro Durazo*. 7th ed. México: Editorial Posada, 1983.

González Meza, José Luis, and Walter López Koehl. *Un asesino en la presidencia?* México: Ediciones Universo, 1987.

González Navarro, Moisés. *Población y sociedad en México (1900–1970)*. Vol. 1. México: Universidad Nacional Autónoma de México, 1974.

Granados Chapa, Miguel Ángel. *Buendía: El primer asesinato de la narcopolítica en México*. México: Grijalbo, 2012.

Grayson, George. *The Politics of Mexican Oil*. Pittsburgh: University of Pittsburgh Press, 1980.

Greene, Kenneth. *Why Dominant Parties Lose: Mexico's Democratization in Comparative Perspective*. New York: Cambridge University Press, 2007.

Guzzi, Líbera, "Medios y democracia: Reflexiones acerca del periodismo público en Colombia." *Chasqui* 122 (2013): 4–12.

Haber, Stephen S., Herbert S. Klein, Noel Maurer, and Kevin J. Middlebrook. *Mexico since 1980*. New York: Cambridge University Press, 2008.

Habermas, Jürgen. *The Structural Transformation of the Public Sphere: An Inquiry into a Category of Bourgeois Society*. Translated by Thomas Burger. Cambridge: Cambridge University Press, 1989.

Hall, Stuart, Chas Critcher, Tony Jefferson, John Clarke, and Brian Roberts. *Policing the Crisis: Mugging, the State, and Law and Order*. New York: Holmes and Meier, 1978.

Hallin, Daniel C., and Paolo Mancini. *Comparing Media Systems: Three Models of Media and Politics*. New York: Cambridge University Press, 2004.

Hayes, Joy Elizabeth. *Radio Nation: Communication, Popular Culture, and Nationalism in Mexico, 1920–1950*. Tucson: University of Arizona Press, 2000.

Hernández Campos, Jorge, Enrique Krauze, Carl Migdail, and Josue Saenz, "A Forum on Mexico's Survival," *Washington Quarterly* 9, no. 1 (1986): 169–84.

Hernández Rodríguez, Rogelio. *El centro dividido: La nueva autonomía de los gobernadores*. México: Colegio de México, 2008.

———. *Historia mínima del PRI*. México: Colegio de México, 2016.

Holston, James. *Insurgent Citizenship: Disjunctions of Democracy and Modernity in Brazil*. Princeton, NJ: Princeton University Press, 2008.

Huerta, Francisco. *Crónica del periodismo civil: La voz del ciudadano*. México: Grijalbo, 1997.

Hughes, Sallie. *Newsrooms in Conflict: Journalism and the Democratization of Mexico*. Pittsburgh: University of Pittsburgh Press, 2006.

Huska, Melanie. "Entertaining Education: Teaching National History in Mexican State-Sponsored Comic Books and Telenovelas, 1963–1996." PhD diss., University of Minnesota, 2013.

Irwin, Robert McKee, Edward J. McCaughan, and Michelle Rocío Nasser. "Introduction: Sexuality and Social Control in Mexico, 1901." In *The Famous 41: Sexu-*

ality and Social Control in Mexico, 1901, edited by Robert McKee Irwin, Edward J. McCaughan, and Michelle Rocío Nasser, 1–18. New York: Palgrave Macmillan, 2003.

Jackson, John. *Real Black: Adventures in Racial Sincerity*. Chicago: University of Chicago Press, 2005.

Johnson, Paul Christopher. *Secrets, Gossip, and Gods: The Transformation of Brazilian Candomblé*. New York: Oxford University Press, 2002.

Joseph, Gilbert M., and Daniel Nugent, eds. *Everyday Forms of State Formation: Revolution and the Negotiation of Rule in Modern Mexico*. Durham, NC: Duke University Press, 1994.

Joseph, Gilbert M., Anne Rubenstein, and Eric Zolov, eds. *Fragments of a Golden Age: The Politics of Culture in Mexico since 1940*. Durham, NC: Duke University Press, 2001.

Joseph, Gilbert M., and Daniela Spenser, eds. *In from the Cold: Latin America's New Encounter with the Cold War*. Durham, NC: Duke University Press, 2008.

Jusionyte, Ieva. "Crimecraft: Journalists, Police, and News Publics in an Argentine Town." *American Ethnologist* 43, no. 3 (2016): 451–64.

Katz, Friedrich. *The Life and Times of Pancho Villa*. Stanford, CA: Stanford University Press, 1998.

Keller, Renata. *Mexico's Cold War: Cuba, the United States, and the Legacy of the Mexican Revolution*. New York: Cambridge University Press, 2015.

———. "Testing the Limits of Censorship? *Política* Magazine and the 'Perfect Dictatorship,' 1960–1967." In *Journalism, Censorship and Satire in Mexico*, edited by Paul Gillingham, Michael Lettieri, and Benjamin T. Smith, 221–35. Albuquerque: University of New Mexico Press, 2018.

Kershaw, Paul. "Averting a Global Financial Crisis: The US, the IMF, and the Mexican Debt Crisis of 1976." *International History Review* 40, no. 2 (2018): 292–314.

Kiddle, Amelia M., and María L. O. Muñoz, eds. *Populism in Twentieth Century Mexico: The Presidencies of Lázaro Cárdenas and Luis Echeverría*. Tucson: University of Arizona Press, 2010.

Knight, Alan. "Cardenismo: Juggernaut or Jalopy?" *Journal of Latin American Studies* 26, no. 1 (1994): 73–107.

———. "Historical Continuities in Social Movements." In *Popular Movements and Political Change in Mexico*, edited by Joe Foweraker and Ann L. Craig, 78–102. Boulder, CO: Lynne Rienner, 1990.

———. "The Myth of the Mexican Revolution." *Past and Present* 209, no. 1 (2010): 223–73.

Kourí, Emilio H. "Interpreting the Expropriation of Indian Pueblo Lands in Porfirian Mexico: The Unexamined Legacies of Andrés Molina Enríquez." *Hispanic American Historical Review* 82, no. 1 (2002): 69–117.

Kram Villarreal, Rachel. "Gladiolas for the Children of Sánchez: Ernesto P. Uruchurtu's Mexico City, 1950–1968." PhD diss., University of Arizona, 2008.

Krauze, Enrique. *Caras de la historia*. México: Planeta, 1983.

———. *Por una democracia sin adjetivos*. México: Joaquín Mortiz / Planeta, 1986.

Kulick, Don, and Charles H. Klein. "Scandalous Acts: The Politics of Shame among Brazilian Travesti Prostitutes." In *Recognition Struggles and Social Movements: Contested Identities, Agency, and Power*, edited by Barbara Hobson, 215–38. New York: Cambridge University Press, 2003.

La Botz, Dan. *Democracy in Mexico: Peasant Rebellion and Political Reform*. Boston, MA: South End Press, 1995.

Langland, Victoria. "Birth Control Pills and Molotov Cocktails: Reading Sex and Revolution in 1968 Brazil." In *In from the Cold: Latin America's New Encounter with the Cold War*, edited by Gilbert M. Joseph and Daniela Spenser, 308–49. Durham, NC: Duke University Press, 2008.

Lawson, Chappell. *Building the Fourth Estate: Democratization and the Rise of a Free Press in Mexico*. Berkeley: University of California Press, 2002.

Leal Martínez, Alejandra. "De pueblo a sociedad civil: El discurso político después del sismo de 1985." *Revista Mexicana de Sociología* 76, no. 3 (2014): 441–69.

Leñero, Vicente. *Los periodistas*, ed. aniversario. México: Joaquín Mortiz, 2006.

León, Juanita. *Country of Bullets: Chronicles of War*. Translated by Guillermo Bleichmar. Albuquerque: University of New Mexico Press, 2009.

Lerner, Daniel. *The Passing of Traditional Society: Modernizing the Middle East*. Glencoe, IL: Free Press, 1958.

Levi, Heather. *The World of Lucha Libre: Secrets, Revelations, and Mexican National Identity*. Durham, NC: Duke University Press, 2008.

Lewis, Oscar. *The Children of Sánchez: Autobiography of a Mexican Family*. 2nd ed. New York: Vintage Books, 1963.

———. *Los hijos de Sánchez: Autobiografía de una familia mexicana*. México: Fondo de Cultura Económica, 1964.

Lindau, Juan D. "Technocrats and Mexico's Political Elite." *Political Science Quarterly* 111, no. 2 (1996): 295–322.

Loaeza, Soledad. *Clases medias y política en México: La querella escolar, 1959–1963*. México: El Colegio de México, 1988.

———. "La política del rumor: México, noviembre-diciembre de 1976." *Foro Internacional* 17, no. 4 (1977): 557–86.

Lomnitz, Claudio. "An Intellectual's Stock in the Factory of Mexico's Ruins," *American Journal of Sociology* 103, no. 4 (1998): 1052–65.

———. "Mexico's First Lynching: Sovereignty, Criminality, Moral Panic." *Critical Historical Studies* 1, no. 1 (2014): 85–123.

———. *The Return of Comrade Flores Magón*. New York: Zone Books, 2014.

———. "Times of Crisis: Historicity, Sacrifice, and the Spectacle of Debacle in Mexico City." *Public Culture* 15, no. 1 (2003): 127–47.

López Portillo, José. *Mis tiempos: Biografía y testimonio politico*. Vols 1 and 2. México: Fernández Editores, 1988.

Loret de Mola, Rafael. *Denuncia: Presidente sin palabra*. México: Grijalbo, 1995.

Lujambio, Alonso. *Federalismo y congreso en el cambio político de México*. México: Universidad Nacional Autónoma de Mexico, 1995.

Magaloni, Beatriz. *Voting for Autocracy: Hegemonic Party Survival and Its Demise in Mexico*. New York: Cambridge University Press, 2008.

Mahieux, Viviane. *Urban Chroniclers in Modern Latin America: The Shared Intimacy of Everyday Life*. Austin: University of Texas Press, 2011.

Martínez, José Luis. *La vieja guardia: Protagonistas del periodismo mexicano*. México: Random House Mondadori, 2005.

Marván, Ignacio L., and J. Aurelio Cuevas. "El movimiento de damnificados de Tlatelolco (septiembre de 1985–marzo de 1986)." *Revista Mexicana de Sociología* 49, no. 4 (1987): 111–40.

Massolo, Alejandra. *Por el amor y coraje: Mujeres en movimientos urbanos de la ciudad de México*. México: El Colegio de México, 1992.

McCormick, Gladys. "The Last Door: Political Prisoners and the Use of Torture in Mexico's Dirty War." *The Americas* 74, no. 1 (2017): 57–81.

———. *The Logic of Compromise in Mexico: How the Countryside Was Key to the Emergence of Authoritarianism*. Chapel Hill: University of North Carolina Press, 2016.

Meade, Everard. "From Sex Strangler to Model Citizen: Mexico's Most Famous Murderer and the Defeat of the Death Penalty." *Mexican Studies / Estudios Mexicanos* 26, no. 2 (2010): 323–77.

Mejido, Manuel. *Con la máquina al hombro*. México: Siglo XXI Editores, 2011.

Mendiola García, Sandra C. *Street Democracy: Vendors, Violence, and Public Space in Late Twentieth-Century Mexico*. Lincoln: University of Nebraska Press, 2017.

Menéndez Rodríguez, Mario. *Yucatán o el genocidio*. México: Fondo de Cultura Popular, 1964.

Miller, Marilyn. "*Guayaberismo* and the Essence of Cool." In *The Latin American Fashion Reader*, edited by Regina A. Root, 213–31. Oxford: Berg, 2005.

Molinar Horcasitas, Juan. *El tiempo de la legitimidad*. México: Cal y Arena, 1991.

Moncada Ochoa, Carlos. *Oficio de muerte: Periodistas asesinados en el país de la impunidad*. México: Grijalbo, 2012.

Monroy Nasr, Rebeca. "De disparos fotográficos: Ezequiel Carrasco, reportero gráfico de la Revolución." In *Los hados de febrero: Visiones artísticas de la decena trágica*, edited by Rafael Olea Franco, 237–58. México: Colegio de México, 2015.

Monsiváis, Carlos. *A ustedes les consta: Antología de la crónica en México*. México: Ediciones Era, 1980.

———. *Carlos Monsiváis*. México: Empresas Editoriales, 1966.

———. *Días de guardar*. 12th ed. México: Ediciones Era, 1988.

———. *Entrada libre: Crónicas de la sociedad que se organiza*. México: Ediciones Era, 1987.

———. *Mexican Postcards*. Translated by John Kraniauskas. London: Verso Books, 1997.

Moraña, Mabel, and Ignacio Sánchez Prado, eds. *El arte de la ironía: Carlos Monsiváis ante la crítica*. México: Ediciones Era, 2007.

Moreno, Olga Leticia. *Qué pasó en Chihuahua?* México: Editores Asociados Mexicanos, 1986.

Mosser, Jason. *The Participatory Journalism of Michael Herr, Norman Mailer, Hunter S. Thompson, and Joan Didion: Creating New Reporting Styles.* Lewiston, NY: Edwin Mellen, 2012.

Mraz, John. *Looking for Mexico: Modern Visual Culture and National Identity.* Durham, NC: Duke University Press, 2009.

Muñoz, María L. O. *Stand up and Fight: Participatory Indigenismo, Populism, and Mobilization in Mexico, 1970–1984.* Tucson: University of Arizona Press, 2016.

Musacchio, Humberto. *Ciudad quebrada.* México: Ediciones Océano, 1985.

Navarro, Aaron W. *Political Intelligence and the Creation of Modern Mexico, 1938–1954.* University Park: Pennsylvania State University Press, 2010.

Necochea López, Raúl. *A History of Family Planning in Twentieth-Century Peru.* Chapel Hill: University of North Carolina Press, 2014.

Nelson, Diane. *Who Counts? The Mathematics of Death and Life after Genocide.* Durham, NC: Duke University Press, 2015.

Nugent, Daniel. *Spent Cartridges of Revolution: An Anthropological History of Namiquipa, Chihuahua.* Chicago: University of Chicago Press, 1993.

Nyhan, Brendan. "Media Scandals Are Political Events: How Contextual Factors Affect Public Controversies over Alleged Misconduct by U.S. Governors." *Political Research Quarterly* 70, no. 1 (March 2017): 223–36.

Ocotitla Saucedo, Pedro. "Movimientos de colonos en Ciudad Nezahualcóyotl: Acción colectiva y política popular, 1945–1975." Master's thesis, Universidad Autónoma Metropolitana-Itzapalapa, 2000.

Ogle, Vanessa. "State Rights against Private Capital: The 'New International Economic Order' and the Struggle over Aid, Trade, and Foreign Investment, 1962–1981." *Humanity* 5, no. 2 (2014): 211–34.

Olcott, Jocelyn. *International Women's Year: The Greatest Consciousness-Raising Event in History.* New York: Oxford University Press, 2017.

Opperman, Stephanie Baker. "Modernization and Rural Health in Mexico: The Case of the Tepalcatepec Commission." *Endeavour* 37, no. 1 (2012): 47–55.

Padilla, Tanalís. *Rural Resistance in the Land of Zapata: The Jaramillista Movement and the Myth of the Pax-Priísta, 1940–1962.* Durham, NC: Duke University Press, 2008.

Padilla, Tanalís, and Louise E. Walker. "In the Archives: History and Politics." *Journal of Iberian and Latin American Research* 19, no. 1 (2013): 1–10.

Pansters, Wil, and Héctor Castillo Berthier. "Violencia e inseguridad en la ciudad de México: Entre la fragmentación y la politización." *Foro Internacional* 47, no. 3 (July–September 2007): 577–615.

Pastor, Rodolfo. "Más *Caras de la historia*." *Historia Mexicana* 33, no. 4 (1984): 540–46.

Paxman, Andrew. "Cooling to Cinema and Warming to Television: State Mass Media Policy, 1940–1964." In *Dictablanda: Politics, Work, and Culture in Mexico, 1938–1968*, edited by Paul Gillingham and Benjamin T. Smith, 299–320. Durham, NC: Duke University Press, 2014.

Pensado, Jaime. *Rebel Mexico: Student Unrest and Authoritarian Political Culture during the Long Sixties*. Stanford, CA: Stanford University Press, 2013.

Phillips, Kendall R. "Introduction." In *Framing Public Memory*, edited by Stephen Howard Browne, Barbara Biesecker, Barbie Zelizer, Charles E. Morris III, and Kendall R. Phillips, 1–14. Tuscaloosa: University of Alabama Press, 2004.

Picazo Sánchez, Leticia. *Una década de video en México 1980–1989: Dependencia extranjera y monopolios nacionales*. México: Editorial Trillas, 1994.

Piccato, Pablo. *A History of Infamy: Crime, Truth, and Justice in Mexico*. Oakland: University of California Press, 2017.

———. "Homicide as Politics in Modern Mexico." *Bulletin of Latin American Research* 32, no. S1 (2013): 104–25.

———. "Murders of Nota Roja: Truth and Justice in Mexican Crime News." *Past and Present* 223 (2014): 195–231.

———. *The Tyranny of Opinion: Honor in the Construction of the Mexican Public Sphere*. Durham, NC: Duke University Press, 2010.

Pieper Mooney, Jadwiga E. *The Politics of Motherhood: Maternity and Women's Rights in Twentieth-Century Chile*. Pittsburgh: University of Pittsburgh Press, 2009.

Pitol, Sergio. "Con Monsiváis, el joven." In *El arte de la ironía: Carlos Monsiváis ante la crítica*, edited by Mabel Moraña and Ignacio M. Sánchez Prado, 339–58. México: Universidad Nacional Autónoma de México / Ediciones Era, 2007.

Polit Dueñas, Gabriela. "Chronicles of Everyday Life in Culiacán, Sinaloa." In *Meanings of Violence in Latin America*, edited by Gabriela Polit Dueñas and María Helena Rueda, 149–68. New York: Palgrave Macmillan, 2011.

Poniatowska, Elena. "The Earthquake: To Carlos Monsiváis." *Oral History Review* 16, no. 1 (1988): 7–20.

———. *Nada, nadie: Las voces del temblor*. México: Ediciones Era, 1988.

———. *La noche de Tlatelolco: Testimonios de historia oral*. México: Ediciones Era, 1971.

———. *Todo empezó el domingo*. México: Fondo de Cultura Económica, 1963.

———. *El tren pasa primero*. México: Alfaguara, 2005.

Poole, Deborah. "'An Image of Our Indian': Type Photographs and Racial Sentiments in Oaxaca, 1920–1940." *Hispanic American Historical Review* 84, no. 1 (2004): 37–82.

Puente Leyva, Jesús. "The Natural Gas Controversy." *Proceedings of the Academy of Political Science* 34, no. 1 (1981): 158–67.

Quiroz, Alberto. *Historias para Oscar Lewis: El reverso de "Los hijos de Sánchez."* México: B. Costa / Amic Editores, 1966.

Radilla Martínez, Andrea, and Claudia E. G. Rangel Lozano, eds. *Desaparición forzada y terrorismo de Estado en México: Memorias de la represión de Atoyac, Guerrero durante la década de los setenta*. México: Plaza y Valdés Editores, 2012.

Ramírez, Luis Alfonso. "Corrupción, empresariado y desarrollo regional en México: El caso yucateco." In *Vicios públicos, virtudes privadas: La corrupción en México*, edited by Claudio Lomnitz, 145–66. México: CIESAS, 2000.

Ramírez, Paul. "'Like Herod's Massacre': Quarantines, Bourbon Reform, and Popular Protest in Oaxaca's Smallpox Epidemic, 1796–1797." *The Americas* 69, no. 2 (2012): 203–35.

Ramírez Saiz, Juan Manuel. *El movimiento urbano popular en México*. 1st ed. México: Siglo XXI Editores, 1986.

Ramos, Samuel. *El perfil del hombre y la cultura en México*. México: P. Robredo, 1938.

Revueltas, José. "TV y cultura en los juegos deportivos de la XIX Olimpiada." *México 68: Reseña Gráfica* 1, no. 33 (1968): 1–16.

Riding, Alan. *Distant Neighbors: A Portrait of the Mexicans*. New York: Alfred A. Knopf, 1985.

Rodríguez Castañeda, Rafael. *El policía: Perseguía, torturaba, mataba*. México: Grijalbo, 2013.

———. *Prensa vendida: Los periodistas y los presidentes: 40 años de relaciones*. México: Grijalbo, 1998.

Rodríguez Kuri, Ariel. "El discurso del miedo: *El Imparcial* y Francisco I. Madero." *Historia Mexicana* 40, no. 4 (1991): 697–740.

———. "Ganar la sede: La política internacional de los juegos olímpicos de 1968." *Historia Mexicana* 64, no. 1 (2014): 243–89.

———. "Secretos de la idiosincrasia: Urbanización y cambio cultural en México, 1950–1970." In *Ciudades mexicanas del siglo XX: Siete estudios históricos*, edited by Carlos Lira Vásquez and Ariel Rodríguez Kuri, 19–51. México: SEP-CONACYT / Colmex / UAM Azcapotzalco, 2009.

Rodríguez Munguía, Jacinto. *La otra guerra secreta: Los archivos prohibidos de la prensa y el poder*. México: Random House Mondadori / Debosillo, 2010.

Roldán, Mary. "Popular Cultural Action, Catholic Transnationalism, and Development in Colombia before Vatican II." In *Local Church, Global Church: Catholic Activism in Latin America from Rerum Novarum to Vatican II*, edited by Stephen J. C. Andes and Julia G. Young, 245–74. Washington, DC: Catholic University of America Press, 2016.

Rosemblatt, Karin Alejandra. "Other Americas: Transnationalism, Scholarship, and the Culture of Poverty in Mexico and the United States." *Hispanic American Historical Review* 89, no. 4 (2009): 603–41.

Ross, Stanley Robert. "Mexico: The Preferred Revolution." In *Politics of Change in Latin America*, edited by Joseph Maier and Richard W. Weatherhead, 140–51. New York: Frederick A. Praeger, 1964.

Roudakova, Natalia. *Losing Pravda: Ethics and the Press in Post-truth Russia*. New York: Cambridge University Press, 2017.

Rubenstein, Anne. *Bad Language, Naked Ladies, and Other Threats to the Nation: A Political History of Comic Books in Mexico*. Durham, NC: Duke University Press, 1998.

———. "Theaters of Masculinity: Moviegoing and Male Roles in Mexico before 1960." In *Masculinity and Sexuality in Modern Mexico*, edited by Víctor M. Macías-González and Anne Rubenstein, 132–54. Albuquerque: University of New Mexico Press, 2012.

Rubin, Jeffrey W. *Decentering the Regime: Ethnicity, Radicalism, and Democracy in Juchitán, Mexico.* Durham, NC: Duke University Press, 1997.

———. "Popular Mobilization and the Myth of State Corporatism." In *Popular Movements and Political Change in Mexico*, edited by Joe Foweraker and Ann L. Craig, 247–67. Boulder, CO: Lynne Rienner, 1990.

Sábato, Hilda. *The Many and the Few: Political Participation in Republican Buenos Aires.* Stanford, CA: Stanford University Press, 2001.

Sackett, Andrew. "Fun in Acapulco? The Politics of Development on the Mexican Riviera." In *Holiday in Mexico: Critical Reflections on Tourism and Tourist Encounters*, edited by Dina Berger and Andrew Grant Wood, 161–82. Durham, NC: Duke University Press, 2010.

Salazar, Jezreel. *La ciudad como texto: La crónica urbana de Carlos Monsiváis.* Monterrey, México: Universidad Autónoma de Nuevo León, 2006.

Salazar-Sutil, Nicolás. "What's in Your Wardrobe, Mr. Morales? A Study in Political Dress." *Popular Communication* 7, no. 2 (2009): 63–78.

Sánchez Prado, Ignacio. "Carlos Monsiváis: Crónica, nación y liberalismo." In *El arte de la ironía: Carlos Monsiváis ante la crítica*, edited by Mabel Moraña and Ignacio Sánchez Prado, 300–336. México: Ediciones Era, 2007.

Saragoza, Alex M., Ana Paula Ambrosi, and Silvia D. Zárate, eds. *Mexico Today: An Encyclopedia of Life in the Republic.* Vol. 1. Santa Barbara, CA: ABC-CLIO, 2012.

Scheper-Hughes, Nancy. *Death without Weeping: The Violence of Everyday Life in Brazil.* Berkeley: University of California Press, 1992.

Scherer García, Julio. *El poder: Historias de familia.* México: Grijalbo, 1990.

———. *Los presidentes.* México: Grijalbo, 1986.

———. *Vivir.* México: Grijalbo, 2012.

Scherer García, Julio, and Carlos Monsiváis. *Parte de guerra, Tlatelolco 1968: Documentos del general Marcelino García Barragán: Los hechos y la historia.* México: Nuevo Siglo / Aguilar, 1999.

———. *Tiempo de saber: Prensa y poder en México.* México: Aguilar, 2003.

Schiller, Naomi. *Channeling the State: Community Media and Popular Politics in Venezuela.* Durham, NC: Duke University Press, 2018.

Schmidt, Samuel. *Humor en serio: Análisis del chiste político en México.* México: Aguilar, 1996.

Schuessler, Michael K. *Elena Poniatowska: An Intimate Biography.* Tucson: University of Arizona Press, 2007.

Scott, James C. *Weapons of the Weak: Everyday Forms of Peasant Resistance.* New Haven, CT: Yale University Press, 1985.

Seelke, Clare Ribando. *Violence against Journalists in Mexico: In Brief.* Washington, DC: Congressional Research Service, 2018.

Serna, Ana María. "Prensa y sociedad en las décadas revolucionarias (1910–1940)." *Secuencia* 88 (2014): 111–49.

———. *"Se solicitan reporteros": Historia oral del periodismo mexicano en la segunda mitad del siglo XX.* México: Instituto Mora, 2015.

Serna, Leslíe, and Coordinadora Única de Damnificados. *Aquí nos quedaremos! Testimonios de la Coordinadora Única de Damnificados: Entrevistas*. México: Universidad Iberoamericana, 1995.

Servín, Elisa. *La oposición política: Otra cara del siglo XX mexicano*. México: CIDE, 2006.

———. "Reclaiming Revolution in Light of the 'Mexican Miracle': Celestino Gasca and the Federacionistas Leales Insurrection of 1961." *The Americas* 66, no. 4 (April 2010): 527–57.

Sheppard, Randal. *A Persistent Revolution: History, Nationalism, and Politics since 1968*. Albuquerque: University of New Mexico Press, 2016.

Sirvent, Carlos. *Encuesta electoral en Chihuahua, 1986*. México: Universidad Nacional Autónoma de México, 1987.

*Situation in Mexico: Hearings before the Subcommittee on Western Hemisphere Affairs of the Committee on Foreign Relations*, 99th Cong., 2nd session (1986).

Sloan, Julia L. "Talking of Tlatelolco: The Power of Collective Memory Suppressed but Not Surrendered." In *Projections of Power in the Americas*, edited by Niels Bjerre-Poulsen, Helene Balslev Clausen, and Jan Gustafsson, 61–88. New York: Routledge, 2012.

Smith, Benjamin T. *The Mexican Press and Civil Society, 1940–1976: Stories from the Newsroom, Stories from the Street*. Chapel Hill: University of North Carolina Press, 2018.

———. "The Paradoxes of the Public Sphere: Journalism, Gender, and Corruption in Mexico, 1940–70." *Journal of Social History* 52, no. 4 (2019): 1330–54.

Smith, S. A. "Talking Toads and Chinless Ghosts: The Politics of 'Superstitious' Rumors in the People's Republic of China, 1961–1965." *American Historical Review* 111, no. 2 (2006): 405–27.

Smulovitz, Catalina, and Enrique Peruzzotti. "Societal Accountability in Latin America," *Journal of Democracy* 11, no. 4 (2000): 147–58.

Snodgrass, Michael. "'We Are All Mexicans Here': Workers, Patriotism, and Union Struggles in Monterrey." In *The Eagle and the Virgin: Nation and Cultural Revolution in Mexico, 1920–1940*, edited by Mary Kay Vaughan and Stephen E. Lewis, 314–34. Durham, NC: Duke University Press, 2008.

Soria, Carlos. "Fundamentos éticos de la presunción de inocencia o la legitimidad del periodismo de denuncia." *Comunicación y Sociedad* 9, nos. 1–2 (1996): 99–219.

Sosa Plata, Gabriel. *Días de radio: Historias de la radio en México*. México: Secretaría de Cultura, 2016.

Sosenski, Susana. "El niño consumidor: Una construcción publicitaria de la prensa mexicana en la década de 1950." In *Ciudadanos inesperados: Espacios de formación de la ciudadanía ayer y hoy*, edited by Ariadna Acevedo Rodrigo and Paula López Caballero, 191–222. México: Colegio de México, 2012.

———. *Niños en acción: El trabajo infantil en la ciudad de México (1920–1934)*. México: El Colegio de México, 2010.

Soto Laveaga, Gabriela. "'Let's Become Fewer': Soap Operas, Contraception, and Nationalizing the Mexican Family in an Overpopulated World." *Sexuality Research and Social Policy* 4, no. 3 (2007): 19–33.

Stephen, Lynn. *Women and Social Movements in Latin America: Power from Below.* Austin: University of Texas Press, 1997.

Strauss, Leo. *Persecution and the Art of Writing.* Westport, CT: Greenwood, 1973.

Stoler, Ann Laura. *Along the Archival Grain: Epistemic Anxieties and Colonial Common Sense.* Princeton, NJ: Princeton University Press, 2009.

Sue, Christina A. *Land of the Cosmic Race: Race Mixture, Racism, and Blackness in Mexico.* New York: Oxford University Press, 2013.

Taibo, Paco Ignacio, II. *'68.* México: Planeta, 1991.

Taussig, Michael. *Defacement: Public Secrecy and the Labor of the Negative.* Stanford, CA: Stanford University Press, 1999.

———. *Shamanism, Colonialism, and the Wild Man: A Study in Terror and Healing.* Chicago: University of Chicago Press, 1987.

Tavera-Fenollosa, Ligia. "Social Movements and Civil Society: The Mexico City 1985 Earthquake Victim Movement." PhD diss., Yale University, 2008.

Ticktin, Miriam. "A World without Innocence," *American Ethnologist* 44, no. 4 (2017): 577–90.

Trejo Delarbe, Raúl. *Crónica del sindicalismo en México, 1976–1988.* México: Siglo XXI Editores, 1990.

———, ed. *Televisa, el quinto poder.* 2nd ed. México: Claves Latinoamericanas, 1985.

Treviño de González, María del Pilar. *Enhorabuena, Chihuahua!* Juárez, Chihuahua: n.p., 1986.

Trumper, Camilo D. *Ephemeral Histories: Public Art, Politics, and the Struggle for the Streets in Chile.* Oakland: University of California Press, 2016.

Tuñón, Julia. *Mujeres de luz y sombra en el cine mexicano: La construcción de una imagen (1939–1952).* México: Colegio de México, 1998.

———. *Women in Mexico: A Past Unveiled.* Translated by Alan Hynds. Austin: University of Texas Press, 1999.

Turner, Frederick C. *Responsible Parenthood: The Politics of Mexico's New Population Policies.* Washington, DC: American Enterprise Institute for Public Policy Research, 1974.

Turner, Frederick Jackson. *The Frontier in American History.* New York: Henry Holt, 1920.

Turner, John Kenneth. *Barbarous Mexico: An Indictment of a Cruel and Corrupt System.* New York: Cassell, 1911.

Urquidi, Víctor. *Los hijos de Jones.* Austin: Institute of Latin American Studies, University of Texas, 1963.

Valle, Luis G. del. "Teología de la Liberación en México." In *El pensamiento social de los católicos mexicanos,* edited by Roberto J. Blancarte, 230–65. México: Fondo de Cultura Económica, 1996.

Van Delden, Maarten. "Conjunciones y disyunciones: La rivalidad entre *Vuelta* y *Nexos.*" In *El laberinto de la solidaridad: Cultura y política en México (1910–2000),* edited by Kristine Vanden Berghe and Maarten van Delden. Amsterdam: Rodopi, 2002.

Vanderwood, Paul. *The Power of God against the Guns of Government: Religious Upheaval in Mexico at the Turn of the Nineteenth Century*. Stanford, CA: Stanford University Press, 1998.

Vaughan, Mary Kay. *Cultural Politics in Revolution: Teachers, Peasants, and Schools in Mexico, 1930–1940*. Tucson: University of Arizona Press, 1997.

———. *Portrait of a Young Painter: Pepe Zúñiga and Mexico City's Rebel Generation*. Durham, NC: Duke University Press, 2014.

Vaughan, Mary Kay, and Stephen E. Lewis, eds. *The Eagle and the Virgin: Nation and Cultural Revolution in Mexico, 1920–1940*. Durham, NC: Duke University Press, 2006.

Vélez-Ibañez, Carlos G. *Rituals of Marginality: Politics, Process, and Culture Change in Urban Central Mexico, 1969–1974*. Berkeley: University of California Press, 1983.

Volpi Escalante, Jorge. *La imaginación y el poder: Una historia intelectual de 1968*. México: Ediciones Era, 1998.

Wahl-Jorgensen, Karin. "Mediated Citizenship(s): An Introduction." *Social Semiotics* 16, no. 2 (2006): 197–203.

Waisbord, Silvio. "Knocking on Newsroom Doors: The Press and Political Scandals in Argentina," *Political Communication* 11, no. 1 (1994): 19–33.

———. *Watchdog Journalism in South America: News, Accountability, and Democracy*. New York: Columbia University Press, 2000.

Walker, Louise E. "Economic Fault Lines and Middle-Class Fears: Tlatelolco, Mexico City, 1985." In *Aftershocks: Earthquakes and Popular Politics in Latin America*, edited by Jürgen Buchenau and Lyman L. Johnson, 184–22. Albuquerque: University of New Mexico Press, 2003.

———. *Waking from the Dream: Mexico's Middle Classes after 1968*. Stanford, CA: Stanford University Press, 2013.

White, Luise. *Speaking with Vampires: Rumor and History in Colonial Africa*. Berkeley: University of California Press, 2000.

Wilkie, James W., and Edna Monzón Wilkie. *Porfirio Muñoz Ledo: Historia oral, 1933–1988*. México: Debate, 2017.

Wilson, Fiona. *De la casa al taller: Mujeres, trabajo y clase social en la industria textil y del vestido, Santiago Tangamandapio*. Zamora, México: Colegio de Michoacán, 1990.

Wilt, David. "Based on a True Story: Reality-Based Exploitation Cinema in Mexico." In *Latsploitation, Exploitation Cinemas, and Latin America*, edited by Victoria Ruétalo and Dolores Tierney. New York: Routledge, 2009.

Womack, John. *Zapata and the Mexican Revolution*. New York: Alfred A. Knopf, 1968.

Wright-Ríos, Edward. *Searching for la Madre Matiana: Prophecy and Popular Culture in Modern Mexico*. Albuquerque: University of New Mexico Press, 2014.

Zeltsman, Corinna. *Ink under the Fingernails: Printing and the Materiality of Politics in Nineteenth-Century Mexico*. Oakland: University of California Press, forthcoming.

Zepeda Lecuona, Guillermo Raúl. *Crimen sin castigo: Procuración de justicia penal y ministerio público en México.* México: Centro de Investigación para el Desarrollo, Fondo de Cultural Económica, 2004.

Zermeño, Sergio. *México, una democracia utópica: El movimiento estudiantil del 68.* México: Siglo XXI Editores, 1978.

Zolov, Eric. "Expanding our Conceptual Horizons: The Shift from an Old to a New Left in Latin America." *A Contracorriente* 5, no. 2 (2008): 47–73.

# INDEX

abortion, 223n48
*Acción* (Chihuahua), 24–25
Agencia Mexicana de Información (AMI), 90, 109–10, 201
agrarian land reform: Díaz Ordaz and, 25–26; Garro's "The Agrarian Problem" and García photo spread, 33–37, 36f; government and U.S. fears, 30–31; history of, 28–29; Rius cartoon "In This Town There Are No Thieves," 33; Yucatán henequen scandal and ejidatario unrest, 25–32, 46–49, 48f
"Agrarian Problem, The" (Garro), 33–35
Aguilar Camín, Héctor, 132, 149, 176, 179–80, 189
Ajoux, Salvador, 170
Alatriste, Gustavo, 50
Alemán, Miguel, 101
Alianza Cívica, 190
Allende, Salvador, 69–70, 187
Álvarez, Luis H., 182
Anaya Sánchez, Federico, 148–49
Aristegui, Carmen, 205
*Asesino en la presidencia?, Un* (González Meza and López), 193–94
Asez Abad, José, 151
austerity policies, 121, 123, 174, 175, 190, 195, 202
Avilés, Alejandro, 185
Ayotla Textil factory labor stoppage, 67
Azcárraga, Emilio, 184

Baeza, Fernando, 175, 181
Banco Agrario de Yucatán (BAY), 26–30
Banco Nacional de Comercio Exterior, 216n31
Banco Nacional de Crédito Ejidal, 216n31
Barreda Solórzano, Luis de la, 122
Barrio, Francisco, 172–73
Bartlett, Manuel, 184
Bay of Campeche oil spill, 97–103
Becerra Acosta, Manuel, 76, 91–92, 147
Becerril, Andrea, 148, 150
Benítez, Fernando, 41, 45, 133, 133f, 225n81
Bernstein, Carl, 203
birth control, 223n48. *See also* family planning
birth rates, Third-World, 60
Blanco Moheno, Roberto, 1, 14
Blancornelas, Jesús, 171
Bolaños, Laura, 187
Bolivia, 60
Borbolla, Carlos, 82
Brazil, 15, 60, 204
Brigada Blanca, 114–15
Buendía, Manuel, 133f; about, 100–101, 232n88; on Acapulco, 1–2; assassination of, 132–35; career of, 109; DFS ties to, 114, 115; Durazo case and, 109–12; Gama case and, 114; leaked documents and, 99–100; on *El Nacional*, 152; on oil spill, 100; "Para Control de Usted" column, 41; radio readings of columns of, 170; "Red

INDEX 275

Buendía (continued)
Privada" column, 90, 109–10, 114, 124–25, 132; Río Tula murders and, 115–17, 127; scandal dynamics and, 15; on sterilization vaccine scandal, 70
Buñuel, Luis, 40
Burelo, Antonio, 154–55
*Buro de Investigación Política* newsletter, 25, 88
Bussi, Hortensia, 69

Calderón, Felipe, 204–5
Camacho Solís, Manuel, 228n30
Camarena, Enrique, 174
Camín, Manuel, 115–16
Cárdenas, Cuauhtémoc, 190
Cárdenas, Lázaro, 29, 81, 96, 199
Carrillo Arena, Guillermo, 143, 246n89
Carrillo Flores, Antonio, 61
Carrillo Gil, Álvar, 41
cartoons, political: on "la crisis," 118–21; "Falso rumor" (Iracheta), 72, 73f; "In This Town There Are No Thieves" (Rius), 33; "Listos con las listas!" (Rius), 119, 119f; "Los infundios" (Iracheta), 74–75, 74f; "Medio siglo de siglas" (Rius), 120, 120f; *Página Uno* cartoon of the PAN, 187; on sterilization vaccine scandal, 72–75, 73f, 74f
Carvajal, Gustavo, 229n31
Casa Blanca scandal, 205
Castañeda, Jorge G., 174
Castillo, Heberto: about, 12, 83–86; activism and journalism, connection between, 80; Buendía and, 100–101, 114; energy talks, 95–96; on González González, 127; *Huele a gas!* (with Rius), 96, 97f, 102, 106; kidnapped and beaten by police, 96; on PAN hunger strikers, 188; Pemex articles, 80, 84–90, 93–94; as politician-journalist, making of, 82–86; publicizing attempts to silence, 87–88; Tlatelolco Massacre and, 11; tortured, 114

Castro, Fidel, 108
Cataño Morlet, Luis, 38–46
Central Campesina Independiente (CCI), 30
Central Intelligence Agency (CIA), U.S., 92, 94f, 174
Centro de Información y Análisis de los Efectos del Sismo (CIASES), 160–61
Centro Nacional de Comunicación Social (CENCOS), 112, 234n19
*Chapulín, El* (Oaxaca City), 25
Chihuahua elections. *See* election fraud, Chihuahua gubernatorial (1986)
circulation of critical news and spectacle, 2–3, 6–7
citizenship: exposé circulation, effects of, 2–3; Krauze's ideal of, 177–78; mediated, 4–8, 201
civil society formation following earthquake. *See* earthquake
class: Durazo and, 126, 128; family planning and, 59–60; sterilization vaccine scandal and, 61–62, 72–73. *See also* poverty
Colegio de Ciencias y Humanidades (CCH) Oriente, 59
Collor de Mello, Fernando, 204
Colosio, Luis Donaldo, 196
Comisión Estatal Electoral de Chihuahua, 250n70
Comité de Defensa Ejidal (CDE), 27–29
Comité de Lucha por la Democracia, 173
Comité Pro Defensa de Presos, Perseguidos, Desaparecidos y Exiliados Políticos, 113
Comunicación e Información, S.A. de C.V. (CISA), 169, 246n2
Conchello, José Ángel, 98
Confederación de Trabajadores de México (CTM), 157
Confederación Nacional Campesina (CNC), 30

Confederación Nacional de Organizaciones Populares (CNOP), 37, 58
Congress, Mexican: Díaz Serrano before, 88–90, 101–3; Durazo case and, 131
corruption: "La Crisis," 117–22; de la Madrid anticorruption platform, 121, 122; evidence tampering as government strategy, 66–67; mediated citizenship and, 4–5; as overriding theme of exposés, 16; PRI investigation into, 121–22; privately acknowledged, 25; *Proceso* and, 79; racialized and gendered explanations of, 21; *Siempre!* cartoons on, 33. *See also* agrarian land reform; earthquake; election fraud, Chihuahua gubernatorial; Pemex oil scandal; police corruption, violence, and repression
Cosío Villegas, Daniel, 178
counterinsurgency campaigns, 113–15
"crisis, la," 118–21
*crónicas* (chronicles), 12, 140–43, 158–65
Cuban Revolution, 4, 32
Cueto, Luis, 170–71
*Cultura en México, La*, 33–34

democratization: "democratic opening," 12, 51–52, 71, 77, 107; PRI and, 2
*denuncia* journalism: balance between concealment and revelation, 136; change in, 203–4; conflicts, internal, 204; history of, 11–13; local and regional vs. national papers, 24–25, 110; meaning of *denuncia*, 10–11; party divisions and, 105; senator's praise for, 131; tensions within, 115; as tool of subversion, 46. *See also* journalism, Mexican; scandal
*dependentistas*, 89
*Día, El*: about, 6, 41; Buendía and, 109; excerpted social science research in, 41; on Lewis case, 41–42; on oil boom, 82; on oil spill, 99; "Para Control de Usted" column (Buendía), 41; on sterilization vaccine scandal, 70; on sweatshops, 151, 156
*Diario de Irapuato*, 171–72
*Diario de Juárez*, 183, 184
*Diario del Sureste*, 32
*Diario de México*, 45
*Diario de Yucatán, El*, 25–32, 49
Díaz, Porfirio, 11, 178
Díaz Ordaz, Gustavo, 24, 25–26, 229n31
Díaz Redondo, Regino, 82–83
Díaz Serrano, Jorge: Buendía assassination and, 132; before Congress, 88–90, 101–3; corruption narratives and, 118; gas pipeline announcement, 84–85; oil reserves and, 80, 85, 228n27; oil spill and, 98–102; PMT accusation against, 95; political downfall and imprisonment of, 103–5; United States and, 92
Dimensión Weld, 150–52, 156
*Dinámica Habitacional*, 141–43
Dirección Federal de Seguridad (DFS): Buendía assassination and, 132–35; Buendía's relationship with, 114, 115; CENCOS and, 112, 234n19; on Durazo case, 135–36; Gama attack, 112–15; importance of, 214n80; intelligence archives of, 18; press monitoring, 24; *El problema henequenero en el estado de Yucatán* report, 29–30; Yucatán ejidatario unrest and, 46
Dirección General de Investigaciones Políticas y Sociales (DGIPS), 18, 24, 56–59, 62, 67, 88
Dirty War, 113, 187. *See also* counterinsurgency campaigns
disappearances, 67, 107, 113, 187
División de Investigaciones para la Prevención de la Delincuencia, 116
Dornbierer, Manú, 196

Durazo, Arturo "El Negro": about, 108; arrest of, 131; assassination plan against de la Madrid, 128; Buendía and, 109–12, 116–17; comic books on, 128–31, 130f; financial corruption and "Parthenon" mansion of, 117–18, 128; gendered, racialized, and classed discourse about, 128–29; González's *Lo negro del Negro Durazo*, 107, 125–27, 135; in radio and film, 127–28, 134; ramifications of scandal, 135–37; Río Tula murders and, 115–17, 134

Ealy Ortiz, Juan Francisco, 185, 196
earthquake (Mexico City, 1985): about, 138–39; broadcast media and, 140–41, 145–46, 155–56, 163; *crónicas* (chronicles), 140–43, 158–65; dark jokes about, 246n89; garment-worker sweatshops and, 146–58; as mediated disaster, 139, 165–66; Monsiváis's "Solidarity" article and mediatization of organized residents, 140–46; official responses, 145–46; public space and representation, contested, 165; unfixed meanings of scandal and, 202
Echeverría, Luis: Allende and, 70; "democratic opening" and, 12, 51–52; Durazo and, 108; *Excélsior* and, 12, 52, 70, 82–83; family planning initiatives, 55; fascism and, 69; financial crisis and, 81; "Granero Político" column (pseudonymous), 17; pardons, 84; PMT and, 96; population control and, 61; press freedom and, 12; urban poor and, 59
economic/financial crises: 1976, 81; 1982, 104, 105–6, 117–18; "la crisis," 117–22; garment workers scandal and, 157–58
Editores Asociados Mexicanos, 129
*ejidatarios* (shareholders of communal land), 27–29

*ejidos* (collectively owned and farmed lands), 26–27
election, presidential (1988), 190–91
election fraud, Chihuahua gubernatorial (1986): about, 167–69; advance framing of fraud, 176–82; censorship and self-censorship, 182–86; forecasting of results, 175–76; hunger strikes, 182, 188; information flows and national vs. regional media, 169–72; observers and removal, 182, 185, 250n70; postelection protests and analysis, 186–89; PRI rallies, 180–81; scandals as potential weapons and, 168; U.S. media and, 172–76, 183–84; U.S. Senate and, 174–75, 188–89
Escuela Nacional de Ciencias Políticas y Sociales, UNAM, 40
*Excélsior*: distribution of, 210n29; earthquake coverage, 145; Echeverría and, 12, 52, 70, 82–83; "F 2.8: La vida en el instante," 35; Gama case and, 114; letter to Granados Chapa, 4–5; Nafinsa loan to found *Unomásuno*, 91; on oil boom, 82; "Red Privada" (Buendía), 90, 109–10, 114, 124–25, 132; on sterilization vaccine scandal, 64–65, 64f, 70–71, 75–76, 77; on sweatshops, 154; on Yucatán unrest, 28–29

family planning, 55, 59–61. See also birth control
Farell Cubillas, Arsenio, 154
fascism, 33, 69, 70, 71, 187
Fasja Dabbad, Jacobo, 157
Federal Bureau of Investigation (FBI), U.S., 39, 43, 128, 131
Félix, Héctor "El Gato," 171
Figueroa, Rubén, 1, 15
film, viewership of, 6
Flores Olea, Víctor, 41
Fondo de Cultura Económica (FCE), 37–39, 44–45

Fox, Vicente, 18
Frente Democrático Nacional, 190, 194
Frente Mexicano por Derechos Humanos, 113
Frente Popular Independiente (FPI), 57, 59
*Frontline* (PBS), 172–73
Fuentes, Carlos, 40, 225n81

Galindo Ochoa, Francisco, 170
Gama, Héctor, 11, 112–15
García, Héctor, 34–36, 36*f*
garment worker sweatshops: accusations against factory owners, 150–51; admission of collusion, 154–55; discovery of, 146–47; economic crisis and, 157–58; *Excélsior* and *Unomásuno* on, 154; gender and, 148, 151–52; independent news bulletins and union, 157; *La Jornada* and Lovera exposés, 147–50; *El Nacional* on, 152–53; refusal of interviews, 155–57
Garro, Elena, 33–35
gender: Durazo case and, 108, 128, 136–37; economically active population percentage, 244n49; explanations of corruption and, 21; garment worker sweatshops and, 148, 151–52; historical concepts of "feminine" and "masculine," 245n75; in journalism, 14, 34, 150, 203; sterilization vaccine scandal and, 61–67
General Population Law (1974), 55
Gershenson, Antonio, 188–89
Gilly, Adolfo, 178–79
Gómez Álvarez, Pablo, 102
González, Antonio Erman, 204
González, Carlos Hank, 110–11, 118
González, Xavier, 162–63
González González, José, 107, 125–27, 135
González Meza, José Luis, 1, 194
graffiti, 95
Granados Chapa, Miguel Ángel, 4–5, 169, 196

Gran Ejido, 29
"Granero Político" (Echeverría pseud.), 17
Guadalupe Zuno, José, 69
Guevara, Ernesto (Ché), 108
Gutiérrez Nájera, Manuel, 158

Habermas, Jürgen, 7–8, 202
Hall, Stuart, 122
Helioflores, 119, 120–21
Helms, Jesse, 174–75
Henequeneros de Yucatán, 29
henequen scandal, Yucatán, 25–32, 46–49
*Heraldo de México, El*, 83, 181
Hermanos Mayo, 35
Hernández Galicia, Joaquín "La Quina," 194–97
Hernández Rivero, Rosa Luz, 148
*hijos de Sánchez, Los* (*The Children of Sánchez*) (Lewis), 37–46
*hombre de razón* ("man of reason"), 72
housing and the urban poor, 37–38, 59
Howard, Georgina, 151
*Huele a gas!* (Castillo and Rius), 96, 97*f*, 102, 106
Huerta, Francisco, 86–87, 127, 196

*iguala* (payments to reporters), 25
*Infierno del Negro Durazo, El*, 128–29
Instituto Mexicano de Petróleo (IMP), 86, 229n31
Instituto Mexicano de Seguridad Social, 55
intelligence archives, 18
International Monetary Fund (IMF), 81, 104, 119–21, 158
Iracheta, Sergio, 72–75, 73*f*, 74*f*
Ixtoc 1 oil spill (Bay of Campeche), 97–103
Iztapalapa, 59–60, 61–62

Jaguar Group, 117
Jaramillo, Rubén, 50

*Jornada, La*: Chihuahua election (1986) and, 169–70, 176, 178–79, 184–85, 189; earthquake *crónicas*, 159–61, 161f; garment workers scandal and, 147–50
Jóseph, Jorge, 133–34
journalism, Mexican: circulation of critical news and spectacle, 2–3, 6–7; co-optation/independence dichotomy, 8–9; gender and, 14, 34, 150, 203; information flows and national vs. regional media, 169–72; literacy and readership, 5–6; muckraking, 79, 80, 90, 171; New Journalism, 13, 158, 203; norms and negotiation, 13–14; press freedom, 12, 51, 101, 134, 183, 196, 205; schools of, 93, 149, 230n52; state support, effects of, 5; violence against journalists, 110–11, 204–5; wire services, 169, 201. See also *denuncia* journalism
Juárez, María Teresa, 94
Jueves de Corpus Massacre, 52
Junco, Alejandro, 171
Junta Local de Conciliación y Arbitraje (JLCA), 154
*Jurado Popular* (TV), 86
Juventud Estudiantil Sindicalista, La, 42

King, Francisco, 171
knowledge production, 64, 72, 77, 203
Krauze, Enrique, 176–79, 187, 189

Lajous, Adrián, 228n27, 229n31
land reform. *See* agrarian land reform
Lara Puerto, Arsenio, 27–28
Lazcano Araujo, Antonio, 160
leaked documents: Pemex scandal and, 79–80, 90–95, 94f, 99–100, 103–4; secrecy and, 19
Ledesma Ramírez, Franco, 216n31
Lerma Candelaria, Miguel, 122
Lewis, Oscar, 37–46, 218n74
liberation theology, 52, 57
Lira, Carmen, 147

literacy, 5–6, 57, 221n23
López Cámara, Francisco, 43, 44
López Koehl, Walter, 1, 194
López Mateos, Adolfo, 27–28, 101, 144
López Narváez, Froylán, 11, 71
López Pérez, Hugo Vladimiro, 149, 154–55
López Portillo, José, 133f; annual address (1979), 101; bank nationalization, 117–18; childhood of, 233n2; corruption narrative and, 118; "la crisis" and, 119–20; Durazo and, 108; González González on, 125; Helioflores cartoon on, 120–21; oil boom and, 80–82; Pemex scandal and, 85, 105; Political Reform laws and, 96–97, 113; *Proceso* and, 83
Lovera, Sara, 14, 19, 148–50, 157
Lozoya, Fernando, 145–46
Lugo Verduzco, Adolfo, 180

Madero, Francisco, 178
Madrid, Miguel de la: anticorruption platform, 121; Chihuahua election (1986) and, 173–74, 188; crime, cultural explanation for, 123; Díaz Serrano and, 104; Durazo and, 118, 128, 131, 136
Magalléan Pérez, Armando, 134
maquiladoras, 170
Márquez, Ramón, 124
Martínez, Hermelinda, 152
Martínez de la Vega, Francisco, 41
Martínez Mejía, Gustavo, 216n31
*Masacre en el Río Tula* (film; Rodríguez), 134
*Más* magazine, 35
mass media: dissent management and, 199; mediated citizenship and, 4; Monsiváis on earthquake and, 140; new publics, creation of, 45–46; transnational spread of, in 1950s and 1960s, 5; urban saturation, 6
Mayares, Mario Enrique, 170

Maza, Enrique, 99, 194–95
memory, public, 201
Méndez, Gregorio, 47
Mendoza, Gilberto, 29
Menéndez Rodríguez, Mario, 25–32, 46–50, 48f, 50, 70, 194
Mexican Revolution. *See* Revolution, Mexican
Mexico City earthquake (1985). *See* earthquake
Meyer, Lorenzo, 189
Mixteco Pastor, Alonso, 163–64
Monsiváis, Carlos: Chihuahua election (1986) petition, 189; CIASES and, 162; *crónica* genre and, 158, 164–65; mother of, 149; Poniatowska compared to, 160; resignation from *Unomásuno*, 147; "Solidarity of the Population Was Actually a Takeover of Power," 140–43, 146; on sterilization scandal, 75–76; Televisa parody, 155–56; violence witnessed by, 11
Moreno, Daniel, 41
Moreno Figueroa, Norma, 189
Movimiento de Liberación Nacional (MLN), 29, 84, 149
Movimiento Restaurador de Colonos, 57
Moya Palencia, Mario, 69
muckraking journalism, 79, 80, 90, 171
Muñoz Ledo, Porfirio, 77, 174–75

*Nacional, El*, 152–53
Nacional Financiera (Nafinsa), 91
Nacos, Los, 128
Naranjo, 82, 96, 97f, 119
Nazar Haro, Miguel, 114–15, 235nn30–31
*negro del Negro Durazo, Lo* (González), 107, 125–27, 135
New International Information Order (NIIO), 184
*Nexos* magazine, 132, 133, 176, 179
Nezahualcóyotl, 52–53, 56–57, 77, 109, 221n23

Niebla, Mario, 184
Nixon, Richard, 70
Nonoalco-Tlatelolco public housing complex, 144
*Norte, El* (Monterrey), 171
*norteños* and regional identity, 177
Notimex, 169, 201
*Novedades*, 82, 102, 159
Novo, Salvador, 158

Obregón, Álvaro, 196
Ocampo, Saúl, 240n6
Ochoa, Guillermo, 171
Oficina de Comunicación Social de la Presidencia (CSP), 170–71
oil policy. *See* Pemex oil scandal
oil spill, Ixtoc 1 (Bay of Campeche), 97–103
Olea Enríquez, Miguel, 47
Olivares Santana, Enrique, 235n30
*Olvidados, Los* (film; Buñuel), 40
Olympics (Summer, 1968, Mexico City), 38, 55
one-party state, 4. *See also* PRI
open secrets, 186; abortions, 72; earthquake and, 165; Echeverría's "Granero Político," 17; one-party state and, 8–10; power of documented, publicized evidence vs., 30; PRI rallies as performance, 180–81; PRI's maintenance of power and, 19; revolutionary shortcomings, 23–24; sweatshops and collusion, 149, 154; torture and clandestine prisons, 113
*Opinión Pública* (Radio ABC), 87
Orfila Reynal, Arnaldo, 38, 44–45, 218n74
Oropeza, Víctor Manuel, 249n58
Ortiz Pinchetti, Francisco, 11, 180–81, 190
Ortiz Pinchetti, José Agustín, 187–88
Oteyza, José Andrés, 92, 98
*Ovaciones*, 80

Pacheco, Cristina, 156
Pagés Llergo, José, 13–14, 23, 32–33
Partido Acción Nacional (PAN): Aguilar Camín on, 179–80; in cartoons, 187; censorship and, 182–83, 186; conference, 118; conspiracies and, 52; democracy movement and Chihuahua mayoralties, 167; Krauze on, 177–79; Ortiz Pinchetti on, 180–81; protests, 168, 173, 182, 186–87; sterilization vaccine scandal and, 68–70; Trejo Delarbe on, 186–87; U.S. interests and, 172–73, 188. *See also* election fraud, Chihuahua gubernatorial
Partido Comunista Mexicano (PCM), 95, 97
Partido Mexicano de los Trabajadores (PMT), 84, 89, 95–97, 101
Partido Revolucionario Institucional (PRI): democratization and, 2; divisions and heterogeneity within, 9–10, 105; elite power sharing and ideological flexibility, 4; logo of, 120, 120*f*; one-party state and, 4; Ortiz Pinchetti on rallies and voters of, 180–81; outside organizing, concern over, 143; population change and, 6; United States and, 173–74. *See also* election fraud, Chihuahua gubernatorial
Partido Socialista Unificado de México, 118
Payán, Víctor, 147
Payán Velver, Carlos, 159
Paz, Octavio, 34, 84, 167, 177, 189
peasants and land reform. *See* agrarian land reform
Pemex oil scandal: accountability, performances of, 86–90; Castillo articles on, 80, 84–90, 93–94; Castillo as politician-journalist, making of, 82–86; Castillo's energy talks, 95–96; Díaz Serrano, political downfall of, 103–5; Díaz Serrano before Congress, 88–89, 101–3; economic crisis and, 104–5; gas pipeline, 84–86, 89, 95–96; *Huele a gas!* (Castillo and Rius), 96, 97*f*, 102, 106; informational supplement by Pemex, 89–90; Ixtoc 1 oil spill (Bay of Campeche), 97–103; leaked documents, 79–80, 90–95, 94*f*, 99–100, 103–4; missing barrels of crude oil, 102; muckraking journalism and, 79, 80, 90; oil boom, reserves, and López Portillo's revenue promises, 80–82, 228n27; popular publics, creation of, 95–97; unfixed meanings of scandal and, 202; wealth redistribution failures and, 106
Peña Nieto, Enrique, 205
Peralta, Cristina, 156
Permargo (Perforadora Marítima del Golfo), 98
Petróleos Mexicanos. *See* Pemex oil scandal
photograph technology, 49
*Picardías del Negro Durazo*, 129–31, 130*f*
Plan for National Development, 98
police corruption, violence, and repression: Buendía and, 124–25; civilian complaints and protests, 108–9; counterinsurgency campaigns, 113, 114–15; crime rates and structural explanations, 122–24; Durazo and, 108–10, 116–19, 125–31; journalist experiences with, 110–11; open secrets, 113; Río Tula murders, 115–17, 119, 127, 134; sexual violence, 129, 131; urbanization and, 107
Policía Federal Judicial (PJF), 108, 113, 116
*Política*, 6, 50; *Sucesos* compared to, 46
Political Reform laws (1977), 96–97, 98, 113
Poniatowska, Elena: about, 12, 14, 159; at el Ateneo de Angangueo, 133, 133*f*; chronicles of earthquake, 159–65; Jóseph on Buendía and, 134; Mon-

siváis compared to, 160; on Pemex, 89–90; Siglo XXI and, 45; Tlatelolco Massacre and, 11
*Por Qué?*, 12, 70, 84
*Por una democracia sin adjetivos* (Krauze), 177
*Porvenir, El*, 171, 182, 185, 189
poverty: in Buñuel's *Los olvidados*, 40; "culture of poverty" thesis, 38, 217n55; discursive feminization of, 151; Echeverría on, 55; in Fuentes's *La region más transparente*, 40; Lewis's *Los hijos de Sánchez*, 37–46; Monsiváis on, 75; technological changes and, 49–50; urbanization and, 37
*Prensa, La*: Buendía and, 109, 134; on crime, 123–24; "Granero Político," 17; Jóseph and, 134; on sterilization vaccine scandal, 66–68, 71–72
*Presente* magazine, 35
Prieto, Guillermo, 158
Prince Alfaro, Jorge, 145–46
*Proceso*: accountability and, 91; cartoons on "la crisis," 119–20, 119*f*, 120*f*; Castillo articles on Pemex, 80, 84–90, 93–94; Chihuahua election (1986) and, 173, 180–81, 188; circulation, 226n3; CISA wire service, 169; founding of, 12, 83; González's *Lo negro del Negro Durazo* and, 125–26; leaked documents and, 92, 94*f*, 103–4; López Portillo and, 101; on mansions, 118; Monsiváis's "Solidarity of the Population Was Actually a Takeover of Power," 140–43, 142*f*, 146; muckraking and, 79; on oil spill, 99; Pemex scandal and, 82, 102; on *Un asesino*, 194
Procuraduría Federal de la Defensa del Trabajo (PFDT), 153, 154
Procuraduría General de la República (PGR), 115, 117, 122, 125, 128, 196
Productora e Importadora de Papel, S. A. (PIPSA), 5, 50, 199

Public Broadcasting Service (PBS) (U.S.), 172–73
publics, creation of, 45–46, 49, 95, 108, 168
public sphere, 7–8, 80, 203, 205
Puente Leyva, Jesús, 87–90

Quinazo, the, 194–97
Quiñones, Horacio, 88

race and racialization: Durazo scandal and, 108, 110, 126–29, 136–37; explanations of corruption and, 21; garment workers and, 164; Habermas and, 7; *hombre de razón* ("man of reason") and, 72; *la indiada* ("the riffraff") and, 83; Krauze's ideal citizen and, 177; Lovera and, 149; "rumor" and, 53; state violence, racially motivated, 53
radio: Buendía column readings, 170; cancellations, 196; *La Causa de las Mujeres* (Radio Educación), 150–51; *Los Expertos Colaboran* (Instituto Mexicano de la Radio), 145–46; *La Hora Nacional*, 199; *Opinión Pública* (Radio ABC), 87; *Palabras sin Reposo* (Radio UNAM), 127; *Participación Ciudadana* (Radio Educación), 163; Pemex scandal and, 86–87; *Radio Mil*, 196; *Voz Pública*, 127, 196
Ramírez, Carlos, 82, 103
Ramírez, Ignacio, 118, 126
Ramírez y Ramírez, Enrique, 41, 45, 134
recording technology, 49–50
*Reforma*, 196, 204
*region más transparente, La* (Fuentes), 40
Resistencia Civil Activa y Pacífica (RECAP), 190
Restrepo, Iván, 133, 133*f*, 147, 159
Restrepo, Laura, 14
Reveles, José, 11, 82, 92

Revolution, Mexican: anniversary of, 23; *Buro de Investigacion Política* on, 25; Castillo on betrayal of revolutionary principles, 96; Chihuahua and, 177; denuncia journalists and, 11; Garro on, 35; gradual opening to criticism of, 32; henequen industry and, 28; invoked in government publicity, 89; political legitimacy via, 36–37; postrevolutionary narratives, 37; social pact of, 4. *See also* agrarian land reform

Reyes Heroles, Jesús, 91–92, 96–97

Rico Galán, Víctor, 33, 46–47

Río Tula murders, 115–17, 119, 127, 134

Rius (Eduardo del Río): *Huele a gas!* (with Castillo), 96, 97f, 102, 106; "In This Town There Are No Thieves," 33; Lewis's *Los hijos de Sánchez* and, 45; "Listos con las listas!," 119, 119f; "Medio siglo de siglas," 120, 120f; Pemex exposés and, 82

Robles, Gustavo, 19

Rodríguez, Antonio, 33, 71

Rodríguez, Ismael, Jr., 134

Rodríguez, Luis Alberto, 148

Rodríguez Castañeda, Rafael, 104

Rojo, Vicente, 45

roundtables, university, 42–43

Ruiz Cortines, Adolfo, 24, 32

Ruiz Massieu, José Francisco, 196

"rumor" vs. "scandal," 53–54

Salanueva, Pascual, 148

Saldaña, Jorge, 86

Salinas, Carlos, 104, 191, 193–97

Salinas, Raúl, 196

Salinas Lozano, Raúl, 193–94

Sánchez, Manuel, 43–44, 50, 218n74

Sánchez, Roberto, 44

Sánchez Azcona, María de Jesús, 152

scandal: definition of, 15; narrative and, 14–17; "rumor" vs. "scandal," 53–54; unfixed meanings of, 202; as vehicle for justice, 199. *See also* agrarian land reform; earthquake; election fraud, Chihuahua gubernatorial; Pemex oil scandal; police corruption, violence, and repression; sterilization vaccine scandal

Scherer García, Julio, 12, 52, 69, 71, 82–83, 125

Scott, James C., 15, 53

secrecy: balance between concealment and revelation, 136; *Buro de Investigación Política* newsletter and, 25; exposure, complicity, and, 10; intelligence reports and, 18–19; leaked documents in Pemex scandal, 79–80, 90–95, 94f, 99–100, 103–4; leaked reports and blurring of "secret" vs. "public" sources, 19; transparency vs., 4, 22. *See also* open secrets

Secretaría de Desarrollo Urbano y Ecología (SEDUE), 143–46

Secretaría de Educación Pública (SEP), 55–56, 59, 73

Secretaría de Salubridad y Asistencia (SSA), 54–57, 65–66

Sepúlveda, Jorge, 169

Serur, Elías, 150

Sesin, Saide, 152

sexual violence, 129, 131

*Siempre!* magazine: about, 6, 32–33; Castillo and, 84; *La Cultura en México*, 33–34; editorial on revolutionary shortcomings (1966), 23; on Lewis debate, 41; political cartoons, 33

Siglo XXI editorial house, 45

Sindicato de Costureras 19 de Septiembre, 157

smallpox vaccination, 63

social sciences, 40–41

Sociedad Mexicana de Geografía y Estadística (SMGE), 38–44

Solana, Luis Javier, 99

*Sol* newspaper chain, 25, 83, 109

Spanish Information Network (SIN), 175

sterilization vaccine scandal: broadsheet depictions and rationality trope, 70–76, 73f, 74f; collective action, threats of violence, and Iztapalapa meeting, 58–63; elsewhere in Latin America, 60–61; media/government offensive and fact-fiction boundary, 63–68; in Nezahualcóyotl, 52–53, 56–57, 77; origins and "Warning Ciudad Nezahualcóyotl Parent" leaflet, 54–58; political blame, 68–70; ramifications of, 76–78; "rumor" vs. "scandal" and, 53–54; spread of, 62, 73
Stoler, Ann Laura, 18
student movements, 51–52, 57, 84, 109, 114, 141, 179–81, 199
*Sucesos para Todos* magazine, 46–49, 48f, 50
sweatshops. *See* garment worker sweatshops
syndication, 7, 90–91, 109–10

technological change, 49–50, 55, 144, 199–200
television: *24 Horas*, 58; *Aquí Nos Tocó Vivir* (Canal Once), 156; earthquake coverage, 140–41, 144–45, 155–56; educational *telenovelas*, 56; elections and, 182, 186, 190; *Hoy Mismo* (Televisa), 171; *Jurado Popular*, 86; Monsiváis's Televisa parody, 155–56; Pemex scandal and, 86; Telesistema Mexicano, 31, 175; Televisa, 55–56, 140–41, 178; Televisa boycott, 190; threats against Televisa, 69; viewership, 6
Tello, Carlos, 176
Tlatelolco Massacre, 11, 51, 67, 69
Tlatelolco neighborhood groups, 144–45
transparency: declassification of intelligence archives, 18; earthquake housing and resident demands for, 144; Gama case and limits of, 112–15;

oil spill and, 85, 98–99; Pemex scandal and, 88; public sphere and, 80; secrecy vs., 4, 22; simulated, 92–93; technology and, 200
Trejo Delarbe, Raúl, 186–87
Treviño, María del Pilar, 167, 169
Turner, Frederick Jackson, 177
Turner, John Kenneth, 28

*Últimas Noticias*, 115, 124
Unión de Periodistas Democráticas (UPD), 189
United States: Chihuahua election (1986) and, 172–76, 183–84; CIA, 92, 174; consuls, 24, 30–31, 46; economy, connectedness of Mexico to, 89; FBI, 39, 43, 128, 131; in *Huele a gas!* booklet, 96; in Mexican public sphere, 203; Senate, 174–75, 188–89
*Universal, El*: Buendía and, 109; Castillo and, 84; Chihuahua election (1986) and, 185, 187; Colosio assassination and, 196; Echeverría and, 83; Gama case and, 113, 114; "Los Intocables" (Mejías), 90; Ocampo story, 240n6; on oil spill, 98; on Pemex scandal, 102; sterilization vaccine scandal and, 71, 77; sterilization vaccine scandal cartoons (Iracheta), 72–75, 73f, 74f
Universidad Nacional Autónoma de México (UNAM), 40–41, 42, 109, 230n52
*Unomásuno*: Chihuahua election (1986) and, 183–84; circulation, 226n3; on Díaz Serrano hearings, 103; founding of, 12, 91; leaked documents and, 92; Nafinsa loan and independence of, 91–92; on police, 113; schism and resignations, 147; on sweatshops, 154
urbanization, 37, 56–57
Uruchurtu, Ernesto, 38

vaccinations. *See* smallpox vaccination; sterilization vaccine scandal

Vallejo, Demetrio, 84, 96
Vallejo, Virginia, 14
Valtierra, Pedro, 160–61, 161f
Vega, Lope de, 47
Velasco, Raúl, 140–41
Veracruz University, 230n52
Villareal, Francisco, 249n58
*Vuelta* magazine, 176, 178, 179

wire services, 169, 201
Woodward, Bob, 203

*Yawar mallku* (film), 60
Yucatán: henequen scandal and Menéndez Rodríguez's *El Diario de Yucatán*, 25–32; protests, strikes, and Menéndez's *Sucesos* articles, 46–49

Zabludovksy, Jacobo, 58, 118
Zamora Batiz, Julio, 175
Zapotec political movement, 182
*Zeta* (Tijuana), 171
Zorrilla, José, 134–35

www.ingramcontent.com/pod-product-compliance
Lightning Source LLC
Chambersburg PA
CBHW070754230426
43665CB00017B/2356